# THE LAND OF
# HOPE AND FEAR

# THE LAND OF HOPE AND FEAR

ISRAEL'S BATTLE FOR ITS INNER SOUL

## Isabel Kershner

ALFRED A. KNOPF | NEW YORK | 2023

Grateful acknowledgment is made to the following
for permission to reprint previously published material:
Vivian Eden: Excerpt from "Bab el Wad" by Haim Gouri,
translated from Hebrew by Vivian Eden. English translation copyright © by Vivian Eden.
The Estate of Haim Gouri: Excerpt from "Civil War" from *Words in My Lovesick Blood*
by Haim Gouri, translated from Hebrew and edited by Stanley F. Cyet.
Originally published by Wayne State University Press, Detroit, Michigan, in 1996.
Janusz Chwierut: Excerpt from letter written by Mayor Janusz Chwierut
addressed to Tova Berlinski, translated by the author.
Reprinted by permission of Janusz Chwierut.

Library of Congress Cataloging-in-Publication Data:
Names: Kershner, Isabel, author.
Title: The land of hope and fear : Israel's battle for its inner soul / Isabel Kershner.
Description: First edition. | New York : Alfred A. Knopf, 2023. | Includes index.
Identifiers: LCCN 2022011916 (print) | LCCN 2022011917 (ebook) |
ISBN 9781101946763 (hardcover) | ISBN 9781101946770 (ebook)
Subjects: LCSH: Israel—History—21st century. |
Israel—Politics and government—21st century.
Classification: LCC DS128.2 .K47 2023 (print) | LCC DS128.2 (ebook) |
DDC 956.9405/5—dc23/eng/20220603
LC record available at https://lccn.loc.gov/2022011916
LC ebook record available at https://lccn.loc.gov/2022011917

Jacket images: (arch) Damien Gan; (birds) tytyeu;
(woman) Adennysyahputra; all Getty Images
Jacket design by Max Rompo

Manufactured in the United States of America

First Edition

For my father, Harold Kershner,

of blessed memory,

and my mother, Doreen Kershner,

may she live a long life,

with love

# CONTENTS

# THE LAND OF
# HOPE AND FEAR

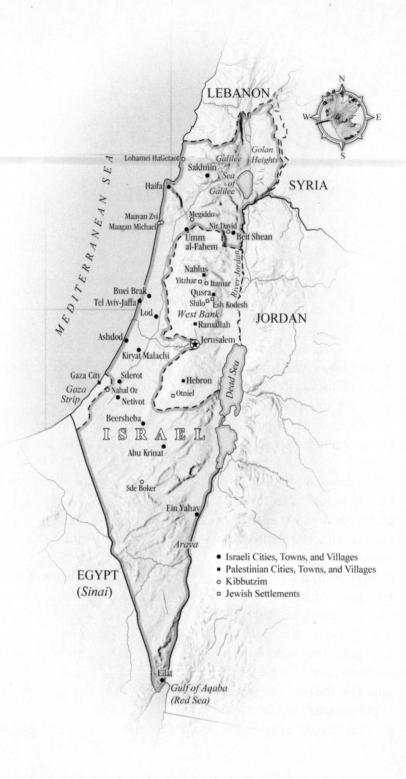

LEBANON

Lohamei HaGetaot ○

Sakhnin ●

*Galilee*

*Golan Heights*

Haifa ●

*Sea of Galilee*

SYRIA

Maayan Zvi ○
Maagan Michael ○

Megiddo ○

● Nir David

Umm al-Fahem ●

● Beit Shean

Nablus ■

Yitzhar □ □ Itamar

Qusra □

Shilo □ □ Esh Kodesh

*West Bank*

Bnei Brak ●
Tel Aviv-Jaffa ●

Lod ●

● Ramallah

*River Jordan*

JORDAN

Ashdod ●

★ Jerusalem

Kiryat Malachi ●

Gaza City ●

Sderot ●

*Gaza Strip*

○ Nahal Oz

Netivot ●

● Hebron

□ Otniel

*Dead Sea*

Beersheba ●

I S R A E L

Abu Krinat ●

Sde Boker ○

Ein Yahav ●

*Arava*

● Israeli Cities, Towns, and Villages
■ Palestinian Cities, Towns, and Villages
○ Kibbutzim
□ Jewish Settlements

EGYPT
(*Sinai*)

*MEDITERRANEAN SEA*

Eilat ●
*Gulf of Aqaba (Red Sea)*

N
W ● E
S

# PROLOGUE

I DRIVE PAST the Israeli prime minister's residence on the leafy corner of Balfour Street in West Jerusalem. The roads are strangely quiet, the house dark: nobody is home. For a year, this busy junction was the epicenter of possibly the most sustained and raucous protest movement in Israel's history, as the country seemed to be tearing itself apart.

On Saturday nights thousands gathered outside the walled, stone-clad mansion where Benjamin Netanyahu, Israel's longest-serving prime minister, was ensconced. The King of Israel to his many admirers, his detractors accused him of having turned Balfour into an imperial castle ruled by members of the royal household. When he was charged with corruption, the Israelis were roughly split between those who believed he had been framed by a liberal deep state and those who desperately wanted to see him go. The protesters of all ages came in costumes, with megaphones and homemade signs, some with flashing lights. They sang, beat on kitchen pots, banged on drums, blew on horns, and chanted for Bibi to quit until they were hoarse. After midnight the hardcore would sit down on the road and brave the jets of police water cannons.

Seven decades after the founding of the state, Israel was doubtless a

modern miracle, a regional superpower and a prosperous and innovative country projecting might to the world. But from the inside it felt
more divided than ever, its population polarized and splintered, an
immigrant start-up nation breaking down into its component parts.

The country had long been shifting to the right. The socialist founders were dying out. Generational change, instead of erasing old resentments and arguments, had brought ideological, religious, ethnic, and
national tensions to the fore. The modern state was supposed to be
an enlightened haven for the Jews in their ancient homeland. Now its
future as a Jewish, liberal democracy was on the line. Too internally
fractured to establish an agreed-upon border with the Palestinians in
the long-occupied territories, the Israelis were entangled in identity
conflicts and culture wars as their toxic politics threatened to trample
the rule of law. Israel had largely learned to live with its outside enemies but seemed less adept at managing itself.

In the spring of 2021 Netanyahu was ousted after a fourth tumultuous election in the space of two years. The lights were turned off
at Balfour as it underwent renovations. A new generation of leaders
emerged. But who were the Israelis and what did they aspire to? This
book takes in the chaotic culmination of Netanyahu's extended run
of a dozen years in power followed by a year of relative, and precarious, normalcy under a fragile new government. Netanyahu's defeat in
2021 initially felt like the end of an era, restoring a veneer of calm and
functional governance. It would not last long. Netanyahu's legacy and
presence continued to cast a long shadow and was likely to affect the
course of the Jewish state in the years to come. Israel's problems did
not end with that election. They would not end with the next one or
go away anytime soon. This is a portrait of a country on the precipice,
battling for its inner soul.

# ONE

# DESERT CORALS

M Y QUEST to explore the soul of the new Israel began with a journey to the biblical wilderness of the southern desert. There, in a
small farming community, lived Assaf Shaham, the native son of hardy
Zionist pioneers who, in the 1950s, had obstinately moved to the Arava,
a sun-scorched, sparsely populated, barren strip of backcountry along
Israel's then-hostile border with Jordan.

A first, chance meeting with Shaham had come years earlier, during
a press tour of the area to promote Israel's expertise in arid agriculture.
Shaham struck me as an archetypal new Israeli: authentic and rooted,
but also worldly and enterprising. He had spent years living elsewhere,
but once he had a family of his own he was drawn back to the remote
community of his birth, Ein Yahav, a tiny speck on the map inhabited
by a few hundred souls.

At first encounter Shaham, a farmer-innovator, seemed to be living
the Zionist dream, and in many ways he was: a bona fide son of the
land whose parents were born at around the same time as the state,
and a product of his generation of high-tech entrepreneurs. The Israel
beyond Ein Yahav had fundamentally changed, divided, and fragmented and was in political turmoil. But perhaps Shaham had cracked
the secret of inner peace and purpose in the Jewish homeland.

My journey began with the ear-popping descent down to the Dead Sea from Jerusalem. The drive from the holy city to the lowest point on earth is a trip through folds of time, but also one through the complex strata of modern Israel. The car sped along the newly asphalted highway in blinding sunlight through the stark, almost primordial landscape of the Judean desert, through an Israeli military checkpoint into the occupied West Bank and past a sprawling Jewish settlement perched along a beige ridgetop, past ramshackle Bedouin encampments of hide tents, tin shacks, and pens for livestock. About halfway down the steep incline a large, turquoise-tiled sign on the roadside marked sea level. An overly adorned camel waited stoically for travelers to take a photo, as if in a picture postcard. The bone-dry hills spread out in the distance like the bed of a waterless ocean.

To the left, the Palestinian oasis town of Jericho lay in a haze. The road twisted rightward, hugging the shore of the receding Dead Sea, glistening with salt. Dramatic beige cliffs lined the other side of the highway, pocked with the dark mouths of caves that once provided refuge for the ancient rebels of the Jewish revolt against the Romans. Through another military checkpoint marking entry back into Israel proper and past the desert fortress of Masada—the deeper toward the earth's core, the thicker the atmosphere became. Beyond the hotel district near ancient Sodom, and after the grotesque, industrial Dead Sea chemical plant, the salt lake was abruptly swallowed up by the Arava desert.

It was still another hour's drive along Route 90 to Ein Yahav, through the moonscape-like Great Rift Valley abutting the Jordanian border. The wind-sculpted cliffs tapered out into a monotonous plain broken only by flat-topped, thorny acacia bushes, providing dappled patches of shade. In this harsh, inhospitable terrain, the Zionist enterprise had been boiled down to its essence, though when I arrived at Ein Yahav it struck me as surprisingly lush. Still a flagship of Jewish settlement in the area, it operated as a *moshav,* a rural cooperative that was a model of old Labor Zionism, the movement that had laid the foundations of the state but had almost become obsolete in twenty-first-century Israel.

Remote by Israeli standards, this being a relatively compact country, Ein Yahav lay about 140 miles from Tel Aviv on the Mediterranean coast. The closest cities, Beersheba and Eilat, were both a ninety-minute drive away. When Assaf's father, Ami Shaham, first arrived in the Arava in 1959, barely more than a decade after the establishment of the state, it was even less accessible. But in those years life here was a mission.

Just a decade earlier, in 1949, Israeli forces had raised an Israeli flag known as the ink flag, hastily drawn on a piece of cloth, over an abandoned British police station in Um Rash-Rash, now Eilat, the southernmost point of the country, in what was considered the final act of the War of Independence. The Arava was still dangerous terrain. Soldiers lay in wait for hours to ambush *fedayeen,* the Palestinian guerrillas who would infiltrate from Jordan. Israelis had to travel Route 90 in convoys, with an army escort.

Ami Shaham was born in 1942 in the coastal city of Netanya. Infused with the ideals of Labor Zionism by his surroundings, he attended the Mikve Israel agricultural school established in the late nineteenth century. Eager to take part in building the state, he left school at seventeen and came south to join a small group of soldiers from the Nahal army brigade who had established a foothold in a former British police fort on the western side of Route 90. In those early years, the Nahal unit combined military service with settling the land. The community consisted of a few miserable shacks near the old fort and was the first agricultural settlement to take hold in this central section of the Arava Valley. The settlers named it Ein Yahav for the nearby Yahav Spring, known in Arabic as Ein Wiba, and they tried to farm the dry, dusty earth where young adventurers before them had failed.

Although settling the borders was one of the pillars of the security concept of the fledgling state, the pragmatic military and settlement authorities at first opposed the central Arava experiment. One Israeli official told the settlers it would be cheaper to put them all up in a Tel Aviv hotel than to bear the cost of sustaining communities in the area. But David Ben-Gurion, the founder of the state and its first prime minister, was a passionate advocate of populating the desert and making it bloom as a central tenet for securing Israel's future.

Few Israelis were then living in the vast expanse between the Dead Sea and Eilat. Tragedy struck the Arava in March 1954 when *fedayeen* attacked a bus on a corkscrew-like desert pass known as Scorpion's Ascent. Eleven passengers were killed on their way back from Eilat's fifth anniversary celebrations. The incident gave added impetus to the Arava settlers' cause. In a landmark speech in 1955 on "The Significance of the Negev," Ben-Gurion declared that it was there "that the people of Israel will be tested" in the spirit of pioneering, science, creativity, and innovation. Israeli control of Eilat, about eighty miles south of Ein Yahav, on the Gulf of Aqaba, was also seen as imperative as a naval gateway to Africa. In 1959, over the objections of the government's settlement commissars, Ben-Gurion signed the letter approving the establishment of Ein Yahav.

Frustrated with the initial results, however, Ami left the outpost to complete his military service and officers' course. He went on to work for three years as the head of the manpower department in Israel's new and highly secret nuclear reactor that had gone up in Dimona, a new town in the Negev desert. Assaf's mother, Shula, was born in 1947 and grew up in Bnei Zion, a *moshav* on the coastal plain. She met Ami during her military service, when she was a young soldier of eighteen, and the pair decided to settle together in Ein Yahav in 1966. Shula, who was still a soldier, had to get special permission to join the Nahal unit in order to move there. "It was the end of the world," she recalled. "There was nothing here. Nothing. You needed a lot of faith."

Ami and Shula married the next year. They were both what was known in the popular vernacular as Sabras, or *tzabarim,* native-born Israeli Jews. The sabra bush, a prickly pear cactus whose fruit wears a thick, spiny armor protecting its soft, juicy interior, grew wild across the country, needing no tending and little water. Though the bush was actually native to South or Central America, the pre-state Zionist pioneers adopted it as a symbol of the children born in the land of Israel, free of an exile mentality and unfettered by European manners. It later came to connote the proverbial Israeli, said to be tough on the outside and sweet and sentimental on the inside, as well as to represent the modern Hebrews' renewed attachment and claim to the land.

In the fall of 1967, flush with victory in the Six-Day War, the Nahal group, by now demobilized, moved their tiny farming cooperative to a permanent location on the eastern side of Route 90, even closer to the Jordanian border. By then, the community consisted of a dozen or so families and a few singles. Two months after the move, Assaf was the first child to be born in the new location. Ein Yahav was off the electricity grid but had a generator. There was no grocery store or telephone line or paved road. It was nearly impossible to push a child's stroller through the sand. Medical emergencies required evacuation by army helicopter. The National Water Carrier—a system of pipes and canals built to bring water from the Sea of Galilee in the north to the arid south, completed in 1964 and a symbol of Zionist pride—did not reach the Arava.

Each family began with a small holding of twenty dunams—five acres—and, according to the principle of Hebrew labor and self-sufficiency, worked the land with their own hands. Once a week a supermarket in Dimona, about fifty miles away, would deliver supplies and the driver would take orders for the following week. Buses or taxis tossed out packages of newspapers on their way to Eilat. The areas along the Jordanian border were mined and residents of the Israeli settlements often spent hours in underground shelters, accessed by trapdoors under their beds, when there were reports of infiltrators, and they would switch off the lights—the only ones in the area—as booms split the air.

Soon more communities sprang up—Hatzeva to the north, Faran to the south. In Ein Yahav, the farmers drilled wells and pumped salty water out of the sand, planted a date grove, and, with the addition of an imported layer of topsoil, learned to tease tomatoes, peppers, melons, and eggplant out of the sunbaked ground. The invention in the 1960s of drip irrigation by Netafim, an industry of Kibbutz Hatzerim in the Negev, and the introduction of hothouses made the seasons almost irrelevant. With its long, hot summers and an average of four days of annual rainfall, the Arava became a dusty petri dish of agricultural improvisation and innovation. The Arava farmers gained the know-how to grow tomatoes in winter and helped turn Israel into a global leader in water conservation and arid agriculture. Over the decades, through grit and determination, the handful of farming communities of the central Arava Valley, with a population of some 3,500, went on to produce more than 60 percent of Israel's fresh vegetables for export.

The Arava farmers experimented with relatively simple technologies like underground water pipe systems to heat or chill the roots of plants, plastic tunnels to regulate the temperature, and net houses to keep out insects. Specializing in bell peppers, the farmers reaped small fortunes, but, in the face of foreign competition and extreme weather, also suffered through years of near financial ruin. As the demand grew for dates, many of the ever-adaptable Arava farmers switched to cultivating Medjool date palms. The founders' original challenge of creating a productive life out of the sand had been accomplished.

For a native of Ein Yahav, Assaf Shaham had seen a lot of the world. His father had held a string of positions in the *moshav* union; he was the first head of the Central Arava Regional Council and was instrumental in bringing water to the region. As an envoy teaching Israeli farming methods, he then took the family for spells in Zambia, Uganda, and Kenya. The family also spent two years as emissaries in New York when Assaf was a teenager. After Israel and Jordan signed a peace treaty in 1994, Ami worked on joint water projects between the two countries.

Like most Jewish Israelis, Assaf was drafted at eighteen for three years of obligatory military service. He served in the 50th Battalion of the Nahal infantry brigade, a favorite with the sons of the kibbutz and *moshav.* Nonetheless, he recalled, that was the first time he met the "other Israel," experiencing a culture shock in his own country. Ein Yahav was a largely homogeneous community of secular, liberal Ashkenazi Jews of European descent, then considered Israel's crème de la crème. But the army was a reflection of a broader Israel: rightists and leftists, religious and secular, veterans and new immigrants, *Ashkenazim* and *Sephardim,* also known as *Mizrahim,* all served together. The *Mizrahim,* or eastern Jews, had emigrated en masse in the 1950s from the mostly Arabic-speaking Islamic world and made up some 50 percent of Israel's Jewish population. Some had come eagerly after the creation of Israel, out of a belief in Zionism, others more reluctantly to flee persecution under the anti-Zionist Arab regimes, leaving their property behind. It was Assaf's first encounter with the Ashkenazi-Sephardi divide. He was unfamiliar with Mizrahi food and culture. On open Saturdays at his army base, the Mizrahi parents, stereotypically warm and effusive compared to their uptight, almost Spartan, Ashkenazi compatriots, would roll up with miraculously hot pots of home-cooked soul food like couscous and kubbeh. Assaf said his parents would arrive "with two cucumbers and a tomato."

The social and cultural collision was compounded by a sudden outburst of violence. In December 1987, a year into Assaf's army service, the first Palestinian intifada, or uprising, broke out, an explosion of twenty years of pent-up frustration since Israel's occupation of the territories of the West Bank and Gaza Strip in the 1967 war. Israeli troops were ordered to respond to stone-throwing Palestinians with beatings and force. Hundreds were killed. (Born soon after the Israeli conquests of the 1967 war, Assaf had never known the smaller-scale Israel without the occupied territories, and within the narrower boundaries set in the 1949 armistice talks.) He said he found the whole army experience overwhelming and disturbing.

After completing his service, he became a feted lighting designer on the Tel Aviv theater, gallery, and museum scene. Having built a career, he then left for a long stint abroad, living in Los Angeles, Fiji, and New Zealand. Being away, he said, he learned the power of identity and belonging. "I learned early that you travel with yourself," he said. "You can't run away from yourself. You will always be an outsider. There comes a point where you are not part of it."

Back in Israel, and in his thirties, he longed for Ein Yahav. It offered a simpler life, intimacy, family, and roots, but without the hardship involved in his parents' first years there. Now there was air conditioning. No place he needed or wanted to go was more than a day's commute away. Hoping to raise his own young family with the same sense of community and belonging he remembered from his childhood, and with the unfettered freedom he felt in the open expanses of the Arava, he persuaded his partner, Rinat Rosenberg, who had grown up in the greener climes of northern Israel, to join him. They built a home near the entrance of the *moshav*—a pale peach stucco villa with blue window frames, a bright green front lawn, and a hammock on the porch. The slanted, tiled roof was covered in solar panels to capture the intense rays of desert sun. The airy and rustic-chic interior soared upward into a double-ceilinged, wood-paneled loft. There was some elemental comfort in the familiarity of it all: Assaf's next-door neighbor was one of the nine peers that had made up his kindergarten and grade-school class.

The Shahams who first settled in Ein Yahav epitomized the romantic image of *Eretz Yisrael Hayafa*, "the beautiful Land of Israel" of old, an idealized place that now largely existed in the nostalgic ballads of kibbutz choirs and army entertainment troops, and where vital young people, living by their values and flush with a sense of purpose, danced the hora in the fields. That Israel was held in the collective, sepia memory as a more innocent, plucky, and heroic country whose exploits inspired international awe. Since then, there had been a changing of the guard. The secular, socialist state builders, the founding elite, were no longer politically or culturally dominant and, pushed off their pedestal, were no longer regarded as national idols. Labor Zionism, which had dominated the country for its first three decades, was in steep decline. The anti-socialist right, in power for much of the past four decades, had become more nationalist and populist, the Jewish population more religious. Farming was barely profitable in the capitalist, free-market economy and the old farmers found themselves on the wrong side of the ideological lines, representing everything that those who came after them despised.

Assaf's parents were the kind of Israelis who had long been considered the salt of the earth. But in this new Israel they were almost a dying breed. Long out of power, marginalized, and even branded the enemy by some, they felt like strangers in their own land. And the feelings of estrangement had grown sharper during the last few years under Netanyahu. Having served his first term as prime minister from 1996 to 1999, the American-educated, telegenic conservative was reelected in 2009 and went on to serve another twelve consecutive years in office. By the summer of 2019, he had surpassed Ben-Gurion's record for years in power. He had much to his credit, having modernized the economy, campaigned against the potential danger of a nuclear-armed Iran, and built Israel up into a country renowned for its prowess in technology and counterintelligence. He had even joined the small pantheon of Israeli leaders who signed agreements with moderate Arab countries when the Trump administration, after failing in its bid to press the Palestinians into accepting a colossal territorial compromise with Israel, ended up brokering normalization deals between Israel and the United Arab Emirates, Bahrain, and Morocco.

Glad to be rid of President Obama after a tetchy eight years of fighting over Iran policy and settlement expansion in the occupied territories, Netanyahu had enthusiastically embraced President Trump, even at the risk of damaging the solid bipartisan support in Washington that Israel had long valued as one of its main strategic assets. The mutual adoration further alienated North American Jews, a majority of whom were liberal and voted Democratic. Netanyahu also allied himself with populist leaders in Europe and beyond, such as Prime Minister Viktor Orbán of Hungary, President Andrzej Duda of Poland, and President Jair Bolsonaro of Brazil, all known for curbing the free press and the courts. Israel seemed on the cusp of becoming a less liberal, or illiberal, democracy.

Netanyahu seemed to play an outsize role on the world stage but his triumphs came at a high price at home. His staying power was largely achieved by exploiting the country's identity politics, by divide and rule and fearmongering. Toward the end of his dozen years in office, the decibels of hate grew louder and reached fever pitch as Netanyahu, under police investigation and then indicted on graft charges, became ever more determined to cling to power. Ultimately, beginning in early 2021, he went on trial on charges of bribery, fraud, and breach of trust. The trial revolved around three cases in which the prime minister stood accused of trading official favors for gifts from wealthy tycoons. Some of the gifts were tangible ones of expensive cigars, the pink Champagne reportedly favored by the prime minister's wife, Sara, and jewelry. The weightiest case, in which he was charged with bribery, involved accusations of a backroom deal with an Israeli media mogul and friend to facilitate a profitable business merger in return for flattering media coverage for the Netanyahu family.

Netanyahu denied all wrongdoing and repeatedly stated that the cases would collapse in court. But at the same time he embarked on a desperate bid to gain some kind of immunity from prosecution or at least to be able to fight his legal battles from the prime minister's office. In attempts to delegitimize the legal process, he launched a Trumpian assault against the very pillars of Israeli democracy, lashing out at the mainstream media, undermining the police and the judiciary, and claiming he'd been framed in a liberal–left-wing conspiracy. Nothing was unholy or off-limits. Netanyahu publicly maligned the police chief, the state prosecutors, and the attorney general, whom he had appointed. He and his supporters accused an elitist deep state of carrying out a witch hunt against him and plotting a "judicial coup" to oust him. He had centralized as much power in his hands as he could, including by putting loyalists in key positions, and the loyalists tried to curb the powers of the once-hallowed Supreme Court. As his critics saw it, Netanyahu prioritized his political and personal interests over those of the country. His strongest detractors accused him of fascism. Among his diehard supporters, anybody who disagreed with the party line was branded a leftist and leftists were branded as traitors. Yair Netanyahu, the elder son, spewed anti-left vitriol on Facebook and Twitter, occasionally even resorting to racist tropes and memes, including one that drew praise from American neo-Nazis and former Ku Klux Klan grand wizard and Holocaust denier David Duke.

Far-right extremists who had previously been considered beyond the pale had been legitimized enough to sit in the Knesset and even to be courted as potential members of the government. Legislation was advanced to clip foreign government funding to left-wing nongovernmental organizations at the forefront of the international struggle against the Israeli occupation of the Palestinians, and to have their leaders ostracized. In what smacked of McCarthyism, right-wing nationalistic organizations exposed academics who might have once signed a petition against the occupation or in favor of boycotting settlement produce, with the goal of disqualifying them for prestigious prizes or appointments.

The national glue, the sense of collective identity and purpose that had brought Assaf back home, seemed to be dissolving. Though Israel was always ideologically split, the majority of Israelis had historically hewn to a common goal of building the state in the face of existential threats from outside enemies. Now that the building was done, and the enemies mostly weakened, Israel seemed to have lost its internal compass.

The second time I met Assaf, we sat on his porch with a latte in the late winter sunshine. He was slender and suntanned, with blue-gray eyes, and fashionably tattooed. To make a living after first arriving in Ein Yahav, he had tried putting his lighting expertise to use, experimenting with the effects of LED lamps on the crop yields in the family hothouses. But he had never really seen himself growing peppers and tomatoes. Eventually he came up with something that no other Israeli had done: In the middle of the desert, he set up a coral farm. In the yard behind his house, water tanks whirred in the sheds that housed his beloved corals. He was experimenting with breeding fish in a small pool out front. It would later be replaced by a turquoise dipping pool. A pioneer for the modern age, he retraced the source of his novel enterprise. He said he had long heard about reserves of underground water in the area that were too saline for ordinary agricultural use and which he had assumed would be similar to the ocean. International restrictions on coral harvesting were tightening, including in the Red Sea to the south. With his lighting skills, he reckoned he could create a twenty-four-hour controlled environment and replicate the natural sunlight that kept corals alive. So he improvised, building the first coral farm in Israel, in the desert of all places, and named it O.K. Coral.

There was nothing charming or exotic about the shipping-container-like sheds from the outside, nor were the corals meant for decorative purposes. Assaf had teamed up with an Israeli entrepreneur, Ohad Schwartz, the founder of CoreBone, a company developing bioactive, coral-based material for bone grafts. Operating out of the Herzliya Industrial Zone, a commercial hub just up the coast from Tel Aviv, CoreBone was tapping into a burgeoning, multibillion-dollar world market in bone replacement and tooth implants.

More than a decade after Assaf established the farm, the corals were growing quietly indoors. Within the confines of lidless metal tanks, tropical fish glided restlessly between orderly rows of miniature coral polyps, some solid like rock, others gently swaying like a watery garden in shades of lilac, pink, and green. Large orbs of light hung low over the tanks, supplemented by smaller white, blue, and green spotlights. The underground reserves turned out to be nothing like seawater, but Assaf, undeterred, used reverse osmosis to purify and reconstitute it to the corals' liking. He also invented a way to breed the corals by surgically sawing off tiny branches and attaching them with superglue to small, round bases he made himself. The sheds offered optimal conditions, more consistent than anything nature had to offer, with no nighttime, no shadows, and no predators to contend with. A tenth generation of farmed corals was growing in the tanks at many times the speed of nature.

Now in his early fifties and the father of teenage twins, Assaf's life seemed like a more bourgeois version of Ben-Gurion's desert dreams. The Arava had become a tranquil border corridor and a symbol of quiet regional cooperation. Traffic accidents and loose camels, rather than enemy ambushes, now presented the greater hazard along Route 90. Dedicated to his business, Assaf said he never left the corals alone for more than twelve hours. The tiny vials of processed coral extract were selling for hundreds of dollars and O.K. Coral had become a destination for visiting coral experts and a stop on public relations tours of the Arava.

So it was all the more surprising, or sobering, to find the private Assaf to be contemplative, cynical, and haunted by fears for his country. It was not the threat of a nuclear Iran that was causing his unease and anxiety, but rather what was happening in Israel and its uncertain future. For decades since the 1967 war, Israeli midwives had been assuring the parents of newborns that by the time the child was eighteen there would be peace and the new offspring would not have to serve in the army. "I tell my children that by the time they get to army age, there is not going to be any country," Assaf said wryly. He added with only a hint of irony that the most important thing an Israeli could own was a foreign passport, "just in case." His twins had obtained German passports by virtue of Ronit's parentage.

Assaf called the angst he was feeling "the heartbreak of failure." The old values were apparently not valued anymore. The contribution of his parents no longer appeared to be appreciated, and they had lost their status. The Shahams found themselves torn between fighting to preserve their place in a transformed society or mentally disconnecting from the rest of the country and focusing on life in their small, tranquil slice of Eden.

The internal fault lines had grown wider as Israel became more established and less of an immigrant nation. By 2022, 79 percent of the Jewish population consisted of native-born Hebrew-speakers. But the country still had no permanent eastern border and no end in sight to the grinding reality of the occupation of the Palestinians. Messianic Jewish settlers hewed to the biblical covenant of the entire Promised Land, enabled by the state. The settlement project had planted half a million Israelis among millions of Palestinians in the West Bank, tying a Gordian knot that was becoming ever harder to untangle and creating what was already a binational reality. Ultra-Orthodox sects listened only to their own rabbis. Palestinian Arab citizens made up a fifth of Israel's population. Almost half the nation's first-graders were either ultra-Orthodox Jews or Arabic-speakers, who did not share the Zionist upbringing of the Jewish mainstream. Slowly, almost undiscernibly, tectonic shifts were taking place below the surface of Israeli society.

Amid the general sense of a national unraveling, Reuven Rivlin, Israel's former president and an old-school Likud party liberal, had leveraged his largely symbolic role and, like an anguished prophet, called for unity and national healing. In a seminal speech in 2015, dubbed "The Four Tribes" speech, he tried to sum up Israel's conundrum and the basis of its social fissures with a presentation that resonated and reshaped the national discourse for years. Aided by a PowerPoint presentation with pie charts, he explained that Israel's demographic makeup had changed. If a clear secular Zionist majority had prevailed from the foundation of the state through to the 1990s, coexisting alongside national-religious, ultra-Orthodox, and Arab minorities, that balance had shifted, he said. Now only about 38 percent of Israel's first-graders were in the secular Jewish school system. Some 15 percent were in the Zionist national-religious system, while the rest were more or less evenly split between the Arab and ultra-Orthodox sectors. He described these four principal Israeli stakeholders as distinct tribes that were fundamentally different from one another but growing closer in size. It was time, he said, to confront this new Israeli order that was restructuring the national identity and what it meant to be an Israeli.

The four "tribes," educated in separate school systems, each had their own curriculum, ethos, and vision, and learned in Hebrew, Arabic, and sometimes Yiddish. Different sectors lived by different calendars—Gregorian, Hebrew lunar, Muslim lunar—and often lived in their own, exclusive enclaves. Some West Bank settlements only accepted members from the Zionist religious camp. Most *kibbutzim* remained avowedly secular. Arab citizens mostly lived in their own towns and villages. The ultra-Orthodox had their own settlements. With no division of religion and state the political system had become increasingly sectoral, with a plethora of small and medium-sized parties catering to different ethnic and religious groups. Elections ended with no clear winner, turning every small party into a potential coalition kingmaker and imbuing them with disproportionate power. That's how, in the spring of 2021, after a fourth inconclusive election in two years, Naftali Bennett, the leader of the boutique right-wing Yamina party, came to succeed Netanyahu with only 6 seats, on a good day, in the 120-seat Knesset. Bennett, the native son of immigrants from the United States and a former high-tech entrepreneur in his late forties, was an almost accidental prime minister, the default candidate who could unify the disparate anti-Netanyahu forces and the first religiously observant premier. His fragile coalition, made up of eight medium- and small-sized parties with clashing ideologies and agendas, was ushered in by a vote of 60 to 59 with one abstention, the only principle binding it together being the desire to end the chaos and keep Netanyahu out of office. Israel had no constitution to chart its core values. The lack of national consensus on key issues prevented one from being written. Instead, there was a body of basic laws that could be amended by a vote of 61 in the Knesset.

Even those killed in Israel's wars were not spared the arguments. In 2017, after more than forty years of anguished discussion and political wrangling, Israel inaugurated, on Jerusalem's Mount Herzl, adjacent to the national cemetery, its first national Hall of Remembrance for its 23,000 fallen soldiers. In this small and intimate country with its conscription army, every one of those deaths left a deep scar, as if the fallen were all relatives. But in the absence of any national consensus, even the most fateful battles were subject to conflicting narratives. When five Arab armies attacked the nascent state immediately upon its declaration of independence in 1948, the Zionists fought and won a war of liberation. To the Palestinians, including those who ended up as citizens of Israel, it was the *Nakba,* or catastrophe. Some 400 Palestinian villages were emptied and destroyed and about 700,000 Palestinians fled the hostilities or were expelled, turning into permanent refugees. The stunning triumph of 1967, when Israel defeated the Egyptian, Syrian, and Jordanian armies in six days and conquered Jerusalem's Old City with its holy sites, the biblical heartland of the West Bank, the Gaza Strip, the Egyptian Sinai, and the strategic Golan Heights, was a sign of divine redemption for some. For others, once the initial euphoria passed, it marked the start of a long, festering, and morally corrosive occupation. The 1982 invasion of Lebanon was officially named Operation Peace for Galilee, but it went far beyond its initially stated goals and many Israelis saw it as Israel's first, controversial "war of choice." It became more commonly known as the First Lebanon War, after it was followed in 2006 by a second one. Inside the memorial monument, where any one word, name, or phrase could spark dissension, the answer was found in simplicity. A spiraling wall of bricks was inscribed only with the names of the dead and the dates on which they died. In the interests of equality, avoiding controversy, and allowing a veneer of unity, there was no mention of the battle in which the soldier fell, or of location or rank. Here, there was no hierarchy of position or ideology, but just a small light by each brick that was illuminated on the anniversary of each individual soldier's death. Remembrance was pared down to a bare, tranquil minimum. After all, consensus over the past could hardly be achieved while the conflict was still so alive. And more awful than the long rows of bricks with names were the empty rows spiraling skyward, waiting to be inscribed with an untold number of new names.

After a while, family holdings in Ein Yahav grew to fifty dunams, equivalent to about twelve acres, and more hands were required. The principle of self-reliance went by the wayside. The remote location and minimum wages were hardly a draw for Israelis, so the farmers came to rely on an imported labor force from Thailand. In the Central Arava, there were more Thai than Israeli adults, and about six Thai workers per family farm. If the workers had the vote, the regional council head would be a Thai, went the local joke. In the afternoons, Thais in brimmed hats would ride around on bicycles and the backs of tractors, lending the mostly bare desert a tropical feel, their faces wrapped with cloth and shielded from the rays of the sun. There was clearly some embarrassment about the phenomenon. Asked how many Thai workers there were in a village or kibbutz, members would give evasive answers such as "enough," or "more than enough." A popular Israeli television drama series called *Yellow Peppers*, set in the Arava, had featured a Thai worker who had almost become part of his employer's family. But the BBC and some human rights organizations uncovered cases of abusive treatment, contending that the Thai farm laborers were often overworked and underpaid, provided with lousy housing conditions, and poorly protected when working with hazardous materials. Local Bedouin had also begun to work on the farms. The reliance on outside labor had perhaps dented any public sympathy for the farmers and their early sacrifices. To many Israelis, the old-school Labor Zionists were out of touch and had an inflated sense of entitlement. In an effort to attract young Israeli blood to the area, Ronit, Assaf's partner, a former spokeswoman for the Central Arava Regional Council, was running a program called Hebrew Labor to encourage demobilized soldiers to work in the packing houses. Dozens had come to the area, their salaries supplemented by government grants and incentives.

Ein Yahav had grown into the largest *moshav* in the Central Arava, with about two hundred families, many of them farmers. Others had branched out into tourism, offering bed-and-breakfast accommodation and desert jeep tours. The population was aging and the schools were short of children. Some families had gone bankrupt. "Farmers will always complain," Assaf said, "if it rains or if it doesn't." But they also felt abandoned in the new Israel.

Assaf's younger brother, Ido, had never even thought about leaving Ein Yahav or of not following in his parents' footsteps and working the land. He said he was too independent to work for anybody else. He had married Hagit, a former classmate in the *moshav*. They had three children and built their own stylish home in Ein Yahav with large picture windows and a wood-burning stove. Ido had tried growing everything: cherry tomatoes, figs, dates, lettuce, cabbage, watermelons, zucchini, cucumbers, eggplant, and, of course, peppers—whatever was in demand, and mostly for export. But with the shekel strong against the euro he was often selling at a loss. Hagit supplemented the family income by selling homemade cakes out of her kitchen, with its double range and a built-in wooden wine rack. The couple also hosted groups for farm-to-table gourmet dinners in their home.

Sitting over bowls of spicy yellow pepper soup served with melting wheels of creamy, locally sourced goat cheese, Ido and Shula, the family matriarch, spoke of the additional challenges they faced as farmers in the modern Jewish state. One of the more bizarre demands revolved around the requirements for being certified as a kosher supplier, meaning one that complied with Jewish dietary laws. On the orders of the state's chief rabbinate, the official religious authority, Shula, an atheist, and the other farmers had to "donate" 1 percent of their produce as a biblical tithe, a priestly offering known as *Terumat Hamaaser*. Since there were no longer any ritually pure Levites or a temple in Jerusalem to receive these offerings, and since it was forbidden to put them to any other use, the rules were that they had to be unceremoniously discarded like garbage.

The Shahams had to constantly reinvent themselves in order to keep up. Exploiting the thermal underground waters, they had experimented with spirulina, a blue-green algae, even before it became a fashionable superfood, then sold it all to a Japanese buyer. Other residents of the Arava had set up fish farms, and Assaf had experimented with raising tilapia in the pond in his garden. Shula went on to establish Israel's first aloe vera farm, starting with two plants that a Protestant priest brought in his bag from Oklahoma in the 1980s, hoping to heal the world. Teaming up with a researcher, Shula began producing aloe-based cosmetics. Others had dreamed of turning the Arava into a center of cannabis growing to supply the medical marijuana industry, but Israel, an early pioneer in research and development, had fallen behind as a producer and the security demands proved too cumbersome for many.

Ido was the more rugged looking son, though he had the same soft, blue-gray eyes as Shula and Assaf. He knew he was living in a kind of bubble in Ein Yahav but said Israeli politics still annoyed him, particularly "the rightists" and "the Orthodox." Ministries had been handed out as political favors based on coalition demands, with suitability or talent rarely a factor. The agriculture minister at the time was a settler dedicated to his constituency in the West Bank. "What does this minister of agriculture consider to be agriculture?" Shula asked rhetorically. "Not us."

Yet Shula herself embodied some of the contradictions that made up the Israeli reality. Like many Israeli families, hers was ideologically conflicted. Her late mother was divorced from her father and had turned religious. Enamored with the messianic settler movement in the late 1970s, she had moved to the West Bank settlement of Kedumim. For twenty years Shula refused to visit her in her home. "I don't want to rule another country," Shula said, referring to the Palestinians. "And if we do," she added, referring to the demographic realities, "we won't have a country."

It had long been a fundamental argument of the Israeli left that the

Zionist vision of a Jewish democracy could only survive by formally separating from the Palestinians—a territorial division between the Jordan River and the Mediterranean Sea creating two states for two peoples, the Jews, or Israelis, and the Palestinians. Otherwise, the argument went, with the number of Palestinians and Jews in the combined areas of Israel, the West Bank, and the Gaza Strip already reaching parity, Israel would eventually have to become one of two things: a single, binational state that granted equal voting rights to the Palestinians, making it democratic but no longer Jewish, or an apartheid-like pariah state of two peoples living in one country under two different regimes and legal systems. The tipping point was fast approaching, and in the eyes of some on the far left, it was already here.

As founder members, the Shaham clan had status in Ein Yahav. They had not come despite the hardship, Shula said, but *because* of it—to settle a strip of empty desert along a hostile border and to see if they could sustain life there. Conditions had since eased up somewhat. Not only did the air conditioners run constantly to banish, or at least dilute, the furnace-like heat of summer, but there was a communal outdoor swimming pool in the middle of the village. A poolside café called Deck Bar served hummus, hamburgers, and pizzas along with chilled beer. There was a library, a basketball court, and a clinic. Even the children had smartphones and could keep up with whatever was going on in Tel Aviv, London, and New York. Most households needed two cars. It was hard to attract new families, perhaps in part because living in Ein Yahav had become more expensive. The *moshav* had tried to market more than eighty plots for private homes in a leveled area between the village and the highway, but this was not your average suburbia and less than half a dozen new houses had gone up, surrounded by wasteland. Setting up a farm required an investment of about half a million dollars—money, Assaf said, that would be hard to recoup. Some newcomers had found it hard to fit in and had left because, Assaf acknowledged, "We were snobs."

The residents celebrated Jewish and national holidays together as social and cultural events, and some had developed their own irreverent traditions, like barbecuing pork on Yom Kippur, the holiest day in the Jewish calendar, when observant and more traditional Jews fast to atone for their sins. Nevertheless, Shula said she felt a common bond with the Jewish people, "after all they did to the Jews in the world." They were, she said, her "tribe," her "family" wherever she went. But she wanted the Jewish state to be just and democratic, citing the Torah's injunction against ill-treating the *ger,* or the stranger, because the Israelites were "strangers in Egypt." She felt less affinity with what Israel had become. After more than five decades of "temporary" occupation and settlement building since 1967, she said, "I believe what we are doing now is not Jewish."

The estrangement felt in Ein Yahav was just a reflection of a broader process in Israel, where, as noted earlier, the Zionist left had become an endangered species. The historic Labor Party, which had long run the country, was reduced to single digits in the 120-seat Knesset. Some pre-election polls had forecast that it might not even win the minimum of 4 seats required to make it past the electoral threshold. By far the largest party in the country was Labor's oldest rival, the right-wing Likud. Labor's descent had been steady and long, marked by historical signposts. Religious fervor had taken over some quarters of the right wing after the conquests of 1967, which left Israel in control of the holy sites of Jerusalem's Old City and the biblical heartland of the West Bank, as if that victory was all part of a messianic plan. Deliverance came again in 1973 after days of near military disaster that many feared would wipe out the country, but the Labor old guard would soon pay the price for the trauma. The legendary Likud leader Menachem Begin swept to power in 1977, upending decades of Labor rule, and went on to make peace with Egypt, eventually returning the Sinai Peninsula to the Egyptians and establishing the principle of land for peace. But he regarded the West Bank and Gaza Strip as integral, inseparable parts of the Land of Israel, and even some security hawks from the left side of the political map were loath to give up the newly acquired strategic depth.

Prime Minister Yitzhak Rabin, the Labor Party leader who made it back into power in 1992, as a former military chief of staff and a liberator of Jerusalem, had all the right security credentials to reach accommodation with Israel's enemies. Yet when he made his "peace of the brave," embarking on the interim Oslo Accords with the Palestinian leader Yasser Arafat in the 1990s, the promise of a final, end-of-claims resolution to the conflict proved short-lived. The early "good years" of

Oslo soon dissolved into murderous violence perpetrated by radicals on both sides bent on derailing the embryonic agreements. Hamas and Islamic Jihad carried out sporadic suicide bombings. Baruch Goldstein, a Brooklyn-born Jewish extremist and physician, gunned down twenty-nine Muslim worshippers in the Cave of the Patriarchs, the Jewish holy site in Hebron also held sacred by Muslims as the Ibrahimi Mosque. In far-right Jewish circles Rabin's territorial concessions to the Palestinians had turned him into a traitor to the Jewish cause, and in November 1995, after attending a peace rally in Tel Aviv, he was assassinated by Yigal Amir, a Jewish zealot who had fed on the incitement of right-wing politicians and sought out the tacit encouragement of militant rabbis. Netanyahu was the leader of the opposition at the time and was blamed by the left for doing too little to calm the atmosphere, and even for taking part in the incitement. The murder rocked Israel's foundations and traumatized the nation. In the Tel Aviv square where Rabin had delivered an emotional speech and sung the popular "Song of Peace" minutes before he was killed, stunned youths gathered around flickering memorial candles. People driving to work the next day cried silently behind their car windows as the radio played the mournful repertoire of Hebrew ballads usually reserved for deaths in war or terrorist attacks, in a requiem for a lost Israel. The Oslo process began to implode. Months after Rabin's murder, in the spring of 1996, a bloody campaign of Palestinian suicide bombings snatched the election from his Labor Party successor, Shimon Peres, and brought Netanyahu to power.

Nobody can say what would have happened had Rabin lived, but after his death the hopes and promises of Oslo swiftly began to shrivel. An abortive, American-brokered effort by another Labor leader, Ehud Barak, to reach a final accommodation with the Palestinians in 2000 exploded into the violence of the second Palestinian intifada. Barak's term was cut short as a cruel and devastating storm of Palestinian suicide bombings ripped through buses and cafés in Israeli cities and sounded a death knell for whatever was left of the leftist Israeli peace camp.

The next few years were excruciating and scarred all those who lived through them. As we brought up two young children in a genteel neighborhood not far from the center of West Jerusalem, the horror was almost on my family's doorstep. The deadly booms of familiar neighborhood cafés and bars blowing up reverberated through the living room followed by a grim chorus of wailing sirens. The drive to school became a nerve-racking exercise in trying to avoid stopping next to a bus at traffic lights for fear it would explode. Tel Aviv's fashionable boulevards were stained with blood. Everybody had their stories of near misses. At least the more fortunate ones. One female suicide bomber wiped out three generations of a family at lunch in a popular restaurant in Haifa known as a symbol of Jewish-Arab coexistence. In Jerusalem, a bride was blown up the night before her wedding together with her father, a renowned emergency room doctor. Schoolchildren were blown apart on buses. In a seminal act of horror, a male suicide bomber disguised as a woman dragged a suitcase into the dining room of a modest hotel near the seaside in Netanya on the eve of Passover and killed thirty civilians, many of them elderly, among them Holocaust survivors. In response, Israel launched its biggest military operation in the West Bank since 1967, reinvading the Palestinian cities, and began building a barrier of concrete walls and steel fences to keep out the suicide bombers. Many Palestinians later lamented the failure of the uprising, which did not serve their goals. Whatever Israeli sympathy they still had dissipated as the left dwindled.

The desert had held a particular allure for Ben-Gurion. With much of the population concentrated in the narrow strip of coastal plain along the Mediterranean, and with the sparsely populated Negev and Arava deserts covering about half the land area of the country, Ben-Gurion had set a personal example by retiring with his wife, Paula, to a modest cabin on the edge of Sde Boker, a remote kibbutz in the Negev desert. He hoped that others would follow. Nicknamed "the Old Man" for much of his life, Ben-Gurion was about thirty years older than the rest of Sde Boker's residents and was given the easier jobs, like measuring precipitation and tending to the lambs. The most important thing he learned from desert life, he said in a lost interview that was rediscovered and aired in a 2016 documentary, *Ben-Gurion, Epilogue,* was the satisfaction of having built something from nothing, knowing "that my friends, and myself, we did it. Everything. It's our creation." The simplicity was also a lesson in the modesty and ideological purity of the early leaders, which sometimes bordered on the fanatical. Assaf recalled that, in those times, his father never let family members use his work-issued car or drop his name, lest anybody think they or he was taking advantage of his position.

In the new Israel such norms rarely applied. Ehud Olmert, a former Jerusalem mayor and Likud politician who moved to the political center and served as prime minister from 2006 to 2009, ended up serving time in prison for corruption. The Netanyahus had become notorious for their penchant for the high life. Economic gaps yawned as the chasm grew between the more prosperous center of the country and the long-neglected "periphery," as the social and geographic margins were known.

In many respects, Israel had exceeded its own expectations, or at least those of its founders. Its population had grown from some 800,000 in the year of its birth to more than 9.5 million by 2022. But its self-definition as a Jewish and democratic state, enshrined in its Declaration of Independence, was being tested and, some critics said, was an impossible contradiction in terms. Increasingly split between those who prioritized its Jewish character and those who put more value on its democracy, the rival camps were no longer so much a matter of right and left as "Jews" and "Israelis." The country had become a simmering cauldron of passions and ethnic divisions, all in an area about the size of New Jersey. The contradictions were on display when the coronavirus hit. Even then, the government response became mired in the country's political and cultural wars as some ultra-Orthodox rabbis flouted lockdown rules and some Arab mayors were seen dancing at large illegal weddings. Israel was initially a global leader in vaccinating its population. Yet at times its COVID infection and mortality rates soared to among the highest per capita in the world.

Assaf had returned to Israel from New Zealand as a young man primarily because he missed the sense of belonging. It was easier to live where you were born, he explained, with your own family, language, and history. Another sibling, a younger sister, was living in her late grandparents' home in Bnei Zion. For Assaf, Ein Yahav, where he went barefoot most of the time, was the ultimate home even if he was sure not to take credit for all it represented. "Look at my parents," he said.

"They were willing to live and die for this country. They had a dream and they did something amazing. I was just born here."

Driving through Ein Yahav one day, I came across a simple but poignant sign stuck on a net house in the middle of the village. It was left over from a farmers' protest of a few years back. "It is in the Negev that the people of Israel and their state will be tested," it read, quoting from Ben-Gurion's 1955 speech, and was illustrated with a sketch of a tractor. A second line encapsulated the collective sentiment of this small community in the desert: "Zionism is not dead (yet)!!!"

Assaf said he did not define himself as a Zionist, because Zionism had already done what it had set out to achieve. At the core of his post-Zionist malaise was the split into camps, or different countries. For Bibi and against Bibi, religious and secular, Jewish and Arab, Jews and Israelis. If the Zionist dream was still alive, it appeared to be in a midlife crisis. Assaf denounced what he called the modern Israeli culture of the *combina*, Hebrew slang for getting a good deal by screwing the system, requiring various degrees of chutzpah, greed, and arrogance. "Eventually there's going to be a civil war here—and I'll be on the losing side," Assaf told me as the political system seemed to be losing its grip in a mad swirl of elections. "I think it's starting already."

The first signs of grassroots protest came in late 2016 with a few dozen activists who demonstrated every Saturday night near the home of the attorney general in the central city of Petah Tikva, accusing him of dragging his feet as he mulled charging Netanyahu with criminal offenses. The charges were filed in 2019. The anti-Netanyahu protests moved to Jerusalem after the government cited COVID in limiting the activities of the courts, leading to the postponement of the opening of Netanyahu's trial, and then of the Knesset. In June 2020, Amir Haskel, a former general and air force pilot and a veteran of the Petah Tikva protests, set up camp on the sidewalk outside the prime minister's residence on Balfour Street and demanded his resignation. A few supporters, many of them grandparents, joined him. After Haskel was arrested for blocking roads and held overnight in a cell, the pensioners began to ask where the young people were. On July 14, Bastille Day, they came out in force and for the next year, on Saturday nights, they filled the streets around Balfour.

People came from all over the country, from all walks of life, with signs and props, some humorous and some obscene, others quoting biblical verses about justice. Netanyahu dismissed the protesters as anarchists. After his son Yair mocked them as aliens, some came dressed as aliens. Mothers in yellow vests came to act as a protective shield between the young protesters and the overly aggressive police. Assaf and Ronit made the two-and-a-half-hour journey several times. "My kids say I'm obsessed. Why do I care so much?" Assaf asked, sitting at the dining room table in Ein Yahav one hot Saturday afternoon as Ronit cooked lunch. "I have a kind of paradise here." He cared because of all that was at stake in his eyes: "The history of my parents and the future of my children."

Here, along the Great Rift Valley, the ground was constantly, if imperceptibly, shifting. Coral reefs thousands of years old were being annihilated. Assaf worried that Israel, a mere seven decades old, could prove just as ephemeral. Its democracy seemed fragile. Politics had taken on a helter-skelter feel. The social solidarity that Israel ultimately depended upon was eroding. "With eyes wide open and with both hands," Assaf said, "we are destroying the foundation of everything we stand on, really fast." Comparing life in Israel to holding the end of a burning match, this small paradise, he said, was also his "private Armageddon." His camp had lost its political clout. The left, he said, constituted 5 percent of the population, if that. "You have to think what it is you can do—not for your country but for yourself," he said sardonically, "because nobody's going to be there for you."

Agriculture was struggling. As food prices for the Israeli consumer rose and rose, the government reached an agreement for agricultural reform that would see a reduction of duties on a range of imported fruits and vegetables while the state would provide the farmers with direct financial support. The Arava was also moving with the times. One family of former pepper growers imported Alpine goats, acclimatized them to the desert, and started producing artisanal French-style goat cheeses, supplying a chain of high-end cafés and delicatessens in central Israel. Another opened a roadside deli serving home-smoked charcuterie and locally brewed craft beer. Glamping sites offered glamorous camping in air-conditioned tents in nature, and an ultra-luxury, ecologically sustainable hotel opened up in the middle of the wilderness, catering to Israel's most wealthy percentile. The old Israel was not coming back. But in the eyes of many Israelis that was not a bad thing.

# TWO

# CIVIL WARS

IN JUNE 1948, Yosef "Yoske" Nachmias, a fighter with the Irgun, the right-wing pre-state underground, had boarded the *Altalena,* an Irgun ship, after it arrived in Israeli waters. It was carrying nearly a thousand young Zionist fighters and immigrants, men and women from Europe, some of them Holocaust survivors.

The ship was loaded with weapons that could help the fledgling state, already at war with the invading Arab armies. David Ben-Gurion was deeply suspicious of the motives of the Irgun's commander in chief, Menachem Begin, his archrival, who had also boarded the ship off the Israeli coast and was refusing to surrender the weapons.

The arrival of the ship brought to a bloody head the long and bitter rivalry between the mainstream pre-state underground, the Haganah, under the direction of Ben-Gurion, and the more militant Irgun. The showdown saw Jews firing on Jews and, ultimately, the soldiers of the newly formed Israel Defense Forces shelling and sinking the vessel. The schism has lasted to this day. To fully understand the left-right ideological gulf between the Shahams of Ein Yahav and the rampant nationalism on the rise in Bibi's Israel requires digging down to the roots of the struggles between the pre-state Zionist schools and undergrounds. The tragedy of the *Altalena,* a blot on the history of the nascent state, would end up strengthening and reaffirming the ultimate bond of Jewish sovereignty, but it also created a new wound that would continue to fester for years to come.

More than seven decades later, that generation of titans, the vital men and women who had fought to establish the Jewish homeland, was fading away, and with them their historic values and moral choices. Each had a story worthy of an action movie or spy thriller, from the uprooted Holocaust survivors who escaped Hitler's ovens to the warrior-poets who shaped modern Hebrew culture. The time was soon approaching when I would no longer be able to hear them, up close, relate their testimonies and memories. My encounters with them were moving and gripping, suffused with so much pride, pain, and glory. They were also tinged with sadness and confusion as the state's founders grappled both with time that was running out and with abiding questions, like whether the Israel they were leaving behind was the one they had hoped for and fought for.

I first spotted Nachmias at the annual memorial ceremony commemorating the *Altalena* passengers who perished, held each June in the tranquil Nahalat Yitzhak cemetery in the leafy Tel Aviv suburb of Givatayim. Modest stone slabs lay in neat rows engraved with the names of the fallen, like Mendel Kaufman, born in Hungary, who was twenty-one at his death, and Eliezer Weitz, sixteen, from Poland. Nachmias stood out in the front row, tall and regal, sporting a jaunty, Indiana Jones–style brimmed leather hat and a mustache. The guests of honor included Prime Minister Netanyahu, President Rivlin, and Moshe Arens, a Likud veteran and a former defense and foreign minister whom the leaders described as a mentor. They had all grown up in Betar, the right-wing youth movement that fed into the Irgun, also known as the Etzel, a Hebrew acronym for *Irgun Tzvai Leumi,* or the National Military Organization. It was Arens who took on Netanyahu as his protégé and nurtured his political career. Once considered the underdogs of the Zionist enterprise, maligned and marginalized by the Labor Zionist elites, the disciples of Ze'ev (Vladimir) Jabotinsky, a Russian Zionist leader and the founder of Betar and the hardline Revisionist school, had risen to power with Begin in 1977 and had remained the dominant force in Israeli politics and government for most of the time since.

Nachmias, ninety-one at the time, suggested we meet at his place of work—the Etzel Museum on the waterfront between Tel Aviv and Jaffa. Now widowed, he volunteered at the museum as a guide and living witness, riding in each day from a retirement home in the Tel Aviv suburb of Ramat Gan. His small office was cluttered with photographs and souvenirs, and he was clearly well loved by the young staffers who clucked around him. He never seemed to tire of telling his story, perhaps even less in the time he had left.

With hindsight, the *Altalena* was sailing into a disaster. Ben-Gurion had declared independence only five weeks earlier and, as expected, the Arab armies had invaded to aid the Palestinian irregular forces. With the birth of the state, Ben-Gurion had established the IDF as a unified, national force that would bring the rival pre-state undergrounds under a single command. Begin signed an agreement to enlist his group's members into its ranks. They were to serve in their own battalions for an interim period, surrender their equipment to the army general command, and swear allegiance to the government headed by Ben-Gurion. But the rival forces were still divided over strategy, ideology, and vision. Ben-Gurion had settled for what was possible, accepting the compromise of the United Nations partition plan of 1947. Begin, a disciple of Jabotinsky's, harbored maximalist territorial ambitions for Jewish control of both sides of the Jordan River. The Irgun had not surrendered its ideology or given up on its long-term aspirations, though it did pledge to confine its activities to the legal and democratic political domain.

"One phase of our war is over," read the Irgun's Order of the Day announcing the paramilitary's integration into the IDF on June 1, 1948. "But the historic mission we have taken upon ourselves goes on. The homeland has been liberated only partially. And we have sworn not to rest or hold our peace until our entire homeland is returned to our people and our entire people is returned to the homeland."

The solidarity of the new state would be put to the test sooner than anyone may have thought. Because of a series of logistical mishaps, the *Altalena* set sail nearly a month later than scheduled, on June 11, from Marseille. It crossed the Mediterranean with some 930 people aboard and was carrying a cargo of thousands of rifles, hundreds of light machine guns, anti-tank and anti-aircraft weapons, half-tracks, and millions of bullets. Begin insisted that 80 percent of the weapons

go to arm the Irgun battalions in the IDF and that the other 20 percent
be earmarked for the Irgun's forces in Jerusalem, which was not yet
under the jurisdiction of the Israeli government.

For Begin it was a matter of honor and prestige, about burnishing
the credentials of the Irgun, which had splintered off from the Haganah in the 1930s, in the Zionist annals. Ben-Gurion saw a conspiracy, apparently convinced that the Irgun was plotting to overthrow
his government, and demanded that Begin hand over the 80 percent
of the weapons that he wanted for the Irgun battalions to the army's
high command. By the time the *Altalena* approached Israel's shores,
on June 20, the Irgun had already agreed to integrate into the IDF, a
temporary truce had come into effect in the Arab-Israeli war, and the
United Nations had imposed a ban on all arms imports. Begin had
announced that the ship had set sail without his knowledge, and that
once he did know, fearing breaching the truce conditions, he had sent
messages seeking to postpone its arrival. The messages went unan-
swered. The vessel was flying a roughly stitched flag of the Jewish state
bearing the emblem of the Irgun: a rifle hoisted over the contours of a
map of a greater Israel, spanning both sides of the Jordan. Scrawled on
it was the Hebrew legend *Rak Kach*—"only thus." The tattered flag was
now on display in a glass case outside Nachmias's office.

Born on November 4, 1925, Nachmias was one of ten siblings. The
family, from the Sephardic Jewish community of Monastir, in the Balkans, had been in Jerusalem for six generations. Known as *Samech
Tet,* the initials for *Sephardim Tehorim,* meaning "pure Sephardis,"
their ancestors had migrated from the Iberian Peninsula around
the time of the Spanish Inquisition. Nachmias grew up in the Betar
youth movement with one foot in the Irgun, he said. At fourteen, he
joined the underground and embarked on his death-cheating life's
journey. The Irgun sent him to join the British Army in its war effort
against the Germans. Before he was fifteen, he said, he was fighting
against the Vichy forces in Lebanon. He then went to Tunisia and Sic-
ily, where he was injured; he was hospitalized in Tripoli. Dreaming
that he'd been hurt, his mother sent him a greeting card, stuffing the
envelope with healing weeds that she had plucked from among the
stones of the Western Wall.

After three years of service abroad, Nachmias returned to Palestine and began moonlighting in the Irgun underground. Well versed in the manners and curses of the British soldiers, he donned a fake mustache to disguise himself and to look older and took part in raids of weapons arsenals at British bases, often sneaking in wearing a British army uniform while the officers were eating lunch. Eventually he was caught, court-martialed, and sentenced to death, but some of his comrades abducted British officers as bargaining chips and his death sentence was commuted to a long prison term. He was moved to the Acre prison, a centuries-old fortress, and escaped in a daring jail break pulled off by the Irgun in 1947. Armed with a false identity, he went back into the underground and became a company commander.

As the *Altalena* approached the Israeli coast, Nachmias was told to go, unarmed, with his company to Kfar Vitkin, a fishing village halfway between Tel Aviv and Haifa. The government had instructed the *Altalena* to anchor, away from the prying eyes of United Nations inspectors, in an area where the Irgun had no foothold. Begin and several other Irgun commanders were in the village too. Such was the secrecy under which the Irgun units operated that Nachmias said he was surprised to meet Yafa, his wife of six months, herself a member of the underground, also waiting on the shore.

Initially, Nachmias recounted, the Irgun fighters sat together with IDF forces they met there, telling stories, like comrades in arms. The *Altalena* dropped anchor in the late afternoon on June 20. Most of the volunteers were brought ashore and put on buses. The ship was sent back out to sea and returned at night so the arms could be unloaded in darkness. "For four or five hours we worked shoulder to shoulder," Nachmias recalled. Then the soldiers melted away and the Irgun fighters were left alone. Feverish discussions were underway in the provisional government. On Ben-Gurion's orders, an IDF brigade commander at Kfar Vitkin gave Begin an ultimatum to forfeit the weapons within ten minutes. Begin refused. Suddenly, Nachmias said, the Irgun fighters came under a burst of fire from the forces they had just been sitting with. Begin, Nachmias, Yafa, and the other Irgun fighters clambered into a landing craft, headed out to the *Altalena,* and set sail for Tel Aviv.

When the ship struck a reef opposite the Frishman Beach, fighting started up again. Begin sent Nachmias ashore to try to negotiate a cease-fire. He raced zigzag across the beach, as bullets kicked up the sand, toward the Red House, the headquarters of Ben-Gurion's Mapai party, which he believed to be the source of the fire. "Who's in command here?" Nachmias shouted as he burst in. A voice called back in surprise. "Yoske? Is that you?" It was the voice of his cousin, Avraham Nehama. The swirling currents of animosity in which the *Altalena* was caught even ran through families. The Irgun commanders were convinced that Ben-Gurion had determined to finish Begin off. One of the main sources of fire was from the headquarters of the Palmach, the elite strike force of the Haganah, located in the Ritz Hotel on the seafront. Yitzhak Rabin, then a young Palmach commander, had dropped by that morning and soon ended up taking command. Rabin later said he did not know who opened fire first, but he recalled in his memoirs that Irgun gunners took up positions on the ship's deck and that fire flew from both sides. The battle lasted several hours. Some IDF soldiers refused orders to fire on fellow Jews. At some point, Nachmias said, Begin ordered the Irgun fighters to stop firing back, famously uttering the iconic words "Never a civil war." Nevertheless, determined to bring the saga to an end, Ben-Gurion ordered the ship to be shelled at 4 p.m.

From the Red House, Nachmias saw the plume of black smoke rising from the belly of the vessel. Assuming that Yafa and Begin were still on board, along with enough weapons to ignite and blow up the ship, he swam madly back out to sea. Dozens of rescue boats had arrived, as if from nowhere, and Yafa was in one of them tending to the wounded. Begin insisted on being the last one off the *Altalena*, but Nachmias said he and a few other fighters put a life belt on the commander and threw him into the water.

By the end of it all, sixteen Irgun fighters and three IDF soldiers were killed in the clashes, an inglorious start for the young nation. For Ben-Gurion and the Labor establishment it was, however, a defining moment, anchoring the principle of one government, one army, and one law, the very foundations of statehood and sovereignty. The disciples of Jabotinsky claimed a moral victory. Begin emerged as their national savior, having ordered his forces to hold their fire, thereby averting a full-blown civil war.

What happened next was no less fateful and would say much about the ability of the Jews to pull together at times of crisis. After all, the independent Jewish state was at stake and there was a larger war to be fought. So, despite their anguish, under Begin's instructions the survivors of the *Altalena* promptly joined the IDF and the war effort against the Arab forces. Like the other survivors, Nachmias and Yafa were taken, dripping wet, to naval headquarters, where they were fingerprinted by the Israeli authorities and soon released. Nachmias enlisted and went to serve in a Palmach brigade. At first, he said, he would joke that he was scared to run ahead in case his comrades decided to shoot him in the back. But there was never any real dilemma. "The IDF became my army," he said. "I was a fighter. There was a war in the land."

The wisdom of putting the common purpose before the sectoral one was a survival instinct that ultimately proved itself and would be repeated at times of war. At the memorial ceremony in the cemetery in Givatayim, the few *Altalena* survivors who were still alive were bolstered by the robust presence of younger generations of the Revisionist camp. No longer the underdogs, Begin's heirs were now the well-established leaders of modern Israel. They had been at the helm of most governments in recent decades. But the trauma and the battle for credit abided among the Betar faithful who had brought their smarting sense of affront with them from their old countries and, here, had added some new causes.

"The tragedy of the *Altalena* left a deep wound in the fabric of our young democracy," Netanyahu declared from the podium that year. "Like all bleeding wounds, if they are not dealt with properly, they can become infected and cause more serious harm. And that's why we are here today, to remember the fallen, to expose the wound to the open air, to sterilize it. To make sure that it heals. It will heal—but it will leave a lasting scar."

As the veterans stood up shakily to sing the Betar anthem, with its rousing lyrics of might and glory, scores of teens who had been bused in from schools and youth movements—girls in skimpy shorts, boys in faded jeans and T-shirts—held up their smartphones to video the scene. The calm within the cemetery walls belied the seething tensions outside. Since the *Altalena* incident, an Israeli prime minister had been assassinated by a Jewish extremist and inciteful, toxic rhetoric was on the rise again.

———

Among an Arab population of more than 1.2 million living in British Mandatory Palestine in 1947, the year before Israeli independence, there were roughly 650,000 Jews, 1 percent of whom would be killed in the 1948 war. Families were often divided in their loyalty to different factions, and, notwithstanding the egalitarian ideals of the state's founders, the waves of immigration determined a national pecking order. The early idealists from eastern Europe revived the Hebrew language of the Bible and prayer into a modern vernacular. Arriving in the late nineteenth century during the Ottoman period, they determined to rid themselves of the Jewish exile mentality, usher in a new and vibrant Hebrew culture, and work the land.

Born David Gruen in 1886, Ben-Gurion insisted on speaking only Hebrew as he grew up in the Polish town of Plonsk, then part of the Russian empire, where his father ran a Hebrew school. First arriving in Palestine in 1906, he worked as a laborer in agricultural settlements and helped found Hashomer, or "the Watchman," the nucleus of an armed defense force guarding the settlements against Arab attack. Hashomer would evolve into the Haganah, the people's paramilitary organization whose emblem, a sword entwined with an olive branch, was later adopted by the IDF. Begin hailed from Brest-Litovsk, Poland, where he was born in 1913, and joined the Betar youth movement at sixteen. Enthralled by Jabotinsky, he made his way to the Middle East in 1943 as a member of the Free Polish Army. Further waves of eastern European Jews flowed into Palestine through the first decades of the twentieth century, many spurred by pogroms and antisemitism. The rise of Nazism brought the German professionals, nicknamed *Yekkes*, a slang term denoting pedantry and punctuality. Then came the Holocaust survivors, some of whom were handed a gun and sent straight from their ships to the front lines to fight for their new homeland.

Despite the paucity of resources at Israel's disposal, Ben-Gurion put a premium on populating the new state; the biblical prophecy of ingathering the exiles became a policy priority. The Law of Return, enacted in 1950, granted automatic citizenship to Jews coming home or seeking refuge. Two decades later, in an amendment ironically based on the principle of Hitler's Nuremberg Laws, automatic citizenship would be extended not only to Jews but to anybody married to a Jew, to the child or grandchild of a Jew and to their spouses, to allow families to remain united but also to ensure safe refuge for anybody subject to persecution because of their Jewish roots.

The *Mizrahim,* the Jews from North Africa and the Middle East, arrived en masse through the 1950s. In subsequent secret operations the government airlifted in immigrants from Yemen and from Ethiopia's ancient Jewish community. The 1990s saw the influx of a million Russians and other residents of the former Soviet Union. Aided by the flight and expulsion of hundreds of thousands of Palestinian refugees in the hostilities surrounding the foundation of the state, Jews soon constituted a clear majority of the country. As Yoske Nachmias was retelling the story of the birth pangs of the nation, Arab citizens constituted about a fifth of the population and more than three-quarters of the Jewish population were native-born Israelis. The rapid formation of an Israeli populace and identity was key to the country's survival and seemed like a miraculous fulfillment of the biblical promise. Immigrants were expected to shed the culture of exile. Ben-Gurion banned Yiddish theater in the 1950s. Jews from Arab lands were made to feel their culture was uncivilized and their spoken tongue the language of the enemy. The strong-arm policies worked. Decades later, Shimon Peres said he had never imagined there would be more Hebrew-speakers in the world than, say, people who spoke Danish.

But the schisms ran deep. The first split from the Haganah came after the massacre of sixty-seven Jews in the holy city of Hebron, revered as the burial place of Abraham and most of the other major biblical patriarchs and matriarchs, during the Arab uprising of 1929. The uprising began in Jerusalem and spread across the country, targeting old Jewish communities as well as the newer Zionist ones. Militant members of the Haganah felt impelled to go "beyond the fences" and take more aggressive, offensive action, even at the risk of killing innocents. The splinter group grew into the Irgun, then a more extreme offshoot known as Lehi, led by Avraham Stern, formed after the Irgun declared a moratorium on its attacks against the British in order to help the war effort against the Germans. Beneath the disputes over tactics and goals lay ideologies imported on the immigrant ships from Europe. Jabotinsky despised Ben-Gurion's extolment of the "proletarian" Hebrew laborer. Ben-Gurion's loyalists viewed Jabotinsky's disciples as bourgeois and fascist. Begin denounced Ben-Gurion as a Bolshevik. Ben-Gurion went so far as to compare Jabotinsky and Begin to Hitler.

"To even understand the intensity of that conflict you have to go back to Europe," Moshe Arens, the Likud elder statesman, told me not long before he died in 2019. "In the middle of building the Zionist entity," he said, "class struggle overruled everything." Arens, a Lithuanian-born American who went by the nickname Misha, had served as the national leader of the Betar youth movement in the United States before immigrating to Israel in 1948. In his book *Flags over the Warsaw Ghetto*, Arens chronicled the rivalry in Poland during World War II between the Zionist socialist force and the right-wing fighters from Betar. That enmity had prevented them from uniting even during the desperate and doomed uprising against the Nazis in the Warsaw Ghetto in 1943, though their ideological differences had become totally irrelevant in the misery of the ghetto, most of whose residents had already been sent to the Treblinka death camp and the gas chambers. Arens said he had written the book in order to redress what he saw as a historical injustice. The socialist state founders had largely erased the role of the Betar fighters in the Warsaw Ghetto uprising, a key symbol of Jewish resistance and heroism during the Holocaust, from the national narrative and Israeli textbooks. Finally, in 2011, after a lifetime of battling for recognition, Juta Harman, one of the last living survivors of the Betar-led resistance organization in the ghetto, was honored by Kibbutz Lohamei HaGetaot, the "Ghetto Fighters'" kibbutz, which was founded near Acre in 1949 by the socialist commanders who survived the uprising. Harman was eighty-nine by the time she was honored.

The visceral enmity between the rival undergrounds in pre-state Palestine peaked with a Haganah crackdown code-named *La Saison*, as in the hunting season. It began in November 1944, after the Lehi gang assassinated Lord Moyne, the British minister for the Middle East, in Cairo, and ran for several months. Declaring the Irgun and the Lehi gang terrorists and traitors who endangered the Zionist project, the Haganah forces went so far as to kidnap some operatives and hand them over to the British authorities. Nachmias said he feared the Haganah more than he feared the British. But once again Begin ordered his forces not to resist or hit back, so as to avoid a civil war.

Nevertheless, after the War of Independence, entering civilian life for the first time, Nachmias had trouble finding employment, lacking the "red book" carried by the ranks of the Mapai, Ben-Gurion's Workers of the Land of Israel party. A former Irgun commander gave him work for a while in Africa. He then saw an advertisement for a job as an air steward with El Al, the national airline. In the job interview, he followed the advice of a friend and remained "silent as a fish" about his days in Betar and the underground. Fluent in several languages, he was hired. His career as an El Al flight steward would last twenty-five years, and he flew whenever Begin flew. On one fifteen-hour flight to Washington, Nachmias recalled, the crew had prepared a bed for Begin in the staff quarters on the upper level of a jumbo jet. Begin, known for his modesty and frugality, insisted on staying in his seat because there weren't beds for everyone. Nachmias did not need to spell out the contrast with the Netanyahus, which was striking: When the couple flew to London to attend the funeral of Margaret Thatcher, sleeping quarters, complete with a double bed, were fitted on the El Al jet for the less-than-five-hour flight, reportedly at a cost of more than $120,000 of taxpayers' money.

Yoske and Yafa Nachmias had two sons, both of whom served in prestigious combat units of the IDF. One barely survived a clash on the Lebanon-Syria border. Nachmias's office was decorated with family photos of his seven grandchildren and seven great-grandchildren. He was animated as long as he was recounting his past escapades and his bit role in the country's history, never sparing the details. He had spoken for hours, with his back to the window, against the backdrop of the sparkling sea, as the beachside promenade teemed with Tel Aviv life, a constant parade of sun worshippers, daytime bar-goers, and skateboarders passing by. He was much less eager to discuss whether the Israel outside was the one he had dreamed of and risked so much for.

The maximalist state that the Irgun had envisioned, stretching eastward across the River Jordan, had not come about, despite the fact that its heirs had held the political upper hand for decades. That was clearly off the table. Now the fight was over the West Bank of the Jordan, where more than two million Palestinians were still hoping to throw off the Israeli occupation and where continued occupation would ultimately endanger the foundational Zionist principle of a Jewish democracy. The Revisionists, sticklers for liberal democracy, had envisioned equal rights for Arabs in sovereign Israeli territory, but including the West Bank in that equation would seriously undermine Israel's Jewish majority. That left the old disciples of the right, like Nachmias, paralyzed in an existential bind. When pressed for his thoughts, all he would say was that his lasting hope was for "peace with everyone," a platitude more suited to a beauty pageant contestant. "If the Palestinians could, they would throw us into the sea," he said. "Our commander, Menachem Begin, would not let us throw them into the sea. Let them dream. We are here." Nachmias was just as reluctant to air criticism of the political leadership, or anything else about his beloved country. "Our commanders said we would be a nation when there were Jewish prostitutes and gangsters," he eventually remarked, drawing on an adage attributed to several early Zionist leaders. Now, he noted wryly, "There are too many of them."

The Likud had clearly grown far from its Jabotinskyite roots, which combined nationalism with liberalism and a strict adherence to democratic values and the rule of law. The party had become more hawkish, booting out most of its so-called princes, the scions of the Irgun commanders and of Jabotinsky's credo. The foundational values, the dignity and glory, had given way to a much cruder populism and even racism. The scandals of the Beitar Jerusalem soccer team provided one stark illustration of that. Founded in 1936 as an affiliate of the Revisionist youth movement, it was the only club in Israel's Premier League to have never fielded an Arab player. When Arcadi Gaydamak, a Russian-Israeli oligarch and the club's owner at the time, secretly hired two Muslim players from Chechnya for the 2012–13 season, the team's hardcore fan group, La Familia, notorious for violence and racism, organized a boycott of the games and burned down the clubhouse. The next crisis came in 2020 after Israel signed its normalization pact with the United Arab Emirates. In one of the first deals to be publicized, the relatively new Beitar owner, Moshe Hogeg, a cryptocurrency executive, tried to sell half the ownership to a somewhat mysterious Muslim sheikh from the Gulf state, Hamad bin Khalifa Al Nahyan, who was presented as a wealthy member of Abu Dhabi's ruling family. But questions were raised about the depth of the sheikh's royal connections and his finances, which were reported to be mostly tied up in nontradeable Venezuelan government bonds. The deal was put on ice, but not before La Familia fans stormed the soccer team's training ground and issued threats against Hogeg.

Israel did emerge from the *Altalena* episode with one government, one army, and one parliament, but it has remained riven by its identity politics. And as Netanyahu fed on them and chipped away at the institutions of the country's liberal democracy, Moshe Arens came to regret having promoted his political career. After Netanyahu's government pushed through the controversial "nation-state" law in 2018 enshrining national self-determination as "unique to the Jewish people" and specifying that Arabic was not an official language but would have a "special status," Arens wrote a searing commentary in *Haaretz,* the liberal-left newspaper, arguing that the law had caused needless damage to Israel and was gratuitously insulting to the country's Arab citizens when Israel's Jewishness was not, in any case, in question.

The Holocaust survivors disembarking from the immigrant ships were not expected to dwell on their trauma. The images of emaciated Jews who had been herded like proverbial sheep to the slaughter did not sit well with the Zionist pioneering ethos. For one thing, the Zionists of the *Yishuv,* who had been building the scaffolding of the state for decades before the Holocaust, with their own sweat and blood, wanted it to be viewed as a legitimate national home for the Jews, not as a project built out of guilt on the ashes of the six million. Nor did the survivors want or have time to wallow in grief. Instead, they threw themselves into fighting for and building the homeland, finding a permanent refuge, and giving their own shattered lives new purpose. The survivors had largely kept the horrors of their past to themselves until Israeli agents captured Adolf Eichmann, an architect of the Final Solution, in Argentina in 1960 and brought him to justice in Israel. It was only during his trial, in 1961, that many Israelis began to hear the shocking testimonies of the survivors for the first time, and for the first time, many survivors began to feel Israeli. And now they, too, were fading away, taking with them some of the grit that had made Israel what it was.

Among the more tangible symbols of the victory and survival was the thriving community of Kibbutz Lohamei HaGetaot, the collective founded by Warsaw Ghetto uprising fighters who survived. They had planned the kibbutz immediately after the war, while they were still in Poland, along with the Ghetto Fighters' House, the world's first Holocaust museum, which would be built adjacent to the kibbutz to commemorate the heroism and the losses. The founders were among those who bore witness at the Eichmann trial. Half a century later, one of them, Dorka Sternberg, a diminutive widow in her nineties with a pixie haircut, sat in her little kibbutz house where she lived with her Filipina caretaker, Sarita, and spilled out her harrowing story as if she were reliving it. Born in the Polish town of Czestochowa, as Devorah Zissel Bram, she was fifteen when the war broke out. Together with her parents, a younger brother of bar mitzvah age, and sister of about eight, she was moved into a ghetto. During an *aktzia*, or roundup, she and her brother were selected to be sent out to a work camp. She saw her mother and sister being led off after a rabbi persuaded them to leave their hiding place, saying they would be killed if they were found but that God would look after them if they came out. Dorka never saw them, or her father, again. They were murdered in the Treblinka concentration camp. Dorka was transferred to a forced labor camp and was first put to work in the fields picking carrots and cabbages. A soldier offered her and her friends a piece of pork sausage once. Coming from a religious, Hasidic background, she examined it, chewed a bit, hesitated, then swallowed it, deciding at that moment that she was parting ways with God, who had failed her family. Her group was then moved back to Czestochowa to work in an arms factory. One day she found herself lined up in the ghetto square in another *aktzia*. Two Jewish youths emerged from a bunker with a handgun. A shot rang out. There was shouting and curses flew in German. The boys were killed on the spot. As a lesson, the soldiers then randomly picked twenty-five young Jews out of the lines, including one of Dorka's girlfriends from their religious youth movement, stood them against a wall, and shot them dead. "I got lucky, I suppose," she said brightly, "because I am here."

Her war ended on January 15, 1945, as the Russians advanced. The Germans said they were taking her group to Germany, but she took her fate into her own hands, hiding in a bathroom, then running. She found others hiding in a carpentry shop, including two girlfriends. It was snowing. A local man with a horse and cart took them to a farmhouse where they were given food and shelter. After walking back to their hometown they were initially dizzy with freedom, Sternberg recalled, but despair soon set in when they found that their families had all perished and they were alone. Salvation came when Yitzhak (Antek) Zuckerman, one of the surviving leaders of the Warsaw Ghetto uprising, came looking to recruit young Jews to set up temporary kibbutz communes in Poland in preparation for moving to the Land of Israel. "We looked to him like a God, an emissary from heaven," Dorka said, recalling a tall figure knocking on their window and gushing with talk of a free people building their homeland. From that moment their lives had new meaning. The young women moved to Warsaw and joined a larger group to set up a temporary commune. On March 20, 1950, Dorka arrived in Israel and went straight to the ghetto fighters' kibbutz that had been founded the year before in the north, by an ancient Roman aqueduct. She became an educator and married one of the activists she had met in Poland. They had two daughters, grandchildren, and great-grandchildren, some still living on the kibbutz. But, of the 150 Holocaust survivors who had made the kibbutz their home, she was one of only two or three who could still tell their stories.

As the survivor generation aged, it was a mark of shame that thousands of them, out of the 240,000 or so who had come to Israel, were living below the poverty line in damp apartments with peeling walls, forced to choose between paying for medication and heating. Neglect by earlier governments and differing categories of benefits depending on the survivors' country of origin or date of arrival in Israel had left many struggling, particularly those from the Soviet Union who had suffered under the Nazis but had not been sent to camps or ghettos and had fallen through the cracks of the Israeli administrations' policies.

By contrast, many of the survivors had undergone an astonishing renaissance in Israel, finding a safe haven, contributing to its culture, building new families, and thriving. Lea Gottlieb, who hid from the Nazis during the German occupation of Hungary, opened a raincoat factory with her husband after arriving at the Port of Haifa in 1949, very much like the one they had left behind. But seeing little rain and only sunshine, they turned to producing designer beachwear and founded Gottex, a company that quickly grew to become a leading Israeli brand name abroad. Kariel Gardosh, a Hungarian survivor whose family was murdered in Auschwitz, became the caricaturist known as Dosh, who created Srulik, a figure in sandals, a blue work shirt, and a blue canvas hat. Srulik became the symbol of what native-born Israelis saw as their quintessential selves—guileless and pioneering, with none of the complexes and pretenses of Europe.

Still, many were stalked and haunted by what they had left behind. Walking into Tova Berlinski's heavily furnished Jerusalem apartment was like entering a gallery of ghosts. On the walls were the portraits she had painted of her late father, a distinguished, pious-looking man with a beard, and her late mother and brother, their features vanishing into the canvas like hazy memories. She painted them that way, she said, because they were gone, murdered in the Holocaust. Born Gusta Wolf, Berlinski grew up the oldest of six children in a Hasidic family in Oswiecim, Poland—a half-Jewish, half-Christian town of about 12,000 residents. The Auschwitz-Birkenau Nazi concentration and death camp would rise up on its outskirts. She met Eliyahu, whom she called Elec, from nearby Sosnowiec, through the Betar youth movement. They married in 1938, when she was twenty-three, and set out for Palestine infused with Zionism and in defiance of the restrictions on immigration imposed by the British authorities. That decision saved their lives, and Tova went on to become a centenarian. We first met when she was 102, a childless widow. She had a sad indifference to her, but her pure white hair was always perfectly coiffed, her face barely wrinkled. Visits were by appointment, because it took some time for her to get dressed for visitors with the help of Jenny, her lively Filipina caregiver. Following Jenny's advice, I would always arrive with some chocolate.

The voyage from Oswiecim was arduous. After the Berlinskis' ship finally anchored off the Mediterranean coast, somewhere between Caesaria and Zichron Yaakov, the passengers stayed on board for three nights waiting for a signal to come ashore. It finally came on the eve of Yom Kippur, from a masked Haganah fighter on a horse. The immigrants disembarked and walked two hours to a fruit-packing house in an orchard. Most of them did not eat the next day, observing the fast. After sundown, buses came to take them wherever they requested. The Berlinskis had no fixed destination and accepted an offer to settle in Netanya, a short ride south along the coast. Tova began work in a canned-food factory. She and Eliyahu were housed in a large hall with other new immigrants, mostly singles. There was little privacy. By day everybody went to work. At night, they got dressed up and went out dancing. The Berlinskis disapproved. "We had come to build the state," Tova said. They asked to be moved.

Their search for a home took them to Betar company headquarters in Rosh Pina, a farming community in the Galilee, then Herzliya, then Tel Aviv. They picked tobacco and oranges. Eliyahu spent a few months in a British jail, fought in the Negev in the 1948 war, then went to work for a government trade office. The couple finally wound up in Jerusalem after Ben-Gurion instructed the government to relocate people from Tel Aviv in order to strengthen Israel's claim to the contested holy city. By then, the Berlinskis had left the Betar movement, finding it too militaristic.

At the beginning of the Second World War, Tova said she was still able to get letters to her family in Poland. Later all contact was lost. Eventually she heard from a sister who survived that her parents and four other siblings had all perished in the Holocaust, most of them in Auschwitz.

Tova had meanwhile studied drama in Tel Aviv and joined the Cameri Theater, where she remembered performing in a Hebrew production of Federico García Lorca's *Blood Wedding*. In Jerusalem she took care of children in the mornings and took afternoon courses at the prestigious Bezalel Academy of Arts and Design. Eliyahu became a lawyer, and as their circumstances improved, they took up hobbies, including ballroom dancing, which they had once considered frivolous.

In the 1970s, she joined the Climate group of Israeli artists, which promoted the idea of local Israeli painting as a rejection of imported art movements, but she soon broke with the group, which then dissolved. She was perhaps best known for her series *Black Flowers,* the subject of a solo exhibition at the Israel Museum in 1995. She said she had painted the somber black and gray blooms, often with their heads bowed, for her parents because there were no graves to visit. She also painted Israeli landscapes, stark and desolate, punctuated by towering cypress trees and heavy rocks. A minimalist still life depicted a pair of empty chairs. The family portraits with vanishing features and faces that faded into geometric patterns were meant as an expression of her pain.

Eliyahu died when Tova was in her eighties. Fifteen years later, settled in her favorite armchair, dressed in a floral summer frock, her smooth hair combed in a perfect bob, she said she still tried to get out each week to the hairdresser's, or to the clinic or to a café to meet friends. With Jenny's encouragement, she had taken up painting again and vibrant colors emerged. A recent work propped up on a ledge by a window depicted a bowl of oranges, a glossy green plant, a blue sky. Another work, dated April 2017, sat on an ornamental easel—an optimistic vista of balcony doors opening onto a rolling desert bathed in the Mediterranean sunlight. In the fall of 2017, a poet friend who ran a private gallery near Tova's home in the leafy German Colony neighborhood of Jerusalem, where she'd lived for more than fifty years, arranged a retrospective and sale of her artwork. The gallery owner and a curator rummaged through piles of paintings Tova kept in spare bedrooms, picking out options for the final exhibit. Among them was a colorful abstract depicting the store Posner that sold candy and ice cream in the Oswiecim of Tova's childhood. She said she could still remember the taste.

Berlinski had been back to Oswiecim several times, to visit a local, non-Jewish family that had been close to her mother. Her grandfather was buried in the cemetery there. Otherwise her family left no trace behind. Their house had been sold and the new occupants had grown a beautiful garden. During Berlinski's last visit in 2006, in a poignant act of closure, she donated a black flower painting to the Auschwitz-Birkenau Museum. A framed letter in Polish hung on her living room wall; it was signed by the mayor of Oswiecim, Janusz Chwierut, congratulating her on reaching the age of 100. "On this extraordinary day," the mayor wrote, "I extend to you greetings from the heart, from the city of your birth, Oswiecim."

Over the years, Berlinski had moved to the left and became active in Peace Now, the Israeli anti-settlement group that was founded in the late 1970s, as Israel was negotiating peace with Egypt, and was still advocating for territorial compromise with the Palestinians. Neatly folded copies of the liberal *Haaretz* newspaper sat on her coffee table. Israel had turned out differently than she expected. There had always been arguments, she said, but people had become more materialistic, a criticism of many of the country's veterans. She feared for Israel's future, between the enemies outside and the internal strife within. "We could lose the country," she said. She had already lost one world. But with all its flaws Israel was still her refuge. The dilemmas and conflicts that racked the rival Zionist movements hardly compared with the torment of those who had escaped Hitler's ovens. There was no peace with the Palestinians, not now, and not for the foreseeable future, but fewer Israelis seemed bothered about that.

The living memory of the Holocaust was naturally fading, though given the resurgence of antisemitism in Europe and elsewhere, and the rampant polarization and poisonous discourse within Israel, it had never seemed more relevant. The Ghetto Fighters' Museum was adapting to the age, moving away from depicting the Holocaust as a static historical event that was only a Jewish tragedy, focusing more on the moral lessons for humanity as a whole and advocating the peaceful resolution of inner conflicts. The Holocaust was held up as a warning sign against the international growth of xenophobia, threats to liberalism and democracy, and the challenge of alternative truth enabled by social media.

In the perpetual political tumult, it was easy to lose sight of Israel's virtues. But perhaps less so for those who had found refuge from calamity here.

"Only this morning I thought to myself how I love it for what it is," Berlinski said of her adopted country. "A religious man can walk around with his *tzitzit* out, and nobody will say a word," she said, referring to the fringed ritual undergarment worn by observant Jewish men. "Here," she added, with piercing, disarming simplicity, "we have the freedom to be what we are."

Haim Gouri, the aging Palmach warrior and national poet, rose from his armchair, plucked the well-worn volume from his crowded library, went straight to the page containing one of his seminal Hebrew poems, "I Am a Civil War," and told me to read it for him out loud. The air bristled with emotion and the awe of the moment. Here was one of Israel's leading intellectuals and a voice of the national conscience asking me to recite one of his most meaningful creations in his presence. I had come one weekday morning to speak to Gouri and his dedicated wife and comrade, Aliza, about a campaign to preserve the memory of the

Palmach, which had been in the news and in which they were involved. But the conversation had instead plumbed the depths of Gouri's conflicted soul.

Born Haim Gurfinkel on October 9, 1923, to Israel and Gila Gurfinkel, who had arrived by ship from the Black Sea city of Odessa four years earlier, Haim had spent his early childhood in Tel Aviv, the first Hebrew city. The family Hebraized their surname to Gouri. Haim's father served as a member of the Knesset from Ben-Gurion's Mapai party from 1949 until 1965, the year he died. Haim had become best known as the voice of the 1948 generation, celebrating camaraderie and commemorating the war dead in his economical but profound and haunting poems. Now, at ninety-three, his thick, white mop of hair with its glorious quiff belied his sapping strength. He was no longer taking his famous walks through the Old City of Jerusalem and was instead shrinking into his trademark blue jeans. He was painfully aware that time was running out and, since I, a former neighbor and journalist, had happened by, there were urgent lessons he wished to impart.

I had taken the opportunity to ask him something that had long intrigued me, to understand him better: What was the source, or the particular event, that had inspired him to compose his poem "Civil War" in the 1950s, eleven lines of almost terse Hebrew verse expressing the search for an elusive justice and the seeming left-wing Zionist condition of the national predicament melding indistinguishably with personal bargaining and torment. He had written it well before the conquest of 1967, which had riven his own conscience, as well as that of the nation. Maybe Gouri, this old wellspring of wisdom, had the answers, with hindsight, that might soothe some of the affliction. Perhaps he could offer some comfort and hope, decipher the problem and its solution. The question had clearly struck a nerve. That's when he fetched the book and asked me to recite. I did so in a trembling voice, conscious of the need to avoid tripping over the pronunciation of the literary Hebrew.

> I'm a civil war
> and half of me fires to the last
> at the walls of the vanquished.

*I'm a court martial*
*working in shifts,*
*its light never dimmed.*
*And those in the right fire on the others in the right.*
*And then it's quiet*
*a calm composed of fatigue and darkness and empty shells.*
*I'm nighttime in a city open*
*to everyone who's hungry.*

After a charged pause, Gouri's eyes glistening with trapped tears, he told me that the line about "those in the right" firing on "the others in the right" was the most important line he had ever written in his life. It was about one half of Gouri firing on the other half of Gouri. And then the memories began to spill out. His personal civil war had originated in an event from his childhood and had never really ended, he said. He related how one day his mother had come out of the house and saw an Arab on a donkey hawking cheap, fine-quality tomatoes and cucumbers. Two Jewish youths came by and told the vendor to clear off; the Zionists were trying to promote Hebrew labor and produce. The Arab stood his ground, so the youths tipped his vegetables out of the crates onto the street. "My mother was extremely Zionistic," Gouri recalled, "but when she saw what had happened, she ran to pick up the tomatoes and cucumbers and returned them to the vendor. She didn't stop crying for two weeks." There was a "terrible contradiction," he said, between the Zionist ideal of Hebrew labor and the socialist, humanistic need for the Arab laborers to have a livelihood. "We have inherited that strife from previous generations," he said. "That was the civil war."

The Gouris called each other by their nicknames, Jourie and Alika. He would rely on her to provide the names and details that eluded him as we talked. She served fruit and cake on plain glass plates from before the age of Ikea. They had lived in the same modest but classic third-floor walk-up since 1961. The apartment was filled with books and art and memories, no doubt. The apartment building, originally constructed by the professional association for working journalists, was in the genteel, well-heeled neighborhood of Talbieh, once the home of Palestinian families who lived in grand villas. Aliza tended to the

plants that turned their small balcony into a suspended green sanctuary. My family had lived across the road from the Gouris for a period of
many years and I would see him going off for his long weekend walks
to the Old City with his close friend, a literary theorist. Occasionally
he would come over and reminisce on our porch.

By the age of twelve Haim was enraptured by the romance of the
pioneering Zionist settlers and went to live in Kibbutz Beit Alfa, one of
the early communal farms, founded in 1922, in the north of the country. He went on to study at the Kadoorie Agricultural High School at
the same time as Yitzhak Rabin. He joined the Palmach as a fighter and
a few years later was sent to Europe to help smuggle Jewish survivors
and refugees to Palestine. Returning in 1948, he fought as a deputy
company commander in the Negev division. He had met Aliza Becker,
an eighteen-year-old casualty officer, in a hospital in Beersheba while
he was visiting a wounded commander there; they married in 1952.

For the Gouris, the 1948 War of Independence had never truly
ended. The reason I had come to visit them that fall morning was
because they were fighting one last, determined battle with their ebb-
ing strength, not against an Arab enemy this time but against what
they viewed as a historic travesty from within. As a young officer in
1948, Aliza had served in the Palmach's legendary Harel Brigade, which
played a critical role in the war, including securing the supply convoys
making their way up the steep and winding road to Jerusalem, captur-
ing the high ground, and breaching the siege of the city. Bab el Wad,
Arabic for "Gate of the Valley" and known in Hebrew as Shaar Hagai,
was a landmark site at a strategic juncture at the foot of the Jerusalem
hills, where the road narrowed into a gorge, making convoys bringing
essential supplies to the besieged Jews of the holy city easy prey for the
Palestinian fighters from the villages in the surrounding hills. One of
Haim's most iconic and haunting poems, "Bab el Wad," commemorated the heroic and terrible sacrifices of the Palmach's battles to open
the road. Set to music, it was often sung by Israelis with the reverence
of a secular hymn. The chorus went:

> Bab el Wad,
> Remember our names for all time.
> Where convoys to the city broke through

*Our dead lie sprawled by the roadside.*
*The iron skeleton, like my comrade, is mute.*

Shaar Hagai had been declared a heritage site for conservation back
in 1979. Drivers speeding up or down the modern highway connecting
Tel Aviv and Jerusalem would pass the spot, marked by a nineteenth-
century, Ottoman-era stone khan, or caravanserai, which used to serve
pilgrims journeying between Jaffa Port and Jerusalem and marked the
beginning of the climb through the narrow pass known as the Jerusalem corridor. The historic khan and the old, empty husks of a few
clumsy armored vehicles left by the roadside had long served as every-
day reminders of the battles and the fallen, along with a few memorial
sites dedicated to specific fighting units tucked into the hills above.
Around 2016, the Netanyahu government came up with new plans
to create a museum and a visitors' center at Shaar Hagai. The problem was that the government intended to name the center in memory
of Rehavam Zeevi, a former Palmach commander and army general
who became a highly controversial, far-right politician and advocated
the transfer of Palestinians to Arab countries. Zeevi was assassinated
by Palestinian militants in a Jerusalem hotel in 2001, at the height of
the Second Intifada. But naming the site for him was deemed nothing short of sacrilegious by the Palmach veterans and their supporters,
who had mostly remained in the liberal, left-wing camp.

Not only had Zeevi's politics been anathema to his old Palmach comrades, but he had played no part in the campaign to secure and open
the road to besieged Jerusalem. The Harel Brigade fighters had taken
tough actions of their own, clearing Palestinian villages that threatened the highway to Jerusalem, blowing up houses, and turning their
residents into refugees, but that was viewed as a wartime imperative
on the way to independence. To make matters worse, Zeevi had gotten
mixed up with criminal gangsters and was accused posthumously of
sexual assault in an Israeli television documentary aired in 2016. The
Gouris were almost beside themselves as they described their personal
anguish, the sense of national affront, and the dishonor the government was doing to history and the memory of the Palmach fighters
who were sacrificed in the battles to open the road in 1948.

Sitting that morning over tea and cake, in the old Jerusalem way, the couple wanted me to feel what they were feeling and to see what they had seen. The stories of 1948 began tumbling out with the kind of urgency and detail the founding generation seemed to excel in, for fear of it being the last time they would be told. In those days, by night, Aliza would hear the dull ring of the gravediggers' spades in the small Palmach cemetery at Kibbutz Qiryat Anavim, in the hills of the Jerusalem corridor, preparing graves for the casualties that morning would bring. There was often an awful dilemma, she said, between preparing adequately for the dead and damaging the fighters' morale by digging too many graves.

Next, Haim urged Aliza to recount the story of the night when a beloved Palmach fighter nicknamed Jimmy, the son of a prominent artist, Menachem Shemi, had been killed in action and she went with a driver to notify his parents so they could part with him before his burial. Aliza and the driver first picked up a relative from Kibbutz Maagan Michael, on the Carmel coast, and went on to the Shemi family's home in Haifa, but found it closed up. They proceeded to the artist's getaway in Safed in the Galilee and, finding him and his wife, rode back with them in silence to the makeshift morgue in the friendly Arab village of Abu Gosh in the Jerusalem corridor. There, Aliza said, Jimmy's father lifted the army blanket from his son's face and drew his portrait. As Aliza described that most intimate moment in the battle for Jerusalem, Haim became emotional, the tears welling up in his eyes. "What we are telling you today is the holy of holies," he insisted, desperate to convey the significance of their final battle for justice at Shaar Hagai.

For weeks prior to my visit, a group of elderly Palmach veterans had been holding protests in the forest by the old khan. The Gouris were planning on attending another protest there that afternoon so I drove there myself to join them. Leaving the Jerusalem–Tel Aviv highway at Beit Shemesh, I made a loop back toward Shaar Hagai. There they were, the veterans, gathering in a clearing in the forest. One came with a hearing aid, another leaning on a walker. Among them were some legendary figures like the commander Eliyahu Sela, still known by his nickname of Raanana. Each had their stories. Pesach Azariyahu, eighty-six, recalled fighting along the road as a youth of sixteen with orphans who had survived the Holocaust. Tovah Ofer, a feisty eighty-seven-year-old and former Palmach medic, reminisced about how she had accompanied the primitively armored convoys and how, when they came under attack, the booms of battle would echo through the hills. The weekly protests, mostly held on Fridays, were organized with the help of the veterans' now-grown children, eager to defend their parents' legacy and place in the national narrative. Their demand: that the planned visitors' center be named, not for Zeevi, but collectively for the fighters of the Palmach who died or risked their lives breaching the road to Jerusalem and escorting the convoys. It was a wrenching sight, these proud heroes picking their way across the muddy ground to make a last stand. The arrival of the Gouris, by now icons of the Palmach, stirred up an additional flurry of excitement, as if royalty had descended on the gathering. Plastic chairs were provided for Haim and Aliza, and Haim was soon called upon to speak. His voice quivering with rage and indignation like a rejected prophet, he threatened to call a hunger strike and declared the government's plan to name the center for Zeevi a "casus belli," as if firing up the troops for a final charge. Someone produced a guitar and the now-emotional crowd, the elders sitting on plastic chairs and their younger cohorts standing around in a circle, began to sing in unison, stirring, full-throated renditions of "Bab el Wad" and "HaReut" ("The Friendship"), another of Gouri's most popular poems that had been set to music long ago and become a hallowed anthem of bygone times.

It was a magical moment that captured, for a few fleeting minutes, the old spirit of comradeship that had forged the new state, just as Gouri's poems of fellowship and camaraderie, and of love and child-hood, drew on and helped forge the language, culture, and emerging identity of the young but divided country. Eventually, after about six months of protests, the government relented and began to look for an alternative site to commemorate Zeevi, who already had at least one bridge and one highway named for him.

Gouri, who became a renowned journalist, novelist, and documen-tary filmmaker, as well as a poet, never stopped struggling with the deep moral dilemmas and inherent contradictions of being an Israeli. The triumph and the territorial conquests of the Six-Day War would sharpen the divisions in Israel and claw at Gouri's conscience. He too was initially swept up in the euphoria after Israel suddenly found itself in control of the biblical heartland of the West Bank and the Old City of Jerusalem, including the Temple Mount, the holiest site in Judaism and once the location of its ancient temples, which is also revered by Muslims as the Noble Sanctuary, the compound now housing the Aqsa Mosque. Like other secular intellectuals of his generation who were steeped in knowledge of the scriptures, Gouri was quickly persuaded by another leading poet, Natan Alterman, to sign up as a member of the newly formed Land of Israel Movement, which maintained that the newly won territories were part of Israel's national heritage and should never be relinquished. Founded by a mix of Labor Zionist and Revisionist intellectuals, the movement rushed to publish its manifesto in the newspapers. Gouri soon regretted having put his name to it and quit. He also lived to regret another episode in the 1970s, when he found himself embroiled in a struggle between the early settlers of the messianic Gush Emunim movement and the Israeli government. On a journalistic mission, he had raced up to Sebastia, in the northern West Bank, where radical settlers were attempting to turn an abandoned train station into the first Jewish outpost in the Samarian hills, an area heavily populated by Palestinians. Shimon Peres, then the defense minister and a Labor hawk, was at the site and, as the atmosphere grew increasingly charged, he drafted Gouri to help with the negotiations. The upshot was that Gouri ended up partially responsible for the settlement of the sensitive area. He had suggested a compromise allowing thirty of the men to remain on a nearby army base, pending a government discussion. Behind the scenes, though, Peres changed the terms to appease the settlers further, allowing thirty families to stay at the army base and essentially sanctioning the first Jewish settlement in Samaria. Both Peres, who became a dove, and Gouri would later insist that their intention had only been to defuse a potentially explosive situation.

Gouri had borne witness to many decisive moments in the building of the country. He was there, in uniform, soon after the 1948 war, when Ben-Gurion gathered a group of Jewish intellectuals around him, convinced that Israel's survival would depend on spiritual superiority as well as military prowess. In 1950, Gouri stormed into Ben-Gurion's office to complain that the police had taken one of his books off the shelves because it hadn't been submitted to the censors prior to publication and it contained the names of army units and commanders that

were still apparently considered military secrets. Two years later Gouri
was there when Menachem Begin fired up a crowd in Jerusalem's Zion
Square and urged them to march on the Knesset. They were protesting
Ben-Gurion's negotiations with Germany for reparations for Holocaust
survivors, which Begin saw as blood money. Begin claimed the police
were coming with "gas bombs," Gouri said, and the protesters stormed
uphill to the old Knesset building, smashed the windows, and tried to
break in. Gouri went on to cover the Eichmann trial for his newspaper. Deeply affected by the survivors' testimonies and courage, which
belied the dismissive early Zionists' image of the "sheep to the slaughter," he made a trilogy of documentaries about the Holocaust, Jewish
immigration to Palestine, and Jewish resistance during World War II.

But nothing seemed to be consuming him as much as the virulent
hatred for the other that was coursing through modern Israeli society,
and Gouri now felt compelled to dig into and expose some of its roots.
On the day of my visit, sitting with his beloved pipe at hand, he suddenly broke into an old Betar ditty set to a Russian folk tune that went
*"Stalin, Hitler, Ben-Gurion / We will send them to their doom / And,
with God's help, Mapai too."* He was determined to shed light on the
ways that the rivalry between the pre-state undergrounds continued to
poison the politics of the new state, and on how things could have perhaps turned out differently, even if it meant reviving some memories
he had long preferred to keep buried. In May 1963, he recalled, just two
years after the Eichmann trial, he had attended a Knesset session that
truly shocked him. He said he heard Ben-Gurion, the prime minister,
accusing Begin's Herut party—a precursor of the Likud—of praising
Hitler. The next day Gouri published a blistering column in *LaMerhav,*
a leftist party newspaper, titled "Shame," criticizing the prime minister's rhetoric. The next morning a messenger knocked on the Gouris'
door in Talbieh and hand-delivered a typed three-page letter marked
"Private" and signed by Ben-Gurion. Gouri said he would have fainted
on the spot had he not been a young man with a strong heart. The letter
was no apology. Instead, the contents offered a rare insight into the pro-
fundity of Ben-Gurion's loathing for Begin and left Gouri reeling. The
original letter was now among Gouri's personal papers in the archive of
the National Library of Israel and he urged me to go read it for myself.

In the hushed archive down in the bowels of the old National Library building on the Givat Ram campus of Hebrew University of Jerusalem, the archivist in charge of Gouri's documents helped me find the manila file I was looking for. Near the bottom of the pile of papers, there it was, the letter, typed in black and white on flimsy paper, the founding father speaking from the grave. Ben-Gurion had written to Gouri that he found his newspaper column "baffling" but unsurprising, saying he understood that covering the Eichmann trial had left a heavy mark. Ben-Gurion then went on to justify his attack on Begin, describing him, no less, as "distinctly Hitlerite: Racist, ready to destroy all the Arabs for the sake of the integrity of the land, sanctifying all means for the sacred goal—absolute power."

Ben-Gurion went on to catalog Begin's "crimes," including the Irgun's deadly bombing of the King David Hotel; the "pogrom" at Deir Yassin, a Palestinian village in the Jerusalem hills; and the *Altalena* episode, which he described as an attempt "to seize power by force." Citing the storming of the Knesset by an "inflamed mob" acting on Begin's instructions, Ben-Gurion wrote that he feared a takeover of Israel by Begin, warning that Begin would replace the army and police command with "his thugs" and "rule like Hitler ruled Germany." Here and there, a typed word was crossed out and corrected by hand. "I have no doubt that Begin hates Hitler," Ben-Gurion continued, "but that hatred does not prove that he is any different from him." He concluded that Gouri had written what he had written out of "decency and good intentions—but in total political blindness."

Gouri had published the letter in Hebrew in the past but was hesitant about publicizing it in English for fear of its effect on the international image of Israel's leaders. However, addressing the internal divisions had become more urgent for him, while he still had time. The political revolution finally came in 1977, bringing Begin and his Likud party to power for the first time. Overturning thirty years of Labor Zionist hegemony, they had ridden in on a wave of rage against the old Mapai establishment following the debacle of the 1973 war, when Israel was caught dangerously off guard, and propelled into power by the resentment of working-class *Mizrahim*, Israel's disadvantaged underclass, who revolted against the old elites. In 1981, when Begin had just been reelected by a narrow margin, there was another knock at the door of the Gouris' apartment. This time the delivery boy was bringing an envelope from Begin, who wanted Gouri to know that Ben-Gurion had sought to reconcile with him in the years before his death. Begin had enclosed a copy of a letter he received from Ben-Gurion in 1969, in which Ben-Gurion had written that, while he opposed some of Begin's positions and actions, he had nothing against him on a personal level. "The more I have gotten to know you in recent years," Ben-Gurion had written, "the more I have come to appreciate you." In addition to the copy of the letter from Ben-Gurion, Begin included a personal note from himself to Gouri. "I have copied the late Mr. Ben-Gurion's letter for you not in order to 'brag,'" he wrote. "But from the moment I received this letter I have always asked myself: Maybe we would really have been spared many tragic and even terrible things had the late Ben-Gurion, of blessed memory, and I been better acquainted with one another."

That opportunity for historic national reconciliation had been missed. The divisions lived on. Gouri lamented that his people were mired in argument. The War of Independence was "still going on," he said, with no sign of peace with the Palestinians and the Israeli right-wing and religious sectors getting stronger. "I don't know where it will end." Sitting in that same Talbieh apartment decades on, Gouri described yet another incident that had left him in turmoil. One Friday a few years back, the Gouris had taken their grandchildren to Tel Aviv to visit a café that was one of Haim's old literary haunts and where he said he was received like a king. It was the summer of 2014 and Israel was in the midst of a deadly war with the rocket-launching Islamic militant groups in Gaza. As Gouri was leaving the café, an anonymous, middle-aged Jewish vendor spotted him, rushed out of his store, and began cursing him in the street. "You writers, you leftists, you kibbutzniks," the vendor inveighed. "It's because of you that they are murdering our sons." Relating the event years later, Haim, long a voice of the national zeitgeist and the Palmach generation who had sanctified Israel's sacrifices of war, was visibly shaken and bewildered as to why writers, leftists, and kibbutzniks would now be blamed for Israel's dead. "Why these three?" he asked. Had they not once epitomized the heroism and spirit on which Israel was built? "I have always been able to decode the Israeli psyche," Gouri said. Now he was distressed that he could no longer decipher his compatriots. "It's a mentality we do not know," Aliza said of the anonymous vendor, trying to comfort Haim and calm him. "You are not the problem," she said, gently. "It is the Israeli psyche that has become more complicated."

Before dawn on the last day of January 2018, Haim Gouri died peacefully at home, surrounded by family. The public paid tribute at a memorial ceremony in the courtyard of the Jerusalem Theater nearby. One of Gouri's three daughters recalled that, when asked how he was, his stock answer was "I fare as well as my people."

With his death it was not only a generation that was passing. Israel was also witnessing the death of ideology. The Labor Party had dwindled into near oblivion, replaced largely by centrist political forces whose main platform was a worthy, if somewhat amorphous, return to some kind of moral decency, sense of unity, and values but who dared not utter a controversial opinion for fear of scaring off whatever nebulous support they could garner from disillusioned soft-right voters. Any prospect of peace with the Palestinians remained elusive. The political leverage afforded by the system of coalition politics encouraged and empowered small parties catering to particular interest groups. So the ideological core of the battle between the camps had waned along with their sense of purpose, morphing into the less glorious, gladiatorial realm of the politics of identity, fear and hate and inherited tribal affiliations that often had less to do with a vision for the future than with the loyalties and resentments from the past. Netanyahu's most loyal base, largely made up of *Mizrahim,* many still smarting over the old arrogance of Mapai, had built something of a personality cult around him as a next-generation Begin. Israeli politics had split into two main blocs that were generally labeled the "Only Bibi" and "Anyone but Bibi" camps.

Sadly, Gouri did not live to hear Prime Minister Netanyahu eulogize him from the podium of the Knesset with heartfelt words that may have redeemed some of Gouri's faith in the broken soul of his country. Netanyahu, the heir of Jabotinsky and Begin, spoke of his respect for those who "fought ferociously for the rebirth of Israel, few against many," describing Gouri as "an extraordinary combination of fighter and man of letters." He spoke of the strong emotions evoked by the songs "Bab el Wad" and "HaReut." And he recalled a meeting he had held with the Palmach veterans, Gouri among them, who came to petition him not to dedicate the Shaar Hagai heritage center to Zeevi but instead to memorialize the fighters who escorted the convoys and breached the siege of Jerusalem. "They each spoke piercingly, emotionally. And then Haim Gouri spoke," Netanyahu said, recalling how Gouri recited Natan Alterman's poem "Remarks by the Breachers of the Road" by heart. "He had lived those days of lead and blood, days in which his friends fell all around him," Netanyahu said of Gouri. "He recited the poem, speaking from his soul, from his heart, and when he finished, there was silence. And then I said, 'The discussion is over. I have made a decision. The memorialization will be as you wish it, as it should be.' I will never forget that moment." When the heritage center at Shaar Hagai finally opened in the spring of 2021, two lines of verse had been mounted in large iron lettering on the façade of the stone khan for travelers on the road to Jerusalem to read, from Gouri's "Bab el Wad": "*Remember our names for all time / Where convoys to the city broke through.*" At least that battle had been won. Gouri, the old Palmach poet-warrior, could rest in peace.

# THREE

# RIVER OF DISCONTENT

THE GENTLE, shallow stream ran for about a mile through the middle of an old kibbutz in the Valley of Springs, a sun-beaten plain about twenty-five miles south of the Sea of Galilee in northern Israel. Its waters were a stunning, inviting aquamarine, the surroundings deceptively serene. For just below the surface lay the ethnic demon, waiting to emerge. And, when it did, the question of who had access to the river became one of the edgier battles between the old Israel and the new one.

More than six decades had passed since the major waves of Mizrahi immigrants arrived and more than forty years since their votes of resentment had helped sweep Menachem Begin into power, unseating the Ashkenazi establishment. Yet the stinging legacy of discrimination still lingered, leaving many feeling marginalized on Israel's socioeconomic and geographic periphery, with less opportunity for advancement. Now and again, usually around election time, the so-called ethnic demon, the manifestation of the country's old Ashkenazi-Mizrahi divide, would be stirred awake by one side or the other in the hopes of reaping some political gain. But, as diversity awareness and social consciousness seeped across Israel's well-guarded borders, a newly assertive generation of *Mizrahim* began to rise up and challenge the system.

Both empowered and disappointed by decades of mostly Likud rule, Israel's *Mizrahim* were having a moment.

Since the fall of 2019, a group of activists had been gathering each Friday outside the locked yellow steel gate at the entrance of the kibbutz Nir David, noisily demanding access to the exquisite sliver of turquoise water known as the Asi Stream. The "Free the Asi" campaigners mostly hailed from the neighboring, working-class town of Beit Shean, a stronghold of Likud and Shas, the ultra-Orthodox Sephardic party, with a distinctly traditional, Mizrahi population. About three miles to the east of the kibbutz, and perched on the edge of the Jordan Rift Valley, the downtrodden town was long a symbol of the less privileged "other Israel." Many of the parents and grandparents of the activists had worked as laborers in the kibbutz fields. The cool waters of the Asi beckoned tantalizingly, but, for anyone except the kibbutz residents or paying guests in the holiday village they had built, the prized beauty spot, which was, by law, state-owned public property, was off-limits.

The kibbutzniks felt they had earned the privilege with their sweat and blood. For nearly ninety years, the socialist founders of Nir David, originally named Tel Amal, and their descendants had been tending to the Asi, initially by clearing the malarial swamps around it and taming the waters into a single channel. They had toiled in the fields and established fish farms. In the mid-1990s, the kibbutz rehabilitated and reinforced the sides of the Asi with concrete and planted the riverbanks with lawns and lush gardens. The members developed the site into a lucrative tourism enterprise by building and renting out waterside holiday chalets. The veterans who inhabited little kibbutz houses along the manicured riverbanks had expected to grow old peacefully, rather than engage in a culture war. "We turned the wasteland into a flourishing garden," lamented Shlomo Glazer, a former secretary of Nir David. "We were too successful."

The battle was emblematic of Israel's oldest struggles and its new ones. Resonating far beyond this peripheral backwater, it reflected the fragmentation, ethnic identity politics, and social upheavals that saw onetime socialists clinging to what they claimed was their private property, and the division that had kept Netanyahu, the heir of Begin in playing on the resentment of self-perceived underdogs, in power for so long.

Once considered the self-sacrificing farmer-warriors who built Israel, the kibbutzniks of Nir David were now viewed as exploiters by a new, more savvy generation of Mizrahi neighbors. The fight over the Asi was, according to Avi Shilon, an Israeli historian of Zionism and a biographer of both Ben-Gurion and Begin, a "quintessential" illustration of the changes in contemporary Israeli society. Israeli *mamlachtiyut,* or the integrity of the state, was so broken, he said, that he feared a time would come when Israelis would mark their Memorial Day by counting how many kibbutzniks and how many *Mizrahim* and how many Orthodox Jews vs. secular Jews had fallen in the country's wars.

Glazer and other Nir David veterans had shepherded the kibbutz through years of legal wrangling over access to the Asi. In the popular image, amplified by social media, the fight was between the old elites of the socialist left and a new, aggressive right made up of rough-and-ready *Bibistim,* supporters of Bibi Netanyahu hailing from his blindly loyal, heavily Mizrahi base that worshipped him in the same way that their parents had worshipped Menachem Begin. The battle quickly took on some ugly ethnic overtones, exposing the depths of mutual prejudice. The Ashkenazi kibbutzniks related in shock how one of the protesters had told them Hitler had not gone far enough. The kibbutzniks dismissed the activists as politically motivated goons. The activists described how supporters of the kibbutz had referred to them as Arabs, terrorists, and baboons.

In fact, the Free the Asi campaign was being waged by an articulate, educated generation of mostly Mizrahi social entrepreneurs. One was a university graduate and information systems analyst; another a committed environmentalist; a third, a businesswoman running a chain of groceries with her husband while also studying political science at a college in the north. They had repackaged their parents' and grandparents' resentments into a potent contest over Zionist narratives and what they viewed as the historically skewed allocation of resources dating back to the early years of the state. They had embarked on a reckoning with what they saw as the old elites' sense of entitlement.

Established in 1936, Tel Amal held a storied place in the annals of Zionist history as the first agricultural "tower and stockade" settlement, set up to withstand Arab attacks in a one-day stealth operation under the noses of the British authorities. Under Ottoman law, any structure with a roof could not be destroyed. The pioneers utilized the new method of rapid construction in putting up surrounding walls and defenses, including a closed guard tower, after an earlier effort at farming there was destroyed by hostile Bedouin tribes in the area. Dozens more tower and stockade settlements would spring up across the land. Tel Amal's humble kibbutz homes first went up along one bank of the stream. As the community grew, its residential areas expanded across to the other side of the river, with a footbridge to link the two parts. When I visited in the spring of 2021, I was escorted through the heavily guarded yellow gate and around the kibbutz by the community's secretary, or chief manager, Lavi Meiri, Shlomo Glazer's successor, who was wary of interlopers. I, too, was struck by the beauty. Butterflies flitted among the brilliantly colored flowers along the riverbank as celestial choral music wafted from one of the kibbutz veterans' homes. It felt like an Arcadia.

Beit Shean, or Beisan as it was known in Arabic, had an even richer history, dating back to antiquity, due to its strategic location between the Levantine interior and the coast, and Jerusalem and the Galilee. An administrative center of the ancient Egyptians, it was ruled by the pharaohs for about three hundred years. Its most recent incarnation was, by comparison, inglorious, having grown out of a slum of tin shacks and huts, known in Hebrew as a *ma'abara,* a transit camp set up to temporarily house the huge influx of immigrants in the 1950s—in Beit Shean's case, from Iraq, then Morocco, then Yemen, then Iran. It evolved into what became known as a development town, a purpose-built city providing permanent housing for the new immigrants and helping settle the territory of the new state through their dispersal across the country. Though a frequent target of Palestinian rocket and mortar fire from Jordan in the late 1960s, Beit Shean's population grew to about 20,000. Its most famous resident, David Levy, a former mayor of Beit Shean, who had immigrated from Morocco in the late 1950s, worked, among other things, picking cotton in kibbutz fields and became a union activist. A charismatic grassroots leader and a father of twelve, he helped bring Begin to power in the revolution of 1977, sealing the bond with the *Mizrahim.* Levy rose through the ranks to serve as the country's foreign minister as well as a deputy prime minister, breaking the ethnic political ceiling. A speaker of Hebrew, Moroccan

Arabic, and French, he was also the butt of many jokes and derided in the old Labor-dominated foreign service for his lack of English. He left government in the early 2000s.

Since then, there have been too many Mizrahi ministers to count. *Mizrahim* have also served as army chiefs of staff, chiefs of police, and Supreme Court justices, though not in the numbers they should have. Moshe Katsav, an Iranian-born politician who started out as another Likud protégé from the development town of Kiryat Malachi, became the eighth president of Israel, though he brought little honor to the office, ending up in jail convicted of rape. Mizrahi culture had moved from the shadows to the mainstream. The Jewish Moroccan holiday of Mimouna at the end of Passover was celebrated nationwide by Israelis of all types with barbecues and parties. Prime ministers never missed a photo op with a Moroccan family in traditional dress holding trays of colorful Moroccan sweets or sticky flat pancakes known as *moufletas*. Netanyahu surrounded himself with a coterie of Mizrahi loyalists he made ministers. The *Mizrahim,* in many respects, had become the new elite, at least in Likud political circles and popular culture.

But none of this erased the humiliation many felt going back to the earliest years of the state. In Israel, old grudges ran deep. The slights got retold like the Passover Haggadah, and the so-called ethnic demon resurfaced in each generation in different shapes and forms. The smarting sense of injustice was fed by a still-yawning socioeconomic gap between "First Israel," roughly defined as the privileged beneficiaries of the old Ashkenazi elites, and the "Second Israel," the disadvantaged geographical and socioeconomic periphery inhabited largely by Mizrahim and bolstered over the years by subsequent waves of poorer immigrants from the former Soviet Union and Ethiopia. First Israel and Second Israel, in the parlance of several prominent Mizrahi intellectuals, often resided just a few meters or miles apart, as in the case of Nir David, with its ample grounds and new neighborhoods of villas, and Beit Shean, whose shabby apartment buildings harked back to a different era. These two Israels often cohabited within mixed households. About half of Israel's Jews were Mizrahi in origin. About a third of Israel's children were being born into families of mixed Ashkenazi-Mizrahi parentage. Some 40 percent of Nir David's population was by now of Mizrahi descent, according to Meiri, the kibbutz secretary, who said that none of his six grandchildren were entirely Ashkenazi. Yet with the state having done too little to address historic inequalities, the bitter fight over access to the Asi had become the latest emblem of the old Ashkenazi-Sephardi class struggle playing out in a nominally classless society.

By law, natural waterways are public property in Israel. But the Asi was in the middle of the kibbutz, and the kibbutzniks said they could not allow their home to be turned into a public park with camping, loud music, and barbecues. The dispute was not only about dipping rights for either side. Deeper down, it was a competition over the Zionist narrative of who suffered more and got historical credit for settling the country and who got to control its resources. Nir David had been founded before the state by hardy pioneers who were joined in the 1940s by a group of Holocaust survivors from Europe. The *Mizrahim* mostly came later, in the decade after the War of Independence, and not always by choice. After Israel's establishment, some were violently expelled when the Arab countries they had lived in for centuries turned hostile. Some left relatively comfortable lives and arrived with nothing. Once in Israel, the *Mizrahim* were often looked down upon as unskilled recipients, or beneficiaries, of those who had come before them—or, in biblical terms, as the drawers of water and hewers of wood.

That version was undergoing a radical, if belated, revision. For the *Mizrahim* also contributed to building the state, suffering the hardships of the transit camps, which grew into development towns. These were often in remote, sparsely inhabited areas of the country that had been emptied by the exodus of the Palestinian refugees. If the *kibbutzim* had sketched out the borders of the new state, the *Mizrahim* helped populate it and, with their traditional Judaism, family-based sense of community, and vibrant diversity, became a main component of the young country's DNA. Perah Hadad, a businesswoman and political science student from Beit Shean and a leader of the Free the Asi campaign, said her parents and grandparents had been too busy trying to get by to focus on such esoteric matters of history. But the children and grandchildren, now young adults, had begun to reassess the past, demanding that their parents be recognized for their contributions to the building of the state and be honored by the state as the "new pioneers." By the mid-1990s, a social justice movement called the Mizrahi Democratic

Rainbow was drawing attention to land issues, and how the boundaries and jurisdictions of local regional councils, drawn up in the early years, unfairly benefited the socialist *kibbutzim* and other rural settlements at the expense of the development towns, planting the roots of the Asi campaign. The development towns often became cramped and run down while kibbutz agricultural land was being rezoned for profitable real estate projects and industry. The Likud, which purported to champion the Mizrahi cause, had been at the country's helm for three of the past four decades. But, given the atmosphere of constant crisis in the region, Israel's fundamental problems were rarely addressed or resolved, including this one. And, with many *Mizrahim* hewing closely to Jewish tradition, eschewing Western liberalism, conscious of the humiliations that their parents endured on arrival, and suspicious of anything smacking of socialism, the ethnic divide, instead of disappearing, was increasingly shaping and defining the character of the new Israel.

Netanyahu, a privileged Ashkenazi, was a master of stoking ethnic tensions to his advantage, cynically playing on the underdog sentiment, not unlike Begin, who was of Polish origin, before him. The *Mizrahim* on the periphery formed the core of the Likud's—and Netanyahu's— loyal base that had kept him in power for so long. And although the "Free the Asi" campaign encompassed all sorts of Israelis, including left-wing social justice activists, the left-wing parties such as Labor and Meretz remained on the sidelines, afraid to go against the Kibbutz Movement, their traditional base of support, despite their purported commitment to social equality. Instead, right-wing forces that thrived on stoking ethnic tensions took up the cause. A lawmaker from Shas went to court against Nir David's closed gate policy. Benjamin Netanyahu's older son, Yair, a regular provocateur, called for the liberation of the Asi on Twitter. The two sides reflected political realities on the ground. In the March 2021 election, Israel's fourth in two years, 93.5 percent of the vote in Beit Shean went to Likud, Shas, and some smaller right-wing or religious parties. In Nir David, a community of about 650 souls, more than 90 percent of the votes were cast for centrist or left-wing parties.

The roots of the profound social, economic, and political gaps between Zionism's "white" Ashkenazi settlers from Europe and the Middle Eastern Sephardic immigrants of the 1950s lay in the rush to populate a young state with scarce resources and to lay claim to the expansive areas beyond the coastal urban centers. In the first three years after the establishment of the state, some 645,000 immigrants arrived, doubling the Jewish population. Many of them remember being doused with a DDT delousing agent on arrival. The authorities directed hundreds of thousands of the new, Arabic-speaking arrivals, as well as some from central Europe, to the squalid, often far-flung transit camps made up of tents, wooden huts, and asbestos shacks. Most were located in the Galilee in the north and the Negev desert in the south, away from the centers of commerce and employment. The conditions were primitive and the families generally large, compounding the economic hardship. As the camps morphed into development towns, rows of soullessly utilitarian government housing projects went up, becoming foci of poverty and offering limited horizons. Many found employment in the local *kibbutzim,* and the towns provided the rural communities with some services.

Mizrahi immigrants who did end up in the major cities often found themselves in gritty neighborhoods. The first outburst of anger came in 1959 in the low-income Haifa neighborhood of Wadi Salib when the police shot and wounded a drunk and disorderly Moroccan Jewish immigrant. False rumors that he had died sparked a furious flash of protests and vandalism that specifically targeted local Mapai offices as symbols of oppression. The line of resistance that began in Wadi Salib led to the emergence of the Israeli Black Panther movement, a defiant, hardcore social-democratic protest group that sprang up in the early 1970s in the neglected, poverty-stricken, and crime-ridden neighborhoods of Musrara and Katamonim in Jerusalem. Inspired by the African American movement, but detested by other *Mizrahim* who had more middle-class aspirations, they rocked the city with a number of tumultuous demonstrations. One of the group's leaders, Reuven Abergel, said he was first arrested at the age of nine for loitering in the genteel Rehavia neighborhood of Jerusalem. When the leaders met with Prime Minister Golda Meir in 1971, she dismissed them as "not nice people." Two years later the arrogance of the leadership at many levels was exposed when the air raid sirens sounded the alarm at two p.m. on Yom Kippur, the holiest day of the Jewish calendar. The colossal intelligence assessment failure that allowed the surprise attack on the Syrian and Egyptian fronts in October 1973 and the trauma of that war would change Israel forever. The subsequent reordering brought Begin to power. Ben-Gurion's melting pot of Israelization and a uniform Hebrew culture was boiling over.

The emergence of eastern pop music served as a kind of social barometer. What the invention of the Philips compact cassette tape did in the 1970s for the Islamic revolution in Iran, enabling Ayatollah Khomeini's sermons to be widely disseminated in the underground, it did for Israel's Mizrahi music scene, giving voice to Israel's underclass. Culturally, it was like adding spice to an old, bland recipe. The New Hebrew culture championed by the Ashkenazi elites ruled the official airwaves and had largely blocked the eastern, or "Mediterranean," sound popular with the Jews from Arab lands from being broadcast. Considered uncouth and lowbrow, it was shunned for years, banished from the Voice of Israel and Army Radio playlists, from Israel's single state television channel, and from mainstream record stores. But the cheaply produced audiocassette liberated the eastern ballads and pop from the smoky backroom clubs and wedding halls, making Mizrahi music cheaply accessible for the mass market of the other Israel. It became known as "bus station music" as the kiosks and stalls around the grimy old Central Bus Station in Tel Aviv became an impromptu mecca for Mizrahi music cassette sales. The latest hits would blare out from tiny stores in the alleys around the always chaotic bus terminal. Fans would snatch the new releases off the shelves. A troubled but talented singer, Zohar Argov, was soon anointed the king of the genre. One of ten children born to working-class immigrants from Yemen, Argov, who changed his family name from Orkabi, grew up in a hardscrabble slum in Rishon LeZion riddled with drugs and crime. His songbird voice was his ticket out. His combinations of the Arabic musical style of *mawwal,* the vocal trills known as *silsulim,* the emotional ballads, catchy tunes, and basic lyrics of love and life became the trademark of Mizrahi pop. Though wildly popular, Argov came to an ignominious end. Twice accused of rape and struggling with drug addiction, he died by suicide in a prison cell. When his demise was announced on the radio news it was the last item before the weather report. By then, though, his most successful songs had broken through the Ashkenazi sound barrier, disrupting and ultimately transforming Israel's pop music scene.

The advent of local commercial television in the early 1990s doubtless played a part, providing the kind of entertainment people wanted, and by the 2000s Mizrahi pop had gone completely mainstream, the biggest hits bringing dance floors alive at even the most Ashkenazi of weddings. In 2012 a *Forbes* billionaires' list placed Eyal Golan, then the most popular Mizrahi singer, of Yemenite and Moroccan origin, as the third-wealthiest person in Israel. Three years later Miri Regev, an ambitious Likud firebrand known for waving a large Israeli flag onstage, became the minister of culture and sports. Born in Israel to a Moroccan father and Sephardic Spanish mother, she promoted a brash blend of nationalist populism and ethnic politics. She bragged that she had never read Chekhov, or Haim Nahman Bialik, and was none the worse for it. She appeared on the cover of a weekend supplement of the popular *Yedioth Ahronoth* newspaper posing with three black panthers. Armed with a government budget, she declared a culture war on the old elites, targeting the theaters, orchestras, and Army Radio playlists. This, she pronounced, was the "Mizrahi War of Independence."

Regev was, however, just jumping on a cultural bandwagon. Anything Moroccan or Yemenite was already "in," the revolution well underway. Years after the deaths of the pioneers of Mizrahi song such as Argov, Ahuva Ozeri, and Ofra Haza, who had become national icons, Israeli filmmakers were producing lovingly crafted documentaries about them. Haza, of Yemenite origin, had gone on to international fame on the world music scene but died tragically at the age of forty-two. After commercial success came a deeper reflection as a young, inquiring, and avant-garde generation of Mizrahi Israelis began revisiting and reclaiming their Arabic roots and reasserting their authentic identity as proud Israelis still chafing against the Ashkenazi ancien régime. One of its protagonists, Khen Elmaleh, had gained some prominence as a unconventional celebrity DJ in the buzzing Mizrahi countercultural scene. She chose to meet me at Café Albi, a self-consciously shabby hangout where she sometimes worked, and near where she then lived, in a not-yet-gentrified section of south Tel Aviv. Albi, colloquial Arabic for "my heart," was a reference to a classic composition of the Egyptian diva Umm Kulthum. The vegetarian/vegan café was popular with the LGBT community, political activists, and African asylum seekers. On a quiet weekday, Arabic pop music played gently in the background.

The mismatched and rickety tables and chairs were mostly empty. Flyers advertising progressive cultural and political events were stuck on the walls, lending the café a club-like atmosphere. Above the bar, along with the choice of basic fare scrawled on a blackboard, hung a striking portrait of a yellow-eyed black panther wearing a shiny tracksuit top and a thick gold chain.

Elmaleh, a native Israeli of Moroccan descent, was thirty-three and pregnant. Born in the mid-1980s in Yokneam Illit, a development town in the hills southeast of Haifa, she was always a bit of a rebel. Eager to become fully fledged Israelis, her parents had played classic establishment crooners at home, like Arik Einstein. Her older brother, Ohad, introduced her to Black American hip-hop and rap when she was a teenager, in the 1990s, and once MTV began broadcasting in Israel, she immersed herself in the rappers' lyrics and video clips. She knew all about Malcolm X before she had heard of the Israeli Black Panthers movement, which was not part of her school curriculum. But when she was in ninth or tenth grade she saw a documentary about the Black Panthers on television. The angry rappers of Compton and Chicago suddenly seemed less relevant; there were authentic Israeli underdogs closer to home. She also discovered that Israel had its own kind of "Black music," she said. It was the beginning of her personal Mizrahi awakening and mission.

Her father, Yitzhak, known as Itzik, or Jackie, came from rural Morocco as a child in the 1950s. His family was placed in the transit camp at Kiryat Shemona, on the border with Lebanon. Elmaleh's grandparents on her mother's side came from Casablanca and Marrakesh to the camp adjacent to Yokneam, an established rural colony set up by early Zionist pioneers from Europe. Her mother, Ilana, was born there. The camp grew into the development town of Yokneam Illit, or Upper Yokneam, its lofty-sounding name belying its humble beginnings. Most residents were employed at the Soltam factory that was set up nearby, producing mortars and artillery for the army as well as stainless steel pots and pans. Elmaleh said that under different circumstances her father could have been a great intellect. But like most of the immigrants in his school he had been channeled into a vocational track to learn carpentry and he quit before graduating. He went to work at a nearby kibbutz, maintaining vehicles and equipment. After his army service, he worked as a handyman and a contractor. He and

Ilana then opened an after-school center at home for children whose parents were at work. Later, a high-tech park would spring up next to Yokneam, a start-up ecosystem with more than a hundred companies and about $5 billion in annual technology exports. But most of the techies came from outside, Elmaleh said, as few of the local residents were equipped for careers in high-tech, instead working in manual jobs, services, and administration.

Elmaleh seemed destined to follow her parents along the path of low expectations. Though hardly remote, Yokneam, she said, felt like "an enclave in the old Ashkenanzi state" on the edge of the Jezreel Valley, a fertile plain dotted with long-established *kibbutzim* rich in land resources. In school, other than a few Russians and Romanians, the students were all Mizrahi—Moroccans, Kurds, and Yemenites. The teachers automatically placed Elmeleh in the vocational track to learn touch-typing and secretarial skills, but she fought to be accepted into the school's small academic stream. "They taught you to be Israel's hewers of wood and drawers of water," she said, echoing a familiar Mizrahi complaint.

Elmaleh's upbringing was typically Mizrahi, she said, meaning traditionally Jewish without Orthodox observance of the rules, and being inherently less rigid and more tolerant. The family would eat shrimp, prohibited for religious Jews, but always said *kiddush,* the blessing over wine, on the Sabbath. At eighteen, most of her peers were eager to enlist for military service, the army being widely viewed as a path to upward mobility and to becoming a fully fledged "Israeli." Her brother, a great source of pride to the family, had served as a combat medic in the paratroopers. Unusually for a Yokneam girl, Elmaleh opted out of the system, claimed that she was Orthodox, and so was easily granted an exemption.

Eager to spread her wings, she first went to Tel Aviv and then Los Angeles, where she sold beauty products from carts in shopping malls. There, she connected through Facebook to the Mizrahi cultural awakening underway in Israel. It was 2012, and Mizrahi music was getting more play and improving in quality. Eyal Golan would soon preside over his own Mizrahi singing contest on the Israeli music channel (and would also have a brush with the law, accused of having sex with underage girls, though for lack of evidence no charges were forthcoming). Elmaleh wanted to be a part of the cultural revolution. She began writing and editing for Café Gibraltar, an Israeli blog devoted to the Mizrahi cultural renewal and world music. Around the same time a young, angry Israeli poet of Yemenite descent, Adi Keissar, was founding a group of like-minded Mizrahi poets called Ars Poetica. A play on the Latin title of Horace's poem, "The Art of Poetry," *Ars*—a word for pimp in Arabic dialect—was also used as a derogatory slang word in Hebrew for a stereotypical lower-class macho and sleazy male, usually of Mizrahi extraction. The female equivalent, *freiha,* based on a common Moroccan woman's name, denoted the stereotype of a peroxided Mizrahi woman with long, elaborately painted nails, figure-hugging clothes, and gaudy makeup and accessories. The trend among the avant-garde was to reclaim and embrace the epithets, with a sense of irony. Ron Kachlili, a Mizrahi intellectual and documentary filmmaker, produced a television series called *Arsim and Frehot,* in which Elmaleh made an appearance. At Café Albi she had consciously adopted the look, with her long hair bleached and showing dark roots, wearing thick gold chains and a nose ring, her long fingernails painted a shimmering silver blue. The cover photo on her Facebook page featured a now-classic photograph of one of Israel's Black Panthers blowing smoke rings against the backdrop of a Panthers poster bearing the legend "Freedom is priceless."

Ars Poetica began organizing evenings in clubs and cafés resonant with defiant poetry and music. Keissar would get up onstage like a punk poet and recite her in-your-face signature poem, *"Ani Ha'Mizrahit,"* meaning "I am the Mizrahi."

Other anti-establishment poets like Roy Hasan, author of *Medinat Ashkenaz* (Ashkenazi State), would appear. In a nod to inclusiveness, Ashkenazi poets were also welcome. The evenings often turned into a *hafla,* Arabic for "party," after Elmaleh came on board as the Ars Poetica DJ. Known for her eclectic playlist of Mizrahi, Arab, and world music, Elmaleh was also the resident DJ at Anna Loulou, a hip bar and club in an old Ottoman cave in Jaffa, which became a haven of coexistence for Israelis and Palestinians, *Ashkenazim* and *Mizrahim,* straights and gays.

It was a glorious period of creative energy and soon Ars Poetica was being feted by the progressive establishment, invited to appear in schools, at arts festivals, and at cultural evenings in the museums. A breakthrough came for Elmaleh in early 2016 when Yaron Dekel, the director of Galgalatz, Army Radio's popular music station, invited her to host a weekly program on Tuesdays from ten p.m. until midnight. Once an Ashkenazi bastion that shunned Zohar Argov, the station was trying to become more multicultural. "My instinct was not to do it," Elmaleh said, fearing being co-opted by the establishment. "But they allowed me in, so I felt I had to. I felt a responsibility." She started out with fusion and progressed gradually to Arab world and Turkish hits, experimenting with what the audience would find acceptable or too hardcore. Nobody interfered with her playlist. But after about a year she was fired for reasons that had more to do with her radical politics than the music. She had written a post on Facebook justifying the death of an Israeli police officer during a controversial eviction raid in a Bedouin village in the Negev that was constructed without the approval of the authorities. The land was to become a new town for religious Jews. "I would also run over a police officer if I were being removed from my home in order to make room for a town built for those more powerful than me," she wrote. She uploaded a famous photograph from 1982 of a Mizrahi resident of a poor neighborhood in south Tel Aviv taken moments after he had been fatally shot by a police officer during a protest against evictions. Dismissed from her radio slot amid a popular backlash, Elmaleh acknowledged the post had been insensitive and deleted it. In the end, it turned out that the Bedouin driver who had run over the police officer, and was himself fatally shot, had done so accidentally after losing control of his car.

The cultural revolution continued. Dudu Tassa, the Israeli grandson of a renowned Iraqi Jewish musician, began to sing in Arabic, as did the Haim sisters of the A-WA band, who drew on their Yemenite heritage to make up an electronic indie desert sound. Nasreen Qadri, an Arab Israeli, won a Mizrahi song contest hosted by Eyal Golan on the music channel and became a new Israeli diva, eventually converting to Judaism. Dikla, a Jewish Israeli of Egyptian-Iraqi origins, sang Umm Kulthum. Elmaleh acknowledged that things had changed since the 1970s. Then, she said, the Israeli Black Panthers "were fighting for their bread, housing, basic conditions. Our generation is not fighting for food, but for cultural representation, for the soul."

More confident than their parents, the activists of her generation were fully Israeli, fluent in both cultures, conceptually bilingual in *Ashkenazit* and *Mizrahit.* The movement, however, defied mainstream

Israeli politics and lacked a political home. Had she been around to vote in 1977, Elmaleh said, she would have voted for Menachem Begin. Now, she said, she voted according to whoever was promoting the most socially aware agenda. That could be confusing. Over the years she had voted for the ultra-Orthodox Shas, which claimed to represent the poor citizens who were transparent to the authorities, but as a party barred women from running for office, and for Balad, a hardline, secular Arab nationalist party. Labor and Meretz were out of bounds as the parties of the liberal, Ashkenazi elite. "They are not my tribe, socially or psychologically," she said. "I will never be part of them."

Politically, Elmaleh was beyond Zionism. For her, the character of Israel was more important than its existence. Harking back to nostalgic memories of how Moroccan Jews and Arabs had lived together in harmony in the past, she envisioned an Israel more integrated into the Middle East, where Jews and Palestinians could simply live together, much like the original Israeli Black Panther founders from the old, drug-ridden Jerusalem border neighborhood of Musrara found kinship with their Muslim neighbors in the Old City. But that was a vague, radical, and unrepresentative vision. Many more *Mizrahim* leaned to the right, holding that "the Arabs" were Israel's enemies and only understood strong-arm tactics and force, as these *Mizrahim* claimed to know from experience. The new Israel was dealing with an identity complex within an identity complex. For many *Mizrahim*, Elmaleh explained, the very term "Mizrahi" had taken on political, leftist, and activist connotations. "Most *Mizrahim* don't want to be described as *Mizrahim*," she declared. "They say, 'What? We are Israelis.'"


The Ashkenazi-Mizrahi divide ought to have become anachronistic. The country's Jewish population was evenly split. Social mobility and intercultural marriage were commonplace. Few third-generation *Mizrahim* pronounced the guttural *het* and *ayin* sounds in Hebrew that gave away their parents' Arabic-speaking origins.

But the bitter debates over educational and economic gaps continued to rear up and roil Israeli society. Some focused on the fact that Ashkenazi Holocaust survivors, including many kibbutz members, received reparations from Germany while Middle Eastern Jews were never compensated for their trauma or property they left behind. Others revolved around the inequality of the original land allocations, or on inherent prejudice. Seven decades after Israel's founding, *Mizrahim* made up only around 9 percent of the academic staff of Israeli universities. A survey of young Israeli adults indicated that the history, heritage, and culture of the Jews from Muslim countries were massively unrepresented in the Israeli education system, with 75 percent saying they could not recall any program or lesson in school that reinforced a positive perception of Mizrahi Jewry. There was a verb in Hebrew slang, *lehishtaknez,* for *Mizrahim* who adopted Ashkenazi habits in a conscious or unconscious effort to get ahead. There were children in development towns who had never met any Ashkenazi Israelis and a few who apparently thought they spoke a different language. Studies showed a still-significant wage disparity of up to 25 percent between Israeli-born Ashkenazi and Mizrahi employees. Among offspring of mixed marriages, those with an obviously Mizrahi surname generally earned less than those with a typically Ashkenazi surname. Bat-El and Yonatan Goldstein, a young "mixed" couple living in Beersheba, revealed in a television documentary how they maneuvered between her Moroccan maiden name, Amr, and his Ashkenazi-sounding one. "He tells me when you fill in forms for student grants, write Amr," Bat-El said, "and when you are applying for a job, write Goldstein." According to Israel's Central Bureau of Statistics, the surname Israelis most frequently sought to change was "Mizrahi," though *Ashkenazim* with surnames like Schwartz frequently Hebraized them to shed their Diaspora origins and sound more Israeli. Elmaleh's parents had tweaked theirs to Elimelech, Hebrew for "My God is King," one of the most popular on the bureau's list of adopted names. Elmaleh had reverted to using her family's original Moroccan name as a statement.

Israel's *Ashkenazim* and *Mizrahim* were increasingly beginning to see each other in terms of black and white, or in what Ruvik Rosenthal, an Israeli linguist, described as the politics of color. Miri Regev had called out what she labeled "the white DNA" of the leaders of the Likud, leading some critics to decry what they saw as the beginnings of Mizrahi racism and prejudice against Ashkenazi Jews. The *Ashkenazim* were sometimes referred to as "the white tribe," while Rosenthal pointed out that army slang for a goody-goody, overly obedient soldier included words like "dairy," "blondie," and "white," the implication being "too Ashkenazi."

If the Mizrahi immigrants had largely kept their resentments to themselves and focused on becoming Israeli, their children and grand-children, first- and second-generation Israelis, began questioning and digging into long-hidden state archives. Some of what they found was shocking: that the cavalier treatment of the Mizrahi immigrants by the old Ashkenazi establishment did not always stem from the mistakes of a young, overburdened, and chaotic bureaucracy, as the mainstream narrative would have it, but also from institutional and systematic poli-cies of discrimination. One highly publicized campaign aimed to shed light on a painful episode known as the "Yemenite babies affair." For decades, about a thousand families, mostly of Yemenite origin, had lived with their doubts and a deep distrust of the authorities, search-ing for children they said had gone missing and suspecting a system-atic scheme to abduct babies from the new immigrants in the 1950s and give them up for adoption by childless Ashkenazi couples. The Yemenites could have been considered easy targets because many of them lacked formal education, and they typically had many children and few means. Many of the missing children had been admitted to clinics or hospitals after falling ill—often a result of the poor sanitary conditions in the transit camps—then been abruptly pronounced dead when their parents came looking for them. Eighteen years later some families had received army call-up papers and voter registration notices for their lost children, who they'd been told were dead, though they were still apparently alive on the official registers. Many parents were never given an official cause of death, never saw the bodies of their infants, and were never able to locate their graves. The campaign was adopted by some Knesset members and prominent journalists, prompting the government to make 200,000 previously classified documents available to the public online in late 2016.

Previous commissions of inquiry had gathered documents that pertained to 1,060 children and included burial certificates for 923 of them. In the cases of 69 children whose parents had contacted the official panels, no records were found and their status was defined as unknown. Those panels had not laid the issue to rest. The calls for a reexamination had come from a new generation of members of the Knesset whose families had missing children and celebrities like Boaz

Sharabi, a popular singer who appeared on television weeping as he spoke of his missing twin sister, Ada. The new effort at transparency by no means answered all the questions, with many other documents lost or still locked up in archives. For some, it stirred old ghosts and dark memories. Avner Tzuri, an insurance agent in Jerusalem in his fifties, eagerly awaited the publication of the digitized documents to try to solve the mystery of his sister Malka, who had disappeared. Their parents, Michael and Kochava Tzuri, had come from Iran, via Iraq, to a transit camp near Hadera, south of Haifa. Malka, at fourteen months, was admitted to a hospital in Haifa on July 19, 1953, after she was found lying unconscious, having apparently ingested oil. When Kochava came to retrieve her the next morning, she was told the child was dead. The family later obtained a certificate from the burial society in Haifa, but when they located the numbered plot they found no sign of a grave. Avner Tzuri was hoping that the newly released protocols of one of the official commissions would answer the questions he has been chasing for years. Instead, he said after examining the online files, the story became even more muddy. The hospital's surgery registry showed that an autopsy had been performed on Malka on July 20. The cemetery records showed she had been buried only three days later, on July 23. "If that was the case, why didn't they let my parents see her body?" asked Tzuri, whose parents were no longer alive. "This only sets off more red lights," he said in exasperation. "It's all lies."

There was still no proof of a systematic plot to kidnap the babies. But the subsequent availability of DNA testing led to some families reuniting with lost relatives they had been told were dead. Finally, in February 2021, the state recognized the tragedy of what it called the Yemenite, Mizrahi, and Balkan Children Affair and approved a financial compensation package for families who were not notified of a child's death or cause of death in real time, or whose child's place of burial had not been located, or who never learned of the fate of the missing child. Some families said that they would not touch the money. The maximum reward per family was set at 200,000 shekels, then the equivalent of about $60,000. In another episode, known as the "ringworm affair," thousands of Mizrahi children were treated for scalp ringworm in the 1950s with irradiation, the standard treatment at the time. After a causal link was found between the X-ray treatment and cancerous growths, rumors abounded that the children had been treated with the radiation as part of an experiment. There was no proof. But the anecdotes of bald neighbors only underscored the depth of mistrust between the Mizrahi immigrant population and the establishment.

More generally in recent years, Israel had begun to make a conscious effort to embrace the Mizrahi cultural revival and to begin to redress the imbalance of the Zionist historical narrative. A committee was formed to examine and enrich the study of Mizrahi culture and heritage in the Israeli school curriculum. Led by Erez Biton, the first Mizrahi poet to win the prestigious Israel Prize for literature in 2015, the committee recommended mandatory study of Mizrahi literature and Sephardi Jewish culture as well as organized school trips to Morocco, Spain, and the Balkans—an alternative to the trips to Poland to visit the Nazi extermination camps. The Education Ministry sponsored a public awareness campaign made up of short TV segments broadcast in prime time. Its messages reinforced positive images of the Mizrahi *aliyah,* or immigration, crediting immigrants from the Arab lands for their contribution to the building of the state, enduring the difficult conditions of the transit camps, and populating the development towns. But even that was not welcomed across the board. Critics said the campaign belatedly honoring the Mizrahi population underscored its otherness.

Yet there were more skeletons to come out of the closet. A pivotal documentary series that aired on Israeli television in 2018, entitled *Saleh, This Is the Land of Israel,* or *The Ancestral Sin* in the English-language version, sent shock waves through the country. It charted the creation of the development towns in the mid-1950s and the state mechanism that compelled unwitting immigrants to remain in them. The director, David Deri, grew up in the development town of Yeruham, a tiny desert backwater south of Beersheba, as one of ten siblings whose parents came from Morocco. The series was heavily based on protocols of meetings of the young state's immigrant absorption officials and agencies, dug out of long-sealed archives, many of which were classified, paired with the recollections of those immigrants who were still alive. The series cast a harsh light on the high-handed, disdainful, and even cruel attitude of the socialist Zionist leaders toward the newcomers from the Arab and Muslim world. It quoted Chaim

Sheba, a revered professor and director of the Health Ministry in the young state, who went on a Jewish Agency mission to Morocco in 1953 and, upon his return, warned against allowing unlimited immigration. "How is it possible to build the future of a nation on such human ruins?" he wrote in one report. "If these are the people with which we fill the houses we are building and the lands we are holding, we will be a non-working nation. One huge welfare bureau." Another settlement official, Aryeh Eliav, described how immigrants were brought by truck, straight off the ships, to the desolate new towns. In several instances, he related, when the dismayed passengers refused to alight at their destination, he instructed the driver to "press the button." The bed of the truck would tilt and dump its human cargo on the ground. One group of immigrants rebelled and refused to go to their assigned destination, so another official recommended threatening them with taking away their children, on the pretext that children had to be provided with shelter by law. The director's own mother described her distress when she saw where the bus had brought her and said she'd refused to get off for hours. In one poignant scene, an aging couple who had arrived earlier, and had been friends and neighbors of Deri's parents for decades, confessed they had been bribed by Jewish Agency officials—with a free cot and some cash—to persuade the Deris to get off the bus. There was nowhere better than Yeruham, they told them, and they would see for themselves in the morning. Inhabitants who wanted to leave were warned that they would receive no housing, jobs, or social benefits elsewhere. Those who left anyway were blacklisted.

The series sparked a furor that resonated for months. Critics found the series divisive and tendentious and accused Deri of being selective in his use of quotations from the protocols. They dug out other quotations uttered by the same officials that showed them in a kinder light; not as racists, but as bureaucrats dealing with the daunting challenge of absorbing massive waves of hundreds of thousands of immigrants with few resources. The government promised to work to declassify more archives. For months, Deri went around the country showing an abridged movie version of his four-part series and engaging with audiences from all sectors of Israeli society.

I attended one such screening one weeknight in the packed auditorium of the venerable Van Leer Institute, an interdisciplinary research center for the study of Israeli society, culture, and education set in pleasant gardens next to the official residence of the country's president in the well-heeled Talbieh neighborhood of Jerusalem. The audience was heavy with Jerusalem intelligentsia, many of them Ashkenazi veterans. Many were moved and let out an audible gasp at the description of immigrants being dumped from the backs of trucks. The stormy debate that followed, with its blend of empathy and indignation, left me fascinated and bewildered as individuals stood up, often on shaky legs and with quavering voices, to argue over who had suffered most. Everybody had had it tough in the early days, the Ashkenazi veterans argued, including those who had drained the swamps before the state was established and those who endured the Nazi concentration camps and came to fight in the 1948 war.

Deri said in response that his tour of the country had been "a journey into Israeliness." For decades, he said, Israelis had debated whether the claims of discrimination by Mizrahi Jews were justified, the phrase "ethnic demon" conjuring up connotations of an imaginary evil. Ashkenazi critics had long accused them of self-pity, dismissing their complaints with a supercilious turn of phrase, "*achlu li, shatu li,*" Hebrew for "they ate and drank what was mine." Finally, Deri told the audience at Van Leer, the archival revelations had proved the reality of institutional discrimination and showed that the eastern immigrants, whether by choice or circumstance, had also played an essential part as pioneers in the building and settling of the state, enduring the hardships of urban living in some of its most remote parts.

Like Deri and eight of his nine siblings, many of the next generation managed to climb their way out of the development towns, though often taking the consciousness of the periphery with them. But the growing prosperity of an emerging Mizrahi middle class combined with the political strength of the Likud on the periphery and the long-held-on power of Likud mayors in some of the development towns had led to a building boom and a social reboot in many of them. Benny Biton, the mayor of Dimona, in the Negev, had been a Likud activist since the early 1980s and was deputy mayor of the desert town when Netanyahu first came to power in 1996. Cranes now dotted the skyline of the town of some 40,000. The local municipality invested 50 percent of its budget in education and, partnering with charitable organizations, was close to closing the educational gap. Speaking shortly before the 2019 fall election, Max Peretz, a former school principal and deputy mayor who held the city's education portfolio, said 90 percent of the town's teenagers went off to the army and college and did not come back. But after years of stagnation, fifteen new factories had gone up and unemployment had dropped significantly. Peretz proudly listed the town's famous offspring: a general, prominent journalists, and television celebrities. "You won't see any homeless here," he said.

Dimona was not alone. Mitzpe Ramon, once a tiny, downtrodden slum on the edge of the stunning Ramon crater that began as a camp for workers building the southern highway, had transformed itself into a buzzing ecotourism destination with a New Age vibe. A luxurious hotel provided employment for local people, while tourism entrepreneurs offered luxury camping and stargazing tours in the desert. Yeruham was also undergoing a revival, with new neighborhoods being created. Considered a failed town in the early 2000s, its turnaround began after a retired general, Amram Mitzna, was appointed to serve as its acting mayor. Residents took back the reins after a few years, and by 2020 a dynamic new mayor, Tal Ohana, had won national accolades for her handling of a coronavirus outbreak in the town, after setting up her own municipal contact tracing system to cut the chain of infection.

The majority of Israel's *Mizrahim* no longer lived in the development towns, which now accounted for only about 10 percent of the country's overall population. Nevertheless, these towns were still associated with the second, other Israel, including the poorer Russian-speaking and Ethiopian immigrants who mostly came in the 1990s, and they still occupied the lower rungs of Israel's socioeconomic ladder, with the central government having invested little in improving their conditions. After the buzz around Deri's documentary and amid the national campaign to recognize the contribution of Mizrahi immigrants to the building of the young state, the Knesset Research Center published a report in 2018 charting the progress of the development towns since the early 1970s. The bleak economic picture that emerged was hardly a badge of honor for the Likud, with workers generally earning about 20 percent less than the national average. Out of the twenty-five development towns on the list, twenty-one ranked in the lower five deciles. In some, college-age students went on to some form of higher education at about half the average national rate.

Yet through it all, the development towns remained bedrocks of support for the Likud. In recent elections, more than 55 percent of Dimona's electorate voted Likud while other residents cast their ballots for Shas, which had also pledged allegiance to Netanyahu. The national divide was sharply illustrated in Rosh Haayin. In the old, low-rise part of town, which grew out of a muddy tent camp for poor Jews airlifted from Yemen into a blue-collar stronghold of largely religious immigrants and their descendants, the residents voted overwhelmingly for the right. The newer neighborhoods that had sprung up since the early 1990s, originally as housing projects for army officers, were bastions of the liberal, secular Israel that voted center-left.

Even in Sderot, a traumatized development town of more than twenty-five thousand residents about a mile from the Gaza border that had been plagued for nearly two decades by Palestinian rocket fire, Likud always came out on top. One of the prime exhibits of the town was the collection of metal tubes and other rocket debris piled up on metal racks in the yard of the police station. The rocket fire was not something one got used to. Whenever I was in the town and the public address system cranked into action with a tinny robotic voice repeating "Color red, color red," denoting incoming rocket fire, my stomach would lurch and seconds of pandemonium and terror would follow on the streets as passersby dropped whatever they were doing and rushed frenziedly to find cover; seconds, because that's all the time it took for a rocket to get there from Gaza. It was barely enough time to unclick a seat belt, grab a cellphone, and get out of a car. Then the double booms of an interception by the Iron Dome anti-rocket system would follow, or worse, a rocket would randomly crash down. With Israel and Hamas stuck in a loop of conflict, a whole generation of children were traumatized on both sides of the border. In Sderot, there was plenty of grumbling about the government not finishing off Hamas, but come election time there was little deliberation about whom to support. Stores in the old commercial center, including Sasson Sara's small grocery store, were routinely festooned with Likud banners and Netanyahu stickers. "It's us or them. Only Likud. Only Netanyahu," one of the campaign posters read.

Sara's parents had opened the store in 1958, a few years after they came from Iraq. Sasson had become something of a local pundit sought out by television crews who came to cover the rocket attacks. The grocery, the first to have opened in the town, did not appear to have changed much in the intervening years. In its cramped and dingy interior an old-fashioned fridge stocked basics like cottage cheese, but none of the fancier Camembert or artisanal goat cheeses to be found in the more affluent areas of First Israel. Like many *Mizrahim,* Sara's explanation of why he remained loyal to the Likud, despite its failure to stop the rockets in its years in power, had less to do with the present than with the humiliations of the past. He first voted for Begin, he said, "For social reasons, and because of the affliction of the *kibbutzim* around here, which controlled everything." The *kibbutzim,* he said, managed the factories in the area and the residents of Sderot were their hired labor, echoing the refrain of the residents of Beit Shean who had been shut out of the Asi at Nir David. "There was a Bolshevik tyranny here. There was a red book. You couldn't work unless you voted Mapai," he claimed, mirroring the experience of the old Irgun fighter Yoske Nachmias, and bearing the grudge and bitter mindset that had perplexed the Palmach fighter Haim Gouri. With Begin's victory in 1977, Sara said, "People suddenly had dignity." Sara denied that the Likud had failed to deliver the goods, citing a new train from Sderot to Tel Aviv, the recent introduction of free dental care for children, and the tough policy against migrants and asylum seekers from Africa. He also identified, like many *Mizrahim,* with the hawkish line against ceding the West Bank to the Palestinians. The takeover of Gaza by Hamas, the rocket-launching Islamic militant group, only bolstered the argument of the right that the liberal left was naive for thinking it could trade land for peace. "It's not about Jews and territory," Sara said. "It's a war of civilizations. It's about the Muslims and Western culture."

The cultural and political chasm was acutely evident in the immediate aftermath of the devastating fifty-day Gaza war during the summer of 2014. In Sderot, residents complained that the army had pushed to end the war too soon. Hamas had not been eliminated, despite the election promises of the politicians. Sara would have rather seen the army bombing Gaza into oblivion, regardless of the extent of the collateral damage. "They shouldn't have checked if there were children in the houses or not," he said, alluding to the military's caution even as it bombed other parts of Gaza into rubble. Sara, a father of five with a son serving in the paratroopers, had a simpler method in mind: "If a Qassam rocket is fired, you flatten the house. Let them turn all of Gaza into a soccer pitch."

A short drive away, in the rural *kibbutzim* along the Gaza border, the residents faced the same problems as Sderot, or worse, being in mortar as well as rocket range. But here they wrestled more with their consciences, recalled the friendships they once had with Palestinian employees and traders from across the fence in Gaza, and, in many cases, advocated some kind of long-term truce with their neighbors. The kibbutz wheat, sunflower, and jojoba fields stretched right up to the Gaza border. Fortified shelters dotted the pathways, often painted with bright murals. If and when the sirens sounded, there were even fewer seconds in which to find shelter. Several kibbutz members, including a four-year-old boy, Daniel Tregerman, of Nahal Oz, had been killed by the rockets and mortars.

It was at Nahal Oz in 1956, soon after it became a kibbutz, that Moshe Dayan, then the military chief of staff, delivered what would become known as one of the defining speeches of Zionism when he eulogized Roi Rotberg, a kibbutz security guard and a young father who was killed in the fields in an ambush by infiltrators from Gaza. Dayan spoke at the funeral of the expectation of rage and thirst for revenge among the refugees across the border and of the cruel fate of the generation of Israelis that had taken over the land where they and their fathers had dwelt, destined to live by the sword. "Without the steel helmet and the cannon's maw," he declared, "we will not be able to plant a tree and build a home."

Nahal Oz, just a few hundred meters from the border, was again marked as a target on a map circulating in Gaza in the spring of 2018, when the Palestinians launched their Great March of Return protest against Israel's eleven-year-long blockade of the Hamas-run coastal territory and to reclaim lost ancestral lands inside Israel. Though the military said the protests were a cover for terrorists intending to breach the border fence and storm nearby Israeli communities, some of the kibbutz members agonized over the scores of Palestinians killed in one day by Israeli fire. Over the following months, black smoke would billow up and envelope the *kibbutzim* along the border as militants launched flaming kites that set the fields ablaze and left huge swaths of charred landscape. Yet in subsequent elections at least 80 percent of the ballots cast in Nahal Oz were for centrist or left-wing parties while in Sderot, a seven-minute drive away, 85 percent voted for Likud and other parties of the nationalist or religious right, reflecting the results in Nir David and Beit Shean, a three-hour drive to the north.

The bond of the Mizrahi base with the Likud, and increasingly, over the years, with Netanyahu, stemmed largely from the emotional attachment to Begin, whose underdog sentiment dated back to his days as the commander of the Irgun. Finding common cause, the right-wing organizations made a point of counting Sephardic Jews among their storied heroes. One legendary case involved an act of self-sacrifice by a pair of fighters named Meir Feinstein and Moshe Barazani. Feinstein, a Jerusalem-born member of the Irgun, was of eastern European origin. Barazani, a Lehi member, had been born in Baghdad to an Iraqi Kurdish family. By the age of nineteen both had engaged in deadly sabotage operations against British rule in Palestine, were captured, imprisoned in the Russian Compound jail in Jerusalem, and sentenced to death. Hours before they were scheduled to go to the gallows, their comrades smuggled in a grenade concealed in a hollowed-out orange. Avoiding harm to a rabbi who had insisted on being with them in their final moments, they placed the grenade between them, embraced each other tightly, and blew themselves up. In a now-iconic instance of how the ethnic demon has been used to great political effect in Israel, the legend of Feinstein and Barazani resurfaced to play a pivotal role in 1981, when Begin was running for reelection. Shimon Peres, his lead opponent, was expecting to wrest Labor back into power, until Dudu Topaz, a popular entertainer drafted to address a Labor rally in Tel Aviv's main square a few days before the June ballot, made a fatal mistake. Whipping up a crowd of thousands, he described the right-leaning *Mizrahim* as *tchach-tchachim,* pejorative slang for riffraff, or lowlifes, and said they were over at the Likud headquarters. "They are barely good enough to serve as guards on a base, if they even enlist," Topaz continued contemptuously, in an effort to burnish the Labor movement's credentials. "The soldiers and commanders of the combat units are right here."

The imperious attempt at flattery backfired, badly, enraging the Mizrahi voters, who mourned their own war dead, and confirming their perception of Ashkenazi arrogance and prejudice. Exploiting the moment, Begin took to the same stage the following night and delivered an impassioned response that is etched in the annals of Israeli political history. "Our *Mizrahim* were courageous fighters, already back in the underground," he roared. "Feinstein was from European origins—what's it called? Ashkenazi. Moshe Barazani was a Sephardi from Iraq." After recounting the story of their death Begin declared in a rousing crescendo, "Ashkenazi? Iraqi? Jews! Brothers! Fighters!"— a winning five words that encapsulated the post-1973-war sense of common fate and became a touchstone of national nostalgia and Begin's political legacy. The crowd burst into rapturous applause and chanted "Begin! Begin! Begin!" When Begin died in 1992, he was not interred along with the other state leaders in the national cemetery on Mount Herzl. Instead, in accordance with his last wish, conveyed in a handwritten note to his secretary, he was buried in the ancient Jewish cemetery on the Mount of Olives, next to Barazani and Feinstein.

But nothing seemed to lay the ethnic demon to rest. It reared its head again in the run-up to the 2015 elections, just as the Labor Party, under the leadership of Isaac Herzog, appeared to be doing surprisingly well in the polls against Likud after years in the doldrums. Though Labor was still widely viewed as a bastion of the old socialist Ashkenazi elite and had never quite recovered from the assassination of Yitzhak Rabin or the suicide bombings of the Second Intifada, many floating voters were seeking change, saying they had grown tired of Netanyahu. Buoyed by the polls, the left held a pre-election rally in that same square in Tel Aviv. Then came another Topaz-like moment. Yair Garbuz, an artist and commentator, got up onstage and lamented that his country had been taken over by "those toting talismans, pagans and those prostrating themselves in supplication on the tombs of the saints." Everybody knew he was talking about the typically traditional and superstitious Mizrahi Jews who would visit mystical rabbis who were dead or alive in search of a blessing for a match, fertility, or their business. Predictably, the speech sparked an uproar. The left wrung its hands while the Likud denounced it as racist and capitalized on it.

Israel had never had a Mizrahi prime minister. For years under Mapai rule, the relatively minor position of minister of police was reserved for a Mizrahi, along with responsibility for the country's Arabic-speaking minorities and the postal service. Polls showed that even the country's *Mizrahim*—or especially the *Mizrahim*—were not in a hurry for a prime minister who was one of their own. On the face of it, it was puzzling how Begin, from Poland, and the American-accented Netanyahu, the seeming epitome of Ashkenazi privilege, had captured the hearts of Mizrahi voters. Even Yitzhak Shamir, the comparatively colorless, if unshakable, Likud leader sandwiched between them, was credited in Likud history with opening up the party to the periphery by establishing party chapters across the country and offering Mizrahi Jews influence in the party's decision-making. Some put it down to an ingrained sense of Mizrahi inferiority, or a brainwashed belief in Ashkenazi superiority, like some political manifestation of Stockholm syndrome, where the oppressed had come to identify with the oppressor. On the pages of the weekend magazine of the leftist newspaper *Haaretz,* intellectuals earnestly debated the reasons why working-class *Mizrahim* found no common ground with Israel's Western-oriented liberals championing equality and universal values, even when left-wing parties chose *Mizrahim* as their leaders in the eternal, if vain, hope of attracting votes from the other Israel.

Instead, the Labor Party ailed under the stewardship of Mizrahi leaders. The collapse of communism and the influx of right-leaning Russians in the 1990s had doubtless benefited the Israeli right, as did the rightward drift of the ultra-Orthodox parties and the political interdependency created between them and Netanyahu. The perennial Iranian threat, instability in the Arab world following the Arab Spring, waves of terrorism, and the perceived intransigence and fecklessness of Palestinian leaders also played their parts. Moreover, Likud members were renowned for their fierce loyalty to their leader, unlike Labor, which was notorious for devouring its party chairpeople. Loyalty to the Likud was also largely inherited, passed down from parents to children.

Despite such challenges, the Labor Party kept trying to appeal to wider segments of the electorate, and particularly to *Mizrahim* on the periphery. In 2017 the party was hoping for salvation in the form of Avi Gabbay, the son of Moroccan immigrants who grew up with seven siblings in a cramped shack in the Talpiot *ma'abara,* or transit camp, in south Jerusalem. Though something of a political novice, he had won the Labor Party's leadership race. Having previously served for a year as the environment minister representing a small, center-right party, he had joined Labor just six months before the party primary. He wasn't the first Mizrahi to hold the position. Benjamin Ben-Eliezer, an Iraqi-born politician, was a Labor leader, as was Amir Peretz, a Moroccan-born trade union leader and Labor veteran from Sderot. Peretz had served as defense minister and was instrumental in the decision to develop the Iron Dome anti-rocket missile defense system but was widely ridiculed for one photograph where he was caught at a military drill in the Golan Heights peering through binoculars with their lens caps on. In an all-Moroccan leadership race, Peretz lost to Gabbay in a runoff.

Labor had not won an election since 1999 but Gabbay, at fifty, suave and with authentic Mizrahi credentials, pledged to bring in new voters from the geographical and social peripheries that had long shunned the party. As a self-made *ma'abara* millionaire, he came with credentials. Identified as a gifted student at a young age, Gabbay was sent to school at the Gymnasia Rehavia, in an affluent neighborhood of Jerusalem, with the children of the city's elite. As a teenager he worked as a waiter in the Knesset canteen. He studied economics and business administration at the Hebrew University of Jerusalem, worked in the budget division of the Ministry of Finance, then went into business. He rose to become the CEO of Bezeq, Israel's telecommunications giant, where his father had worked as a technician. He liked to say that he did not need opinion polls to gauge the mood in the country but just had to speak to his relatives. His wife was a teacher. His siblings, who endorsed him in a primary campaign video, included a taxi driver, a special education assistant, and an aluminum trader. Avi was described as "the diamond" of the family. He tried to appeal to the soft center-right with policies and statements that upset traditional Laborites. He also tried to capitalize on his Moroccan roots. Protesting some legislation that Netanyahu loyalists were pushing to hinder police investigations against public figures, Gabbay said, in a snide reference to Netanyahu, "While my grandmother did not study at MIT, she would say this is a *hashuma*. In Moroccan, that means shame." He put Netanyahu's successes down to good campaigning and manipulation.

Gabbay traveled the length and breadth of Israel, engaging with audiences in nightly town hall meetings, including in Likud strongholds like Kiryat Malachi, where no Labor candidate had bothered, or dared, set foot in twenty years. In the previous election, 6 percent of the town's voters had cast a ballot for Labor while some 90 percent voted for right-leaning or religious parties. He de-emphasized the party's liberal approach and focused more on what he called "being Jewish." Teaming up with Tzipi Livni and her small centrist party, he winked at the soft right by naming their joint slate the Zionist Union. The ploys didn't work. By the end of 2020, opinion polls indicated that the historic Labor Party would not even pass the electoral threshold and gain enough votes to enter the Knesset.

Gabbay had rightly identified one of Labor's lacunas, even if he was unable to fill it. The Mizrahi base was more attached to tradition if not strictly observant in its Judaism. Neither religious by the Orthodox establishment's standards nor fully secular, many *Mizrahim* made up the more nebulous category of sentimental, traditional Jews who would make *kiddush* and go to synagogue on the Sabbath, then host a karaoke party or attend a soccer match. These included the amulet kissers who prostrated themselves on the tombs of the saints even as they became increasingly prosperous and kept up with the latest trends. Catering to a market of overstretched businesspeople and frequent fliers, one enterprising purveyor of prayers had, for example, created a smartphone application called Tikkun, a word implying spiritual repair, providing customers with the chance to offer supplications remotely at holy sites or order up blessings from rabbis. The menu included options ranging from fertility to success in business to warding off the evil eye, all payable by credit card online. Blessings could be received in audio or video form. "The blessing of a holy man has the power to change nature even against apparent reason," the app's website promised. The ethereal entrepreneur who created the app acknowledged that people like Yair Garbuz might ridicule the idea, but he said they were not his target audience in any case.

It was from this pool of traditional *Mizrahim* that Shas drew its support. Founded in 1984, Shas, a Hebrew acronym for *Shomrei Sefarad*, or the Sephardic Guardians, said its main agenda was "returning the crown to its former glory," meaning restoring Sephardic pride, and promoting social justice. It set out with relatively dovish views toward the peace process but became more hawkish over the years in right-wing governments. Shas won over many in the community by establishing its own state-funded ultra-Orthodox education network after years of discrimination in the Ashkenazi system. At its peak, in 1999, Shas won a record 17 seats in the 120-seat Knesset and has been a lynchpin in most government coalitions since it was established. Its spiritual leader, Rabbi Ovadia Yosef, a Baghdad-born Torah scholar, was instantly recognizable in his trademark gold-embroidered robe, exotic turban, and dark glasses. Embodying a particular blend of religion, tradition, populism, and ethnic identity he sometimes employed unorthodox methods playing on a potent mix of faith, superstition, and resentment. In 2003, he promised voters that a ballot for Shas would guarantee them a place in heaven. A decade later, the Central Elections Commission fined Shas for violating campaign laws by distributing amulets and blessings and again in 2020 for handing out charms promising protection from the coronavirus. When Rabbi Yosef died in 2013, an estimated 700,000 people—almost one-tenth of the population of Israel—crowded the streets and rooftops of Jerusalem along the route of his funeral procession.

The political wunderkind of Shas, Aryeh Deri, was born in 1959 to a wealthy, secular family in Meknes, Morocco, and came with them to Israel as a child. A sharp operator, he became the minister of interior at the age of twenty-nine. His stellar career was interrupted in 2000 when he was convicted of bribery and fraud and handed a three-year jail sentence, of which he served twenty-two months. His imprisonment only heightened the Shas public's sense of ethnic discrimination and persecution and spawned a soulful hit song, "Hu Zakai," Hebrew for "he's innocent." Years after his release he made a political comeback. After the Garbuz slipup, he tried to capitalize with a newly polarizing campaign slogan, "A Mizrahi votes Mizrahi." Around 2015, Deri added a Moroccan family surname to his name, becoming Aryeh Machluf Deri. Understanding the will of its voters, Shas bound itself ever more tightly to Netanyahu, readily signing loyalty pledges to keep him in office. When Deri was later convicted on charges of tax evasion and, in early 2022, reached a lenient plea deal with the authorities, which some Israelis viewed as a possible precursor to a similar deal for Netanyahu, Deri, who got off with a suspended prison sentence and a fine, again pulled out the ethnic card, declaring that, if his name was not Machluf, the matter would have ended with a tax assessment.

In search of the essence of Bibi's base in the other Israel, I drove south to Netivot, in the western Negev, between Gaza and Beersheba. An otherwise drab city of about 37,000 souls, it was best known as a mystical center of Mizrahi Judaism and as the home of the tomb of a venerated Moroccan rabbi, Israel Abuhatzeira, popularly known as the Baba Sali. Born in Morocco in the late nineteenth century, he died in Netivot at the age of ninety-four, in the 1980s. Several of his descendants had set themselves up as mystics and became popular with Israeli politicians, police commanders, tycoons, and celebrities. Some mystics went by technical nicknames denoting their particular talents. Rabbi Yaacov Ifargan, revered by adherents for his diagnostic and healing powers, was known as "The X-Ray," for example. Other members of the dynasty were given the monikers of MRI, CT, and Ultrasound for the supposed medical miracles they performed. On the security front, a nephew credited with causing the collapse of Hamas's underground tunnels in Gaza became known as the "tunnel rabbi."

I hadn't known quite what to expect on my first visit to the tomb, wanting to find typical members of Bibi's base ahead of one of the recent elections, and to try to figure out why they apparently did not care that the prime minister had been accused of bribery, fraud, and abuses of power in a series of corruption scandals. But I hadn't expected the gift shop. The approach to the tomb was desolate, the entire complex rundown and shabby. A large sign near the entrance promised a milliondollar renovation. But inside the store the shelves were loaded like an oriental cave of treasures. On offer were Baba Sali votive candles, key rings, books of psalms, and arak, the Levantine aniseed-flavored liquor. Available in three varieties, the bottles were graced with labels bearing the portrait of the wizened holy man himself, his face loosely framed by a white scarf and a wispy beard. The tomb itself drew supplicants from all economic strata and areas of Israel. Hailed as the political equivalent of the miracle-working rabbi, Bibi was the unrivaled king here, revered for the sense of stability and national security that he brought, for his oratory skills at the United Nations, and for his stature as an international player. The more the arrogant likes of Garbuz insulted his loyal base, and the legal establishment pursued him, the more defiantly, it seemed, the *Bibistim* professed their love for him.

Among the trickle of visitors one ordinary weekday was Iris Gattegno, forty-eight, who stood out from the other staidly attired pilgrims with her blond hair pulled back in a ponytail, tight jeans, a body-hugging black top, and large sunglasses. She flounced into the store with the air of a big shot and bought up candles that she would later toss into a large and smoldering barbecue pit, as was the custom, while uttering supplications. She introduced herself as "Iris Gattegno, yes, Gattegno of the biscuits and of the YOO Towers," her prestigious address in Tel Aviv. Presumably she belonged to the family of the Gattegno kosher cookie firm that produced Israeli classics like half-chocolate-coated wine cookies. She said she visited the tomb often and had come "to pray for my love for the Jews, for Israel, and for Bibi." Off to the side, a family was celebrating a bar mitzvah with grilled meat and loud music. "There is nobody like him. Nobody can deliver a speech like him. There is nobody more handsome, charming and wise," Gattegno gushed, performing like a caricature of a *Bibist*. Bibi, she declared, was "chosen by God," and was struggling to survive in "a nest of scorpions," but she insisted that "envy and evil will not prevail."

The allegations of corruption had clearly made little impression on Netanyahu's core base. The loathing of the old elites had transformed into a belief in an Ashkenazi deep state, a cabal that was using the judiciary and the mainstream media to persecute and bring down the prime minister. Netanyahu himself fueled such sentiments with Machiavellian vigor, railing about a witch hunt and a putsch and insisting he had been framed by the police and the attorney general—despite the fact that the police chief who had spearheaded the investigations and the attorney general who brought the charges against him were both his own, handpicked appointments. Avishay Ben Haim, a religious affairs analyst on Channel 13 news and a Netanyahu supporter of Moroccan descent, peddled a provocative theory with a passion bordering on the comical about the ongoing hegemony of First Israel and its deeply embedded, nefarious designs to keep down the Bibi-loving Second Israel. He described the cases against Netanyahu as "legal violence," and as Ashkenazi revenge for the political upset of Begin's victory in 1977. Critics ridiculed the theory, pointing out how far the *Mizrahim* had come and noting that Ehud Olmert, Netanyahu's predecessor and a former Likud prince, had been sent to prison for bribery even though he had quit the Likud, turned to the left, and became the darling of First Israel by seeking an eleventh-hour peace deal with the Palestinians as the state prosecutors closed in.

Despite the panning by the critics, when Ben Haim's book *Second Israel: The Sweet Gospel, the Bitter Oppression* was published in the spring of 2022, as Bennett's government was already falling apart, Netanyahu warmly recommended the book in a video for Israel's annual Book Week. Pulling it off his shelf, Netanyahu pointedly described it as thought provoking. Likud loyalists had already branded Bennett's government as representing First Israel. One politician from the anti-Netanyahu camp, Zvi Hauser, remarked on Twitter that Netanyahu had not recommended reading Herzl or Jabotinsky and had "even forgotten Churchill. For Book Week, of all people, he recommended Ben Haim," Hauser wrote. "Netanyahu 2022 model. The rest are details."

The rest of Netivot was a mixture of religious, ramshackle neighborhoods and flashy villas of the newly rich. In the dismal town square, where the heat of the sun was beating down with the intensity of summer one March afternoon, Yoram Korkevados, forty-eight, a premier local butcher, attempted to decipher Netanyahu's popularity. A native of Netivot, Korkevados's parents came from Tamatert, near Marrakesh. He had visited Morocco for a three-week roots tour. The Moroccan king, he said, had at least half a dozen palaces, "and nobody opens their mouth. Here, what a noise over a few cigars." Crediting Netanyahu for his world standing, a flourishing economy, and security, he dismissed the corruption allegations as an invention of the media. The family meat business boasted a vibrant Facebook page hawking delicacies such as stuffed spleen and foie gras. Korkevados's parents were among the first to settle in Netivot, and the family had come far. "They came with nothing, out of ideology, to be in the Land of Israel," he said. "We are like the Blacks in America." He said he had watched *Saleh*—the series had become the talk of the development towns. "That's exactly what my mother told me had happened!" he exclaimed. "They unloaded them here off a truck. They brought them at night. There was sand and more sand."

At the crossroads of Western, Mediterranean, and Middle Eastern civilizations, the fusion that invigorated Israel's vibrant new cuisine and pop culture did not always translate so easily into the political realm and worldviews. In these parts, Netanyahu's popularity appeared to defy the laws of gravity. The deeper he sank in graft allegations, the more his political stock went up. Even as his trial got underway and the coronavirus pandemic ravaged the economy, his political wizardry kept confounding his rivals. In Kiryat Malachi, another inland city of some 25,000 residents, north of Netivot, there was a similar consensus. "We are all Bibi," said Erez Madar, a fashionable hairdresser in his early thirties who ran a salon off the city square. "Let him have a cigar," he added. "He deserves an airplane."

Founded in 1952, Kiryat Malachi grew out of a *ma'abara* on the grounds of an abandoned British army camp and a former Arab village named Qastina. The earliest settlers arrived in the middle of the night to find a few empty tents in a patch of weeds and thorns, according to the city's website. Within a year the tent encampment had grown to house three hundred families. Most had been traders and came with nothing other than their beds and a few days' supply of staples provided by the Jewish Agency. Each family was allotted a small patch of land. There was little work or income to be had in the area, but some found jobs paving roads and building housing. The town was grandly named Kiryat Malachi, Hebrew for "the City of Angels," in honor of the Los Angeles Jewish community, which adopted the immigrant backwater, whose most famous scion was probably Moshe Katsav, the political protégé and disgraced president.

Thousands of newer immigrants have since arrived from the former Soviet Union and Ethiopia. The streets around the square were lined with crumbling old tenements, but the town had expanded, with neighborhoods of neat, single-family homes and attractive apartment blocks going up around a park.

One weekday morning, a group of half a dozen old-timers had gathered around a simple metal table outside a national lottery kiosk in the forlorn city square, with small glasses of black coffee and the newspaper. This was their daily "parliament," an old Israeli tradition of meeting the same friends at a regular time and place to hold forth on current events. Yehuda Ayyash, fifty-eight, a local greengrocer born to Moroccan immigrants, was passing around a copy of that morning's *Israel Hayom*, the daily tabloid giveaway financed by the late Sheldon Adelson who died in 2021, the conservative American casino magnate and a generous backer of Netanyahu. The latest in-house opinion poll splashed over the front page showed another spike in support for Netanyahu and the Likud. "The worse they treat us the stronger we get," Ayyash, clean-shaven in a short-sleeved shirt and wearing a white skullcap, almost gloated, egged on by his friends. One wore a pink polo shirt and aviator glasses. Another, bearded and dressed in the black-and-white uniform of the ultra-Orthodox, with a black velvet skullcap, leaned on a walking stick. Ayyash then launched into an impassioned soliloquy about why he and his ilk would not forgive the old Ashkenazi establishment and would never vote Labor. "The left is cruel," he said. "You saw *Saleh*? That's the left. We experienced it as kids. We are scared of them. We are not B'Tselem."

By B'Tselem, he meant the veteran Israeli human rights organization that monitored violations of Palestinian rights in the occupied territories and was widely vilified on the right as the embodiment of Western liberalism and naivete. Here, a deeply held distrust of Arabs prevailed and mixed with the resentments and humiliation of the past and a more traditional Jewish outlook. "We want Eretz Yisrael. Jerusalem," Ayyash continued. There was, he said, "something wrong with the DNA" of the Israeli left who defended the Palestinians. "They are not Jewish," he declared. Nor were income gaps between the *Mizrahim* and *Ashkenazim* the point, he said, but a matter of values. "The *Sephardim* won't change their skin, even if there is no food in the house. They can't, out of fear. It's like someone who has been burned. My parents were burned. We grew up here in shacks. They tossed us out here. There was half a meter of water on the ground in winter from the rain. There was no drainage. My mother sat with six children on her lap to keep them dry." And, in a local version of the battle over the River Asi running through Kibbutz Nir David, Ayyash decried what he called the "theft" of tens of thousands of dunams of land by the thirty or so families of the prosperous neighboring farming community of Beer Tuvia, originally founded by Jews from Europe. Kiryat Malachi was fighting for the land, he said. It was payback time.

The words came coursing out, filled with years of bitterness, as if nothing had changed. Ethnicity was irrelevant in choosing a leader, Ayyash insisted, explaining, "We are not racists. We are rightists." The anger, almost unfathomable to outsiders, was not mitigated by the fact that Ayyash's five children, all married, had done well enough. They all lived around the area in homes they had built in the nearby *moshavim*. "They all support Likud," he added, proudly. "It's genetics. I don't need to tell them anything."

Netanyahu had led the Likud into opposition before, in 1999 and again in 2006, when the party suffered a stinging defeat against Ehud Olmert's Kadima, winning only twelve seats. After dragging the country through four inconclusive elections in the space of two years, from 2019 to 2021, ultimately losing the government, there were rumblings from the opposition benches of a party leadership race shaping up. There was no primary vote on the horizon, and most would-be successors did not dare to declare their candidacy so long as Netanyahu was in charge. The roster of prime candidates was a predictable lineup of Ashkenazi men such as Nir Barkat, Israel Katz, Yuli Edelstein, and Gilad Erdan. Miri Regev had had enough. In an interview spread over seven pages of *Yedioth Ahronoth*'s weekend magazine, she declared herself a leader of the new Mizrahi elite. Not coincidentally, she was photographed in a black-and-white polka-dot dress. "Tell me," she was quoted as saying, "this state has existed for seventy-three years. In most senior positions there are no *Mizrahim*. There has never been a Mizrahi prime minister. Something is wrong here." The day after Netanyahu, she said, there would be a reckoning. "If the Likudniks keep choosing leaders with white DNA," she said, "another Likud will rise up." At the same time, acknowledging another Israeli reality, she described her own marriage to an Ashkenazi man, Dror, whose family had Hebraized their original surname, Zeidler, to Regev, as "the true Israeli story. The combination of east and west."


It was a sunny Mimouna holiday in the spring of 2021. The "Free the Asi" campaign was in its third year. Both the protesters and the kibbutz had uploaded slick, online presentations of their legal claims and positions, both presenting maps of the area going back to the 1880s. The dispute over access to the stream that ran through the heart of the kibbutz appeared no closer to resolution. Nati Vaknin, the information systems analyst, and Perah Hadad were outside the locked yellow gate at the entrance of Nir David setting up for a festive and rowdy protest. A DJ blasted loud Moroccan pop music through a powerful sound system. Benefactors, including the family of the lawyer working pro bono for the campaign, also a native of Beit Shean, had provided plates of traditional sweets and piles of *moufletas*. "Open your gates and open your hearts!" Vaknin bellowed through a microphone, inviting the kibbutzniks to come out and join the party. Livestreaming the event on social media, he urged people to come from all over the country.

In the end, an eclectic mix of about two dozen Israelis stopped by. Both the kibbutzniks and the protest leaders made a point of displaying huge Israeli flags, each signaling that they represented the true Israel. After a couple of hours outside the gate, the protesters moved down the road to a point where the Asi petered out into an irrigation channel outside the kibbutz. Clambering down a steep incline, they launched a flotilla of a whimsical chain of inflatable rafts tethered together by a flimsy rope and set off upstream toward the forbidden Eden at the heart of the kibbutz. The ragtag crew included day trippers and children. Vaknin waded ahead with a bullhorn and hailed them as the "new pioneers."

Having spent an hour in the tranquility of the kibbutz with the veterans earlier that morning, and now floating along in a plastic dinghy with the protesters, I was torn over whose side I was on. Our dinghy hit a sharp rock lurking under the surface and began to take on water. We disembarked near the kibbutz cemetery, at the edge of the houses. The children splashed around in the water and chased ducks under the grim eye of private security guards hired by the kibbutz. Some of the wet interlopers sauntered off in the direction of the manicured lawns. Vaknin, whose parents came from Morocco, still lived in Beit Shean but had become quite a media personality as the face of the campaign to free the Asi. Lavi Meiri, the kibbutz secretary, was convinced Vaknin was headed for politics, something that Vaknin, who described himself as being right of the Likud, denied. I asked Vaknin if he considered himself First Israel or Second Israel. "I'm a Sabra!" he fired back.

Months later, the legal wrangling dragged on and the case looked like it was headed to the Supreme Court. Hoping to turn down the heat, the kibbutz agreed to a temporary compromise. A fenced-off green bank on the edge of the kibbutz was opened to the public during set hours and allowed in four hundred visitors at a time. The kibbutzniks built defenses, laying a thick, black rubber float, like an oil pipeline, across the river as an informal barrier to deter intrusions by the bathers from outside into the residential and touristic areas of the kibbutz. Vaknin, for his part, would urge the bathers from outside to cross the boundary, explaining that it was perfectly legal, and desirable, to swim through the middle of the kibbutz. The battle was not over. The river flowed on.

# FOUR

# A TALE OF TWO *KIBBUTZIM*

THE TUG OF NOSTALGIA led me back to Maayan Zvi, a kibbutz on the Carmel Ridge, adjacent to the town of Zichron Yaakov just south of Haifa, where I had spent much of my gap year studying Hebrew at its then-renowned *ulpan,* or language school, and volunteering in the 1980s. After many years away I was filled with curiosity and anticipation as I drove the familiar hairpin turns on the steep road up to the kibbutz and through the gate. I parked and headed straight to the dining hall that I remembered in my halcyon days as a sparkling jewel and the beating heart of communal life in the kibbutz. This was where everyone gathered in their work clothes for a breakfast of semolina, eggs, and vegetables they would chop fastidiously on their plate into a colorful salad, or spruced up for festive Friday night dinners at long tables set with cloths and baskets of ready-sliced challah. This was where news was swapped, important meetings held, and festivals celebrated.

The *ulpan* students were also expected to work and I had put in many hours of dining room duty, cleaning the tables and floors and scrubbing the toilets. The menial, if stress-free, labor was made more palatable by the near-majestic surroundings. The modernist, imposing dining hall was perched on the edge of a ridge overlooking the sparkling Mediterranean, its floor-to-ceiling windows and a wraparound balcony offering breathtaking, panoramic views along the coast. Down below, a patchwork of green fields and mirror-like, rectangular fish-ponds melded into the glinting sea that stretched out to a horizon of dazzling sunsets.

Now that I had returned, I found a scene of dereliction. My throat tightened. I had heard that things had changed, but I was not expecting this. The view was still there but the building was padlocked and deserted. I made my way up some outside stairs and peered through the now-grimy windows. The once sun-kissed communal dining room was crammed with old, obsolete machinery and piles of junk gathering dust.

Gone were the old engine rooms of kibbutz life: the small offices on the ground floor of the building once staffed by stern commissars drawing up daily work rosters and guarding the keys for the small pool of cars. Later, as I walked around this new version of the kibbutz, it appeared that most of the residents had private cars parked in their driveways. Old apartments had been renovated and expanded. The kibbutz had sold off land to developers and rows of single-family villas had gone up on the eastern side, blending seamlessly into the residential neighborhoods of Zichron Yaakov. Stylish private homes had also replaced an old block of studio apartments and wooden cabins that had once housed the young, single kibbutzniks, as well as all but one of the *ulpan* buildings, an iconic part of Maayan Zvi's history. Unlike the dark commissary where kibbutz members could once buy basics such as a comb, beer, or a packet of cheap cookies, a brightly lit supermarket had opened adjacent to the abandoned dining hall, stocked with the best that suburban Israel had to offer. Its shelves were stacked with an array of fine local wines and foreign liquor. A tempting fresh bakery section sold artisanal spelt and sourdough loaves. There were takeout trays of sushi and a freezer section stocked with tortellini and *gyoza*.

The abandoned dining room and the supermarket, in almost surreal juxtaposition, were the new faces of Maayan Zvi, founded as a farming commune a decade before the foundation of the state on the purist ideology of Zionist socialism. By the time I got there in the 1980s there were rumors of impending financial ruin. Maayan Zvi's attempts at industry and its agricultural endeavors did not succeed, let alone flourish. There were whispers about bad luck and bad management. In the end, the kibbutz had gone bankrupt. It remained a kibbutz only in name but had reinvented itself as a fully privatized residential community and, essentially, a real estate enterprise prized for its stunning location.

By contrast, just within sight on the coast down below, an old rival, Kibbutz Maagan Michael, was still striving to fulfill its original mission as an egalitarian commune, and it was thriving. Its Midas-like plastics industry had made it a fortune, its success serving as an omnipresent rebuke and reminder of Maayan Zvi's failure. The prosperous Maagan Michael had an almost mythical reputation of aloofness, and during my time at Maayan Zvi, the poor relative, I had never set foot there. But unlike Maayan Zvi, Maagan Michael had managed to survive as an authentic kibbutz based on socialist values. Its wealth had afforded it the luxury of adhering as closely as possible to the Marxist axiom underpinning the idea of the kibbutz: Each according to their ability and each according to their need. That model, once the embodiment of Zionist pragmatism, romanticism, idealism, and pioneering spirit, had become something of an anachronism in Israel.

The divergent paths taken by these two *kibbutzim* were emblematic of Israel's internal wrestling with its past, its present, and its consciousness. The country had gone through social, political, and economic revolutions since its foundation. The whole landscape had been transformed since Degania Aleph, the first Zionist socialist farming collective, was established in 1909 on the southern shore of the Sea of Galilee, the prototype of the utopian human experiment that would become known as the kibbutz. The kibbutz rose up to fulfill the needs and mission of the nascent state, providing food, taking possession of newly acquired lands, planting roots, and marking Israel's future borders. After the farmer-fighters, the next generations of kibbutzniks stood out as the Sabra elite, the warriors and pilots who filled the top ranks of the military, having been brought up collectively and nurtured on selfless values, their contribution and achievements far surpassing their numbers given that they accounted for a fraction of the population.

More than a century later, the Soviet Union had come and gone. Communism had all but passed from the world. In Israel, the upheaval that brought Likud to power in 1977 ushered in an anti-socialist era, in part fueled by Mizrahi resentment against the old elites. And, as Israel struggled with inflation and moved toward a free-market economy, the kibbutzniks fell so far from grace that some detractors came to curse them as "parasites" and a drain on resources, and eventually even usurpers, as in the case of Nir David. About three-quarters of the 250 or so *kibbutzim* dotted around the country had undergone some degree of privatization in recent decades, in a reflection of the broader materialism, the decline of leftist ideology, and the redefinition of modern Israel.

Yet the utopian dream had not been fully dismantled. Some kibbutzniks described this rather as a new phase in the experiment. Adapting with the times, *kibbutzim* still offered residents a close-knit community life even as they were expected to depend on themselves. And incredibly, rather than being seen as dinosaurs, many *kibbutzim* were experiencing something of a revival, with waiting lists of Israelis wanting to move in. For many, the newer, less puritanical version of the kibbutz offered a suburban, semi-bourgeois lifestyle in a rural community without the irksome egalitarianism or the hardship of toiling in the fields.

Maayan Zvi, the kibbutz of my memories, was founded in 1938 by members of the Young Maccabee movement, immigrants from Germany, where Nazi persecution of the Jews was sharply escalating. Originally named Kibbutz Maayan, meaning a spring, the nucleus of the group had already spent a year in training at Degania Aleph, then another two years working as day laborers in other early Zionist settlements as part of the campaign for Hebrew-only labor, and as guards against Arab attack. The Maayan group suffered its first casualty during the Arab Revolt, the Palestinian nationalist uprising against British rule, Jewish immigration, land purchases, and other efforts to build the Jewish national home that broke out in 1936 and lasted three years.

Amid the troubles, on August 30, 1938, the Maayan group arrived at the spot allocated for their own settlement, on the former marshes of the coastal plain below Zichron Yaakov, along the old Tel Aviv–Haifa road, sandwiched between the Carmel mountain ridge and the seashore. Part of their mission was to defend the road and the nearby railroad. The swampland had been purchased and drained by PICA, the Palestine Jewish Colonization Association founded by Baron

Edmond de Rothschild, and redeemed for agriculture. It consisted of a two-hundred-dunam, or fifty-acre, orchard surrounded by eucalyptus forest and another five hundred dunams for intensive crop farming. The group arrived with a military escort for fear of resistance from the nearby Arab villages of Furedeis, Tantura, and Kabera. The orchard was known as Nazlah, for the name of a village to the north. The August 31, 1938, edition of *Davar*, the Zionist Labor movement's main organ, reported on the inauguration of Maayan, which followed the model of Tel Amal as a tower-and-stockade settlement, referring to the rapid construction method meant to circumvent British building regulations and provide protection. Immediately upon arrival, the *Davar* correspondent reported, the Maayan workers set about hooking up to Zichron's water supply. Electricity workers came from Hadera to install a cable. One group of workers burned the weeds and thorns while another drove metal stakes into the ground and stretched barbed wire between them. A third group erected prefabricated wooden panels filled with gravel to create an instant stockade. There were celebratory speeches in the shade of the eucalyptus trees about building the Zionist enterprise, despite the danger, and "conquering the wilderness." Before the afternoon was out, travelers along the road would have seen the new settlement already in place.

In 1942 the group moved their living quarters up the hill to escape the malaria-carrying mosquitoes that lingered in the former swamplands. The kibbutz name was lengthened to Maayan Zvi in honor of Zvi Frank, a PICA official. In late 1947, reinforcements arrived on boats from Europe, part of the illegal immigration of young refugees from Germany, Austria, and Czechoslovakia who had been rescued from the Nazis and taken to safety in England, among them my inspirational *ulpan* teacher, Walter Braun.

One of the few members left with an institutional memory of Maayan Zvi's history was Shoshana Haber, a no-nonsense nonagenarian. On my subsequent visit, she picked me up at the kibbutz entrance in her two-seat electric scooter car. As she sped us along the pathways I clung on for dear life, relieved when she pulled into a parking spot outside her bungalow. A widow, Haber was one of the last surviving members of the founding generation. My *ulpan* teacher and adopted kibbutz parents had passed away years before. With a thick mop of white hair, Haber was still vital. A large picture window in her living room, one of the only improvements she'd made to the dwelling, took in the sea view. But even the view had changed. Down below, a shopping mall had sprung up between the fields and fishponds of Maayan Zvi and Maagan Michael, housing a multi-screen cinema complex and lighting up the night sky with a neon glow. A few miles off the coast, marring the sunsets, the gray skeleton of a natural gas rig rose out of the sea to process the recently discovered riches of the Leviathan gas reservoir. Haber had invested most of her life here and I was expecting her to reminisce about the more virtuous past. Yet once we were settled in her small living room she proved surprisingly unsentimental about the collapse of the egalitarian kibbutz.

Haber had arrived in Palestine with her family from Germany in 1935, soon after the rise of Hitler. They settled in Haifa, which was small and intimate then, she said. She played mostly with her Arab neighbors and learned to speak Arabic before Hebrew. She first arrived at Maayan Zvi in 1947 as a twelfth-grader when her class was sent to volunteer in the kibbutz fields, because most of the men were away fighting. She fell in love with the nature and freedom and decided to stay. She slept in a tent and worked alone in the fields with a couple of mules. She also put in shifts on kitchen duty, in the laundry, and in the sewing workshop. The women used to sit and repair the communal work clothes on sewing machines in a corner of the original kibbutz dining room, which was then a simple wooden shack. In 1949, in that same dining room, she married Avi, an Austrian who had arrived on an immigrant boat.

Haber went on to manage the sewing workshop and created a niche business selling clothes that she would bring from Tel Aviv. She then worked in one of Maayan Zvi's factories as a packer until she was seventy-six. She did not receive a salary, just the usual kibbutz stipend, like everybody else. "We worked because it was ours," she said. As newlyweds, Avi and Shoshana adopted a seven-year-old Turkish girl who had arrived as part of a kibbutz program to take in orphaned immigrants. They went on to have two daughters and a son. The adopted child was the only one to remain on the kibbutz. The children were reared in the communal system of children's houses, one of the more controversial aspects of the old kibbutz life that was mostly phased out decades ago. The idea had been to raise the children in as egalitarian an environment as possible while freeing up both parents for work. Children would spend a few hours in the late afternoon with their families and would go back to the children's house at bedtime. The younger boys and girls would cohabit and shower together. As adults, some of the products of that system remembered it as having been fun, like living in a year-round summer camp. Others recalled suffering through nightmares alone and were scarred by a sense of parental abandonment. Haber said she had asked her children and they had all told her they enjoyed the experience. When they were young, she said, she had carved out more family time by bringing prepared food home every evening from the communal dining room for a family supper, before returning the children to their houses for bedtime. She never learned to cook.

The kibbutz had provided for all their needs, though Haber said the secretariat never had spare cash to go around. Her brother started to send her fifty shekels a week from Haifa, thinking she could use the extra money, but she sent it back. There was nothing left of the old kibbutz, she said, adding, "Today, it's all money, money, money." If, in the past, the members used to gather in the dining room for general meetings where matters of principle and fateful decisions were discussed, the arguments nowadays were over property ownership and family inheritance rights. One topic Haber was less eager to hold forth on was the *renta,* the Holocaust reparations from Germany that had fueled the kibbutz in its good years. There had been a kibbutz member whose job it was to work on obtaining the reparations, she said, and she was a recipient herself, though she refused to disclose the sum. Haber qualified on the grounds that she never got to go to school in Germany, which she found amusing. The money was still being deposited in her bank account every month, she said, "as if I'd ever go to university now!" The *renta* may have been the best thing and the worst thing that had happened to Maayan Zvi. Some members said the reparations had built the dining room and the swimming pool and gave the kibbutzniks a good life for a while. But the payouts had also allowed the kibbutz to coast along until the older members began to die off and the money ran out. An ugly dispute over the *renta* had made it into the national press. "Kibbutz Maayan Zvi Riven by Row over *Renta* Payments," read the headline in a July 2001 article in *Haaretz.* According to the story, about a hundred of the 290 kibbutz members received reparations amounting in total to some half a million dollars a year, and some of them had stopped turning the money over to the kibbutz coffers. In response, the kibbutz treasury had started sanctioning those members by sending them bills for anything beyond the most basic medical care.

One of the starkest illustrations of the disintegration of Maayan Zvi was that Haber, after a lifetime as a member of the kibbutz, spent much of the week alone. Her son had spent forty years in the United States but had returned to live in a private villa in the new neighborhood on the edge of the kibbutz. The other two daughters had left Maayan Zvi. All the family, including grandchildren and great-grandchildren, would crowd into Haber's little bungalow on Friday afternoons for coffee and cake. And on Wednesdays there was a club for veteran members who met around sunset in a corner of the vestibule beneath the defunct dining room, with lectures and singing. But when Haber came down with shingles a few years ago, she said she sat and cried alone until the state's national insurance system stepped in. Help came in the form of Suad, a young mother of three from the nearby Arab town of Furedeis. Haber had been there only once, with a friend to buy a cake. But she raved about Suad, who cooked and kept Haber company for a few hours three times a week. And when Haber needed a cleaner, Suad would arrange for one to come from Furedeis. Some other elderly kibbutz founders who could no longer cope alone had live-in caregivers from far-flung places such as Sri Lanka or the Philippines. The principle of Hebrew labor had obviously long gone by the wayside. "Thank goodness for the Filipinos!" Haber exclaimed.

In the years before the founding of the state, the *kibbutzim* were an effective tool for establishing a Jewish presence and, after 1948, for establishing Israeli sovereignty over tracts of empty or abandoned and appropriated land, as well as for marking the new country's boundaries. Even though the *kibbutzim* accounted for only about 5 percent of the population when the state was founded, their role was considered so important that every political party had to claim some. Seven different kibbutz movements, or federations, including a religious one, came into being, vying with one another ideologically and politically. An internal crisis in one of the movements even led a few *kibbutzim* to split like amoebas in the 1950s. Physical or virtual lines were drawn through some communities divided by opposing schools of thought.

By the start of the new millennium, however, the secular *kibbutzim,* numbering more than 250, had come to coexist under the roof of a unified Kibbutz Movement federation. It was run out of the modernist headquarters inaugurated in the 1960s at 13 Leonardo da Vinci Street in downtown Tel Aviv, close to the old heart of Hebrew government. The three-quarters of *kibbutzim* that had gone through the privatization process, some to more extreme degrees than others, were now labeled "renewed" *kibbutzim* and were refashioned as largely decentralized communities where families were responsible for their own income and ideology, though they often retained a few cooperative assets and a social welfare program. The other quarter, Maagan Michael among them, still operated as a kind of collective, even if the children were no longer reared in communal children's houses and even if outside contractors were running the banana plantations, the dining room, and the laundry, since even the most principled Israeli egalitarians had a growing aversion to manual labor.

Renewed kibbutz households were expected to be self-sufficient, and those still working on the kibbutz received differential salaries depending on their jobs and level of responsibility. Members would pay a tax of about 5 percent of their earnings into a mutual assistance fund used to maintain the public spaces and provide a financial safety net for other members in need. Loans were also available on comfortable terms. No kibbutz member would be destitute or starve. But the unique experiment that had captured the world's imagination, that had been synonymous with pioneering Zionism and had, in the early decades, produced many of the country's top warriors and leaders, intellectuals, and artists, had lost its moral clout and influence. The country had grown up around the *kibbutzim,* with expanding cities almost devouring some of them. Many ordinary Israelis had come to regard them as remnants of the old Ashkenazi elite with their sense of entitlement.

Nir Meir, the twice-elected secretary of the Kibbutz Movement, traced the history of the kibbutz's fall from grace and its loss of prestige back decades. Hailing from kibbutz aristocracy, both he and his wife were third-generation members of Kvutzat Shiller, a kibbutz founded in 1927 in central Israel. Dressed for our meeting in an oversized blue shirt reminiscent of vintage kibbutz work clothes and the uniform of the socialist Zionist youth movements, he sat in an office on the top floor of the building on Leonardo da Vinci Street and, like a well-practiced teacher, drew charts on a board to illustrate the plethora of movements and splits over the years.

Surprisingly, he began the story of decline with Ben-Gurion, who decreed in the 1950s that at least some of the *kibbutzim* must employ outside labor. He had complained in the Knesset that the *kibbutzim* had not done enough to help absorb the waves of new immigrants and saw them as a means of employment and at least a meager income for some of the residents of the transit camps and development towns. But that, too, led to resentment as Mizrahi immigrants toiled in kibbutz factories, workshops, and fields while the party-connected kibbutzniks were perceived as lording it over them as managers. And in many cases socialism ended at the kibbutz gate. As a rule, the *kibbutzim* did not open their swimming pools for the use of underprivileged children from poor, neighboring communities. In an echo of the dispute over the Asi Stream at Nir David, Meir explained that there had to be limits, or it would be difficult to close the floodgates.

The 1960s saw the beginnings of industry taking over from kibbutz agriculture, and the start of a steady dilution of the staunch kibbutz value system. Volunteers began to pour in from abroad, particularly after the Six-Day War in 1967, as the Israeli victory drew international attention. Degania Aleph would be among the first *kibbutzim* to bar volunteers two decades later because they were seen as a bad influence. "The volunteers bring in a spirit of instability, of hedonism, of cosmopolitanism, which our children are not mature enough to absorb," Eitan Peretz, the secretary of Degania Aleph, told the Associated Press at the time, adding that several kibbutz members had married non-Jewish volunteers and moved abroad. The political revolution of 1977 that brought Menachem Begin to power upended the old socialist order. Israel's economy was already sliding into the crisis that would lead to increasing privatization on a national level. After his reelection in 1981, Begin, who was then championing new settlement in the occupied territories, appeared to have set his sights on the *kibbutzim*. In one holiday eve interview in the fall of that year, Begin was asked about the polarization between the *Ashkenazim* and *Mizrahim* that had characterized the election campaign. In his reply Begin turned on the *kibbutzim*, accusing them of snobbery toward the immigrant communities that lived nearby. Citing a television clip of a member of Manara, a kibbutz near the Lebanese border, speaking to a reporter while swimming laps, Begin denounced kibbutz members as living "like millionaires lolling around their swimming pools."

The state builders of old increasingly came to be seen as a drain on national resources. As inflation soared up to 450 percent in the 1980s, the *kibbutzim*, whose main income by then came from industrial ventures, began collapsing under the weight of high-interest bank loans. Shimon Peres, as prime minister, came up with a rescue plan that included a massive debt cancellation and restructuring agreement among the kibbutz federations, the banks, and the government. It took until 2013 for the debts to be finally resolved. By then, the world had also changed, with the crumbling of the Soviet Union and globalization. Though the *kibbutzim* still punched above their weight by growing nearly half the country's agricultural produce, Israeli agriculture was, for the most part, hardly profitable. Though there were more people than ever living on *kibbutzim*, by 2020 they accounted for only 1 percent of the total population. And the campaign against Kibbutz Nir David, Meir, the Movement secretary, said, showed that "someone has an interest in turning it into a war."

In the old days, Meir said, the state's covenant with the *kibbutzim* could be summed up as " 'Go where we send you and we'll make sure you can live.' That was the deal." Now, with the country built, the sense of purpose had faded. The main goal now, he said, was simply "to remain us. It's a constant battle, all of the time."

Even Sde Boker, Ben-Gurion's remote kibbutz in the Negev desert, had felt the winds of change. His humble green cabin had become a museum attesting to his frugality. The only evidence that he was no ordinary kibbutz member was to be found in his office, where the walls were lined with a five-thousand-book library including volumes on world history, geography, philosophy, security, and the Talmud. In the kitchen, stuck on the wall by an iconic, Israeli-made Amcor fridge, was a handwritten menu: a four p.m. snack of *nes al halav,* Hebrew for instant coffee on a warm milky base, and two slices of cake, to be followed by a light evening meal of tomato juice and a soft-boiled egg.

More than six decades after its founding in 1952, however, Sde Boker was no longer the austere place it once was. Though it was one of the minority of *kibbutzim* that had maintained a traditional communal structure and had not been significantly privatized, it had moved with the times. Well-kept green lawns and vivid blooms defied the scorching desert heat. Someone had opened a winery producing desert wines. Near the entrance of the kibbutz, Café Paula, named for Ben-Gurion's no-nonsense wife, served cappuccinos, pizza, and quiche and sold a local artisanal brand of individually wrapped soaps and lip balms. A notice board outside the kibbutz dining room advertised Pilates classes, the services of a cosmetician, and an acoustic concert by a popular artist to be held in a pub at a nearby kibbutz. The agenda posted for an upcoming kibbutz members' meeting included an update on the construction of a high-end hotel and holiday cabins, a partnership with a private developer on kibbutz land. When it opened, the hotel boasted a pampering spa with a Turkish bath and was advertised as within walking distance of Ben-Gurion's cabin.

Aviva Popper, the manager of the kibbutz's archive, had come to Sde Boker from Tel Aviv in 1957, at the age of eighteen. She and her husband, Uzi, had both arrived with one of the IDF's Nahal settlement groups. Of their four children, only one, a daughter, had remained on the kibbutz and now had four children of her own. After riding up to the small archive building on a bicycle, Popper settled behind her desk. Shelves were stacked with file boxes, film cartridges, and photographs. She had overseen the production of a slick, four-hundred-page album to mark Sde Boker's fiftieth anniversary and voluntarily produced a kibbutz newsletter. As the unofficial chronicler of the kibbutz, she said it was important to keep people informed about what was going on in the present, and also for posterity. In the past, she said, members had worked wherever they were told, whether in the vegetable patches, the kitchen, or the weaving workshop, where sheep's wool was spun into rugs. Today, she said, "everyone does what they want." Nor did the principle of self-sufficiency apply. A sticky-tape factory hired outside workers. Three Bedouin men were employed in the kibbutz kitchen. The newer members mostly shunned menial labor and preferred to work outside the kibbutz.

Popper recalled that the Ben-Gurions would eat their lunch in the communal dining room every day. There would usually be a vegetable soup and always a dessert of fruit in summer or a pudding in winter. Sometimes the kibbutzniks would eat *ptitim*—an Israeli orzo-like rice-shaped pasta still popularly known as "Ben-Gurion's rice," because the Osem food company developed it at his request during the austerity years of the 1950s, when real rice was scarce. Other occasions when the regular kibbutz residents might have encountered the aging father of the nation were during his long daily walks or on his birthdays, when Paula invited all the members to drop by the cabin and wish him *mazel tov*. Residents could also cadge a rare ride in a vehicle when he went to Tel Aviv. Now Sde Boker had a fleet of more than twenty cars for the members' use, and if the demand outstripped the supply the kibbutz would rent additional vehicles.

In the old days, when money was short, Popper said, everyone shared the little that there was. The kibbutz grocery stocked basics like tooth-paste. People took food home from the dining room. Electricity was unlimited. Now members had to pay for what they consumed. Since they also had to pay for newspaper subscriptions, only Popper and one other member still subscribed to *Haaretz*. Ironically, as in many other *kibbutzim,* the most read newspaper had become *Israel Hayom,* the right-wing free giveaway that Sheldon Adelson had financed with the original goal of helping Netanyahu return to power.

"People like the comfortable life now," Popper said, adding that the new maxim was "each according to their will." "I wouldn't have led that revolution," she said, "but I am enjoying the fruits of it." When it came to the rest of the country, she was disappointed at what she viewed as the lack of social justice and of even a desire for peace. The *am segula,* or consecrated, model society envisioned by the prophets and Ben-Gurion was, she said, "a long way off."

Like Maagan Michael, some other *kibbutzim* developed successful industries and sold their stakes to outside investors in multimillion-dollar exits. Among them was Lohamei HaGetaot, or the Ghetto Fight-ers' kibbutz, founded by the surviving commanders of the Warsaw

Ghetto uprising. Dorka Sternberg, the Holocaust survivor from the Polish town of Czestochowa, said that when she first came to the kibbutz near Acre in 1950 there was a "messianic" feeling in the air and a sense of being able to repair the world. Seventy years later it was still a cooperative, but no longer egalitarian. Its main industry, the Tivall factory, producing vegetarian, meat-substitute products and ever-popular corn schnitzels, was sold to Osem, the Israeli food giant, which was then bought by the Swiss Nestlé conglomerate.

In Hatzerim in the Negev, the Netafim factory began producing innovative drip irrigation equipment in the 1960s and became a world leader in the field before a Mexican company in 2017 bought 80 percent of the business, which was valued at $1.9 billion. Tnuva, which started as a central dairy cooperative created in the 1920s by the kibbutz leadership for distribution and export, was partially sold to foreign and Israeli investors as part of the recovery program, providing the kibbutz movement with $500 million to establish pension funds. In 2006 a Chinese food conglomerate bought the controlling holding for a reported $2.5 billion. The climbing price of cottage cheese, an Israeli staple and a Tnuva classic, became a symbol of the rising cost of living and helped spark the social justice protests of 2011 that at their peak brought almost half a million Israelis out onto the streets.

As the *kibbutzim* adapted and reformed, they experienced a kind of revival. After many of their young generation left for the city in the 1980s and 1990s, the early 2000s saw a reverse trend born of a hankering for tranquility and quality of life. Just as the West Bank ideological settlements offered religious Zionists a like-minded community, kibbutz life still offered disillusioned or harassed urban Israelis a measure of social solidarity, values, and good schools in a pastoral atmosphere. Many *kibbutzim* were suddenly bursting at the seams, with little spare housing and waiting lists even for their own sons and daughters who wished to return. The new neighborhoods that had been built were often oversubscribed. Even Nahal Oz, the kibbutz within Palestinian mortar range on the border with the Gaza Strip, quickly found sixteen families to replace those who had left the kibbutz in trauma after the fifty-day war in the summer of 2014.

Some *kibbutzim*, like Maayan Zvi, were selling plots to outsiders who built homes there and paid for kibbutz services but had no stake in the community assets. Others took in new blood as full kibbutz members. The coronavirus pandemic only added to the demand, with low infection rates inside the *kibbutzim,* which offered a respite from urban restrictions and lockdowns. Some registered a 100 percent increase in inquiries. The only thing preventing even greater expansion, according to Meir, the Kibbutz Movement secretary, were limits placed by the government on new zoning and building permits.

For Maayan Zvi, the billionaires down the hill in Maagan Michael, just visible from Shoshana Haber's picture window, would serve as a constant reminder of what went wrong and what could have been. Haber herself remembered having lunch in Maagan Michael's fabled dining room once, when she went to fetch a daughter from the school she attended there. The spread, Haber recalled, was far superior to anything served in Maayan Zvi, even on the Sabbath. There was chicken cooked at least three ways and as much steak as you could eat, she marveled, repeating the word "Steaks!" for dramatic effect.

Established eleven years after Maayan Zvi, in 1949, Maagan Michael started out with the humble goal of becoming a fishing commune, given its location on the coast. Its founding group acquired four fishing boats, but seafaring proved to be hard and unprofitable, and by the 1960s the kibbutz was in crisis. Established on the marshy land known as the Kabara swamps, the soil was highly saline, making it unsuitable for many crops. So the enterprising kibbutzniks dug ponds and turned to fish farming. Then, as in many *kibbutzim,* as the founders aged and could no longer manage such physical labor, they turned their attention to finding a suitable, clean industry. Thanks to the efforts of one astute kibbutz member, Itzik Kantor, they came up with Plasson, a plastics factory established in 1963 that introduced injection molding production to Israel as well as innovative pipe fittings, automatic drinking and feeding systems for chicken coops, and the plastic toilet tank. Plasson expanded and became an international company. Listed on the Tel Aviv Stock Exchange since 1997, it has a presence on five continents, more than twenty-five overseas subsidiaries, and annual returns exceeding a billion shekels, with net profits of tens of millions of dollars.

For Maayan Zvi up the hill, it was a sore case of bad business judg-

ment and missed opportunity. Early on, when Plasson was struggling to pay for machinery, the factory founders made their way up
to Maayan Zvi with a proposition. They were hoping that Maayan Zvi
would invest and become a partner in the business. Maayan Zvi was
considered the rich neighbor at the time, with scores of its members
receiving Holocaust reparations from Germany. But Maayan Zvi had
already made some failed investments. Reluctant to take a chance on
Plasson, its managers turned down the request from Maagan Michael.
Maayan Zvi started its own industry, setting up factories called Scopus
and Meprolight that produced optical lenses and night vision sights
for weapons. Proving unprofitable, they were eventually sold off, and
ultimately the kibbutz collapsed under its crippling debts. The shuttered Scopus building still stood, forlorn, in the middle of Maayan Zvi.
Meanwhile, down at sea level, Plasson brought Maagan Michael vast
wealth.

Curious to see how the other half lived, I went to meet Tsafrir
Sasson, a forty-something friend of a friend and a native of Maagan
Michael who still lived there with his wife, Dana, and their two children. Maagan Michael had long had a reputation in Maayan Zvi not
only for being wealthy, but also for bringing up their youth in a kind
of ideological and physical boot camp, conjuring up the notion of a
Hebrew Sparta. A turn off the coastal road led to the kibbutz entrance,
where a guard cursorily checked incoming vehicles and directed them
to a central parking lot, as the narrow pathways inside the residential
part of the kibbutz were off-limits to cars and reserved for pedestrians
and bicycles. Sasson rode up to meet me on his bicycle and immediately invited me to lunch at the renowned dining room, one of the few
kibbutz dining halls still operating throughout the week. The canteen-
style buffet was appealing and abundant. We filled our trays and, in
at least one nod to changing times, registered the meals at a checkout
counter on Sasson's kibbutz account. They cost an almost symbolic $3
each for a delicious meal of trout with chimichurri and a bountiful
choice of sides.

At a table out on a shaded terrace Sasson began to parse the pros
and cons of life in a kibbutz that had essentially remained a kibbutz,
though he and Dana both worked in professions outside the community. Tsafrir Sasson was a development engineer at a start-up creat-

ing a new generation of ultrasonic air freshener near Netanya. Dana
worked as the principal of an agricultural school in nearby Zichron
Yaakov. Together, the Sassons earned more than double the average
income that members employed outside the kibbutz were expected to
bring in. But their salaries went straight into the kibbutz coffers and
the kibbutz treasury then paid them the same monthly stipend that all
the other members received, regardless of position or workload. Cali-
brated only to account for family size, their monthly budget was suf-
ficient for a reasonably high day-to-day standard of living, Sasson said,
but did not stretch to include foreign vacations. Such extras required
working overtime or external assistance. Sasson's mother had received
a small family inheritance that had paid for a family bar mitzvah trip
to Nepal a year earlier. For despite its riches Maagan Michael prided
itself on maintaining what the members now described as "conservative" kibbutz values and a modest, simple lifestyle, shunning unbridled
materialism. Some of the profits of Plasson, the plastics factory, went
into the kibbutz, but they were not divvied up among the members.
Instead the money became savings for the members and their children.
Dispelling any notions of a luxurious lifestyle, Sasson said, "There are
no gold taps in our houses."

More important to Sasson was the peace of mind, the sense of psychological and social well-being that came with belonging to a tight-
knit community with a considerable financial safety net. Maagan
Michael also offered the kind of natural beauty, personal security, and
serenity that was hard to quantify in monetary terms. In the residential
interior of the kibbutz, there was an air of idyllic tranquility. Young
parents pedaled along the sunny pathways with infants perched on the
back of their bicycles. Children roamed freely in packs, in complete
safety. At the communal laundry, workers sorted piles of clean, neatly
folded clothes into members' cubby holes. A special bin was labeled for
dog blankets. But beneath the veneer of this social paradise by the sea
lurked all the usual human complexes, peccadilloes, grievances, and
misgivings, Sasson said, revealing that he and his wife had occasionally
debated leaving the kibbutz. There was no doubt that the quality of life
they enjoyed on a daily basis was almost unbeatable, but it had its limits in terms of personal choices. "The cost," Sasson said, "is freedom."

Maagan Michael seemed to exist in a cocoon-like time warp. It was proud of its origins, and an exhibit in the central gardens around the old water tower, made up of large boards with Hebrew text, told of the history of the place, accompanied by grainy archival photographs. The founders, a cluster of two dozen German and Austrian youths, had formed a Scouts group that first trained for kibbutz life in Ein Gev, near Tiberias, by the Sea of Galilee, in the early 1940s. After joining up with two other local pioneering groups, they went to work in the Ayalon Institute, a secret facility run by the Haganah to produce illegal ammunition in preparation for the coming 1948 war. It was a heroic part of Zionist history: The workers toiled underground, beneath a mock kibbutz in Rehovot built to fool the British authorities, at perpetual risk of being discovered or blown up. "I doubt there was a more daring enterprise in the *Yishuv*," David Ben-Gurion once wrote of the Ayalon project. "And I don't know what was greater—the modesty of the workers or their courage?!"

When the enlarged group of 154 adults and 47 children laid the cornerstone for their own kibbutz on the Mediterranean coast, the lofty founding manifesto spoke of a seafaring community that would struggle to tame the waves to earn their daily bread and, as a brigade of the Hebrew Labor youth movement, would strive to fulfill the dual values of work and creativity. Along with the lush greenery, small placards inscribed with poems were planted along the pathways.

The area was inhabited by the Arab Al Ghawarina tribe, which had lived off fishing since the previous century. After draining the Kabara swamps in the 1920s, PICA built the village of Jisr al-Zarqa for the tribe, adjacent to where Maagan Michael would be established. By Maagan Michael's account, the neighboring Jewish settlements of Zichron Yaakov and Binyamina had become dependent on the tribe's labor and made sure the village survived the 1948 war intact. After the war, Jisr al-Zarqa was the only Arab village left along the seashore.

Unlike Maayan Zvi up the hill, Maagan Michael clearly treasured its history and was dotted with memorabilia. The old wooden cabin that served as the first dining room had been lovingly preserved. While the privatized residential properties of Maayan Zvi had been divided up between the members and many had since been extended or renovated, even the highest achieving members of Maagan Michael lived in modest and uniform kibbutz houses and apartments in the old quarter of the kibbutz, though Tsafrir Sasson and his family lived in a taste-ful new home in a recently built neighborhood a short walk from the beach. More than half his class had remained on the kibbutz, so he was surrounded by friends he had had since childhood.

Sasson, for one, had great admiration for the older members of Maa-gan Michael, including its military heroes and now legendary entrepre-neurs, and also for the values of humility and thriftiness and the work ethic they had instilled. Like all the kibbutz children, Sasson learned to sail on the sea, and as a teenager he worked in agriculture and in the kibbutz carpentry shop. Once, he recalled, his mother needed to go to the hospital but his father couldn't find an available kibbutz car in time, so they walked to the highway and hitched a ride. When Sasson asked why they didn't just call a cab, his father said it hadn't occurred to them.

The accomplishments of the founding generation and their ingenu-ity and acumen had allowed him a more carefree life. Nowadays there was no shortage of numbered, communally owned cars in the parking lot for the members' use. In general, life was less puritanical and dog-matic. Sasson drove a private car to and from work and paid a small tax on it to the kibbutz treasury. Members no longer had to perform din-ing room duty. It had been outsourced to an outside company though the kibbutzniks remained the managers. As in Maayan Zvi, the banana plantations of Maagan Michael had been leased out to a contractor, apparently because not enough kibbutz members were willing to work there, despite their egalitarian ideals.

The early efforts to erase the individual and quash private ambition had also been eased. If in the past kibbutz committees would decide everything for their members and send people to study only disci-plines that would be of use to the commune, the offspring of Maagan Michael could now choose to study whatever they wanted and the kib-butz would pay for it. One of the first to benefit, Sasson had studied plastics engineering at the Shenkar College of Engineering, Design and Art in Tel Aviv, then gone on to obtain an MBA. One of the larg-est *kibbutzim,* with 1,000 members and some 2,000 residents, Maagan Michael had outgrown holding general meetings in the dining room. Instead, notices about upcoming decisions were sent around to mem-bers digitally and they voted on their smartphones. Sasson missed the tough debates. Now, he said, the only arguing took the form of some sparring on a kibbutz Facebook group. In another sign of change, he found some spiritual and intellectual stimulation attending a discussion group on the weekly Torah portion that took place in the kibbutz, a bastion of secularism where religion was once anathema.

He said he missed the passion and drive of the pioneering generation. Like the rest of Israel, the kibbutz had been built and was thriving. It was hard to see what was left to be achieved, what more there was to strive for. "There is no longer any objective," Sasson said. "Nobody is asking hard questions." Instead, the kibbutz was coasting along on Plasson's success from decades before. He still craved some intangible, ideological nourishment or spirit. Despite the security and largely stress-free life that the tight-knit community had bestowed upon him and his family, he was bothered by a niggling thought: "Now what?"

Despite the desolation of Maayan Zvi's dining room and the dismantling of the communal structure, nobody there seemed to be lamenting the privatization and basic disintegration of the traditional kibbutz. Instead, many of the second generation appeared at peace with its demise and even preferred it in its new form, as if they had been liberated. Tamar Goldbach, whose parents were among the founders of Maayan Zvi, having come from Austria and Czechoslovakia, was typically unsentimental. Free-spirited and fiercely independent by nature, with long, hippie-style hair reaching below her waist, she had come and gone from Maayan Zvi as an adult, her built-in wanderlust clashing with the once-rigid expectations of the egalitarian kibbutz. As a young child, Goldbach remembered growing up in the communal children's houses as a frightening experience. "I was one of those who used to run home," she said. "I had nightmares." It was more fun as a teenager, living with her peer group of classmates who were "like brothers and sisters." Her parents, she said, were only youths themselves when they arrived from Europe and the kibbutz replaced their family. One of three daughters, two of whom no longer lived on the kibbutz, she had attended high school in Maagan Michael, down the hill, left for her army service in the north, then embarked on her post-army travels that never really ended. Returning to the kibbutz after years in South Africa, where she trained in iridology, an alternative medicine technique based on reading the iris of the eye to determine health issues, she had inherited her late parents' bungalow with a spacious veranda overlooking the sea. She set up her private iridology clinic in the basement. She still spent months of each year in India, which had become her second home. The renewed kibbutz allowed her that freedom. She was back living in Maayan Zvi as an heir, not a member. "Inheritance law trumps kibbutz rules," she said. It probably helped that one of her sisters was a lawyer.

Goldbach had come to reject the very concept of the traditional kibbutz that had nurtured her. "There's no such thing as equality," she pronounced. "People were not born with equal abilities. It cannot be flattened out. It's good that change has come."

Also enjoying the change were Uki and Shulamit Arbel, stalwarts of the community. Now in their early seventies, they were living in a smart, ultra-modern apartment in a small complex that had recently been built at the top of the kibbutz rise, near where the *ulpan* had stood. Grandchildren were playing Ping-Pong on the large dining table in the air-conditioned living room with floor-to-ceiling windows offering stunning views of the Mediterranean. We went out to sit on the large veranda. Uki, the son of founders of the kibbutz, grew up there and went on to work in the banana plantations down in the coastal plain as well as in the Scopus factory. Shulamit also grew up on the kibbutz and became its nurse. Since the kibbutz economy was dismantled, Uki had been running his own security company. The old system, he said, had invited "a lot of parasites who lived on the account of others." But he was sure that if not for the *kibbutzim,* which drew the borders, there would be no state of Israel.

If Maayan Zvi had any kind of a future as a community, it was perhaps in the hands of members of the younger generation who could still appreciate what it had once been, someone like Amitai Ashkenazi, a native of Maayan Zvi who was born during its heyday in the early 1980s. In 2002, as he was finishing his army service, outside management "said they were closing the gates," he said. What was said by many to be one of the crueler, more brutal privatization plans designed to rescue the *kibbutzim* as they floundered in an increasingly capitalist country was applied to Maayan Zvi. Ashkenazi went to Switzerland to work in security for two years in order to make money.

Returning to Israel, he graduated from Tel Aviv University's Depart-

# FIVE

# OUTPOST MILLENNIALS

T HE STYLISH wooden chalet with the red-tiled roof looked out over a sweeping vista of rolling hills. At around $200 a night, midweek, its spa-like, pine interior slept up to eight and included a vibrating massage chair, a pampering Jacuzzi tub, and free Wi-Fi. French windows opened onto a wooden deck. Acres of vineyards stretched across the valley below. For an additional charge, Inbal, the hostess, would provide a wholesome breakfast. A heated indoor swimming pool encased in a quaint stone building could be booked in advance for the guests' private use.

The mountain villa's Airbnb listing was vague on location: The *Bikta B'Kerem*, or "Cottage in a Vineyard," was described as being in "Shilo, Jerusalem District, Israel." Arrival by taxi or private car was recommended. A click on the Airbnb map erroneously placed the pastoral retreat in Shiloh, Illinois. In fact, as a couple of guest reviews quickly revealed, the luxury cabin was situated in Esh Kodesh, a settler outpost on a rugged hilltop deep in the occupied West Bank that was illegally built, even by Israeli standards. An hour's drive from Jerusalem, the outpost lay up several miles of winding roads from the established "mother settlement" of Shilo, in what the settlers referred to as Samaria. Once a hardscrabble frontier post suitable for only the hardiest and most radical of settlers, it was reimagining itself as a laid-back holiday ment of Film and Television Studies and became a filmmaker. His first short film, *Till the End of the Day,* shot in 2014, was a disturbing coming-of-age story set along the tense border between the fishponds of Maagan Michael and the poor, neighboring Arab fishing village of Jisr al-Zarqa. It was screened at international film festivals. Later, as a thirty-something screenwriter and director, Ashkenazi and two other filmmakers also from kibbutz backgrounds co-created *Kibbutznikim,* an ironic, thirty-six-part cable television daily drama following the escapades of a group of former classmates from a fictional kibbutz that had collapsed, called Maayan Haim. Dispossessed by the new management, and plotting some payback, they create an alternative commune by squatting in an old hangar in Tel Aviv owned by the kibbutz.

The initial trauma of the privatization of Maayan Zvi had faded in Ashkenazi's mind over the years. And in an odd twist the new spirit of individualism that had taken over there had made it an attractive proposition. Married with a baby, Ashkenazi was already living a few miles to the south and was planning to move the family to Maayan Zvi, the place he still called home. Development plans were afoot for 163 new apartments along with holiday chalets and commercial space to be built on the site of the ghostly Scopus factory.

As Ashkenazi reminisced about the past, the tale of Maayan Zvi and Maagan Michael began to sound like a classic case of sibling rivalry, with equal parts love and envy. Ashkenazi, like all the other children from Maayan Zvi, had attended the regional kibbutz school in Maagan Michael and maintained many friendships with classmates down on the coast. Quite a few of his peer group from Maayan Zvi had married members of Maagan Michael and settled there. Each of the *kibbutzim* had its pros and cons. "There is always some jealousy when it comes to Maagan Michael," he acknowledged. "They are the successful kibbutz. We are the ones who went bankrupt. But the paradox is that to me, Maayan Zvi is in a much better place."

He described Maagan Michael as being stuck in its own bubble and riddled with social problems under the surface. After years of urban living, Ashkenazi considered the traditional model of communal life practiced by Maagan Michael as "out" in the 2020s. "They don't really understand what independence is," he said, adding wryly, "The problem with Maagan Michael is that it is still a kibbutz."

retreat, even though the area had more of a reputation for militancy and violence.

One of a string of outposts in the Shilo Valley, a picturesque area of the northern West Bank with a rich biblical history, Esh Kodesh, which was about twenty years old, featured sporadically in reports about gun-toting, messianic settlers at war with their Palestinian neighbors. Grainy Palestinian cellphone footage sometimes captured images of armed settler men descending the mountainsides with unkempt beards, flowing sidelocks, and large skullcaps, their faces wrapped in T-shirts. Clashes with farmers in the fields around Esh Kodesh, between the Palestinian villages of Qaryut, Jalud, and Qusra, had occasionally turned deadly amid mutual recriminations about the uprooting of olive trees and vandalization of crops.

Yet Inbal Zeev, the Airbnb host, and her neighbors sold an alternative reality of a mostly tranquil, bucolic idyll in which the Palestinian villages, in plain view on the opposite slopes, hardly figured. Brushing off the outpost's image of violence, she and other residents pointed to one incident a few years back when Esh Kodesh residents were suspected of torching six cars in Qusra. More than a decade had passed since the so-called hilltop youths of the northern West Bank spawned the "price tag" policy, a doctrine of revenge whereby any act of Palestinian terrorism against the settlers or any effort by Israeli security forces to curb illegal construction in the settlements would be met by settlers exacting a price against Palestinian property. The Israeli police eventually concluded that in the Qusra case local Palestinians had tried to stage a "price tag" attack, supposedly to collect insurance. On that occasion, at least, the settlers were apparently blameless.

Magical thinking was intrinsic to Israel's settlement enterprise. It had long gotten by on the government's marketing of its decades-old occupation of the West Bank to the world as temporary, along with its settlement project, pending a negotiated resolution of the Israeli-Palestinian conflict, while simultaneously striving for permanence. As the pioneering phase and outsize influence of the *kibbutzim* had waned, the ideologically and religiously inspired settlers took up the standard of redrawing the borders. At times they did so with the open encouragement and full support of the government; at others, with a nod and a wink. Often, the leadership simply equivocated or turned a blind eye, leaving it up to the military to deal with the situation on the ground, afraid to rein in the religious Zionist patriots out of political expediency.

The upshot was that more than half a century after the Six-Day War the settlement enterprise was nearing the point of no return, making any eventual partition of the territory almost impossible. Mainstream Israelis, chronically divided and convinced by years of violence and political fearmongering that there was no Palestinian partner for peace, had sunk into a state of inertia. The settlers exploited the vacuum. Meanwhile Israel remained paralyzed, with no plan and no vision of an endgame for the most fundamental challenge to its future.

The mind tricks began in the first decade after the territorial conquests of 1967. The Labor governments set their sights on settling the Jordan Valley as Israel's eastern security border, as well as building a Greater Jerusalem. But Moshe Levinger, a firebrand rabbi who viewed the victory of 1967 as a sign of redemption, moved a group of settlers into the Park Hotel in the newly conquered holy city of Hebron to celebrate the Passover holiday the following year and refused to leave. The government caved. The group remained in an Israeli military compound in the city until the adjacent settlement of Kiryat Arba was established with government approval.

Many other Israelis at that time viewed the newly acquired territories as a valuable bargaining chip to be exchanged for peace with the Arab enemies when circumstances allowed. Ben-Gurion, once out of power, had stated that in return for a true peace he would give up all the territories except for the Golan Heights in the north, Jerusalem, and the West Bank city of Hebron, distinguishing between his belief in Israel's rights to all the land and the pragmatic need to forgo some of those rights and concede some of the land. But after the Likud's political revolution of 1977 the hawkish security concept of Ariel Sharon—which demanded Israeli control of the high ground of the West Bank—dovetailed with the old, right-wing Revisionist designs for a Greater Israel. The messianic mission was underway to settle all the land that God had promised to the Israelites and ensure that no Palestinian state would rise up there.

By the early 2020s, more than 440,000 Jewish settlers were living in 132 officially established settlements and a similar number of unauthorized settler outposts dotted throughout the West Bank, which was

home to more than 2.7 million Palestinians. The numbers were somewhat deceptive. Up to a third of the West Bank settlers were ultra-
Orthodox Jews living in two rapidly expanding urban settlements,
Beitar Illit and Modiin Illit, located just across the 1967 lines. Many
of them, ambivalent about Zionism to begin with, were there for economic and social reasons, and not out of political ideology. Under any
proposed final status map with the Palestinians, it was long assumed
that these two settlements could easily be incorporated into Israel and
would not pose an obstacle to partition within the framework of the
long-accepted paradigm of a two-state solution. Many secular residents of other urban settlements were less motivated by ideology than
by cheaper housing within easy commuting distance of Israeli cities,
and more than 70 percent of the West Bank settlers were estimated to
live within Israeli-defined settlement blocs that were mostly close to
the 1967 boundary and that successive Israeli governments had long
assumed would be incorporated into Israel, with border adjustments
and possible land swaps, as part of any negotiated deal.

Overall, however, the Israelis and Palestinians were at a demographic tipping point, with more-or-less parity in the number of Jews
and Arabs living between the Jordan River and the Mediterranean
Sea. The century-long struggle over the land was only becoming more
intractable. The Israeli Zionist left had long warned that the dream was
at stake and that Israel could not have it both ways: Without partition
into two separate homelands for Jews and Palestinians, Israel's self-
definition as a Jewish democracy, however compromised those terms
were, could not be sustained and Israel would inevitably become a
binational country. If all the Palestinians were given equal rights and
the vote in Israel, it would not have a Jewish majority. Without partition and without allowing Palestinians to vote for the government
that controlled fundamental aspects of their lives, Israel's claim to be a
democracy would eventually implode. The temporary occupation had
gone on so long that many critics were already describing the separate statuses of Israel and the occupied territories as a fiction meant
to obscure what was already a binational, one-state reality. Instead of
a light unto the nations, Israel was being cast by its harshest liberal-
left critics and human rights groups such as B'Tselem, Human Rights
Watch, and Amnesty International as a single-state entity and territory

that had already veered into a system of varying degrees of "Jewish supremacy" or racial "domination" over the Palestinians in different geographical areas that, they asserted, fit international definitions of apartheid and crimes against humanity.

With a weak Palestinian leadership split between the increasingly autocratic Palestinian Authority in the West Bank and Hamas-run Gaza, and after years without any semblance of a peace process, Israel, more than seventy years after its founding, was more divided over its endgame than it was on the eve of its independence. Esh Kodesh and a rash of other settlement outposts had stepped into the void to try to determine the outcome and doom Israel to victory, or at least to deepen the entanglement of the Israeli-Palestinian conflict.

The outpost project began during Netanyahu's first term in office in the late 1990s, as a delayed response to the Oslo process, then to counteract a declared settlement freeze under Prime Minister Rabin and the Wye Plantation talks, where the United States pressed Netanyahu into conceding more territory to the Palestinians. The Israeli government had made a commitment to Washington not to establish new settlements at the time, so Ariel Sharon, as Netanyahu's foreign minister, urged the settlers to "run and grab" the hilltops. Setting up the outposts became a stealth operation carried out with seeming spontaneity, without any formal Israeli government decision, but with significant help from government officials and bureaucrats working below the radar. This state-within-a state was made up of settlement advocates either exploiting their executive powers or working in full collusion with the government while allowing it some deniability, though the pirate settlement points were hardly invisible.

The founders of Esh Kodesh, a few fervent young men, moved to the spot around 1999 or 2000 and slept in an abandoned bus on a bare hilltop. The outpost was initially labeled N.G. 827, or Migdalim South, in an effort to pass it off as a new neighborhood of an existing settlement, Migdalim, about three miles away. It was eventually renamed Esh Kodesh, which means holy fire, in memory of Esh Kodesh Gilmore, a young security guard who was gunned down by Palestinians in October 2000 at the Israeli National Insurance Institute office in East Jerusalem; the settler movement had adopted a doctrine that erecting new settlements was the appropriate response to Palestinian terrorism.

Twenty years on, seventy families were living in Esh Kodesh in a variety of trailers, prefabricated villas, and other types of mobile homes. That was because the outpost was still in legal limbo in Israeli terms while most of the world considered the entire settlement enterprise a violation of international law. Despite the initial connection to Migdalim, the Israeli military, the ultimate power in the occupied territories, had included Esh Kodesh within the boundary of Shilo on its maps. The Israeli government had since declared its intention to authorize the outpost and the area had been zoned into housing lots. Residents said they paid property tax to the local settler council. Yet the process of retroactively authorizing the outpost had been drawn out over years and had still not been completed. So there were still no building permits for the residents, and therefore no mortgages available to build permanent homes on firm foundations.

Nevertheless, these outpost settlers had created a deceptive normality and an illusion of permanence. Several of them had extended their prefabricated houses and covered them in pale peach stucco. Other houses were clad in beige stone dug out of the earth and embellished with arched windows, in the style of a Tuscan villa. The unpaved paths were all labeled with handcrafted mosaic street signs. Gardens were planted with maturing fruit trees. The pathway of Inbal Zeev's stone-clad family home, a short distance from the Airbnb chalet, was inlaid with colored glass marbles that glinted in the sun like magical gemstones. Esh Kodesh residents sold organic vegetables and produced boutique quality wines. One man produced gluten-free buckwheat pita bread, another managed major city construction projects in Israel. A woman briefly ran a sushi business, while other residents worked in high-tech. Extracurricular activities for the children included horseback riding and after-school acrobatics in a circus tent set up by an outpost entrepreneur in a former sheep pen. Doors were left unlocked. Outpost children clambered up on the roof of the old, painted bus in what was now a central park and playground. Fearless three-year-olds peddled about in front yards and along the paths, unattended, on tricycles.

These were the outpost millennials, the yuppie pioneering elite of the religious Zionist movement. Many of them left comfortable backgrounds for this windy, inhospitable high ground, drawn by nature and the idea of starting something new as part of a tight-knit community of like-minded ideologues. Firm in the belief that this land was their God-given birthright, they were on a mission to reclaim it. If decades of diplomacy had given the Palestinians the impression that this land would one day form the heart of a future Palestinian state, the outposts aimed to disrupt that. "Primarily, we came here out of ideology," Inbal said, pointing vaguely out toward Jalud, the Palestinian village that spilled down the opposite hill and contained some ancient ruins. "We are restoring Jewish settlement here." Undoubtedly, for many young settler families, there was the additional allure of cheap housing. The rent for a trailer home here was about $250 a month, a fraction of the price of a couple of rooms in Tel Aviv. That was an important factor, because unlike Western millennials, who tended to stay home and marry late, if at all, these Generation Y settlers married young and many were already grandparents by their early forties.

Inbal Zeev had married at nineteen and moved here in 2006 with her husband, Benaya, a carpenter. He had grown up in the radical Jewish settlement in the center of Hebron, she in central Israel. They had first met in another outpost to the north, the majestically named Gvaot Olam, or Hills of Eternity, set up by Avri Ran, a charismatic guru of the hilltop youth. Ran and his ilk had first emerged in the 1990s, pushing the boundaries of the established settlements after Israel began ceding territory to the Palestinians under the terms of the Oslo Accords, the interim peace agreements that brought the PLO leadership back from exile, established the Palestinian Authority, and was supposed to have led to a permanent agreement within five years. Gvaot Olam, a private ranch-cum-commune in the high terrain south of Nablus, had an almost mystical ambiance, enhanced by sculptures and wind chimes. A main producer of organic eggs, it attracted dozens of religious youths seeking freedom and adventure. But Ran and his followers were also notorious for run-ins with the law and assaults on local Palestinians who dared venture onto land near the outpost. There were reports of shootings, beatings, and the poisoning of livestock. From there, the Zeevs had followed friends to Esh Kodesh, joining the first five families that moved from the bus into mobile homes. Fourteen years later, they were in their mid-thirties and bringing up seven children. Inbal ran the B&B. Benaya helped build the swimming pool.

Sitting at the dining table of the holiday cottage between paying guests, Inbal served fresh fruit shakes made by one of her young sons. She was attired in modest but fashionable color-coordinated settler chic: a flowery print dress over black leggings, her dark hair tucked into a maroon, volumized turban known as a *bobo*. The idea to build the guest cottage had first emerged when reports of clashes between the local settlers and Palestinians began to flood the media a few years ago, she said. The residents of Esh Kodesh and neighboring outposts such as Adei Ad, Yishuv Hada'at, Achiya, and Kida were, she said, being "portrayed as fanatics." Insisting that the wild image of the outposts was unjustified, she said Esh Kodesh residents were "with the state" all the way, to the point where one neighbor had snitched to the authorities about another's illegal construction. But realizing that they were losing the sympathy of ordinary Israelis, she said, she and her husband decided, "We have to bring them to us."

Products of the religious-Zionist education system, the outpost settlers in Esh Kodesh and elsewhere marveled that they were fulfilling the prophecies of Jeremiah, quoting verses like "Again you will plant vineyards on the hills of Samaria," and "Your children will return to their borders." Revered as the site where Joshua and the children of Israel erected their first tabernacle after entering the Promised Land, an archaeological dig in Shilo had turned up a family burial plot and ritual baths from the Second Temple period. The ruins of a Byzantine church had been repurposed into an events and banquet hall. Thousands of pilgrims were bused to a raised, round, UFO-like visitors' center that stuck out of the landscape incongruously but offered panoramic views of the surrounding area and a sound-and-light show. A gift store sold model tabernacles and Arks of the Covenant.

These hardy Jews with basically bourgeois aspirations had inserted themselves into the very crux of the Israeli-Palestinian conflict. They competed over every dunam with generations of Palestinians. As concerned as they were with nurturing an image of being ordinary Israelis, they did not care in the least about international opinion. Collective Palestinian rights did not appear in their scriptures. Successive governments had backed them up. The official position was that the West Bank was disputed, not occupied, since it had not been previously ruled by the Palestinians or any other legal sovereign. And while the Geneva Conventions prohibited the deportation or transfer of an occupier's population into occupied territory, Israel argued that its settlers had all gone there voluntarily.

By the 2020s, the original hilltop youths who spearheaded the illegal outpost construction had grown up and had children of their own. The outpost population numbered about 20,000 and the political right had begun to refer to the unauthorized outposts as "young settlement," euphemistically masking its outlaw beginnings with a new layer of respectability. For communities like Esh Kodesh, which had already undergone a degree of gentrification, it was time to think long term. The goal was to be counted as normal—not as a semi-permanent settlement of stone-clad prefabricated homes but as an integral, inseparable part of Israel.

There was a moment in time, through the combined efforts of the Trump and Netanyahu administrations, when the prospect had appeared tantalizingly close and possible. Along with the recognition of Jerusalem as Israel's capital and the subsequent move of the American embassy to the city, the gifts the Trump administration had bestowed on Israel, if only to shore up Trump's Evangelical base, included an unexpected pronouncement in late 2019 by Secretary of State Mike Pompeo that the administration no longer considered Israel's settlements in the West Bank to be inconsistent with international law. And when Trump finally unfurled his long-awaited "Peace to Prosperity" plan for the resolution of the Israel-Palestinian conflict in early 2020, few believed it would bring prosperity or peace, but for Netanyahu it legitimized the idea of annexing and applying Israeli sovereignty over large swaths of West Bank territory, including every settlement and outpost, unlike any American final status proposal that had come before.

The Oslo Accords had divvied up the West Bank into three administrative zones known as Areas A, B, and C, according to varying degrees of Israeli and Palestinian Authority civilian and security control. Though the definitions had frayed over the years, the Palestinians exercised limited self-rule in Areas A and B while Israel fully controlled Area C, the 60 percent of the West Bank where all the Israeli settlements were located. But as Inbal Zeev put it, "Our Torah doesn't differentiate between A, B, and C." The settlers had exulted at Trump's election in 2016—Naftali Bennett, then the minister of education, declared that the era of the Palestinian state was over—but the celebrations proved premature. When the Trump administration unveiled its "Vision for Peace," a proposal for a final settlement, in early 2020, it was heavily tilted in favor of Israel, offering it the prospect of annexing about 30 percent of the West Bank, including every settlement point, as Netanyahu had improbably promised his voters. But it also offered the Palestinians a conditional, demilitarized, and fragmented mini-state to be made up of the Gaza Strip and some 70 percent of the West Bank territory pockmarked with Israeli enclaves, barely contiguous in parts and all to be surrounded by Israeli sovereign land. The Palestinian capital was to consist of an unimposing village on the eastern edge of Jerusalem, Abu Dis, as well as a few disconnected slum neighborhoods and a refugee camp on the northern outskirts of the city. Not a single settler was to be uprooted. Yet even that was not enough for some of the settlers: The plan created a split within the movement between pragmatists who advocated taking what they could get in terms of annexation and trusting that the Palestinians would never reach the required benchmarks to qualify for statehood, and the movement's more rigid wing, which rejected the plan outright. The rejectionists decried the idea that some fifteen settlements would have been left stranded like islands within Palestinian territory, tethered to Israel by narrow roads like balloons on a string, and they refused to accept the principle of Palestinian sovereignty or statehood, however restricted, in any area of the West Bank, considering all of the land to be Jewish patrimony.

The Palestinians and their president, Mahmoud Abbas, an ailing octogenarian, had already rejected far more generous American-brokered proposals. Loath to go down in history as conceding on any fundamental Palestinian principles, Abbas had previously gone AWOL whenever it was time to sign on the dotted line. Unsurprisingly, he furiously rejected the Trump plan, calling it a "conspiracy" and comparing the offered polka-dotted Palestinian statelet to Swiss cheese.

Trump, Abbas, Netanyahu, and the settlers were in many respects fighting yesterday's diplomatic war over the outlines of a two-state solution. What they had not taken into account, and were seemingly oblivious to, was the Palestinian millennial factor and the changing human landscape on the other side of the lines. For a young, educated, and social-media-savvy generation of Palestinians was speaking a new language, not of future borders and minor land swaps, but of freedom, rights, and justice. Local campaigns led by self-made Instagram activists, such as the sustained protest against evictions of Palestinian families from homes reclaimed by Jews in coveted areas of East Jerusalem, were suddenly drawing international celebrity support from online influencers such as supermodels Gigi and Bella Hadid and Dua Lipa, the pop star dating their brother. Like the outpost settlers, these Palestinians had no recollection of a time when Israel was not in control of the West Bank. They detested what they perceived to be a corrupt and feckless Palestinian Authority and viewed the old guard led by Abbas as a miserable subcontractor for the Israeli occupiers. They had largely lost hope in a viable, independent state of their own, given the spread and entrenchment of the settlement project. Like the settlers, they did not articulate a clear, unified position regarding the endgame. They simply canceled each other. "I think the key thing that has changed is Palestinian agency," said Fadi Quran, a thirty-something grassroots activist and community organizer in the West Bank. "In the past, throughout my activism, when Palestinians were usually interviewed on TV, the key line was, When is the international community coming in to save us? When will Israel be held accountable? When will the Arabs come and rescue us? Now the discourse of the young is, We've got this," he told me. Buoyed by the international momentum of rights and social justice movements like Black Lives Matter, he said, and working quietly to avoid attention or arrest by the Palestinian Authority or Israel, each small victory was consciousness-building and each celebrity social media post was empowering. There was a new unity that cut across factionalized Palestinian politics and society. "It's not about how it looks in the end, but how to get there," he said. "We are flipping the game on its head. Instead of drawing borders, we are focusing on values."

There were also the Palestinian youths and adults who, egged on by the glorification of the perpetrators of the last attack or the hate-filled corners of social media, grabbed knives or cleavers or makeshift machine guns crafted on lathes in the West Bank and set out to kill Israelis. They, too, seemed to have little faith in their leaders. The waves of deadly terrorist attacks in 2015 to 2016 and in the spring of 2022 were largely carried out by Arab assailants who had no known affiliations with organized Palestinian political or militant factions and were acting almost aimlessly, whether out of a deep loathing or personal frustration, with unclear political goals. Acting solo or in pairs, they were referred to by the Israeli security authorities as "lone wolves."

Inbal Zeev was reluctant to talk politics, conveniently saying that was not her department. While some settler women, like veteran settlement entrepreneur Daniella Weiss, were feisty and vocal advocates of the cause, others demurred, saying they left the politics to their husbands. But Esh Kodesh had an official spokesman, Aaron Katsof, who welcomed me into his home with the swashbuckling confidence of a local sheriff. The silver cowboy buckle on his jeans belt, his leather holster, and the revolver on his hip added to the image. Barring those accessories, Katsof, a California native with preppy spectacles, would not have looked out of place in an Israeli tech firm. In his mid-thirties and a father of six, he ground his own specialty coffee beans, served his wife's homemade buckwheat, oat, and chia cookies, and marketed Esh Kodesh as an orchard-laden Eden, as if for the Good Life channel.

The Katsofs had been living in Tel Aviv and looking around for somewhere new to settle when Aaron's second cousin, Akiva HaCohen, a hilltop activist widely credited as an architect of the price tag doctrine, had recommended Esh Kodesh as a good fit. The Katsofs moved in around 2010 when there were just ten families living at the outpost in trailers. He said he felt like the American pioneers who went west in search of a better future for their children. Since then, he had built extensions onto his family trailer, tiled the floors, lined the ceiling with pinewood, and installed a wood-burning stove, lending it the air of a spacious ranch house. Self-assured to the point of cockiness, Katsof listed his other pursuits, including serving as an officer in the reserves, founding and running a premilitary program in Tel Aviv for foreign volunteers, studying for a degree in Arabic, and tending to his vineyards. He produced cabernet sauvignon for export under the label "Settlers Cellar," which was advertised online for up to $60 a bottle. He had also founded a nonprofit that collected donations from American Evangelical Christians, cashing in on an unholy alliance that had been building for years and had, at times, divided the settler movement. Some favored taking whatever support they could get.

Others were more wary of the doomsday scenario of the Evangelicals, whose interpretation of prophecy involved the conversion of Jews to Christianity on Judgment Day, and they were reluctant to be cast in the role they'd been assigned come Armageddon. The ministries of the American preacher John Hagee had donated $1.5 million toward a sports and recreational complex in the settlement of Ariel, with a huge swimming pool and other state-of-the art facilities. Other Evangelicals took a humbler approach, dispatching volunteers to help settlers in the Samarian hills harvest their vineyards. The alliance reached a peak during the Trump administration, culminating in the opening ceremony of the United States Embassy in Jerusalem, where both Pastor Hagee and another controversial Evangelical pastor, Robert Jeffress, a Southern Baptist, delivered prayers and benedictions.

Katsof's next project was to develop a "country club," he said, using the suburban Israeli term for a neighborhood swimming pool, sports, and recreational complex, though the Israeli versions lacked the golf courses and any of the snobbish connotations of country clubs abroad. "We are in heaven here," he declared. A long list of people were waiting to move into Esh Kodesh, according to Katsof, echoing the new popularity of the *kibbutzim* with Israelis looking for space, clean air, and a community, though obviously appealing to a very different constituency of national religious Zionists. Katsof's goal was to dispel the image of Esh Kodesh as a stronghold of crazies and fanatics and present it as a middle-class, if alternative, paradise. He recounted how the outpost hosted a barbecue for the soldiers guarding the area during a recent holiday. As the home-smoked meats and fine wines came out, Katsof said, the father of one of the soldiers asked where the "real" settlers were, meaning the extremists. "Hey, you're in Esh Kodesh!" Katsof replied, meaning you don't get more authentic than that. He then pulled up photos on his smartphone of his fifteen-year-old daughter galloping on horseback past an emerald vineyard in the valley below, her long mane of blond hair flowing behind her. This, he said, was the "new settler." In fact, his children were not settlers, he said, but natives of Samaria, having been born there.

The Palestinian neighbors within sight from the verandas of Esh Kodesh hardly featured in the consciousness of Katsof and other residents, or at least that was the impression they liked to create, even though according to the Trump map the border of one chunk of the Palestinian mini-state would have run through the fields about three hundred meters from Katsof's patio. He would almost have been able to kick a soccer ball from his backyard across the valley into enemy territory.

Naturally, the view from the surrounding Palestinian villages looked very different. If the Palestinian residents were largely invisible to the settlers, the armed settlers of the outposts loomed large to the Palestinians as arrogant and aggressive usurpers of land that was not theirs to take. One Saturday afternoon in early 2021 an Israeli human rights organization, Yesh Din, posted video images provided by the Qusra village council of a menacing line of settlers appearing on a rise above the farmland on the edge of the village. They had come from the direction of Esh Kodesh, according to a Yesh Din field-worker. The Palestinian farmers said the settlers had stolen agricultural equipment and a stone-throwing clash ensued. A car was set on fire.

An intimate war was being fought in the area and sometimes it turned deadly. One of its Palestinian casualties, Mahmoud Zaal, a forty-eight-year-old farmer from Qusra, had waged his own quiet campaign to defend his land and stop settlers from claiming it. A family man living in a modest home in the village, he had planted six rugged acres with pistachio, fig, apricot, apple, and olive trees, as well as vines and berries for the birds, turning it, too, into a paradise, according to one of his cousins.

I visited the Zaal home while the family was in mourning, in late 2017. Mahmoud had been shot and killed on his beloved patch of the hillside by a settler armed with an M-16, said his son, Awad, who had been with his father at the time and witnessed the shooting. The suspected perpetrator was accompanying his own young son and his classmates on a bar mitzvah hike in the area. The party had set out from nearby Migdalim and were heading to the outpost of Kida. As always, the circumstances of Zaal's death were a matter of dispute. The settlers' version was that the children on the hike had come under attack from Palestinian youths pelting them with stones from above and that the shooter had fired into the air to save their lives. Awad said his father had gone out to farm alone that November morning, but had called him to come quickly because a settler with an M-16 was approaching. The settler ordered them off their land, Awad said, but they refused to leave. The settler then shot in the air, repeated the demand, then fired once more, hitting Mahmoud in the upper torso before fleeing downhill. The stone throwing broke out later, he said. The Israeli police carried out a cursory investigation and apparently accepted the settlers' claim that any shooting had been carried out in self-defense. Mahmoud's relatives took me out to the muddy land around the village, which since Mahmoud's killing had been the scene of repeated clashes between the local Palestinian youths and the Israeli security forces. We clambered down to a cave where the bar mitzvah group had sheltered from the stone-throwers. Settlers had repeatedly tried to return to the cave, to make a point or to stake a claim. The local Palestinian villagers had staked a counterclaim, planting the path below the cave with tiny olive saplings. The dirt between the spindly trees was strewn with bullet casings. Here, on the stony ground and away from the maps, ownership extended only as far as the last furrow.

The earliest settlements had sprung up under the Labor governments in the territories conquered by Israel in the Six-Day War. The first initiative came from the scions of Zionist pioneers who had been massacred in the battles of 1948 in Kfar Etzion, a religious kibbutz just south of Jerusalem in the West Bank. By the end of the fighting in 1967, Israel had conquered the Jordanian-held territory, including the area known as the Etzion bloc, and the sons of the original settlers had returned to the Jewish-owned land there. Yigal Allon, who was the minister of labor in 1967, then formulated a plan that envisaged Israel annexing the Jordan Valley, the Etzion bloc, a strip near the holy city of Hebron, and other strategic but sparsely populated areas of the West Bank while returning the densely populated Palestinian areas to Jordan. The Israeli government moved immediately to expand Jerusalem's city limits, ringing the capital from the east with massive new Jewish neighborhood-settlements.

The Allon plan did not lead to any negotiated arrangement and the subsequent shock of the 1973 war spurred into action the messianic zealots of Gush Emunim, the Bloc of the Faithful, a fervently ideological Jewish settlement group. They viewed the triumph of 1967 as a sign of redemption and the settlement of the newly won territories as a sacred mission. Adopting the dunam-by-dunam, goat-by-goat approach of the old Mapai state-builders, they forced the government's hand by placing facts on the ground. Determined to push into the heavily Arab-populated biblical heartland of the West Bank, they called the territory by its biblical names, Judea and Samaria. One early deception was carried out by the group of radical settlers who had moved into a hotel in the southern West Bank city of Hebron for Passover and refused to leave. The operation carried out by the group of fanatics holed up in the abandoned train station near Sebastia, in the hills around Nablus in the northern West Bank, involving Haim Gouri, the poet and journalist, also forced the government's hand in allowing the first modern Jewish settlement in the northern West Bank, or Samaria.

But it was after Likud's ascendance to power in 1977 that the settlement enterprise moved into high gear. The foreign-looking red-tiled roofs of settlement homes sprang up like mushrooms across the West Bank hills. Government incentives beckoned ordinary Israelis across the lines in search of "quality of life," offering an affordable, single-family home with a yard often within easy commuting distance of Israel proper. Nearly half a century later, the West Bank settlements were home to Israeli families spanning three and even four generations. Ariel, an urban settlement of 20,000 or so residents founded in the late 1970s by secular security hawks, sat in the center of the West Bank with the goal of preventing any Palestinian contiguity. It now boasted a bustling university attended by thousands of students, many of them Arab Israelis, and two new shopping malls. Many of its residents were secular immigrants from the former Soviet Union who were mostly not there out of ideology.

The Green Line, or 1967 boundary, had over the years been all but obliterated from public consciousness or Israeli discourse. A trans-Samarian highway sped from the coastal plain to Ariel and was fully integrated with Israel's central road system. Television anchors, military officers, and civil servants who used to refer to the West Bank as "the territories" in Hebrew now routinely referred to the area as the biblical Judea and Samaria. Ariel was just a dot on the weather maps along with Tel Aviv and Beersheba. Still, the idea of unilaterally annexing the territory was a step that no Israeli leader had taken in all the decades since the conquest, aware of the likely fury of the international community and the boost such a move would give to those detractors who already saw Israel, or at least the West Bank, as an apartheid regime and called for boycotts and sanctions.

One of the first settler leaders to see President Trump and his cohorts as false messiahs rather than saviors was Yochai Damri, a founding member of the settlement of Otniel in the desert borderlands of the southern West Bank. The twice-elected mayor of the Mount Hebron Regional Council, he stationed himself in the vanguard of a counterintuitive battle against the Trump plan by those who were supposed to be its main beneficiaries. By the spring of 2020 Damri, in his midfifties, had turned his spacious office on the third floor of the regional council building into an operations room where he projected onto the wall PowerPoint presentations filled with graphics showing why a hasty annexation move would put in mortal danger not only the settlement enterprise but the whole of Israel. He seemed to prefer the current ambiguity to any clearly defined separation of the West Bank into areas of Israeli and Palestinian sovereign territory. To prove his point, he displayed maps filled with arrows that showed that the range of potential Palestinian rocket fire from what were supposed to become the permanent Palestinian areas of the West Bank included most Israeli cities, often with warning times of mere seconds.

Damri, a native of Beersheba, had moved to the West Bank with his family in the early 1980s. He was then eighteen and his parents, who were having "a midlife crisis," were looking to join a new community. The settlement division of the World Zionist Organization suggested the southern Judean hills around the city of Hebron, and in November 1983 Damri found himself with his parents and younger siblings in a tiny mobile home on a lonely, beige hill with no running water or electricity. They joined seven other families who made up Otniel's founding nucleus, or *garin*. There wasn't much there at the time, just a fitful generator, one public pay phone, and communal showers. "It was a very special time," he recalled. "A pioneering period. The state had sent us."

He met his future wife, Yael, who was one of the only other teens on the mountain. Barely four decades later, four generations of Damris were living in Otniel, including two of Yochai Damri's married children and three grandchildren. Otniel had developed into a middle-class, religious community of single-family villas on avenues lined with mature trees. From the inside it looked and felt like suburbia, though it was jammed between the Palestinian villages of Yata and Dahariya. The settlement was home to a large religious Zionist yeshiva with a program for religious soldiers combining service with Torah study. Damri's sister was living in Kiryat Arba, abutting Hebron. "I have lived here for forty-three years—and so have the Arabs. In the end, we are not leaving this place and they are not leaving," said Damri.

Under the Trump plan, Otniel was slated to become one of the fifteen island-enclaves stranded in the midst of a putative Palestinian state. Damri failed to see how the settlement-enclaves would sustain them-selves, left to dry out like grapes on a vine. There was no infrastructure for high-rise construction in Otniel, he said, adding that the elevator up to his office was the only one in the settlements of the area. In his view, the Trump map was just a covert way of evacuating or deporting the settlers in isolated settlements without paying them compensation.

For the settlers, the main battle in recent years was for full control of Area C, the 60 percent of the West Bank under exclusive Israeli authority. They were livid that the Palestinians had adopted the settlers' tactic of establishing facts on the ground, and Damri sent me out with an aide for a tour of the area. Looking out from Mitzpe Yair, an illegal outpost on a wild and thorny ridge in the South Hebron hills named for another settler who was killed in the area, the aide pointed to a string of what he called Palestinian "outposts" that he said had sprung up over the past decade on the empty slopes down below. The Palestin-ians and the settlers were in a race to "fill in the gaps," he said. Otniel had always tried to project an image of tolerance, but even in these desert vistas that stretched for miles the earth was tinged with blood. Dafna Meir, a nurse and mother of six from Otniel, was stabbed to death in 2016 at her doorway by a Palestinian youth from a neighbor-ing village. Months later, a neighbor from the same leafy street, Rabbi Michael "Miki" Mark, a father of ten and the beloved director-general of Otniel's yeshiva, was gunned down while driving on the main high-way one Sabbath eve.

Despite the obvious hostility of the Palestinians toward their occu-piers, Damri had decided not to dwell on such lofty issues as the final status of the territories. Instead, he advocated what he saw as a more attainable, pragmatic model of "good-neighborliness" for all the residents of the area, Jewish and Arab. With Palestinian and Israeli built-up areas together covering only a small portion of the West Bank, he argued, there was "plenty of room for all for many years to come." The idea sounded disarmingly innocent, though it was clearly meant to cement the settlement project as a permanent, ever-expanding part of the landscape. To make settler life in the remote Hebron hills more comfortable, Damri had already built new sports facilities and tripled the bus lines. The first Jewish supermarket "since the days of Abraham" had opened up by the council building.

Whether these creature comforts had attracted residents or not, or whether natural growth was responsible, the local settler population had doubled in recent years to 10,500 souls. Damri was convinced that ordinary Palestinians, too, were far more concerned with earning a livelihood, and health and education services, than about national aspirations. At some level he may have been right. Fatigued by the never-ending conflict, with little confidence in their jaded leaders and resentful of the Palestinian Authority's culture of patronage and corruption, tens of thousands of Palestinians already worked as day laborers in Israel, in the settlement industrial zones, and even in construction building settlement homes. Damri had plans for two new industrial zones that would employ local Palestinians in high- and low-tech. He said he was looking into building a private, Israeli-managed hospital that could cater to wealthy Palestinians who currently traveled to Tel Aviv or abroad for quality medical treatment. He was not agonizing over Israel's conundrum of becoming a binational state or one accused of apartheid. The Palestinians already had a flag and a de facto "state" in the Palestinian cities that made up roughly 18 percent of the West Bank; they could vote for their own representatives in the Palestinian Authority. Damri preferred to give up on annexation rather than accept the vision of Palestinian statehood offered by the Trump plan. And he urged patience. The mystical number, or critical mass, of settlers that would ensure Jewish sovereignty in the West Bank, he said, was 600,000. He arrived at that number by citing the biblical censuses of the book of Numbers, in which 600,000 Israelite males able to bear arms symbolized the totality of a nation. It was no coincidence, he said,

that the Jewish population on the eve of Israeli independence numbered a little over 600,000. There were already about 500,000 Jews living in Judea and Samaria, he said, "so it will take us another three, four,
or five years. We are not far off." When the settlements of East Jerusalem were added, Damri's target number had already been surpassed.

If there was one thing that both the ideological settlers and their
critics could agree on, it was that the Trump map was, in effect, a
delusional recipe for a bloodbath. Yitzhar, in the northern West Bank,
one of the most radical of all of the established settlements, had also
been slated to become an enclave. An uncompromising community
of 270 families southwest of Nablus, it was home to the Od Yosef Hai
yeshiva, a notorious hotbed of racism and extremism. The outposts
it had spawned spread across the hills around the mother settlement.
Akiva HaCohen, Katsof's cousin, lived in one of them, Shalhevet-ya,
when he was not under a secret service administrative order banning
him from the area. Yitzhar's hilltop youths were notoriously wild. They
did not restrict their price tag attacks to their Palestinian neighbors but
were also known for puncturing the tires of Israeli army vehicles and
stoning members of the security forces who came to demolish illegal
structures. The slightly older leadership of the mother settlement had
been trying to clean up its image. Matanya Gavrieli, twenty-seven, a
member of Yitzhar's council and manager of the yeshiva, told me he
had been channeling the youths into more "wholesome" pursuits such
as renovating a nearby (and disputed) spring that had been vandalized
by local Palestinians. His intense, bearded look gave no hint that he
was also a co-founder of a group that made satirical, right-wing political videos for social media and had even starred in some of them.

Gavrieli was personally torn over the Trump plan, which contained
both a blessing and a curse. On the positive side, a U.S. president was
recognizing Jewish rights to what Gavrieli called "the land of our ancestors" and sovereignty there. But there were the dangers of being in such
hostile surroundings. His wife carried a pistol. He said he still needed
to get a gun license. As individuals, Gavrieli and the other settlers of
Yitzhar could be disarmingly pleasant. They just lived, or pretended
to live, in a parallel universe. Ora Tubi, another resident in her forties,
embodied that combination of scripture-based faith, grit, and a hint
of New Age sensibility to be found in the most isolated of settlements.

Stylishly accessorized with a matching dark dress and hair covering, large, hooped earrings, and a nose stud, Tubi organized spiritual workshops for women and sold health products. Her husband, Ezri, made spiritual rap music clips. The living room of their modest, orderly home was lined with shelves of the requisite holy books. The bathroom featured a pretty plastic toilet seat inlaid with seashells, and there was a trampoline in the yard for the children. She was not oblivious to her surroundings. Her family from central Israel did not visit much, she said, afraid of the drive through the West Bank and the Palestinian town of Hawara. She viewed the Palestinians in the area as "guests." Good guests, she said, meaning those who peacefully accepted the sovereignty of their Jewish landlords, should be treated well.

But the Palestinians were not always "good guests" in these parts, where neighbors were enemies. One of the most brutal acts of terrorism in the area had occurred one Friday night in 2011, when two teenagers from Awarta, a sprawling Palestinian village in the hills off the main road running through Hawara, crossed a valley at night and cut through the perimeter fence of the settlement of Itamar. They entered the home of the Fogel family—the door was unlocked—and stabbed and shot five members of the family to death: Ehud Fogel, who was known as Udi; his wife, Ruth; and three of their children, Yoav, eleven, Elad, four, and Hadas, a baby girl of three months, all murdered in their beds. On the somber Saturday night, after the end of Sabbath, the settlement opened its gate to reporters. I watched as emergency workers carried out the dead one by one in black body bags. In all, at least twenty residents of Itamar have been killed in attacks since the settlement was established in 1984. The unlocked doors were a token of how cocooned the settlers felt within their own communities of like-minded people, where children's tricycles, infants' car seats, and other paraphernalia of family life were routinely left out on porches and front lawns in a show of trust. The residents told me that with each bloody attack their community, though heartbroken, was strengthened. Even amid the shock of the latest bloodshed, Moshe Goldsmith, a rabbi who was then the mayor of Itamar, spoke of the Jews' "legitimate right to the Land of Israel," adding, "the Bible is our deed."

Nearly a decade later, I went back to visit the Goldsmiths, who welcomed me into the cozy kitchen of their home with homemade iced tea and chocolate chip and peanut butter cookies. American born and bred, Moshe and Leah had come as newlyweds from Brooklyn in the mid-1980s and soon joined the founding *garin,* or settlement nucleus, of Itamar, moving into a small, prefabricated home that Leah described as being "perched on a bald hill overlooking no-man's land." They built a spacious, permanent family home with a living room window that looked out onto Mount Gerizim and Mount Ebal, the two mountains framing the Palestinian city of Nablus, where, according to the book of Joshua, the Israelites were to proclaim God's blessings for those who obeyed the commandments and curses for those who disobeyed his law. The Goldsmiths were running the Friends of Itamar organization, lecturing to and raising money from Christians in the United States, among others. Leah, who spoke with the fervor of a preacher even while sitting at the kitchen table, described the Jews in these parts as a "stiff-necked people," borrowing a biblical phrase for stubbornness. They were here to stay.

The Goldsmiths were still considered *mamlachti,* or the type of set-tlers who respected Israeli law and ultimately would put belonging to the state before their ideology. But on the extreme margins of the settle-ment movement there was a new generation of hilltop youths who had gone beyond the price tag doctrine and advocating Jewish sovereignty over the West Bank. Instead, a loose fringe group had emerged to agi-tate against and overthrow Israel's democratic system. The *mamlachti* settler leaders had long dismissed the extremists as social dropouts and delinquents with no real hierarchy, organizational skills, or follow-ing, but they had proved to be dangerous and bent on avenging Jewish blood. In one unusually horrific episode in July 2015, a young extremist carried out an arson attack in the dead of night on a Palestinian home in the heart of the village of Duma, a few miles east of Shilo and Esh Kodesh. An infant, Ali Dawabsheh, was burned to death at the scene. His parents, Saad and Riham, died of their wounds an agonizing few weeks later. Ali's older brother, Ahmed, was critically wounded but survived the inferno.

Weeks later, Israel's Shin Bet internal security agency exposed a shadowy, anarchistic network operating in the hilltops whose mani-festo, "The Revolt," urged fomenting chaos to bring about the collapse of the state and its replacement with a Jewish kingdom based on the laws of the Torah. Non-Jews were to be expelled, the Third Temple was to be built in Jerusalem where the Aqsa Mosque now stood, and religious observance was to be enforced, initially in public spaces. The Shin Bet identified the ringleader as Meir Ettinger, an activist in his early twenties and a grandson of Meir Kahane, the slain American-Israeli rabbi considered the father of far-right Jewish militancy. The perpetrator, or perpetrators, of the Duma arson attack appeared to have followed the exact instructions for such an activity laid out in "The Revolt"'s handbook. Nearly five years later Amiram Ben Uliel, a young settler, was convicted of the Duma murders, which the Israeli authorities condemned as an act of Jewish terrorism. He had been living with his wife and baby in a truck in Adei Ad, another of the Shilo Valley outposts, at the time of the attack. He told investigators it was meant to avenge the fatal shooting of another young settler, Malachi Rosenfeld, in the Shilo area that summer. But Ben Uliel's defenders, including Aaron Katsof in Esh Kodesh, insisted he'd been framed. His confession, they said, was extracted under torture after the Shin Bet was authorized to employ "special" counterterrorism methods in his interrogation. According to this alternative version, the Dawabshehs were the victims of an internal village feud, though even Ben Uliel's defense lawyers had not made such a claim.

Settler violence was nothing new. Members of the Jewish underground in the 1980s had bombed and maimed Palestinian mayors, gunned down students at an Islamic college in Hebron, and plotted to blow up Jerusalem's Dome of the Rock. The perpetrators, educated army veterans, had served short prison terms, then were pardoned and became members of the settlement movement's aristocracy. The likes of Meir Ettinger and Amiram Ben Uliel were more worrying, even to some of the veterans of the 1980s underground. They were widely viewed as ignorant and lawless young men whom the army did not want in its ranks. They may only have numbered in the dozens or hundreds, as far as the Shin Bet could tell. But the established settler leadership and the security forces had done too little to rein them in. And even if the majority of settlers eschewed such terrible acts of violence as the Duma murders, the extremists often found shelter and succor in the outposts where their ideology fell on more sympathetic ears.

Like Otniel and Yitzhar, Itamar was slated under the Trump plan to remain in place as an isolated enclave. For the Goldsmiths, it was a nightmare. "Any plan with a mention of a Palestinian state is a tragedy," Moshe Goldsmith said. "We want peace, but we are not willing to commit suicide, and we will never agree to something like that, giving up our homeland." Ultimately, for the settlers, the internal schism over the plan's promise of annexation and its curse of Palestinian statehood proved superfluous. For Trump's vision had come to naught even before Trump lost the 2020 presidential election and ended his term in a blaze of violence and accusations of insurrection.

After unveiling the plan, Trump's Middle East peace team, led by his son-in-law, Jared Kushner, had indicated that the administration would immediately green-light Israeli annexation of up to 30 percent of the West Bank, including every point of settlement, so long as there was an Israeli consensus in favor of the plan. But the ideological settlers, it turned out, had not managed to gain the sympathy of all of mainstream Israel and the outlying settlements still remained outside public consensus. The Netanyahu government itself was split, with the centrists of the Blue and White party, who shared power with the Likud party at the time, opposed to the unilateral annexation of West Bank territory. Then, with annexation stuck anyway, the United Arab Emirates, an under-the-table ally of Israel in the anti-Iranian axis, stepped in with a groundbreaking proposition offering Israel the full normalization of ties and diplomatic relations with the Emirates in return for shelving its annexation plans, as well as Netanyahu's quiet agreement with the American administration's plan to sell the Emirates a package of advanced weapons, including F-35 stealth fighter jets and Reaper drones. Netanyahu, who had always been wary of rocking the boat, and especially with such a momentous move that would have caused an international backlash, grabbed the opportunity to present himself as a peacemaker who managed to reach agreements with Arab leaders while bypassing the Palestinians. So the ill-conceived Netanyahu-Trump plan for annexation, which had been sketched out without any proper Israeli staff work, strategic planning, or consultations with the military, was rapidly dumped by both parties in favor of the Abraham Accords, the normalization agreements that allowed Israel to establish formal and full diplomatic relations with the United Arab Emirates and Bahrain, then Morocco, as well as a preliminary deal with Sudan.

Mainstream Israelis were happy, much preferring to shop and vacation in the emirate of Dubai than in a West Bank outpost like Esh Kodesh. The settler leaders from the Samarian Regional Council jumped on the bandwagon themselves and began marketing settlement products in Dubai. But just the talk of annexation, along with discriminatory land allocations, separate justice systems for Jewish settlers and Palestinians in the West Bank, and many other grievances, was enough to spur leading human rights organizations to brand Israel internationally as a state practicing apartheid in the West Bank and, though to a lesser degree, within Israel itself.

In a last-ditch effort to salvage something before President Biden took office in January 2021, the same settler leaders who had gone to Washington to celebrate the unveiling of the now-defunct Trump plan joined a hunger strike outside the prime minister's office in Jerusalem. They were trying to pressure Netanyahu's government into regularizing the status of a few dozen, or even just two or three, illegal outposts and allow them a normal electricity supply and permits for permanent housing. Even those efforts came to naught. Katsof, the spokesman of Esh Kodesh, had joined the delegation of settlers to Washington, but once annexation got bogged down in the details he had smugly shrugged it off as something the settlers could just as easily live without. Equally dismissive of the doomsday scenarios of the end of the Zionist dream and the Jewish and democratic state, and undeterred by labels of apartheid, he declared that while the politicians "danced around" and people philosophized, "We are here, building, planting trees and having children." The outpost settlers had adopted the Arabic concept of *sumud,* or steadfastness and sticking to the land, the West Bank Palestinians' fundamental tool of resistance.

The settlers and the supporters of the illegal outposts, or "young settlement," continued to lobby the government and establish their presence, as they put it, by "creating more facts on the ground." When the last, chaotic months of Netanyahu's fifth term finally gave way to the diverse coalition led by Naftali Bennett in the spring of 2021, the former government left a poisoned gift in the form of a new outpost, Evyatar, which had sprung up in record time near the Ariel Junction in the central West Bank while the army and the rest of Israel were distracted by an abrupt but deadly eleven-day-long air war with Gaza. Within weeks, fifty families had moved in. They asphalted roads, assigned them street names, and clad hastily erected sheds with stone. The idea was to lay a political minefield for the new coalition whose incoherent array of partners ranged from Bennett's boutique, pro-settlement Yamina party to the leftist, anti-settlement Meretz, taking in the small Arab, Islamic party Raam along the way. The military declared the outpost blatantly illegal and argued for its immediate removal. The far-rightist provocateurs who sat in the opposition were angling for a violent showdown. In a bind, the fragile new government could not risk a forced evacuation, nor could it be seen to capitulate to the radical settlers and allow them to determine priorities for the IDF's deployment in the West Bank. Several Palestinians from the nearby village of Beta were killed by Israeli army fire while protesting the takeover of land the rural village claimed as its own. Like in Sebastia five decades earlier, the immediate crisis was averted when the government reached a compromise with the settlers, who agreed to leave quietly while the buildings and the army that had been forced to come to protect them remained on the site. The government promised to allow the establishment of a permanent yeshiva in Evyatar and to fast-track a probe of the legal status of the land. The settlers would be allowed to return and build permanent homes on any parts that were found to be state land. The government had handed the settlers a victory of sorts, albeit one that was deferred.

With Israel's occupation of the West Bank more than half a century old and still no clear vision emerging from the government, the feasibility and fate of the two-state solution, and the future character of Israel, largely depended upon the initiative of the settlers and their enablers. Fewer and fewer Palestinians or Israelis were able to envisage any realistic solution based on partition. In a sign of diplomatic exhaustion, the international community sufficed with issuing routine condemnations of Israeli settlement building and demolitions along with platitudes about maintaining the option of a two-state solution. Israel's vaunted Supreme Court had taken a convoluted position regarding the country's settlement policies, having long refrained from ruling on the legality of Israel's government-sanctioned settlements, caught between preserving its international reputation and avoiding a headlong confrontation with the government.

The court did initially sanction Israel's limited seizure of West Bank lands on security grounds, but it declared the legality of settlements in general to be non-justiciable and a political matter for the government. When it ruled that privately owned Palestinian property was sacrosanct and could not be used for the settlements, Israel set about seeking out and declaring huge swaths of West Bank land as public, or "state," lands. But over five decades, 99.76 percent of the territory it had defined as public land had been used to benefit the settlements. Only 0.24 percent was earmarked for Palestinian use according to Peace Now's Settlement Watch monitoring group.

Nor was there anything random about the seemingly spontaneous outpost project, as the new dots on the map began to spread across strategic areas. Shimon Riklin, a self-declared "outpost entrepreneur," set up his first pirate settlement, Mitzpe Danny, in 1998 on a hill overlooking the Jordan Valley, just across the road from the established settlement of Maaleh Michmash, where he lived, east of the Palestinian administrative capital of Ramallah. By the time I met Riklin, a gregarious and natural raconteur, at a café in a Jerusalem shopping mall, he had reinvented himself as a high-profile, right-wing media personality. He appeared eager to take credit for his past exploits. He said he had helped Netanyahu win the 1996 election, then watched him being squeezed by the United States to make territorial concessions to the Palestinians. Riklin, the son of a Lehi fighter, felt it was time to "go out of the fences," he said, and expand the settlers' footprint in order to ensure their future in the area. One starry night, after the Sabbath, he recounted, he brought three trailers up to the hill opposite his settlement, accompanied by dozens of enthusiastic youths. Looking out over the hills that night, he said, he felt like Mufasa in Disney's *Lion King* surveying his realm. The next morning, he said, the army arrived but were clueless as to what to do, so they left. Riklin's wife and toddler joined him on the hilltop, then another family moved in. Within a couple of weeks, the local regional settler council brought in generators and water tanks. The housing minister soon promised a road and electricity, according to Riklin. Encouraged, he went on to set up three more outposts, what he called the "next generation" of settlement, or settlement 2.0. "I jumped from hill to hill," he said, until the authorities eventually stopped him.

It may have sounded like a freelance initiative, but the depth of official Israeli collusion and the illegal diversion of government funds was later exposed in a report on the outposts that was commissioned by the Sharon government in the hope of alleviating American pressure. The conclusions, published in 2005, were shocking. The author, Talya Sasson, a former prosecutor in the state attorney's office, described the regional settler councils as the likely "engine" behind the decision to establish the outposts, aided by a network of officials in the World Zionist Organization's settlement division, who overstepped their executive authority, and the Ministry of Housing and Construction. Housing ministers had either provided support or turned a blind eye. The settlers were even calling the shots when it came to army deployment, since the IDF was bound to protect them wherever they were living. All this, Sasson wrote, came along with "massive" state financing. In addition to the 125 settlements established with government approval, Sasson counted more than a hundred new outposts, including many wholly or partially established on private Palestinian land or on land whose ownership was in doubt.

Floods of petitions to the Supreme Court forced the state to declare where it stood on the outpost issue. In its first responses to the court, the state agreed that outposts should be evacuated but also kept delaying such action, arguing on security grounds that it was never a convenient time. By 2011, during Netanyahu's second term in office, a new "combined policy" was quietly introduced. Israel would remove unauthorized structures built on privately owned Palestinian land but would also begin retroactively legalizing construction on public land. In some ways, the anti-settlement activists' campaign against government ambiguity had boomeranged. One local settler council sent a bouquet of flowers to Peace Now, the anti-settlement group, after its petition to remove some new construction ended up with the government sanctioning other construction. The council attached a note: "We will happily consider naming a street 'Peace Now' in the new neighborhoods." By Netanyahu's fourth term, twenty years after the first outposts were established, more than a third of them had been retroactively "legalized" by the government or were in the process.

Mitzpe Danny, Riklin's first outpost, was named for Danny Frei, a British immigrant and Riklin's neighbor in Maale Michmash who was stabbed to death by a Palestinian in his settlement home. Mitzpe Danny and its neighboring outposts grabbed the high ground along the strategic Allon Road, a winding route named for Yigal Allon, the Israeli general and politician, which ran from the Ramallah district down to the Jordan Valley and offered breathtaking views all the way from Jerusalem's Mount of Olives to Jordan. At a scenic lookout point in Mitzpe Danny, an audio system described Jewish settlement of the area as the fulfillment of Jeremiah's prophecy: "Thy children shall return to their own border." Twenty years after its establishment, Mitzpe Danny was home to about forty Orthodox Jewish families. The army's planning branch had advanced plans for 180 permanent housing units there as part of an overall legalization effort. The outpost was retroactively authorized as a "neighborhood" of Maale Michmash in the spring of 2022.

In order to counter the damaging Sasson report, Netanyahu commissioned another report from a conservative committee that he appointed in 2012, led by Edmund Levy, a retired Supreme Court judge. Unsurprisingly, it came to starkly different conclusions, including that the West Bank was not occupied, since there had been no internationally recognized sovereign there before 1967. There was no impediment, therefore, to approving the outposts built on state, or public, land with the "implied" agreement of senior Israeli officials. Settler activists had radicalized the Likud from within, turning the ruling party of much of the past decades into a settler lobby. Netanyahu, in his bid to harness the electoral potential of every last right-wing voter, eventually legitimized far-right political partners like Itamar Ben-Gvir, an ultra-nationalist agitator and Kahane disciple who had hung a portrait of Baruch Goldstein, the perpetrator of the 1994 Hebron massacre, in his salon.

The seasoned settler leaders understood that Netanyahu's embrace was probably less about ideology and more for political expediency as he clung to power. But they knew how to exploit his electoral needs and increasingly pulled him into political territory he had long avoided. So after years of blocking legislation known as the "Regularization Law," which would allow Israel to forcibly transfer Palestinian private property to settlers in return for compensation, Netanyahu finally capitulated to pressure from the settler lobby and the law was enacted in 2017. The government had to decide if it stood with the cops or the thieves, said Michael Sfard, an Israeli human rights lawyer who had represented scores of Palestinian landowners in Israel's Supreme Court on behalf of Yesh Din. "In the end," Sfard said, "the Netanyahu government crossed the Rubicon and joined the thieves."

Esh Kodesh, one of the string of outposts commanding the hilltops east of Shilo, like beads on a chain, provided a contiguous east–west axis of Jewish settlement from Ariel, in the center of the West Bank, to the northern section of the Jordan Valley. In a declaration to the court in 2015, the state had said it intended to legalize Esh Kodesh. Five years later, that still had not happened. Katsof, the outpost's spokesman, said it was easier for the government just not to decide. In a bone thrown to the settlers shortly before the March 2020 election, the prime minister's office issued a directive allowing several outposts that were "on their way to being regularized," including Esh Kodesh, to hook up to the national electricity grid, ensuring a reliable energy supply and an end to the frequent blackouts. The letter, dated February 23, 2020, was posted on Esh Kodesh's Facebook page. Three months later, however, Israel's Supreme Court struck down the 2017 Regularization Law, on the grounds that its purpose was to legalize "unlawful acts perpetrated by one specific population," meaning the Jewish settlers, "while harming the rights of another," the Palestinians. Airbnb, meanwhile, came under mounting pressure from Palestinian officials, anti-settlement advocates, and human rights groups for advertising holiday chalets in the occupied territories and the illegal outposts, until it announced in 2018 that it would remove its West Bank settlement listings. Legal challenges in the United States accused the online rental company of discrimination and forced it to reverse its decision. Airbnb pledged to donate to charity any profits it made from West Bank rentals. Years of efforts by the international, pro-Palestinian boycott, divestment, and sanctions movement were hardly felt on the ground, as the settlers remained focused on building.

At the peak of a wild and windy mountain in the heart of the West Bank once stood Amona, a flagship settlement and jewel of the outpost enterprise and a symbol of settler resistance. Then, after an exhaustive legal battle and a brief holdout against a phalanx of Israeli security officers, it was gone. Its eventual removal, in 2017, was both a lesson in the ephemeral impermanence of the outposts, many of which were little more than trailer parks, and, ultimately, a lesson in the settlers' endurance and entrenchment.

The first time I visited Amona I was directed to the home of Avichay Buaron, a lawyer who lived with his family in a well-established, much-expanded mobile home not far from the entrance to the outpost. He was leading Amona's public and legal campaign against the settlement's looming demolition after the Supreme Court had eventually ruled that the entire outpost was illegally constructed on privately owned Palestinian land. Buaron had moved to the hilltop in 1996 as a law student "for the fun of it," sharing a trailer with a few male friends. Some female students arrived on the hilltop and the outpost turned into a kind of commune. "Then the weddings started," Buaron said. Hovering above the established mother settlement of Ofra, which was home to veteran members of the settler aristocracy, as well as the dismantled Jewish underground, Amona was a youthful, romantic wilderness with panoramic views perched about three thousand feet above sea level, beckoning the next generation of settlers who were searching for a meaningful existence. Buaron met his wife, Ofra, there. A daughter of the mother settlement down below, she had been named in its honor. They had seven children, who all grew up in the outpost.

I had turned up without an appointment, but Buaron was home and was happy to bring out his thick files to try to illustrate how Amona had been set up in all innocence and with the tacit blessing of the authorities. The outpost's founders, he said, had been told by officials that the hill was abandoned Palestinian property. And if there had been any uncertainty about its future, the doubts dissipated in 2001 when the Housing Ministry okayed a neighborhood of permanent houses to be constructed with foundations. Five years later, however, the courts ruled that the first nine houses under construction were on private Palestinian land and ordered them to be torn down. That blow came at a volatile time. The settlers were already traumatized and enraged by Israel's 2005 unilateral withdrawal from Gaza, which had been engineered by none other than Prime Minister Ariel Sharon, the former champion of the West Bank hilltops. Its scenes of settler families being dragged out of their homes was wrenching for many Israelis. Their communities, green and oddly insulated from the misery of much of the rest of the densely packed Palestinian coastal enclave, were reduced to rubble. Many of the young settlers, in particular, felt betrayed—not only by the Israeli government and the state, but also by the more establishment leadership of the YESHA council, the settlers' umbrella organization, which had agreed to a quiet evacuation from the Gaza settlements, as well as from four settlements in the northern West Bank, in return for ample government compensation. The settler youth, disgusted by what they saw as a shameful capitulation to a cruel government edict, were determined to deter the government from thoughts of any similar debacle or withdrawal in the West Bank. Amona became the new frontline cause in their ongoing struggle for self-preservation, so when the bulldozers moved in for the first time, in 2006, to demolish the nine houses of the fledgling new neighborhood, the stage was set for an emotional and explosive showdown. A pitched battle ensued between the outpost residents and their supporters who had gathered on the mountain and were hurling stones and cinderblocks, and the mounted and baton-wielding Israeli police officers who arrived in full riot gear. Scores were left injured on both sides, including two right-wing legislators, one of whom later called the clash a "pogrom." There was more to come. A Supreme Court ruling subsequently determined that the entire outpost was sitting on private property and had to be evacuated. Some of the claimants were living in plain sight of Avichay Buaron's living room, in the Palestinian villages in the surrounding hills.

One of the claimants was Maryam Hassan Abd al-Karim Hamad, a wrinkled and wizened widow in her eighties who inhabited a simple, domed room in her family compound in the Palestinian village of Silwad. As we spoke and feasted on plump, sweet grapes from the vine outside, grandchildren ran in and out. Chickens scratched around in the yard. Hamad said her husband had bequeathed to their six children his property on the hill where Amona stood. Michael Sfard, the lawyer for Yesh Din, was representing the family in an Israeli court. "The lawyer once told us they wanted to give us alternative land," Hamad said of the Israelis. "We refused." Reminiscing about how her family would plant grains one year and vegetables—tomatoes, cucumbers, zucchini, okra—the next, she added, "We put the blood of our hearts into our land." Another resident of Silwad, Atallah Abd al-Hafez Hamed, sixty-three, said that he and his three siblings had inherited an eight-acre plot on the edge of Amona from their father. It was once planted with grapevines. The family stopped working the land in the 1980s, he said, because the only access to it was through Ofra and, in any case, the grapes went bad from disease. If the land was returned to the family, he said, he would plant it with apple and almond trees. After laying out the family's case in a narrow reception room of his home, Hamed drove with his sister, Huda Qurr'an, to the edge of the village, crossed over Route 60, the main north–south highway, and parked the car to pose for photographs as close to the mountain as they dared to go. Picking their way among the rocks and boulders, they pointed up to the top of the mountain, using the trees near the peak as markers to identify their land.

The Amona settlers, who were then officially considered trespassers, fought the legal battle for as long as they could. Amona had become a test case, Buaron said, after years in which the government policy had been to turn a blind eye. His binders were filled with documents, maps, and photographs tracking the development of the outpost as proof of the infrastructure that the authorities had provided. "The legal norms were less developed then," he explained. "The legal norms have changed." Buaron's *caravilla,* or prefabricated mobile home, had expanded with his family and looked more or less like a permanent structure. He said he had tried to purchase the plot on which it stood, paying more than $100,000 through middlemen to a man in Jordan who was the supposed owner, in an example of the kind of shady land dealing the settlers were engaged in. Israeli military officials later informed Buaron that the "seller" was a fake and that the property was not his to sell.

In a desperate effort to stay put, Buaron drafted a first version of the regularization law intended to compel Palestinian landowners whose property had been taken over to accept alternative land or compensation instead. But the attorney general ruled that such a law could not apply retroactively to Amona, whose fate had already been decided by the Supreme Court. Next, Israeli officials tried to seek out unclaimed plots of land adjacent to the outpost that may have been owned by absentee Palestinians, with the intention of offering them to the settlers as alternative locations for their trailers, "Like on a chessboard," Buaron said. But real, living Palestinians came forward to claim them all.

When the legal and political processes were exhausted, evacuation day finally arrived in early 2017. The outpost residents put up passive resistance, insisting on being carried out of their homes. Hundreds of youths from yeshivas and other settlements had converged on the outpost ahead of time to try to resist the operation; they holed up in the synagogue and in residents' homes. A communal trailer served as separate quarters for the girls who prepared vats of soup. It was winter. The mountaintop was lashed by wind and rain and the outpost had turned into a muddy youth camp seething with anger. Tamar Nizri, one of the matriarchs of Amona, urged the security forces to refuse orders. Her husband, Yohayada Nizri, had risen to national fame as a finalist on the Israeli *MasterChef* program with his mouthwatering Sabbath dishes and would go on to open a wine bar in Shilo. One of their daughters, Rivka, had married at eighteen, weeks before the evacuation, and she and her husband had been renovating a trailer in Amona.

A whole generation had grown up in the outpost, but soon it was all over. Some youths barricaded themselves inside trailers and threw objects or liquids out of the windows at the police officers. Many parents had sent their youngest children away to grandparents to spare them the trauma. By the end of the day, the outpost had been evacuated. Dozens of activists were driven away on buses by the security forces. Most of the residents moved into dorms in a hostel in Ofra awaiting their next move. Amona was razed within two days but the settlers did not give up on their mission. Instead, they leveraged their wrath and the right-wing government's guilt over the evacuation into securing approval for the construction of the first new, openly authorized Israeli settlement in thirty years, to be named Amichai, Hebrew for "my nation lives."

Two years after the evacuation, thirty-six of Amona's forty families had been rehoused in neat rows of government-issued *caravillas* in Amichai, a few miles north of Ofra and Amona in the Shilo Valley. Amichai's asphalted main road and paved sidewalks had none of the wild, unkempt soul of Amona. The next time I met Buaron, at a juice stall in Jerusalem, near his office, he said he had settled into his new home in Amichai but described it as "a second love" and wistfully remembered Amona as "a place close to heaven." His children would still go up to Amona, he said, to sit around a bonfire, sometimes with sleeping bags. Occasionally the army would come to evacuate a few trailers and tents as some youths tried to return. Buaron hadn't given up the idea either. He said that some "warm-hearted" Jewish donors from abroad had put up more than $1 million to purchase ten acres of the mountain from owners who were in Jordan. The plan, he said, was "to have it in Jewish hands," adding, "Maybe our children can start it anew."

One hot afternoon in 2020, after visiting Amichai, I decided on a whim to drive back up the mountain. Three years had passed since the evacuation of Amona, but it lived on in Waze, the navigation app, which guided me through Ofra to the foot of the hill. At the top of the steep, narrow road only a stone boulder bearing the name Amona provided any hint of the community that had resided here for more than two decades. Nature had reclaimed the site in all its spring glory. Tall grass and weeds obscured the old trailer and mobile home lots, bathing the mountaintop in a rippling sea of green. It had become a magical sanctuary of wild roses and butterflies, its profound, ghostly silence broken by birdsong.

It turned out that I was not alone. As I was leaving, I came across a young settler couple, Chana and Aharon, sitting on an abandoned old couch in a small clearing. A few torn mattresses, scruffy chairs, and other bits of junk were strewn around. I joined them for a while. They were on a date, discussing marriage plans. Aharon, an off-duty soldier in a T-shirt and jeans, had come with a large assault rifle, which was propped up by his side. Though the couple were not originally from Amona, they had been there for the evacuation. Chana, who worked as a youth counselor in Amichai, said she longed to come to live on this mountaintop one day, adding dreamily that "it was paradise."

Both sides, it seemed, had their patches of paradise in this land of perpetual conflict. One of the last traces of Amona was a fenced-off rectangular plot planted with a few rows of vines that belonged to a former Jewish resident of the razed outpost. Despite having won their case, the Palestinian farmers had not been able to return. The army had declared the area a closed military zone, both to prevent attempts by settlers to rebuild the outpost and to avoid inevitable friction between settlers and Palestinians. But the mountain stood firm, like a silent sentinel in the heart of the occupied West Bank.

# SIX

# SABRAS AND OLIVE TREES

THE STREET in Lod resembled a scene from midway through an apocalyptic movie. More than a dozen burned-out shells of Jewish-owned cars were lined up in a row where they had been parked along the sidewalk. The hulk of an incinerated Arab-owned truck stood stranded on a patch of wasteland. Arsonists from one side or the other had vandalized Igael Tumarkin's 1970s stone-and-steel Peace Monument, a rare piece of public art around these parts. Most of the Arab and Jewish residents of the neighborhood had either fled town or were keeping off the empty streets. The urban detritus spoke of a two-headed, if lopsided, pogrom. A few dazed Jewish locals gathered in the yard of a charred school building, seeking safety in numbers. A clutch of Border Police officers who had been called in from the West Bank stood guard in full riot gear on the street corner. The air was heavy with suspense, shock, and fear, and tinged with a lingering odor of soot. This sudden paroxysm of violence had not broken out over the Green Line, in the hostile terrain of East Jerusalem or the West Bank, but in Ramat Eshkol, a hardscrabble neighborhood of dilapidated apartment blocks in the center of Lod, a mixed Jewish-Arab city ten miles southeast of Tel Aviv and ten minutes from Ben-Gurion International Airport. Few places were closer to the heart of sovereign Israel.

It was May 2021, toward the end of the holy Muslim fasting month of Ramadan, and the flash of rage and destruction had seemingly burst out of nowhere. Tensions had been mounting all month between the Israeli police and Palestinians in Jerusalem, culminating in an early morning police raid of the Aqsa Mosque compound, where protesters had holed up. The Muslim holy month had coincided with several sensitive dates in the Jewish calendar, including the annual Memorial and Independence Days, and Jerusalem Day, marking Israel's conquest of the eastern part of the city along with its Muslim, Christian, and Jewish holy sites in the 1967 Six-Day War. Ultra-nationalist Jews were planning a provocative victory march with flags through the Muslim Quarter of the Old City. At dusk, Hamas, presenting itself as the defender of Jerusalem and following an ultimatum, fired a salvo of rockets toward the holy city in a defiant challenge to Israel that would set off a deadly eleven-day air war with Gaza. The troubles in Lod started after evening prayers in a mosque in the old town center. Angry Arab youths had spilled out into the square and raised a Palestinian flag atop a pylon in solidarity with Palestinians in Jerusalem and Gaza. The police reacted forcefully, dispersing them with tear gas and stun grenades, but it was as if a fuse had been lit, unleashing years of pent-up frustrations among Israel's own Palestinian Arab minority over discriminatory land and housing policies and what many described as built-in prejudice and racism.

Long humiliated, resentful, and enraged Arab residents, full citizens of the state, turned on their Jewish neighbors, sparking a three-day blaze of intercommunal violence, the worst that Israel had seen in decades. Jewish nationalists soon went into revenge mode. Mobs made up of racist La Familia ultras associated with Jerusalem's Beitar soccer club, radical armed settlers, and other thugs quickly formed via WhatsApp groups and other social networks and moved into Lod. Tearing like a twister through the country's mixed cities and beyond, the storm sucked in communities and businesses long held up as models of coexistence, exposing the country's deepest ethnic and national fault lines. It left at least four dead in its wake—two Arabs and two Jews—as well as a trail of mutual suspicion. The first to be killed was Mousa Hassouneh, an Arab from Lod, fatally shot by Jewish residents who told investigators they were acting in self-defense when protesters surged toward them; the suspects were soon out on bail. Yigal Yehoshua, a Jewish resident of a small community near Lod, succumbed to his wounds after a brick was thrown at his head as he drove home through the city. An elderly Jewish rocket scientist died in an Arab arson attack that destroyed a Jewish-owned, lovingly restored boutique hotel in Acre in the north. An Arab driver was pulled from his car and nearly beaten to death by Jewish vigilantes on the streets of Bat Yam, down the coast from Tel Aviv. Others marched through Haifa chanting "Death to Arabs." An Arab teen was fatally shot in a car in Umm al-Fahem, in central Israel, by errant police fire, according to his family. A Palestinian boy of twelve was almost burned to death when Arab assailants in Jaffa threw a Molotov cocktail through the window of his family apartment, mistaking it for a Jewish home. The violence spread to the Arab towns of the Galilee in the north. Bedouin torched and ambushed Jewish cars with stones in the southern Negev desert. A Jewish man was stabbed on his way to morning prayers—on the sidewalk where I stood a couple of hours later in Lod.

As I drove out of Lod after the second day of violence, Border Police officers were blocking off the entrances to the city shortly before a nighttime curfew was to come into force and surrounded the square with armored vehicles. A smattering of left-wing peace activists stood at the main junction on the highway holding messages of conciliation on hastily scrawled placards. Inside the city, Palestinian youths and men wrapped in keffiyehs had set up their own roadblocks of burning tires, simulating a domestic pop-up intifada. I slowed down and waved through an open window with a hopeful smile; a helpful protester kicked aside a couple of tires to let me pass.

Through a veil of smoke and an anarchic rampage of stone-throwing, shooting, torching, and near lynching, the Israelis on both sides were getting a glimpse of their national nightmare. Reuven Rivlin's seven-year term as president had started with a call for a tribal truce and a new Israeli order. Now, as his term was coming to an end, alarmed by the violence, he invoked the specter of civil war. Not in the sense of the anguished, poetic, personal struggles of Haim Gouri, or even the Israeli-Palestinian struggle over the future of the occupied territories, but a domestic hell of guns and knives and fists and fire, an inferno of bloodletting between the country's Jews and Arabs, and in the mixed cities like Lod, literally between next-door neighbors who shared stairwells and yards.

Like the Jews, Israel's Palestinian Arab citizens were the progeny of trauma—in their case, the trauma of 1948. They were the remnants and descendants of the *Nakba* generation. Exodus Street, the epicenter of the violence in Lod, conjured up images for Jewish Israelis of the heroic story of the ship that tried in 1947 to break the British blockade and bring thousands of Holocaust survivors to Palestine—and the subsequent book and movie, Zionist cultural icons. The street name must have had other connotations for its Arab residents.

After the Arab leadership rejected the United Nations partition plan in 1947, and with the end of the British Mandate for Palestine, Israel declared independence in May 1948, aware that war was about to break out. The Arab armies invaded. Some 700,000 Palestinian Arabs fled or were driven by Zionist forces from their homes. Many had assumed it would be a temporary absence until the war died down, but David Ben-Gurion's new state, which had won more territory than the original partition plan afforded it, closed the door to any refugees who wanted to return. The bonus areas won by Israel in the war included Beersheba in the south, the Galilee region in the north, and Lod. Most of the refugees ended up in camps within marching distance of the boundaries of the new Jewish state. Israel destroyed some 400 abandoned Arab villages, ensuring that their inhabitants, and the internally displaced, had nowhere to return to. Only about 156,000 Palestinians remained behind. Despite the best efforts of the new state to erase the memory, the lay of the land still gave up its secrets and traces of the past.

More than seventy years later, Israel's Arab minority now made up a fifth of the population, numbering about 1.8 million people, and the self-contradiction of being an Arab citizen of the Jewish state, or a Palestinian citizen of Israel, as many preferred to be known, was coming to a crux. Long treated with suspicion by the broader Arab world because of their connection with Israel, and still viewed as a demographic or security threat in some Jewish quarters, this hybrid community, mostly Muslim but also including Christians, semi-nomadic Bedouin, Circassians, and Druze, had largely forged a separate identity, or identity crisis, of their own. The Jewish Israeli majority was constantly seeking signs of "Israelization," an affirmation of the Arabic-speaking minority's loyalty and sense of belonging, despite years of discrimination underscoring its otherness, and holding up a mirror to Israel's equally conflicted self-image as a Jewish democracy. At the same time, among the young, progressive, and connected generation of Arab activists in Israel, sympathy and solidarity with the broader Palestinian population outside the borders only grew stronger, aligned in spirit and, at times, in blood. The same duality saw the Palestinian citizens increasingly participating in the country's politics, society, and culture, whether by joining an Israeli government, by increasing visibility in the mainstream Israeli media, or by running the local pharmacy. A breakthrough came in 2007 with a popular television comedy series, *Avodah Aravit*, Hebrew for "Arab labor" and slang for shoddy workmanship, the satirical creation of Arab Israeli author Sayed Kashua that brought endearing and self-deprecating Arab characters, Arabic dialogue, and the identity struggles of Arab Israelis to prime-time TV. Arab home cooks and chanteuses consistently won hearts on popular reality cooking and singing shows. The coronavirus crisis highlighted the extraordinary cooperation between Jewish and Arab medical staff in Israeli hospitals, long models of successful integration.

Yet at the same time Israel's Arab citizens were living a confounding dichotomy, battling a rampant scourge of illegal weapons trading and gangland-style murders within their own communities, and harboring explosive levels of pent-up resentment that always threatened to burst outward.

It was little coincidence that Lod, and the Ramat Eshkol neighborhood in particular, bore the initial brunt of the violence. The city was built on the deepest foundations of both Jewish history and the trauma of the Israeli-Palestinian conflict. Lod was also reputed to be the crime capital of Israel. In its most recent incarnation, because of its central location, cheap housing, and fluctuating demographic balance, Ramat Eshkol had become a magnet for young and ideological religious Zionists who wanted to settle back in Israel and make parts of it more Jewish.

Ancient Lod traced its history to Canaanite times and was mentioned in the Bible. It became a center of trade and early rabbinic scholarship. The Arab city, with its late medieval Mamluk-era structures, had been built on the ruins of the Roman and Byzantine city. Two centuries later, among the shabby buildings of Ramat Eshkol, with laundry hanging out and garbage-strewn yards, archaeologists unearthed an exquisite, late-Roman-era mosaic floor with colorful depictions of birds, fish, exotic animals, and merchant ships that probably adorned a grand villa here, conjuring up a more glorious past. Before the *Nakba*, Lod was an important Arab town known as Lydda, strategically placed along the highway between Jaffa and Jerusalem. Lod, like Acre, was meant to have remained under Arab rule according to the United Nations partition plan of 1947, but it was conquered in a bloody battle led by Palmach forces in July 1948. The majority of the Palestinian residents were compelled to leave on the personal orders of Ben-Gurion, according to some historical accounts, and were offered safe passage out to become refugees. At least 250 of Lod's men, women, and children were killed in the fighting; more died of exhaustion and dehydration on the march east in the summer heat.

Today, Lod is a city of some 80,000 people, some 70 percent of them Jews and the rest Arabs, mostly Muslims and a few hundred Christians. Much of Arab Lod was demolished in the 1950s. Aside from the remnants of the pre-1948 Palestinian community, Bedouin displaced from the Negev desert arrived in the following decades, as did families of Palestinians from the West Bank who had collaborated with Israel, seeking safe refuge and further complicating relations in the city. The Arab community was further upset by the influx of the nationalist religious Zionists. While the newcomers built an entirely new neighborhood of apartment blocks, the homes of Arab families built without the proper permits were under demolition orders.

The first to arrive were two families from the West Bank settlement of Beit El in 1995. They were the pioneers of a new movement known as *Garin Torani*, Hebrew for "Torah Nucleus," and they arrived with the express intention of "Judaizing" the city. It was a kind of inverse settlement enterprise aimed at tipping the demographic, not in the West Bank, but in the few mixed Jewish-Arab cities in Israel proper. The movement fanned out to nearby Ramleh, then Jaffa, and had grown over the years to encompass thousands of Orthodox families in dozens of Israeli towns and cities, many of them predominantly Jewish, but socioeconomically weak, neglected, and in need of a lift. With the settlement project of the West Bank now firmly entrenched, and many young Orthodox couples looking for a life of community, values, volunteering, and meaning, a new challenge became enriching tough neighborhoods within Israel with good works and their religious Zionist brand of Judaism. By 2021, about seventy *Garin Torani* hubs stretched from the desert town of Yeruham in the south to Kiryat Shemona on the northern border with Lebanon.

Ramat Eshkol was also 70 percent Jewish at one time, its public housing association blocks inhabited by some poor Arab families and more equally poor Jewish immigrants, including from the former Soviet Union and Ethiopia. But as the neighborhood went further downhill, it was abandoned by many of its Jewish residents and the Jewish-Arab ratio was reversed. Ramat Eshkol became about 70 percent Arab. From 2012, it became a target for the *Garin Torani* movement. By 2021, the *Garin Torani* community in Lod numbered about 1,200 people. Scores of religious nationalist families rented or bought apartments lining a warren of streets near Lod's old quarter, sharing the stairwells with longtime Arab residents. Many of the newcomers marked their presence by hanging Israeli flags out of their windows, even when it was not Independence Day. The Jewish mayor was sympathetic—a religious rightist, one of his flagship battles was an attempt to lower the volume of the calls to prayer from the city's minarets. A religious pre-army academy, where teenage boys could spend a year strengthening their religious education before performing military service, and an Orthodox boys' elementary school went up on Exodus Street. The newcomers called it coexistence, appropriating the language of the decimated Israeli peace movement, and spoke enthusiastically of running voluntary programs and distributing food packages for the benefit of both Jewish and Arab families. "Coexistence is not standing on the road with a placard," Avi Rockach, the tall, articulate, kippa-wearing leader of the Lod nucleus, told me, mocking liberal Israeli peace activists. "It is getting up and saying good morning to your Arab neighbor and lending each other milk when necessary. We are living it."

He may have thought so, or have liked to think so. But he was speaking while sitting in the yard of the charred elementary school after two nights of wanton violence had convulsed the neighborhood where the dueling nationalisms were playing out. Synagogues had been burned and firebombed. Video had circulated showing a dozen bystanders in the parking lot across the road fleeing from long bursts of gunfire as an invisible shooter aimed at them from an apartment. A kippa-wearing medic was hit in the leg and had to be evacuated by his colleagues. Tahel Harris, a twenty-seven-year-old Jew in a stylish dress, her fair hair caught up in a colorful *bobo,* related how she, her husband, and two infant children had been besieged in their apartment behind locked doors in an old building with a mix of Arab and Jewish residents across from the school while Arab mobs set cars alight in the street below and threw stones, and as bursts of gunfire split the air. Harris had grown up in the settlement of Maale Michmash. The family had moved to Lod two years earlier to live in a community closer to the university where Tahel's husband was studying. She said she had cleared and planted the small garden at the entrance to the building. The flowering plants in the troughs had survived. But one of the stone steps from the street had been smashed, to provide ammunition for the stone throwers. Not everything had been perfect, she said, but all the residents of the mixed building had enjoyed the garden and she had thought they were good neighbors. "I don't know where they were last night," she said, adding that she would not ask them because she was scared to hear the reply.

Young yeshiva students were offering journalists tours of the Jewish sites of destruction. One stop was the Dadon family's second-floor walkup. Arab rioters—possibly neighbors—apparently unable to break down the front door, had bashed a hole through the wall of the cramped apartment from the stairwell, entered near the kitchen, took what they wanted, then set it on fire. The young couple, he a musician, she a baker and homemaker, had left town. Only an old upright piano and a metalwork calligraphy ornament of a short prayer affixed to the wall had survived.

Behind Exodus Street, in the patch of wasteland where the burned-out truck and Tumarkin's monument stood, several of the Palestinian "collaborator" families resided in semi-permanent-looking dwellings cobbled together from tin and cement blocks, like in a shantytown. One destroyed car lay on its side. The men, tough-looking and suspicious of outsiders, were taciturn and hostile. The women, agitated and traumatized, sought the kindness of strangers, or at least a sympathetic ear. Jewish vigilantes had raided the neighborhood the night before, they related, burning vehicles, firing at the dwellings, and setting the entrance to one home on fire. "We ran out of the house without clothes on. It was burning," said Shirin al-Hinawi, a thirty-three-year-old resident of the house. She worked for Osem, a major Israeli food company, displaying its stock in a supermarket in Bat Yam. Tears spilled down her cheeks as she described the family's desperate calls to the police, with no response. "Nobody came to defend us," she said. "Nobody cared if we died or not." She did hear from colleagues at Osem who called to offer their help and support. The police would later say they were overwhelmed with calls at the time and could not place an officer by every doorway, Jewish or Arab. But while the Arab attacks on Jewish property were well known to the police, at least one police spokesman who had offered to tour the scenes of destruction in Lod with me said he had not heard about the Jewish gang attack on Hinawi's neighborhood. "We are not living in Gaza. I'm an Israeli citizen," Hinawi cried, trembling and in despair. "And we didn't do anything."

The *Garin Torani* residents of Lod were indignant. This was nothing like the controversial West Bank "settlement," they said, and where could they live if not in Lod, in the heart of central Israel? But many of the Palestinian citizens of Lod called them "settlers" and viewed them as invaders who had come to replace them. Ramat Eshkol was a stone's throw from the Dahamshe Mosque in the old core of the city, at the center of its *Nakba* narrative. During the capture of Lod, grenades had been thrown from within the mosque, according to some accounts, and Palmach forces fired an anti-tank shell into the building, where many of the town's residents were being detained or had taken shelter. Dozens were said to have been killed. Here, the century of conflict was boiled down to its essence. The Arab residents were living with a smarting sense of injustice, prejudice, and an ingrained fear of displacement. The Torah Jews, seen here as the new settlers, were steadily growing their presence in the mixed apartment blocks, coming from all over to snap up any available flats, however run-down, and creating a real-estate boom that had doubled their value, tempting more apartment owners to sell and pricing out the locals. Weeks before the May violence erupted, two Arab homes built without permission in a nearby neighborhood were demolished by the authorities.

Rami Salameh, twenty-four, an Arab resident of another mixed building on Exodus Street, scoffed at the idea of good neighborliness.

He was sitting under a tree in the yard, eating a takeout shawarma and fries, his eyes hidden behind aviator glasses. A building contractor, he volunteered that he had served four years in prison for the possession of illegal weapons, a piece of his biography he conveyed matter-of-factly, not as a boast, but just to make clear where we were. It was necessary to be armed, he said, because the Arab community was riddled with its own problems and brutality that sucked you in, whether you liked it or not. In recent years, two Arabs had been shot dead by other Arabs in the parking lot just behind us, and many more had been shot in the legs in feuds over money or honor, Salameh said, adding bitterly that the police and the Jews had not cared, so long as the guns were not being turned on them. But what gutted him was the attitude of the "settlers" that now made up half the residents of the building, where he, his parents, and ten siblings lived in two adjoining apartments. "When I say good morning or *shabbat shalom* or happy holidays to them, they don't answer me," he said of the Jewish neighbors who had moved in over the past five or six years. He said he had invested thousands of shekels in fixing up the garden around the building, fencing it off from the street and mounting security cameras and buying garden benches—"I put them here for everyone, without discrimination"—though none of the "settler" neighbors had agreed to chip in. And when his mother came down one morning to speak to one of them about the children throwing their Popsicle wrappers in the garden, he immediately turned the conversation to real estate, asking her about an empty apartment in the building. "It's all they think about," Salameh said. The building's interior was dark and dingy. One apartment had a name on the door, "Cohen." The door of the apartment above it had an Arabic sticker on it that read *Subhan Allah*, "Praise be to God."

Salameh, who was born in a building with sixteen apartments, said it was always mixed, with Arab families living alongside Jewish Ethiopians, Russians, and others. His family had moved twenty-five years earlier from Jaljuliya, an Arab town in the Triangle, an area of central-eastern Israel with a large Arab population. He described how, as a youth, he and his Arab friends were kept out of the school grounds across the road as his Jewish neighbors played soccer there. He didn't know then it was called discrimination. But after the fatal shooting of Mousa Hassouneh, an acquaintance, in another *Garin Torani* neighborhood nearby, Salameh said he felt like "a brother had been killed in cold blood." The day before he had joined the funeral, one of hundreds of men who followed the coffin in a procession through the streets. Defying the police instructions, they insisted on bringing the body down Exodus Street. "We wanted to show them the guy they had killed," Salameh explained, though nobody from the street had been accused of firing the shots. There, the funeral procession devolved into a riot as the mourners threw stones at the police, who tried to disperse them with tear gas and stun grenades. "If all of Lod brought out its weapons there wouldn't be a single police officer left," he said ominously, in what may not have been much of an overstatement. "There are more Katyushas here than in Gaza," he said, referring to the rockets that fly over Israel's borders. "But I don't want Gaza here. I only hope for peace and love."

After a few days of nighttime curfews and police roundups, the worst intercommunal violence to have rocked Israel in decades petered out as abruptly as it had started. Both sides shrank back from the brink in fear of what lay beyond, although nothing had been resolved. Lod's new neighborhoods spread out from the old core of the town and the street names resonated with conquest: Beitar Fighters Street, Paratroopers Street, Navy Commandos Street, and, at the entrance of what remained of the Old City, the scene of the bloodshed in 1948, Palmach Square. The city's broad avenues were now lined with utilitarian apartment blocks and some better-off neighborhoods with rows of single-family homes. But modern Israel tapered off at the entrance to an even rougher neighborhood known as HaRakevet, Hebrew for "the railroad," giving way to narrow, dusty alleys, tin-roofed cinderblock homes, and fenced-off compounds. HaRakevet, which resembled a refugee camp and housed a few Arab railroad workers who had remained in their homes after the expulsion of 1948, was now ridden with drugs and crime. I had driven around there a few months before the violence broke out. An emaciated man rummaged through a garbage can; a youth with a wisp of facial hair sat on a stoop surrounded by police officers, his slim wrists encased in clunky metal handcuffs. The atmosphere was menacing. A decade-old blood feud between two families had left a trail of bodies. In one particularly brazen revenge attack in late 2020, one teenage boy was killed and another critically wounded as they headed north up

Route 6, a main highway, to seek refuge with relatives. They were shot while riding in a convoy escorted by three police cars.

The children of HaRakevet were growing up literally on the wrong side of the tracks. Getting to the neighborhood entailed a perilous crossing of an eight-track-wide railroad junction. Plans for a pedestrian tunnel or footbridge had never materialized. Unlike the growing Arab middle classes who endeavored to send their children to private schools in Israel and summer schools and universities abroad, HaRakevet belonged to that half of the Arab community whose children lived below the poverty line. Long-standing educational and budget gaps had already created a built-in inequality. The Arab state schools routinely scored near the bottom of the charts in international tests compared to their Jewish counterparts—excluding the autonomous ultra-Orthodox boys' schools that shunned secular studies and did not even take the tests. Arab local authorities tended to be poorer than Jewish ones and were unable to provide matching funds for government-subsidized enrichment programs. Even the quality of the Arabic language was suffering, with the number of Arabic-language teaching hours set by the state failing to take into account the complexities of literacy in the literary as opposed to the colloquial form of the language, meaning that many Arab pupils left school without high-level proficiency in either Arabic or Hebrew, let alone English.

It was here, on the front lines of HaRakevet, that Shirin Natour-Hafi, a Muslim Arab native of Lod and an Arab educator, was trying to bring about a revolution and, as the determined principal of the first Arab ORT high school of science and engineering, help close the gaps. The ORT school system, a global Jewish educational network, originally sought to teach Russian Jews essential trades in the nineteenth century and was now focused on STEM education, particularly in underprivileged communities in Israel. Natour-Hafi was pioneering the first ORT school in an Arab locality. Born in Lod to an established Arab family— her father worked in an Israeli insurance company and then became a lawyer—she had attended local Jewish schools and went on to study Hebrew literature at Bar Ilan University. After turning to teaching, she worked in Jewish schools in the area until she felt an urge to return to her fold, spurred by an encounter with racism. Sitting in her office dressed casually in jeans, she recalled the experience of trying to purchase a house in Lod with her husband, Muhammad, a banker. She said the first few sellers told them, "You and your husband seem very nice, but we won't sell to Arabs." The insult set Natour-Hafi off on a journey back into her own society, believing that education was the best weapon against violence and racism. With her background in Hebrew literature, she said she understood the anxiety of the other side and the fear of assimilation; the Jewish DNA that she said was influenced by a tragic history.

Teaching, she said, was a form of *tikkun olam,* a Hebrew concept meaning repairing the world; a way of empowering people to rise above hatred and knee-jerk responses. "Saving one child is saving a family in ten years' time, and a whole clan in twenty years," she said of her mission. Natour-Hafi had become something of a role model in educational circles. She had taught at a Jewish ORT school in Lod, and in 2009, at the age of thirty-four, had become the founding principal of the first Arab one. At first, some of the parents were suspicious of her, she said, viewing her as "too Ashkenazi." A decade later, the school moved into its new, permanent building in HaRakevet, with 1,300 students, male and female, from grades seven to twelve. Some girls wore a black hijab, or Muslim head covering. All the students were neatly turned out and the school was spotless. Along with COVID-awareness notices to abide by hygiene, an exhibit in the lobby celebrated medieval scientists and other role models from the Islamic world, including Fatima al-Samarqandi, a twelfth-century female scholar and jurist from Samarkand, and Ibn Sina, known in the West as Avicenna, the Persian physician and philosopher.

Natour-Hafi broadcast an impressive blend of authority, energy, and compassion. She greeted pupils by name and dropped into a teachers' potluck lunchtime gathering, sampling their home cooking and insisting on a group photograph. When a pupil had not shown up for an important biology test that morning, she had gone to his home to fetch him. Looking out of an upper-floor window over the rickety homes of HaRekevet, she said, of the pupil, "You see the house and you realize how hard it must be to get out of bed in the morning."

In Natour-Hafi's view, the main division in contemporary Israel was less between Jews and Arabs than between the rich and poor, the educated and uneducated. She said her own three children were receiving an education similar to those living in the best Jewish neighborhoods of Jerusalem, while children on the Jewish and Arab social margins were similarly disadvantaged. The difference for Jewish teens, she said, came when they enlisted for army service, which helped fix some of the glaring educational gaps and shortfalls. Her school, a beacon of hope, had won many Jewish supporters from industry, and it was aided in its operation by an effective volunteer steering committee. During the coronavirus crisis, one organization donated fifteen computers to help poor students with remote learning. But Natour-Hafi had to navigate the kind of sensitive cultural and political minefields that came with the territory.

The year before, on Yom HaZikaron, Israel's annual memorial day for its fallen soldiers and victims of terrorism, Natour-Hafi had wondered how to handle the issue of "the siren" that wails out across the country at eleven a.m., marking a nationwide two-minute silence. Mainstream Jewish Israelis would stop whatever they were doing and stand at attention. Traffic would come to a standstill. It would not ordinarily be an issue for an Arab school to ignore the siren and carry on as usual. Many Palestinian citizens would object to displays of respect for the soldiers who fell in bloody wars against other Arabs—and not least since the Israeli government had, years earlier, passed the so-called *Nakba* law, denying government funding to bodies or institutions that commemorated Nakba Day, the anniversary of Israel's establishment, "as a day of mourning." But there was a Jewish teacher in the school who would be teaching an architecture class that morning. If the pupils had been ordered to stand, Natour-Hafi said, they would likely have rebelled. So, fifteen minutes before the siren was due to sound, Natour-Hafi entered the architecture class and spoke "to their hearts" about respect for the bereaved families and the principle of honoring the dead. As the siren began to wail, the whole class spontaneously rose to its feet. The rest of the school continued as normal. Asked if the school marked Nakba Day in some way, she said it was better not to talk about it.

The continual state of identity crisis was illustrated, she said, by the fact that students left school with high-level proficiency in neither Arabic nor Hebrew. But, she said, "Over the last ten years, we've learned to live with it and not spend too much time on it." Arab society itself was far from homogeneous and had undergone significant generational changes affecting its contract with the Jewish state. The older generation, she said, was "still busy with the pain and loss and has not been liberated from it." The middle, forty-plus generation of Arab citizens still felt it was "a kind of betrayal" to engage too much. But the young generation, she said, "sees there is no choice. You are no longer considered a collaborator if you work in a government office." When it came to advancing the community, Natour-Hafi said, with a new confidence, "I learned from the *Haredim*," referring to the country's ultra-Orthodox Jews. "I don't have to identify with the values of the state in order to demand what I'm entitled to."

The rows of olive trees shimmered, iridescent in the late afternoon sun. The broad, green valley basked in quiet splendor. The acres of orchards, long claimed by the nearby Arab towns of Sakhnin, Arraba, and Deir Hana, nestled in the rolling countryside of the Lower Galilee in northern Israel. Like any old battlefield, oblivious and long overgrown, the tranquility of the valley gave lie to a blood-tainted history. Known locally as El Mal, it was sandwiched in a dip between two tiny Jewish communities, Maaleh Tzvia and Lotem, established by the Israeli government in the 1970s as hilltop "lookouts," perched above the Arab villages as part of what was then a national project to "Judaize" the Galilee. The state's intention was to tip the demographic balance in the heavily Arab-populated Galilee by building more Jewish communities. That involved designs to expropriate swaths of land, including property that was privately owned by Palestinian citizens of this area in what became sovereign Israel. A government decision in February 1976 to close the lands of El Mal to the Arab villagers and block their ability to farm there, as part of the Judaization plan, was one of the catalysts of Israel's Arab awakening.

In a phrase widely attributed to some early Zionists, and before them Christian Restorationists, Palestine was "for a people without a land, a land without people." Herbert Samuel, a British Jewish liberal who served as the first high commissioner of the Mandatory government in Palestine, presented an interim report to the League of Nations in the summer of 1921, a year after his arrival, in which he described a country "exhausted by war" that was "under-developed and under-populated."

Though he may not have been entirely impartial, he depicted Palestine as a kind of wasteland where the townspeople were "in severe distress," cultivated land was left untilled, woodlands had almost disappeared, and orange groves were parched and in ruins. Juxtaposing this scene of devastation with the agricultural colonies being set up by the Zionist Jewish immigrants who fled the persecutions in Russia, on land purchased with funds collected in Europe and America, he extolled their modern methods, which developed the culture and trade of Jaffa oranges as well as the cultivation of the vines and export of wine. Samuel went on to contrast what he called "the reality, the strength and the idealism of this movement" and its pleasant villages with the "primitive conditions of life and work" surrounding them. By then, Britain had already decided to support the establishment of a national home for the Jewish people in Palestine. Jewish communities, however small, had maintained a constant presence in the Holy Land since the days of antiquity, and the immigrant pioneers saw their endeavors not as colonization but as a homecoming. But a clash was inevitable, with the national aspirations of one party awakening the nationalism of the other. Deadly Arab riots broke out in 1929, sparked by a dispute over access to the Western Wall in Jerusalem. The Arab Revolt of 1936–1939 against Jewish immigration and land purchases and for Arab independence was aimed against both the Zionists and the British authorities.

By the time the 1948 war was over, the Palestinian population was even further depleted. And once the state was established, the Israeli government placed the Arab communities living in the north, the south, and the Triangle under military rule, their daily lives and movements proscribed by military governors. The grip was soon lifted from Jaffa, Lod, and Ramleh but the other Arab-populated areas remained under the military regime until 1966. A decade later, the threat of the mass expropriation of land around El Mal jolted the Palestinian Arab citizens into their first act of political resistance. Already traumatized by dispossession and expulsion, local Arab leaders called a general strike for March 30, 1976, to defend the lands. During marches and protests held that day, six Arab citizens were shot and killed in clashes with the Israeli security forces and scores were injured. A pivotal moment, it became known as Land Day, and is marked each year with anniversary marches, lectures, and cultural events in a binding ritual observed by

Palestinians living in Israel and beyond, symbolizing a cardinal but largely peaceful struggle for their rights in the land. The new sense of solidarity in the face of adversity also spawned a distinct, new Middle Eastern identity: that of the Arab Israeli or Israeli Palestinian.

Full Israeli citizens by right, who largely identified as Palestinian in sentiment and nationality, they lived with the suspicion, in some Jewish quarters, of being a fifth column, and were treated as a demographic threat or felt compelled to prove their loyalty to Israel. They spoke Arabic at home and in school and for the most part could not identify with the national symbols such as the flag, its design based on a Jewish prayer shawl with a blue Star of David, or the stirring lyrics of the national anthem, which spoke of the Jewish soul yearning for Zion. They were torn by the ongoing Palestinian conflict and the occupation of the 1967 territories. Some nationalist Jews believed in stripping Arab citizens of the right to participate in Israeli elections and to send representatives to the Knesset. Prime Minister Netanyahu had certainly played his part in the delegitimization of the Arab parliamentarians, describing them as terrorist sympathizers and running scaremongering campaigns warning his right-wing base that the choice was between "Bibi or Tibi," referring to Ahmad Tibi, a veteran Arab lawmaker and obstetrician whose surname happened to rhyme. Nor did Netanyahu spare the Arab electorate. Halfway through election day in 2015, he was spooked by what looked like a sluggish turnout by his voters. In a ploy to rally his base he released a notorious video falsely claiming that leftists were busing Arab voters to the polls in droves. Accused of incitement and racism, he later apologized.

But Israel's Arab minority was already on a very different trajectory, a rapidly changing society that, despite the inherent gaps, was more educated, modernized, and politically savvy. By 2020, more than 40 percent of the students at Haifa University were Arab, the highest ratio for any university in the country. Many were striving to become more integrated into mainstream Israeli society. And, in a dizzying turnaround reflecting Netanyahu's desperation to remain in office, even he began canvassing Arab voters during the 2021 election campaign, unabashedly posting beaming videos of himself on social media showing how his Arab fans on the campaign trail greeted him as Abu Yair, father of Yair, his elder son. When that election, the fourth in two years, again ended inconclusively, with neither he nor his oppo-nents able to muster a majority, Netanyahu tried to make up his num-bers by courting Mansour Abbas, the leader of the United Arab List, a small Islamic party also known by its Hebrew acronym, Raam, which had won four seats. Ultimately, he ended up koshering the way for his rivals to bring the Islamist party into the alternative government led by Naftali Bennett—the first direct participation of an independent Arab party in a governing coalition in decades. And given its razor-thin parliamentary majority of one, or two on a good day, each one of its eight partners, including Raam, had the power to bring down the government. That made Abbas, a conservative on social issues and an advocate for new levels of government support for the Arab minority and moderation in the Palestinian conflict, one of the most influential politicians in the country.

Few Israeli Jews driving the country roads of the Galilee would have heard of El Mal or been aware of its existence. I was taken there by Bayan Sayed Ahmad, a modest, if dapper, student at Haifa University and a son of the nearby Arab town of Sakhnin. For him, El Mal was a rich canvas of living history. His family had land and olive orchards there. Each fall, grandparents, aunts, uncles, and cousins would all turn out for three or four days for the olive harvest. It was a joyous occa-sion, and a triumph nearly four decades after the sacrifices of Land Day. The elders would sit in the shade and drink coffee, watching all the activity. There were family picnics. Ahmad's father had two dozen trees that produced enough high-quality olive oil for the year, he said, and sometimes even a surplus. Extended families like Ahmad's had divided up the orchards into smaller lots, with tall trees marking the family borders. The dirt path leading into the valley off the asphalted country road was lined with thorny sabra bushes—hardy cacti glo-riously abloom with rosy clusters of prickly pears. Sabra bushes had very different connotations for the native Arabs than they did for the Jews. They traditionally demarcated the borders of Palestinian lands and villages. The plant's name in colloquial Arabic, *sabr*, also means patience, and symbolized steadfastness on the land. Impervious to time, the weather, and human designs, the cacti endured across the

Israeli countryside, often marking the boundaries of the Palestinian ghost villages that were erased in 1948. The sabra bushes bore witness, remaining long after the inhabitants had gone.

Ahmad, twenty, a friend of a friend, had kindly and eagerly taken me on a tour of his hometown, proudly showing off its landmarks: the historic old city with its steep lanes, churches, and mosques, the impressive new municipal building, and Doha Stadium, the pride of Sakhnin, built with funds from Israeli institutions and the Qatari Olympic Committee after the now legendary home soccer team, Bnei Sakhnin, won the Israeli State Cup in 2004. Ahmad's life was an increasingly typical blend of cultures. He was studying for a BA in business and economics, commuting by bus daily to classes, and, like everyone else in his town, he was an avid fan of Bnei Sakhnin. He volunteered in local cultural and youth organizations and danced with a traditional folkloric *debka* troupe. Before college, he worked to earn money in the Lee Cooper and Homestyle stores franchised by his father and an uncle on Sakhnin's high street, honing his Hebrew while engaging with Jewish customers and regional managers. His father was also the deputy principal of a local school and his mother a teacher. Together, they watched reality shows like *Survivor* and *Big Brother* on Israeli television, further improving his Hebrew.

The vast majority of Sakhnin's 30,000 or so residents were Muslim, like the Ahmad family, but the city had a richly diverse history. The hilly old core, where the streets gave way to narrow alleyways, contained an old church, a restored mosque, and a Palestinian folklore museum. Ahmad had been part of an effort by young activists to revitalize the old city by holding a Ramadan festival there. The busy main street running the length of the city still had the feel of a low-rise, Galilean Arab town, but it featured smartly renovated stores selling international and Israeli brands. Simple eateries offering traditional Arabic street food attracted a loyal Jewish clientele from the surrounding area. Young, fashionable locals like Ahmad preferred the new Tulip café, a more cosmopolitan, glass-fronted venue that offered eastern, western, and fusion "comfort food," including its Instagrammable flagship dish of salmon sprayed with gold dust, specialty milkshakes, and Starbucks-style frappés.

At the same time the municipality had infused the town with its own ethnic imprint. The uniform street signs and house numbers were decorated with the city's emblem, an olive sprig, a universal symbol of peace but also a statement of Palestinian pride and steadfastness on the land. Another icon of Sakhnin was the Land Day monument, unveiled in 1978 on a rise in the Muslim cemetery near the town's entrance. One of the first national monuments erected to commemorate the struggle of the Arab citizens of Israel, some experts have credited it with embodying the beginnings of an Arab Israeli collective memory and consciousness. The large sarcophagus-shaped block of stone is carved with figures weeping, lying still, and tending to the land and engraved with the names of the dead, three of whom were from Sakhnin. A collaboration between an Arab artist, Abed Abedi, and a Jewish sculptor, Gershon Knipsel, the monument is also etched with the artists' words: "They sacrificed themselves so that we could live . . . Thus, they live."

Ahmad was now navigating Israel's social, ethnic labyrinth. He had attended a private high school in Sakhnin, like most whose parents could afford the fees. He was a representative on the national student council and had made some Jewish friends through a regional dialogue group that had brought together groups of Jewish and Arab high school students from the area for about a dozen meetings. When the Jewish teens visited Sakhnin he took them to an ice cream parlor. At eighteen, their lives went on different trajectories. He worked in his father's stores for a year and spent a few months with relatives in Germany before starting university. His Jewish compatriots were drafted into the army. He said he did not resent them for their service, since it was obligatory and a simple reality of life here. But at university he felt the gap between himself and the older, more experienced, post-army Jewish students. "I have seen a little bit of life," he said. "But they have a different way of thinking." He found the former soldiers to be more independent. Many had taken long, adventurous trips abroad, the post-army expedition to the Far East or South America having become something of a rite of passage. They spoke better English, a second language for them and for Ahmad a third. In general, he said, the former soldiers came more prepared and had scored better on the college entrance exams. For him, serving in the IDF was out of the question. "If I could join an army in another country, I would be happy to do it," he said. But the Israeli-Palestinian conflict was too personal.

Even performing national service by volunteering in the community was not acceptable to most of the Arab population if the program was administered by the Ministry of Defense.

With his trim, fashionable beard and hazel eyes, dressed in jeans, a pristine white fitted T-shirt, and sneakers, Ahmad looked the part of an Israeli student. He lived with his parents in a stylish house in a new neighborhood on the edge of Sakhnin but was planning to rent a place with other students in Haifa the following year. An older brother, an engineer, was already living there. A married older sister had studied at Hebrew University in Jerusalem and had settled back in Sakhnin. Ahmad was generally comfortable at university, where his first-year class was roughly half Jewish and half Arab. At times, he said, the teacher or other students might ask the Arab students not to speak in Arabic around them because they did not understand it.

Ahmad was born a few months before another traumatic watershed event in the annals of the Palestinians of Israel: the October 2000 riots, when twelve unarmed Arab citizens were fatally shot by Israeli security forces during protests they held in solidarity with the Palestinians of East Jerusalem, the West Bank, and Gaza at the outset of the Second Intifada. A Gaza resident protesting in Israel at the time was the thirteenth fatality. Over that bloody weekend, like twenty years later in Lod, it felt as if Israel itself was unraveling. A governmental commission of inquiry that investigated the police response exposed an institutional pattern of government discrimination, prejudice, and neglect of the Arab minority over decades, expressed among other things in the chronic underfunding of Arab municipalities and schools, widening the social gaps and deepening poverty.

"They want the young generation to forget all that," Ahmad said of the state's approach to commemorating the anniversaries of the *Nakba* and the October riots. "We haven't." While the state-funded Arabic schools and institutions were barred from holding any formal Nakba Day ceremonies, Ahmad said pupils in Sakhnin would simply not show up for class that day and would hold quiet rallies outside. Local organizations would host events and bring survivors to tell their stories, and Facebook and social media provided newer platforms for sharing emotions. Once, Ahmad and a group of friends visited the ruins of a destroyed village where a *moshav* now stood, a few miles from Sakhnin. They found graves, but no old houses. Then the police came and told them they had to leave.

Soft-spoken, mild-mannered, and respectful of his parents, Ahmad said he followed a lot of people from the wider Arab world on Facebook and Instagram. A short drive away across the pre-1967 lines, in the occupied West Bank, the Palestinians were more or less strangers to him. Ahmad had occasionally been shopping in the northern West Bank cities of Jenin and Nablus, a weekend activity for many Palestinian citizens of Israel. Some from Sakhnin went to study at West Bank universities. But all Israeli citizens had been barred from entering the Hamas-run Gaza Strip ever since Ahmad was a child, and he had never visited the coastal enclave.

The Palestinians outside Israel referred to those inside as the Palestinians, or Arabs, of 1948. It had never been an easy relationship. Some of the Palestinians in the West Bank still related to the Arab Israelis as traitors and quislings, adding to their conflicted identity. "They overcharge us for coffee, they think we live the good life, like in Dubai, as if we are millionaires," Ahmad said. It was all relative. Others, he said, were more welcoming and "ask how we get along here." He said being branded a traitor was hurtful. "Some people want to change history. We are the ones who stayed, despite it all. If we weren't here Israel would be entirely Jewish. They wouldn't have left a single olive tree, there would be no trace of us here. We try to preserve the memory."

In the eyes of many Israelis, the Palestinians of 1948, or the Arab citizens, were put to the test in the fall of 2021 when six Palestinian security prisoners escaped from the Gilboa prison in the north. Five of them belonged to the extremist, Iranian-backed Islamic Jihad and were mostly convicted on charges of terrorism and killing Israelis. The sixth was Zakaria Zubeidi, a celebrity grassroots commander of the Fatah-affiliated Al Aqsa Martyrs' Brigades who had long flirted with the radical left in Israel. He was a gun-toting, swaggering symbol of the Second Intifada from the Jenin refugee camp, a hotbed of militancy in the northern West Bank, a few miles over the Green Line south of the prison. Dashing, though his face was pockmarked, apparently from an explosion that occurred during a work accident, he was rumored to have escaped several Israeli assassination attempts. When I met him once in the West Bank, he was casually taking delivery of a supermarket-style plastic shopping bag heavy with bullets. He had had a Jewish Israeli girlfriend who repudiated Zionism, and he was a household name in Israel. Amnestied at some point, despite his record of involvement in terrorism, he was also involved in political theater and cultural resistance, literally, as a founder of the refugee camp's Freedom Theater. But Zubeidi had been arrested again and charged with firing on two civilian buses in 2018 and 2019 near the central West Bank settlement of Beit El.

The jailbreak was almost farcical. Over months, the six had dug their way out from under the prison wall using dishes and tools fashioned from saucepan handles. Nobody had noticed, even when the sewage system kept backing up from all the sand and earth that was being dumped in it. They emerged from a hole outside an empty prison watchtower after one a.m. The guard who was meant to be watching the security camera footage was watching television. But once the prisoners were outside and on the lam, there was no plan. They headed for a nearby Arab Israeli village, Naoura, hoping for help, including some means of transportation to Jenin, but the local mosque officials would not even let them make a phone call. They then split into three pairs and went their separate ways, scavenging for food and sleeping rough in Arab areas of northern Israel. Within days, four of the escapees, including Zubeidi, had been rounded up, two in Nazareth and two in a village on Mount Tabor. Whether out of loyalty or fear, the local Arab residents had not offered any succor. Israel's minister of public security publicly thanked unnamed Arab citizens for tipping off the police. It turned out that one of the Israeli officers involved in the capture was a Muslim. Palestinians from the West Bank and Gaza, whose social networks had burst with pride over the initial escape, exploded with anger, describing the Palestinian Israelis as traitors to the cause.

Even the local Arabic vernacular was becoming "Israelized," while a couple of prominent Arab Israeli authors who had been educated in elite Hebrew schools preferred to write in Hebrew. Ahmad said he tried to avoid peppering his Arabic with Hebrew words, but it was hard. Arabs routinely used the Hebrew terms for air conditioner, remote control, café, apartment, traffic light, and, in the lingo of the occupation, checkpoint and roadblock. Listing the Hebrew words that he often used, Ahmad included *sababa*—Hebrew slang for "cool," or "awesome"—apparently unaware that the word had its roots in Arabic. Israeli Jews had adopted many Arab colloquialisms as part of their vernacular. The linguistic fusion reflected a complex and evolving sense of self, place, and belonging. For Ahmad, being an Israeli was a natural condition but one that still needed clarification. When people abroad asked him where he was from, he would reply, "Israel. And then," he said, "I try to explain."

At the end of our tour of Sakhnin Ahmad had shyly raised the idea of taking me to El Mal. It was his mother's idea, he said, adding that it was about a twenty-minute drive away. We stopped en route at a picturesque spring where a young Arab family was enjoying the cool, green water gathered in a stone pool. As we turned off the road onto the bumpy path and approached the olive orchards, the peace and silence created an aura of reverence. Ahmad fondly recalled the joyous family picnics at olive harvesttime. The sacrifices of Land Day had not been in vain. As we drove back onto the smooth highway, Ahmad snapped back into the present. "The younger generation is less connected to the land," he pronounced matter-of-factly, "because we have options." A century after Herbert Samuel's damning report about the Palestinians' agricultural endeavors, as we drove through Deir Hana, the Arab village closest to El Mal, Ahmad noted that it was renowned for its number of doctors.

The Arab minority in Israel had never quite managed to realize its full electoral potential. Voter turnout was routinely lower than that of the Jewish Israelis, whether because of a lack of trust in their own politicians or cynicism about the system. And the more the Arab minority sought equality and integration, the blunter the Jewish nationalist rhetoric, even in the Knesset. As prime minister in 2015, Netanyahu had promoted a cross-ministry five-year economic development plan allocating $4 billion to advance the Arab community. But any sense of goodwill dissipated about halfway through, in the summer of 2018, when he promoted and passed one of the most controversial—and arguably superfluous—laws on Israel's books under pressure from ultra-right-wingers in his government. Named "Basic Law: Israel—The Nation State of the Jewish People," it was an addition to the body of basic laws that together formed the closest thing to an Israeli constitution and dealt a blow to the Arab Israeli psyche, despite the largely symbolic nature of most of its provisions. The law enshrined the right to self-determination in Israel as being "unique to the Jewish People." It omitted any mention of equality or democracy, which critics viewed as elevating the state's Jewish character above those principles. Its supporters argued that they were anchored in other basic laws, although equality was not explicitly mentioned anywhere and was only extrapolated by the interpretation of Israel's Supreme Court. This strengthened the conviction of many Arab citizens that Israel could not be both Jewish and democratic. The law also effectively downgraded Arabic from a second state language to one with a "special status." It described promoting Jewish settlement as a "national value," without specifying where. Its clauses affirmed the openness of the state for Jewish immigration and the ingathering of exiles and the status of the flag; the national anthem, "Hatikvah"; and the Hebrew calendar, alongside the Gregorian one, as official calendars of Israel. Netanyahu hailed the passage of the law as "a defining moment in the annals of Zionism and the history of the state of Israel." Arab representatives ripped up copies of the bill and denounced it as the anchoring of racism, fascism, discrimination, and Jewish privilege. Ahmad Tibi and Ayman Odeh, the leader of the Joint List, an alliance of predominantly Arab parties, called it apartheid. Jewish critics, Jabotinskyites among them, said the Knesset would have done better to stick to Israel's Declaration of Independence of 1948, which did ensure complete equality of social and political rights for "all its inhabitants."

For decades, the Israeli authorities had tried to minimize the influence of the Arabic-speaking minority with a divide-and-rule policy, splitting it into its various components of Muslims, Christians, Druze, Bedouin, and Circassians, and referring to them collectively as "the minorities." Each of the communities does indeed have distinct identities, characteristics, and interests, but nothing galvanized them as much as the Nation State Law. Perhaps most aggrieved by the legislation was the Druze sect, which practices a largely secret religion resulting from a schism with Islam. The Druze are concentrated in a couple of dozen villages in northern Israel and are part of a larger people spread across the region; an element of their creed is loyalty to the government of whichever country they find themselves in. This made the Israeli Druze more Zionistic and patriotic than many Jewish citizens, in contrast to most Arabic-speaking Israelis. Accounting for little more than 1.5 percent of the population, they had thrown their lot in with the Jews even before the state was established. Druze males are conscripted into the IDF and have made an outsize contribution to national security. On the edge of Daliyat el-Carmel, one of the Druze villages nestled in the green hills of the Carmel region south of Haifa, a national monument is engraved with the names of more than 420 Druze soldiers and security personnel who fell while fighting for Israel. The Druze and the Jews had long described their alliance as a "covenant of blood" and themselves as "blood brothers," even though many Druze complained of discrimination when it came to building permits, despite their army service.

At the height of the rage over the passage of the law, I met Shadi Nasraldeen, a Druze native of Daliyat el-Carmel. He worked as a manager at the memorial site after retiring from a twenty-six-year army career. His brother, Lutfi, had been killed in the Gaza war of 2014 and his name was engraved on the glass wall of the monument. "It is enough of patting us on the shoulder and saying 'You are our brothers, we love you,'" Nasraldeen said. "We are the first to run into battle and to die on the flag. It's as if the Israeli people simply abandoned us." The hurt spread over the village. Near a holy shrine in the old village center, Anan Shami, a young Druze who ran a cellular phone shop and lab, said the covenant of blood stretched back to ancient times when Jethro, a chief prophet in the Druze religion, had crossed the Red Sea with Moses, his son-in-law. Sporting a generous, Druze-style moustache and dressed in traditional baggy pants and a white cap, Shami related how his father had fought on the side of the Zionists in the 1948 and 1967 wars, his brother in the Second Lebanon War, and he in Gaza in 2014. "Tell the war dead in the cemetery that they made you second-class casualties," he said bitterly. "For what were they killed? What were they fighting for?"

This was not the first law to enrage the Arab citizens. A 2017 act, dubbed the Kaminitz Law and meant to increase enforcement against unauthorized building, was broadly seen as targeting the Arab public. Other laws were explicitly created to ensure that Israel remained a sovereign Jewish refuge, chief among them the Law of Return, guaranteeing Jews the automatic right to immigrate and become Israeli citizens, as well as anyone with a Jewish parent or grandparent, and their spouses. There was no such law for Palestinians. Yet the more divisive Israeli politics became, and the more Arab politicians became targets of toxic, right-wing discourse, the more Arab voters were shaken out of their apathy. Running in an alliance as the Joint List, the Arab representatives made their biggest gains in the September 2020 election, winning a record 15 seats out of 120 in the Knesset.

Independent Arab parties had traditionally not been invited to join any Israeli government coalition, nor had they wanted to do so. The government did not want to be seen as "relying" on Arab politicians for sensitive military decisions. The Arab parties historically did not want to share responsibility for going to war or for the occupation of the Palestinian territories. Ayman Odeh, both the leader of the Joint List and the head of one of its components, Hadash, the former communist party of Israel, was no exception, although he had made much headway in reaching beyond Arab politics to a broader Israeli audience at the time with his calm demeanor and his commonsensical and non-abrasive talk about building bridges. These attributes made him a favored guest on prime-time television panels and quiz shows, where he displayed his intimate knowledge of Zionism and popular Hebrew culture.

Months after that election victory, I sat for a quick breakfast with Odeh in a fashionable café on Tel Aviv's Dubnov Street, a block from army headquarters, the opera house, and the city's museum. He was between stops on a tight schedule, having just come from an Arab protest on the border of Tel Aviv and Jaffa, where the authorities were planning to build on what locals contended was still-consecrated ground of an old Muslim cemetery. The lot was just across the road from the seafront Etzel Museum, where a stone monument on the lawn commemorated the right-wing underground's "liberators of Jaffa." Odeh ordered the "health breakfast" of omelet with herbs, low-fat white cheese, and a chopped salad—the kind that the Jews called Israeli salad, and Arabs called Arab salad. Asked what he called it, Odeh retorted, "Did my grandmother not eat a salad like this?"

Odeh grew up in the Kababir neighborhood of Haifa, the mixed port city, and still lived there surrounded by extended family. His wife, Nardine Aseli, a physician, had lost a younger brother, Asel, to police fire during the protests in October 2000 near his home in Arraba. Only seventeen at the time, Asel was a star student and a beloved member of Seeds of Peace, a coexistence program for Arab and Jewish youths. He was shot while wearing his green Seeds of Peace T-shirt. Energetic and raven-haired in his mid-forties, Odeh had swept onto the political scene with a refreshing blend of firm principles, a rare amicability, and familiarity with Jewish sensibilities. His political credentials were impeccable. Since boyhood, he had been influenced by the communist Hadash, a Hebrew acronym for the Democratic Front for Peace and Equality, the party he would eventually lead. Founded in 1977 as a joint Arab-Jewish party by veterans of the Land Day and Black Panther protests, it was now predominantly Arab and the largest component of the Joint List. Odeh was in his early teens during the first Palestinian intifada in the late 1980s and demonstrated in solidarity with the Palestinians "until the Shabak caught up with me when I was fifteen." The Shabak, as Israel's domestic security service is commonly called, summoned him repeatedly for questioning, sending him into a depression. Once he got back on his feet and returned to activism, like many of his generation, he said, he briefly flirted with the more hardline approach propagated by Azmi Bishara, a charismatic Arab Israeli intellectual and the founder of Balad, an Arab nationalist party that was more vocal in its support for Palestinian resistance and became a home for the more provocative Arab politicians. Bishara later resigned from the Knesset and skipped the country amid allegations of aiding the enemy during the 2006 Second Lebanon War and of money laundering, accusations he denied; he wound up in Qatar.

But by the age of twenty-three Odeh was serving as a representative of Hadash on the Haifa city council and became notorious as the "bad boy" of his hometown. He campaigned unsuccessfully for HaZionut (Zionism) Boulevard, a central artery running from the low port area up the slope of Mount Carmel, with its dazzling Bahai temple and gardens, to revert to its original, Arabic name, Al Jabal (Mountain) Street.

In those days, he said, the discourse over the incompatibility of Israel's symbols was potent among the Arab population. Now he was more concerned with content. One turning point came when an Arab resident of Wadi Nisnas in Haifa told him that his positions as a young firebrand were harming local interests by disturbing the day-to-day fabric of coexistence. Odeh likened that awakening to the moment when Malcolm X rejected a white woman's pleas to join the Black cause, dismissing her as a "white devil," and later regretted it. Odeh's political journey led him to a deeper understanding of his sense of place and belonging in his homeland. "I didn't come to Israel. Israel came to me," he said. "I was here before '48. I am very secure in my national identity." That security led him to appreciate how multiculturalism could enrich a society and a country. "I choose it," he insisted. "I want it."

Odeh's guiding principle was a dual struggle for peace and equality, born out of what he called a "100 percent joint interest" shared by Israel's Jewish majority and Arab minority; equality because social justice was a prerequisite for stability, and peace because the Arab citizens were not going anywhere. Palestinian Israelis repeatedly stated in surveys that they would rather remain as citizens of Israel than become part of any putative independent Palestinian state across the borders, and the establishment of a Palestinian state alongside Israel was "the only realistic solution," according to Odeh. Though young progressives were coming to favor the idea of a single, binational state with equal rights for all between the Jordan River and the Mediterranean Sea, the GDP per capita in the Palestinian territories was about a tenth of Israel's, and the Arab Israeli mainstream preferred Israeli democracy, for all its flaws, over the arbitrary rule of the Palestinian Authority or Hamas.

If he sounded naïve to some Jews, his moderate message, relative youth, and articulateness in both Arabic and Hebrew energized the Arab electorate and attracted some more left-wing Jewish voters. Emboldened, the Joint List began to take a more active role. After the September 2019 election, its Knesset members, other than the Balad representatives, took the extraordinary step of openly endorsing a former army chief, Benny Gantz, for the job of prime minister in an effort to oust Netanyahu. Nevertheless, when Gantz had the chance to form a minority government with the outside support of the Joint List, that prospect was foiled by two defectors from his centrist Blue and White party whose votes were critical for obtaining a majority.

As comfortable quoting Jabotinsky, modern Hebrew poets, and verses from the book of Psalms as he was quoting Martin Luther King Jr., Odeh seemed to lay as much importance on reaching out to Jewish Israelis as to his mostly Arab constituency. It was a high-wire act. He was bitterly criticized for boycotting the 2016 funeral of Shimon Peres, the peacemaker who was also the father of Israel's nuclear weapons program, though Mahmoud Abbas, president of the Palestinian Authority, attended. Four years later he was being praised for his humanity when he visited the mourning family of an Israeli Jew, Michael Ben Zikri, from the southern port city of Ashdod, who had drowned while saving a Bedouin woman and three Bedouin children who were about to be dragged into the depths in a dangerous lagoon.

Odeh was walking an equally precarious tightrope across the fault lines of Arab society, given the internal divisions among the moderates, the more strident nationalists, and the Islamic conservatives. When Julia Zaher, the owner of Al Arz tahini factory in Nazareth, the "capital" of Arab Israel in the Galilee, decided to donate some profits to an Arabic hotline for gay youths, conservative Arabs called for a boycott of the product. Arab shopkeepers launched a social media campaign, posting video clips of themselves taking tubs of Al Arz tahini off their shelves and throwing them into the garbage, and denouncing aid for "perverts." Arab and Jewish liberals urged supporters to go out and buy the sesame paste. Israel's gay Palestinians had collectively and courageously been tiptoeing out of the closet. Weeks before the tahini war thousands had attended the funeral of an openly gay, internationally acclaimed dancer, Ayman Safia, a Palestinian from northern Israel, who had drowned while swimming in the Mediterranean. His family held a secular burial ceremony after Muslim clerics reportedly refused to officiate. Aida Touma-Suleiman, a Hadash lawmaker and longtime women's rights activist, gave her full support to Al Arz, praising Zaher on Twitter "for making a clear statement to our public: that LGBT rights are human rights." But Odeh was caught between his principles and his political instincts. He issued a mealy-mouthed response on Facebook, condemning the boycott of Al Arz without voicing any explicit support for the gay community. Muhammad Zoabi, a gay Arab activist, told Odeh to choose whose side he was on. In an article on *Ynet*, a popular Hebrew news site, Zoabi wrote, "Is it really so hard for the person who offers himself as an alternative, for democracy and equality, to say that there is no democracy and equality without equality for the LGBT community?"

After the Joint List won its fifteen seats in the Knesset in September 2020, the question was where to go from there. Deep change, Odeh said, required a political leap into a broader partnership with what remained of the Jewish left. The Zionist Israeli left would never win a majority and form a government again unless it joined forces with Arab parties. But Arab society was as splintered within as the country was as a whole. By the election of 2021, the conservative Islamic party, Raam, had split off from the Joint List, in part over the other Arab parties' refusal to vote down bills dealing with LGBT rights, and was running under its own steam. And defying all expectations, it was not the bridge-building Odeh, but Raam's Mansour Abbas, a jovial dentist from Maghar, a mixed Galilean town with a Druze majority and Christian and Muslim minorities, who crossed the political Rubicon. Capitalizing on the electoral deadlock after three inconclusive ballots had failed to produce a government, he indicated that he would be willing to go with either the pro-Netanyahu or the anti-Netanyahu bloc, depending on who could offer the most for the Arab minority, thus displaying a keen talent for Israeli coalition haggling and becoming the Jewish state's most unlikely kingmaker.

A week after garnering four seats in the March 2021 election, Abbas presided over what many would describe as a historic moment in Israeli politics and society. He made a speech, in Hebrew, aired live by the main television channels, riveting the nation as if he were the new prime minister. Flanked by the green flags of the Islamic movement, Abbas spoke of Jewish-Arab coexistence, security, and the desire for integration and brotherhood, steering clear of any mention of the occupation, the Arab citizens' Palestinian identity, discriminatory laws, or anything else that could be considered discordant to Jewish ears. He also quoted a Quranic verse about a shared life in the Holy Land.

It was enough to charm those in the Netanyahu camp who had previously vilified Abbas and the other Arab politicians as supporters of terrorism. Sensing a possible lifeline, Netanyahu's ultra-Orthodox allies also appeared to find more common cause with the socially conservative Raam than with the Zionist, secularist leftists of the Meretz party. In the end, Netanyahu's alliance with the far-right religious Zionists foiled his chances of forming a majority coalition as they ruled out sitting in a government with Raam or even one dependent on the outside support of Raam. Instead, Abbas helped crown Naftali Bennett, the more malleable rightist leader who had leveraged himself into the top spot of the anti-Netanyahu bloc. Raam became the first independent Arab party to participate in an Israeli governing coalition, and Abbas made possible what would become the most diverse, if short-lived, government in Israeli history. Breaking a political taboo, Abbas accepted the reality of Israel as a Jewish state and rejected the assertions of apartheid, saying he would not describe it that way. Nick-named the "kumbaya coalition" by some for its message of national unity and inclusion, the Bennett government imploded after a year, strained by policy issues from the inside and under relentless outside pressure from the Netanyahu camp. But Raam had redefined the politi-cal map, giving an Arab party a stake in national decision-making.

Along with canceling or amending the Kaminitz Law and allocating far more resources to the Arab public, the most urgent item topping the Arab political agenda was the need to address the plague of crime and gun violence in Arab towns and mixed cities all over the country. The problem had been creeping up for years and had burst onto the national agenda in a blaze of bloodletting and murder, much of the violence the result of Mafia-like Arab criminal gangs running protec-tion rackets and brutally enforcing debt collection after lending money on the gray market. Surveys showed that a majority of Arab citizens felt unsafe in their own neighborhoods. Aided greatly by government neglect, the internecine killings had spiraled from a reported fifty-eight in 2013 to about a hundred in 2020 and accounted for about 70 percent of all homicides in the country. Many Arabs blamed the Israeli police, accusing them of turning a blind eye and saying it suited the govern-ment to let the Arabs kill each other. When the police did intervene, the results could be tragic. While they ambushed armed suspects in the northern Arab city of Tamra one night in February 2021, an inno-cent nursing student, Ahmad Hijazi, was killed in the crossfire when he ran out of a friend's house, having heard calls for help from one of the injured gunmen. Hijazi's friend's brother, Muhammad Armoush, a doctor, had rushed out after him and been shot in the foot, but he recovered. Residents and Arab leaders excoriated the police for open-ing fire in the middle of a residential area.

Months later, sitting at dusk on the Armoush family's porch, over-looking the scene of the shootout, Muhammad recalled the night of violence. Two nights earlier, masked gunmen had fired at the house across the road and warned the owner they would be back two days later to collect money. When they returned, armed with at least one M16 assault rifle and other firearms, a police SWAT team was waiting in ambush. One of the gunmen was killed. Another was severely wounded and arrested. A third escaped. Everybody knew who he was. Armoush said all three were from the neighborhood and the fugitive was a distant relative. But everyone claimed ignorance, stating that the gunman had been masked. Months later he was still on the loose.

Nowhere was safe. Jaffa, the ancient, once-bustling port known in Arabic as the Bride of the Sea, or the Bride of Palestine, was now a mixed Arab-Jewish locality that was still gritty in parts, while undergoing rapid gentrification, attracting Jewish and Palestinian artists, gays, and bohemians. Historic buildings had been converted into luxury boutique hotels, art galleries, and restaurants. On the day I met Odeh, a small group of well-built men, black T-shirts stretched tight across their bulky chests, stood vigil in the afternoon on the sidewalk outside the Abu Seif family compound on Jaffa's Rabbi Rubinstein Street, a nondescript residential street pocked with trees and bursts of bougainvillea a few blocks in from the seashore. There was a mourning tent for men across the street. The women mourned indoors. A few days earlier, in broad daylight, an Arab gunman on a motorcycle had fatally shot a twenty-year-old man and critically wounded a twelve-year-old boy from the Abu Seif family. The boy was still in the hospital. Asked if they knew who was behind the hit, the men, sullen and laconic, replied with impatient tut-tuts, warding off any further questions. These were just the latest victims in a long-running feud that, a year earlier, had cost the life of Sabria Abu Saif, a matriarch of the family, aged around seventy, who was shot to death on Machrozet Street, on the other side of the family compound. A year before that, five-year-old Walid Abu Saif was critically wounded by bullets that had apparently missed their mark.

Most of the deaths resulted from feuds involving the criminal underworld or petty disputes over land, money, or a perceived insult. A lack of building permits and space for new housing in cramped Arab cities and towns led to violent land disputes, sometimes over a parking spot. Along with the lack of formal permits and land registration, the traditional, cash-based economy that persisted in Arab society and the scarcity of Israeli bank branches in Arab localities precluded normal banking, including obtaining mortgages or loans, making the Arab population vulnerable to loan sharks and extortion. Government money allocated to the local municipal authorities ended up in the

pockets of the gangs. Israel's Arabs were also becoming more prosperous and opening up small businesses, and the criminals went where
the money was. After the police wiped out most of the major Jewish
crime families in the mid-2010s, Arab criminal networks stepped in to
fill the vacuum, with a ready supply of poorly educated, aimless Arab
youths looking for easy money ready to serve as their foot soldiers.
And in another sign of lawlessness, combined with the traditional conservatism of many parts of Arab society, women were being murdered
in so-called honor killings for as little as speaking to a male on the
phone.

The Arab leadership was powerless and begged the government and
the police to take on the organized gangs. In an impassioned Knesset speech in late 2020, Odeh was on the verge of tears as he pleaded
for a government plan for the collection of illegal weapons, 70 percent of which he said came from the military. Arab elders opined that
the young generation no longer took any notice of their parents or
respected their authority. Divorces were up. Traditional family structures were breaking down. Petty arguments quickly turned into a
deadly settling of scores because weapons were apparently as easy to
come by as a new pair of sneakers. Aside from those stolen from the
IDF, Israel's state comptroller identified three other sources: smuggled
weapons that come across the border from Jordan, improvised weapons manufactured on the West Bank, and airsoft pellet guns that could
be ordered from Amazon and adapted to fire real bullets. Nobody
knew how many guns were out there. Estimates ranged from tens of
thousands up to hundreds of thousands. The entire Arab population of
Israel numbered less than two million.

Bereaved Arab mothers held heartbreaking protests and marched
from Haifa to Jerusalem demanding an end to the bloodletting. One
of them, Watfa Jabali, from Taibeh, in central Israel, had lost a son to
violence. Saad Jabali, twenty-six, the father of a baby girl, was shot to
death in broad daylight one day in November 2018 while he worked
in the family's grocery store. Watfa saw it happening in real time on
CCTV while she was upstairs in the family's apartment. We met three
years later in her small store across the road where she sold fabrics and
Palestinian embroidery and did upholstery. Warm and strong, she was
determined to keep speaking out and protesting, she said, not because

she believed it would make any difference, but for her own psychological well-being and to honor her son, whom she described as always active.

The house had been shot at twice before, she said, but the police had not acted. After her son's fatal shooting, she said she knocked on every door in the search for justice. Four and a half months after the murder, the gunman and his accomplice, a minor, were arrested. Jabali knew the gunman. She said he was one of the nine children of a troublesome family who had rented the house next to theirs, and who had eventually been kicked out by the landlord. Jabali said her family's "mistake" was to have rented the apartment for themselves a few months later. The former neighbors accused the Jabalis of having kicked them out. "They said we were the settlers who took their house," Watfa Jabali said. By her account, the killer was one of the sons who came back to exact revenge.

Like many other Arab citizens, Jabali said it was inconceivable that the state, which boasted the most sophisticated intelligence tools in the Middle East, and could steal the Iranian nuclear archives from a warehouse in Tehran, was unable to locate a few domestic criminals. Arab politicians noted that the police had been very effective at rounding up hundreds of Arab suspects in the days after the May 2021 outburst of intercommunal Arab-Jewish mob violence and had even managed to collect footage from security cameras, something that seemed to elude the officers investigating internecine Arab murders. Many also noted how the police and security forces had managed to round up the six escaped Palestinian prisoners within a week, four of them in Arab areas of northern Israel and even the two who had made it to the West Bank city of Jenin.

The police, for their part, complained that their investigations were hampered by codes of silence and fear of revenge in the Arab sector. Terrified of retribution, witnesses rarely came forward with information. Crime scenes and camera footage were tampered with. Whether a result of police neglect or the Arab community's lack of trust and cooperation, out of more than 3,300 shootings in Arab communities in 2019, only 5 percent resulted in charges and less than a quarter of the murders were ever solved.

But the intercommunal violence of May 2021 at least served as a wake-up call. The authorities realized what the implications would be if Arab citizens turned their illegal weapons on the Jewish public. Within his first hundred days, Prime Minister Bennett announced that eradicating Arab gun violence was a national priority. After another bloody episode in Taibeh in September 2021, when a gunman feasting at a pre-wedding henna party suddenly sprayed a group of guests with bullets, killing one and injuring five more, Omer Bar-Lev, Israel's minister of public security, who was tasked with overseeing the police, posted an impassioned thread on Twitter in which he decried what he said had been "the prevailing assumption that as long as they are killing each other, that's their problem." But governments had made promises before and officials said that implementing the plan and addressing the root causes of the violence would take years.

The pre-wedding killing had been one of at least sixteen homicides in Israel's Arab localities that month and one of nearly a hundred already that year. The groom, the killer, and the victim, all in their twenties, had grown up together in the same part of town. The gunman, who was unmasked during the attack, which was meant to avenge his own injury in a shooting months earlier, was soon arrested, but the father of the groom assumed there would be little evidence to convict him. Sitting in the family's dim reception room the day after the funeral and a joyless wedding, he said there would be no witnesses because "some people walk around with guns and some people walk around with fear." Public outrage reached a new peak months later when stray bullets from criminals hit a three-year-old boy, Ammar Hujayrat, in the neck, killing him as he played with his young cousins in his village's new playground.

For many Arab professionals and intellectuals, there was no refuge. Unable and unwilling to blend into the Israeli mainstream and abandon their collective Palestinian aspirations, they also felt trapped and even threatened by the conservatism, anarchy, and sense of abandonment prevailing in Arab society. Some said they felt more at home when they were abroad and talked about leaving the country. Others said the time had come for civil disobedience.

The most neglected, poorest, and weakest group in Israel, as well as one of the fastest growing, was the Bedouin community, which numbered more than 200,000 people and made up about a third of the population of the Negev. An ancient culture, these semi-nomads had subsisted in the harsh desert environment for thousands of years, raising livestock, wandering in search of pastures, and pitching tents under the stars. But over the past half century, under Israeli rule, Bedouin society had undergone a dizzying process of modernization. The erection of modern borders, the imposition of military rule in the early years of the state, and the encroachment of economic and technological change in the region had put an end to the traditional migrations when the Bedouin tribespeople would wander across the southern Negev desert and the Sinai Peninsula for weeks on camelback, trying their luck at planting grains in the winter and returning months later for the harvest.

Daham Al Atawneh, a retired publisher who was born in the Negev in 1945, and who had spent years working for the BBC in London before returning to his village of Houra, told me that the men of his tribe only began to swap their traditional robes for shirts and pants after military rule was lifted in the 1960s and as the Bedouin came more into contact with other Israelis. Fifty years later the rhythms of a simple desert life that had survived almost unchanged for thousands of years had all but vanished. The concept of distance and remoteness changed with the advent of the transistor radio, then cars, then mobile phones.

Though the old culture remained a source of pride for many Bedouin in Israel, the social structures were fast breaking down. The Israeli government worked to corral the Bedouin into purpose-built urban centers that nevertheless lacked adequate infrastructure, arguing that the state could not provide basic services to every encampment dotted across the wilderness, including formal education, which the younger Bedouin came to value. Bedouin complained that the Israelis exploited their lack of formal land deeds: Having been a largely illiterate society with an oral tradition of poetry and one of justice for settling disputes, many lost their ancestral lands overnight.

By the 2000s, about half the community had moved into unlovely urban centers at the government's urging. The other half lived in dozens of villages and encampments scattered across the southern desert, tin-roofed shanty towns unrecognized by the Israeli authorities that were not even hooked up to the national electricity grid. Locked in a protracted land dispute with the central government, many lived under the constant threat of demolition orders.

A society within a society within a society in flux, Bedouin families were typically large and some still practiced polygamy, bearing
multiple offspring and receiving child support from the state. With
the breakdown of old social structures, the towns had become foci
of lawlessness and poverty, with the worst educational levels and life
expectancy in the country. The largest Bedouin urban center, Rahat, a
mostly drab, low-rise town of 70,000, was often the scene of shootouts
and considered a dangerous no-go zone by many outsiders. So I was
intrigued when I saw an advertisement in a Hebrew newspaper inviting Israelis to come on a "Ramadan Nights" excursion to Rahat. Four
busloads of curious Jewish tourists turned up. Rahat's mayor, Talal
al-Krenawi, welcomed them and said he was opening up the town in
an effort to boost its image and economy. The tour included stops at the
un-picturesque market, a *debka* performance by a youth troupe in the
community center, a sweet-making workshop, and home hospitality,
with the town's families hosting *iftar* meals to break the fast at sunset,
seating the guests at long tables in their courtyards. Rahat was hardly
likely to become a tourist destination, but it was far more welcoming
than one might have thought. For the group I joined, the highlight
was our irreverent local tour guide, Laila al-Huzayel, a feisty mother
of five, who was eager to divulge the local gossip between stops along
the way, to the obvious amusement of the bus driver—including about
her own rocky marriage to a local, abusive good-for-nothing, by her
account. Married off at sixteen, she had later gone to get an education.
Dressed in tight jeans and with long, painted nails, she declared herself to be secular but proud of her Muslim heritage. Mocking the local
men's predilection for polygamy, she said that the Prophet Muhammad
had good social reasons for taking four wives, referring to the ancient
system of taking care of war widows. "Our men—they don't pray, they
don't fast, but they marry four wives," she blurted out.

Economic integration did not necessarily lead to social integration
or acceptance—not for the Bedouin and not for the Arabic-speaking
fifth of the population in general. In some Jewish quarters, discrimination and racism were considered normal. In the northern, predominantly Jewish town of Afula, the right-wing base was determined to
preserve its "non-mixed" character. In the summer of 2019, the mayor
and council members joined far-right extremists from Lehava, a hard-

core, racist, anti-assimilationist group, to protest the sale of an apartment to an Arab family. When Lucy Aharish, a high-profile television personality who had grown up in an Arab Muslim family in the largely Jewish city of Beersheba, married Tzahi Halevi, a prominent Jewish actor who starred in the Netflix series *Fauda,* some right-wing politicians publicly denounced the union. Personal success was not any guarantee against ugly behavior. Ishmael Khaldi, a Bedouin from northern Israel, had spent part of his childhood tending sheep then went on to graduate from the cadet course at the Israeli Ministry of Foreign Affairs and become a diplomat. Assigned to the Israeli embassy in London, he had represented Israel and was noted for his battles against the pro-Palestinian international boycott movement. Yet back in Jerusalem, he made the newspapers after he was pinned to the ground by irate guards at the Central Bus Station. They said he had provoked them by filming them on his phone after he was asked to undergo a security check. The incident occurred three weeks after the killing of George Floyd by police in Minneapolis, prompting the "I can't breathe" protests. In a complaint to the police, Khaldi said the officers had knelt on his back and neck. "I screamed that I was choking and that I couldn't breathe," he said. In his case there was a happy ending. His superiors backed him up and soon after the incident Khaldi was appointed Israel's first-ever Bedouin ambassador and posted to Eritrea.

Trying to make sense of the outburst of ethnic violence in May 2021, one veteran Arab Israeli analyst and activist promoting equality and a shared society, Mohammad Darawshe, explained the dichotomy of acceptance and repudiation this way: "From nine to five we know how to live with each other, and to form partnerships," he told me. "But after five we go back to our own dens where identity components take control, even within mixed apartment blocks."

Maryam Abu Shakra was dying of cancer. She had not been told that her days were numbered, but she probably sensed it. As her elderly friends dropped by, one after the other, to tacitly bid her farewell, one of her grown sons, Said, began photographing and filming their reminiscences and documenting the pieces of her story before she took it to the grave. It was the beginning of what would turn into an ambitious project to preserve the memory of Palestinian life in the area before and after the *Nakba*.

Maryam was married at twelve to Abed, when the British were still ruling Palestine, and lived in Al Lajoun, a northern Palestinian village of more than 1,000 souls in the Jezreel Valley, by the ancient site of Megiddo, or as it was known in Greek, Armageddon. Ancient battles had been fought there and a more recent one, though the Final Battle of the End of Days was yet to come. Under the original UN partition plan rejected by the Arab nations, Al Lajoun, with its boys' school, white stone mosque, fields, and orchards, was supposed to remain part of the planned Arab state. But in April 1948, as the Haganah forces approached, then conquered the village, quashing the resistance, the residents fled their homes. Maryam, about sixteen at the time, was in the middle of cooking and had covered the food to keep it warm, believing they would soon be back. Abed, a truck driver, stole back into the village once to retrieve the food. A couple of days later he came back again, hoping to fetch more of their belongings, but by then the house had been blown up along with everything inside—a measure taken by the Palmach units to ensure that the villagers would not return. Some of them left for Jordan and Syria; one of Said's grandfathers died in Syria at the age of 110. But like most of the residents of Al Lajoun, the Abu Shakras joined the villagers who became "internally displaced" and moved to Umm al-Fahem, an Arab town just fifteen minutes' drive away on today's roads. Bordering the northern flank of the West Bank, Umm al-Fahem was in the hands of the Arab forces at the end of the 1948 war, but it ended up under Israel's control after the 1949 armistice negotiations with Jordan. Maryam bore eight children, one of whom died very young. After Abed's truck overturned, leaving him bankrupt, he went to work as a forest keeper for the Jewish National Fund, the Zionist quasi-governmental organization founded in 1901 to purchase and reclaim land for Jewish settlement, partly through a vast afforestation project that marked out the borders, blocked the spread of Arab towns, and redeemed and greened what was seen as a desolate land. Abed died first, at sixty-two. Maryam lived into her late seventies and died around 2010.

Said Abu Shakra was born in 1956, eight years after the establishment of the state, and he described himself as "second generation" in terms of the *Nakba*. Like the Holocaust survivors, he said, many of the first generation kept their trauma to themselves and only began telling their stories as they grew old. Abu Shakra, the director of a groundbreaking art gallery in Umm al-Fahem, embarked on a mission to gather the memories from a generation that was dying out.

The gallery, exhibiting Palestinian and Israeli art, was first established in 1996 in a modest, four-story building with little aesthetic value from the outside, but with panoramic views across the town. It was a somewhat incongruous institution in the landscape of Umm al-Fahem, better known for its radical politics as the home of the northern, more militant branch of the Islamic Movement in Israel, which, unlike Mansour Abbas's so-called southern branch, did not participate in Israel's general elections. Umm al-Fahem was now a populous Arab city of more than 50,000 souls and was the stronghold of Sheikh Raed Salah, the firebrand leader of the northern branch and a former mayor of the town. A cousin of Said, he had been famous for his provocative "Al Aqsa is in Danger" campaigns, holding mass rallies in the local soccer stadium to protest what he said were Israeli plans to cement Jewish control over the contested holy site in Jerusalem known to Jews as the Temple Mount and Muslims as the Noble Sanctuary. Sheikh Raed, as he was popularly known, had been in and out of prison for offenses connected to inciting violence, and the northern branch of the Islamic Movement was eventually outlawed by the Israeli authorities.

Most Israeli Jews still considered Umm al-Fahem to be hostile territory and dangerous. One once asked me if I went there armed, or with a bodyguard. In recent years, though, the city had undergone a partial makeover. A vast new shopping mall dominated the entrance to the city from Route 65, a junction that had seen deadly riots in 2000, its outer wall advertising all the leading Israeli retail brands. The main road winding up to the old center was lined with shiny new storefronts. A Pierre Cardin Kids shop was opening up, a toy store featured a Disney *Frozen II*–themed window display, and there was no shortage of espresso bars.

Said Abu Shakra was from a family of artists whose work was on permanent display in the gallery. A brother, Walid Abu Shakra, a renowned artist and a Sufi sheikh, had recently died in London. Said's late cousin, Asim Abu Shakra, who was a brother of Sheikh Raed, was known for his self-portraits and for his works featuring a recurrent motif—the sabra, the prickly pear cactus, which he depicted sometimes in the wild and sometimes as a domestic potted plant. He had moved to Tel Aviv to study art in the early 1980s, and his work was embraced early on as part of the canon of Israeli art and was exhibited in the Israel Museum in Jerusalem. The museum archive described his use of the sabra as a reappropriation of the symbol adopted by native-born Jews of the Land of Israel, a "loaded image" that was both collective and individual. The sabra motif, according to one expert, blended the "tragic displacement of the Palestinians from their lands and villages resulting from Israel's War of Independence in 1948 and the personal tragedy that struck the artist when he was diagnosed with the cancer that killed him." He died at just twenty-nine in 1990.

As well as preserving the family's artistic heritage, the gallery tried to capture whatever traces were left of the Palestinian history in the land. Since it also exhibited the work of contemporary Jewish artists and hosted Jewish groups for tours and lectures, it had become a potent symbol of Arab-Jewish coexistence. One exhibit on display in 2020 featured the work of Elisheva Frankfort-Smith, a photographer who moved to the British Mandate of Palestine from the Netherlands in 1936 and spent many years in Kibbutz Maagan Michael on the Carmel coast. Her haunting works revisited the remnants of seven abandoned and destroyed Palestinian villages, including Al Lajoun, the Abu Shakras' ancestral village. One image was of olive trees twisted by age and surrounded by cacti, another of an old wall scrawled with graffiti. The name of the village, Al Lajoun, appeared there along with the first words of an iconic poem by Mahmoud Darwish, the Palestinian national poet of exile: "On this land, this is what makes life worth living."

The upper floor of the gallery had become the hub of a growing historical archive. Racing against time after his mother's passing, Said Abu Shakra had filmed six hundred interviews with elders of Umm al-Fahem and the surrounding villages that zigzagged across Route 65 and Wadi Ara, a valley that formed the backbone of eastern Israel. He also collected old photographs and was building what he described as the first publicly available oral and visual archive of the Palestinian *Nakba* generation in Israel. He had trained a team to gather more testimonies and digitize, scan, and catalog the materials. He realized he had started late. Flicking through images of the proud but gnarled faces and withering figures of elderly Palestinian women and men dressed in traditional robes, embroidered thobes, or dresses, and headdresses, he said most of the subjects had since died. "I managed to salvage a part," he said. "Not enough, but it's better than nothing." There were black-and-white images of destroyed villages and stone ruins; of the Israeli forces entering Umm al-Fahem for the first time as residents came out onto the rooftops and balconies and stood with their arms folded, as instructed; of an Israeli flag raised on a hilltop; of village notables shaking hands with the military governor; of a dirt track traveled by camel that is now Route 65, the highway plied by cars speeding through Wadi Ara. Said Abu Shakra had published two valuable books of history, testimonies, and images with the help of a Palestinian historian and a Jewish Israeli photographer and curator.

Sitting at a large wooden table in his office surrounded by piles of documents, books, and artifacts in glass display cases, Said remarked that everything had changed, not only the politics and the socio-economics, but the whole fabric and culture of Arab society in Israel. If the children once served the family, he said, the attention was now all focused on the child. The individual mattered more than the home. The Muslim Arab birth rate had dropped significantly. In the 1960s Israel's Muslims averaged about nine children per family, though the Christian birth rate was always lower. Half a century later, in 2018, the Jewish fertility rate overtook the overall Arab fertility rate for the first time in Israel, with Jewish women averaging 3.05 children and Arab women averaging 3.04. The rising cost of living as well as aspirations of upward mobility led more Arab women to get college degrees and go to work. Arab women had fewer options to work in manual labor than men, experts said, meaning that more women went into higher education. Their education and earning power were now counted as assets by prospective husbands, while social media and online dating sites were replacing the traditional practice of parental matchmaking. The gender discrepancy in levels of education was said to be causing problems in many marriages. But divorced Arab women no longer slinked off to live out their days in their parents' homes, Abu Shakra said, and often they got remarried.

The social transformation was evident in Abu Shakra's own family. His wife, Siham, had fought to become the first female principal of a school in Umm al-Fahem. Teaching was now predominantly a women's profession in Arab society. The couple's five grown children were scattered among Germany, Canada, and Rehovot, a predominantly Jewish city in central Israel. One daughter was a doctor, another a therapist.

And yet despite the progress, for many Arab Israelis, their future in the country felt unassured. Israeli nationalists had increasingly promoted the idea of ceding the towns of the Triangle, including Umm al-Fahem, under any future partition deal with the Palestinians. The idea was to exchange them for the West Bank Jewish settlement blocs in a bald-faced bid to bolster Israel's Jewish majority. The proposal had been included as an option in the dreaded Trump plan, which had been closely coordinated with Israeli leaders. Under the military regime, between 1948 and 1966, the mayor of Umm al-Fahem had pledged loyalty to Israel in return for citizenship for the town's inhabitants. The contract, Abu Shakra said, was based on the principle of equality for all citizens described in Israel's Declaration of Independence. Seventy years later, Israel was more prosperous and secure than it might have imagined, but he felt that the fundamental basis for the relationship was again in question.

"They cannot tell us on the one hand that you have to be loyal to Israel, and on the other, that you are here on probation, and one day you won't be here," Abu Shakra said. The Nation State Law had dealt a particular blow, he said, to people in his camp who had long advocated dialogue and resisted those who rejected Israel. "What was so bad before?" he asked in exasperation. "They just came to say you are not one of the tribe. That the Jews are more important and will get more."

Caught right in the middle of the Israeli-Palestinian conflict, he said he faced pressure from the pro-Palestinian, anti-Israel Boycott, Divestment and Sanctions movement because the gallery received Israeli government funding. He said he had explained to his critics that he paid taxes in Israel and was entitled to some rights and benefits, to no avail. He had also been criticized for translating his books on Palestinian history into Hebrew. "What's the harm in a Jew knowing my history?" he asked, defiantly. "It strengthens my presence here." To qualify for Arab funding, he said, "you have to prove you are a radical Palestinian. But I am part of the state!" Therein lay a truism that transcended any funding shortfall: Despite it all, the Arab minority in Israel was by now much closer to the Jewish majority in Israel than to any Arab country. Abu Shakra had still not lost hope, in the people if not in the leadership. He had a business to run, and new summer exhibits to show of Jewish and Arab artists. Four weeks after the deadly flash of Jewish-Arab violence that rocked Israel in May 2021, he sent out a WhatsApp message inviting the patrons of his gallery to a festive reopening. "Shalom, my dear people," he wrote in Hebrew. "We are returning to routine life and activities that express the spirit of togetherness and partnership."

Abu Shakra said he often went walking around the area where Al Lajoun had stood. In 1949, a year after his parents fled the village, Kibbutz Megiddo was established on its lands. Heading north from Umm al-Fahem, the slopes above the smooth section of Route 65 were lined with a patchwork of old olive orchards and pine forests planted by the Jewish National Fund. Israel's Jews tended to view the landscape differently from Israel's Arabs, blinkering themselves from the remnants of the destroyed Palestinian villages. There was nothing to be done. One people could not have sustained their ownership or sovereignty in this land without defeating the other. Most Jews saw no point in disturbing that skeleton in the national closet. The ruins of Al Lajoun were slowly being overtaken by foliage. Aging sabra bushes that once marked the village land boundaries continued to branch out in the shade of a planted pine forest. An attempt by Palestinians to reclaim the land was rejected by Israel's Supreme Court in 2010 on the grounds that the afforestation constituted acquisition under Israel's land laws. At the entrance to Kibbutz Megiddo, old farm implements were placed like sculptures, turning Zionist pioneering into public art. Abu Shakra's lifelong dream was to turn his gallery into a full-fledged museum of Palestinian art and culture. Sifting through his archive of fading black-and-white images, he recalled the old Zionist adage of "for a people without a land, a land without people." "There was a people here," he said. "We have the photos."

# SEVEN

# HAREDI AND ISRAELI:
# HAVING IT ALL

W HEN THE TALMUDIC SAGES gathered in ancient times for their
all-night seder in Bnei Brak to recount the Passover miracle
for all the generations of the Children of Israel, they probably weren't
thinking of Yanki Farber. A fast-talking, black-velvet-kippa-wearing
native of Bnei Brak, a suburb of Tel Aviv, in the modern era, Farber,
forty, was the foreign correspondent of *Behadrei Haredim,* a leading
ultra-Orthodox Hebrew digital news site. Its name, which roughly
translates as "inside Haredi chambers," promised to take the reader into
the inner sanctums of the Haredi world—"Haredi" being the Hebrew
term for the ultra-Orthodox, referring to those stringently observant
Jews who fear, or tremble, before God. *Behadrei*'s newsroom was situated in a faux-chic gray and glass building abutting a grimy gas station
on the industrial edge of the city, which bordered the eastern neighborhoods of Tel Aviv. Having just arrived for his night shift, Farber fired a
volley of voice messages into his smartphone, shooting instructions to
an unseen underling.

One of fifteen siblings and a father of four, married to Clara, a
homemaker, Farber had lived his entire life in this crowded town of
more than 200,000 mostly Haredi residents, and the undisputed capital of ultra-Orthodoxy in Israel. The title of foreign correspondent was

a bit wishful. His dispatches, including items from the Arab world with any hint of a Jewish angle or interest, were largely plucked from the cybersphere. Somewhat unorthodoxly, he subscribed to *The New York Times, The Washington Post,* and the British *Daily Mail,* the latter, he said, being the best at dishing up the dirt. His Twitter banner at the time read "Gevalt," a Yiddish cry of alarm and protest that was often used during panicked political campaigns to rally voters during elections and translated as "Oy vey," but with a weightier sense of doom.

We met during the first wave of the coronavirus pandemic, at the peak of fear. The infection was raging through Israel's ultra-Orthodox community, fueled by the typically crowded living conditions as large families crammed into small, airless apartments and by the Haredi way of life that revolved around communal prayers and gatherings, coupled with a misplaced faith in some rabbis who put the community's spiritual welfare above physical well-being. The first year of the plague promised to be a watershed for the ultra-Orthodox and their place in Israeli society, testing their willingness to conform, defer to central government, and integrate against the desire for isolationism and autonomy, and pitting life in the shtetl against allegiance to the country.

The rapidly expanding Haredi population posed one of the greatest internal challenges to modern Israel. Those who trembled before God had little ingrained respect for the state, many being ambivalent about Jewish sovereignty preceding the arrival of the Messiah, or even rabidly anti-Zionist. By the early 2020s, the Haredi sector made up at least 12 percent of the general population, and 16 percent of draft-age Israelis, though most *Haredim* shunned military service. Half the men chose full-time Torah study over formal work, living off government stipends and stirring the resentment of taxpaying Israelis. With Arab birth rates dropping, Israeli economists and demographers increasingly focused on the Haredi effect while projections suggested that within a few decades, between the *Haredim* and the Arabs of 1948, more than half of all Israelis would not be Zionists.

At the same time, the Haredi politicians and rabbis had no qualms about exploiting their voting power and the leverage that coalition politics gave them in affairs of religion and state. Netanyahu had turned the Haredi parties into what he called his "natural partners," and they repaid him with loyalty, sticking with him to the end in coalition negotiations even at the price of following him into the opposition. But the fragile one-year government of change led by Naftali Bennett and his centrist partner Yair Lapid was also reluctant to take any drastic anti-Haredi action, as they hoped to shore up or broaden their own shaky coalition with the addition of a Haredi party at some point. Israel's culture wars were coming to a head, but the nature of Israeli democracy seemed to preclude solutions for dealing with them.

For decades, the ultra-Orthodox had built their own walls of seclusion to keep at bay the influence and temptations of secular Zionism. But the ground was now quaking under Bnei Brak and other Haredi strongholds. The material world was slowly, relentlessly getting through. One Hasidic scion of the anti-Zionist Toldos Aharon sect, which was headquartered in Jerusalem's Mea Shearim, a hotbed of extremist Hasidic sects, explained the core of the Haredi conundrum to me this way: In the absence of the Messiah, the *Haredim* had never expected the secular Zionist state to survive over time. Similarly, the secular state builders had never counted on the tenacity of the ultra-Orthodox citizens, expecting them eventually to blend in and secularize. Seventy years on, both Israel and the *Haredim* had survived; even thrived. Israel had grown into a regional nuclear and cybernetic superpower. Yet the Messiah had still not materialized.

A mighty internal tug-of-war was underway as the *Haredim* increasingly became Israeli and the Israeli population became increasingly Haredi. The pandemic brought with it a sharp increase in Internet use, which chipped at the walls of the self-imposed ghettoes of the mind. Ultra-conservative rabbis railed against change, the zealous guardians of the flipside of the start-up nation. But unlike Amish people living in rural Ohio or Pennsylvania the *Haredim* mostly lived in the inner cities in the heart of Israel, or in populous urban West Bank settlements just over the 1967 lines, ready to be incorporated into Israel in any territorial agreement with the Palestinians. Bnei Brak itself abutted the well-heeled, liberal Tel Aviv suburb of Ramat Gan, and the desire for seclusion had its limits. When, at the height of the pandemic, the mayor of Ramat Gan erected makeshift fences in an effort to keep out the Haredi neighbors, the ultra-Orthodox mayor of Bnei Brak accused his counterpart next door of erecting a ghetto in a move reminiscent of the darkest times in Jewish history.

The *Haredim* were far from monolithic; there were Haredi groups who tried to build bridges and others intent on burning them. Farber was a member of one of the largest, the "Lithuanian" branch of ultra-Orthodoxy, the black Borsalino-hatted school generally viewed as the more dour and intellectually rigid, with a tradition that prized full-time Talmudic study and scholarship above all else for the men, while the women went to work. The main opposing Hasidic branch was generally more spiritually and emotionally inspired. Its *rebbes* and disciples donned the theatrical silk coats and fur *shtreimels,* or hats, often associated with old Polish nobility on Sabbaths and holidays. But Hasidic men were encouraged to work and earn a living. The *Haredim* had always been splintered among a plethora of rabbinic courts and dynasties. Personal enmities and rival doctrines stretched back over centuries to the shtetls and grand yeshivas of central and eastern Europe. Some managed to reconstitute themselves after the Holocaust. Others were obliterated. Now largely divided between two main camps, the "Lithuanians" and the Hasidim, distinctions remained but the enmity had faded to the point where the "Lithuanian" party, Degel HaTorah, and the Hasidic Agudat Yisrael had joined forces and had run together in Israeli elections since the early 1990s as the United Torah Judaism alliance.

Despite his Lithuanian roots, Farber had been schooled in the Hasidic Satmar system, one of the strictest, anti-Zionist sects, which originated in Hungary. The Satmars utterly despised the state of Israel, viewing Jewish statehood as an ungodly abomination and a premature and arrogant escapade that should not have preceded, and might even have delayed, the arrival of the Messiah. "It was anti-anti," Farber said of his schooling in the sect, "so I went 'pro.'" In the rapidly expanding and ever-shifting ultra-Orthodox world, the conservative, yeshiva-bound Haredi masses who were less rabidly anti-Zionist but just wary and ambivalent called themselves the "mainstream." Farber had gone one step further and become what the mainstream referred to as a "blue shirt": code for a modern, working Haredi male who had opted out of full-time Torah study and ditched the sector's formal black-pants-and-white-shirt uniform in favor of the polo shirt—or as one more mainstream Haredi put it, the "Tommy Hilfiger" look. Farber's polo shirt was, in this instance, a faded light blue with a white collar and trimmings. Beardless and without any hint of sidelocks, he was sporting day-old stubble.

Unlike the vast majority of *Haredim* who voted for the ultra-Orthodox parties, as per their rabbis' instructions—and with an obedience that, to many, was the very essence of being a Haredi—Farber openly declared himself a Likud supporter, indicative of a new flexibility around the edges of the community and a desire to belong to the country rather than deny it after it had existed more than seventy years. Like some other Haredi journalists, he had become a kind of interpreter of the Haredi world to the Israeli mainstream and of the Israel that lay outside to the *Haredim*. He had just opened an additional political news site of his own, where he could post what he called his "less Haredi content." He advertised it as "uncensored" and "Israeli and Zionist," and pledged to provide "the stories they don't want you to hear."

The first Lithuanian Jews arrived in the Holy Land at the end of the eighteenth century as religious emissaries and spiritual pioneers. Most rabbinic courts, however, stayed behind in Europe and were decimated in the Holocaust. Some rabbis accompanied their flocks to the gas chambers. Others were spirited out of the inferno to the nascent state of Israel or to safe havens like America. Having escaped, they strove to fulfill the *mitzvah,* or Torah commandment, to be fruitful and multiply and they created a new creed around rebuilding the ranks of Torah scholarship and, with the intensity of avengers, replacing with large families the six million who had been wiped out by the Nazis.

The Zionist bargaining with the ultra-Orthodox predated the state. In June 1947, in order to persuade the ultra-Orthodox Agudat Yisrael party not to oppose its establishment, Ben-Gurion sent them a letter known as the "status quo" agreement in which the future prime minister of secular socialism ensured the place of religion in the new society. Among other things, he promised that Saturday, the Sabbath, would be the statutory day off for Jews, that religious law would govern all Jewish marriage and divorce, that only kosher food would be served in all official kitchens, such as that of the army, and that the Haredi educational institutions would be allowed to maintain their autonomy regarding what was to be taught. Clearly there would be no Darwinism. Nor, it turned out, would there be much of any other science or core curriculum that was taught in the regular state schools. Ben-Gurion also granted a deferment of military service for four hundred yeshiva students in a gesture to help rebuild the ranks of Torah scholarship that had been wiped out by the Holocaust and in a further attempt to buy quiet from the pre-state *Haredim* in the Holy Land, whose anti-Zionism would probably have in any case worked against turning them into good soldiers. But the status quo agreement was vague and broad enough to allow any number of permutations to creep into the delicate relationship between religion and state, and seven decades later the so-called Sabbath wars still flared up now and again over issues like public transportation and regulating commercial activity on Saturdays, occasionally leading to violent clashes with the police.

As the *Haredim* struggled with their own internal dialectic, they found little sympathy among the secular, traditional, and even modern Orthodox Israelis. Some taxpaying middle-class Israelis described the non-working Haredi men as parasites, and they were broadly viewed as a looming socioeconomic threat given their large families of seven children or more, the rabbis' shunning of secular education, the community's ever-expanding voting power, and the seemingly glacial pace of change.

The *Haredim* largely spoke Hebrew, though the more extreme considered it a holy tongue that should be reserved for prayer. In the *Talmud Torah* schools and young children's *cheders* of the independent Haredi education system, and in the alleyways of Mea Shearim, the lingua franca was often Yiddish. Math, science, and English were generally considered a waste of time for boys destined for yeshiva life. If the secular core curriculum was taught at all beyond eighth grade, and then only to secure some portion of state funding, there was little outside supervision to ensure standards and compliance. Pupils came out of the system ill-equipped and lacking the basic tools to succeed in a modern economy.

And if Ben-Gurion had originally assumed that ultra-Orthodoxy would be swept away by the wonders of secular Zionism and that exemption from the draft would no longer be an issue, that was not to be the case, as the four hundred turned into tens of thousands. Some adjustments were made in the 1950s and 1960s, including the introduction of quotas for the number of annual yeshiva student deferments, in an effort to maintain a veneer of egalitarianism. But those were revoked after the Likud revolution of 1977, when the ultra-Orthodox gained political leverage by joining the coalition. There was an additional glitch in the arrangement. In order to qualify for deferment and eventual exemption, the Torah students had to remain in the yeshiva, full-time, well into their twenties, delaying—and in many cases, enabled by government stipends, aborting—their entry into the labor market.

Agudat Yisrael had joined Ben-Gurion's first governments just long enough to secure the basics, such as independent education and deferment of military service for yeshiva students. They quit government in 1952, only returning with the rise of the Likud a quarter century later. From then on, the ultra-Orthodox parties grew into a formidable political force, willing to participate in the democratic process in order to guard essential interests like budgets, minimizing desecration of the Sabbath, and fighting against liberal values. Orthodox Sephardic Jews became a potent political force multiplier with the establishment of the Shas party in the early 1980s, tapping into the rising trend of identity politics, building up its popularity by providing sectoral educational and social services with added extras like free lunches, and harnessing the underdog sentiment of many of Israel's more traditional Mizrahi Jews, who voted for the party even though they themselves were not strictly Orthodox. The Shas school system largely imitated the Ashkenazi ultra-Orthodox one but filled a gap because Mizrahi applicants were often discriminated against in the Ashkenazi establishments. Gifted and ambitious Mizrahi students fought for the few places allotted them in the elite Ashkenazi yeshivas, while the Shas politicians adopted the black-and-white uniform of their ultra-Orthodox Ashkenazi peers.

At first, Shas was open to peace overtures and compromises with the Palestinians, wary of alienating Israel internationally and placing paramount importance on avoiding loss of life. In more recent years, though, along with the rest of the Haredi bloc, Shas, too, has moved rightward and forged a tight alliance with Netanyahu's Likud. The Haredi parties got political clout and, in return, long underpinned Netanyahu's grip on power, remaining his last stalwarts even as other, once-solid coalition allies began to split off in the wake of Netanyahu's legal troubles.

Among the Haredi public, voter turnout was significantly higher than among the general population and loyalty was key. Adherents told me that voting according to the dictate of one's rabbi was the very essence of being a Haredi, and that only the Haredi parties could be trusted to look after Haredi interests.

The Haredi politicians, who were coalition kingmakers, acted as intermediaries between their communities and the state, ensuring the flow of budgets to maintain the ultra-Orthodox lifestyle—or as critics, even from within the community, put it, to keep the ultra-Orthodox masses ignorant, dependent, and poor. For years, secular Israeli politicians and analysts had been making doomsday predictions based on the high Haredi birth rates and low work patterns. In the early 2000s more than 60 percent of ultra-Orthodox men did not work, compared with 15 percent in the general population. About 56 percent of the Haredi population was living below the poverty line, mostly dependent on welfare payments like income support, child allowances, and state stipends for those studying in *kollel*s, yeshivas for married men, as well as charity. Bnei Brak was ranked as the poorest city in Israel with the lowest household income and expenditure. About a quarter of household income in the city came from allowances and subsidies— more than double the national average, according to government data. Yet when a maverick Shas politician, Chaim Amsellem, argued back in 2010 that full-time, state-supported Torah study should be reserved for exceptional scholars destined to become rabbis or religious judges, while the rest should go out and earn a living, he was ousted from the party, was labeled "Amalek"—the biblical embodiment of all evil—in the party newspaper, and had to be assigned a bodyguard.

A decade later, by 2020, the rate of working Haredi men had risen slightly, to above 50 percent, while the rate of Haredi women who went to work had jumped to 76 percent, albeit in mostly low-income jobs. After years of legal challenges and Supreme Court rulings demanding an amended military draft law that would regulate the Haredi service and conform with the principle of equality, and, by definition, get more ultra-Orthodox males out of the yeshivas and equipped to enter the workforce, modest quotas for Haredi enlistment were introduced, but the Haredi politicians vehemently opposed any imposition of sanctions on individuals or yeshivas that did not live up to the quotas. The quotas were supposed to increase gradually over several years, though the targets remained unambitious at just a few thousand a year. Even so, army officials were caught deliberately inflating the numbers of Haredi recruits in the path of least resistance. Within its first hundred days, the Bennett-Lapid government of change attempted its first reform, promoting legislation to lower the age of exemption for yeshiva students from twenty-four to twenty-one, temporarily, and on the condition that those who left the yeshivas did so for an approved professional or vocational training program or to work in emergency services, with a view to entering the workforce and pending a new and comprehensive military draft law.

Some *Haredim* said the government plan would not have much impact. Despite years of government investment in programs to help educate and integrate *Haredim* into the workforce, progress had been halting. Less than 10 percent of Haredi men and 12 percent of women studied in regular higher education institutions. And then, about half the women and three-quarters of the men dropped out before qualifying for a degree or diploma. The prospects were a national economic horror show. With an average of 7.1 children per family, as opposed to less than 3 in the general population, about 19 percent of all Israel's children in 2015 were Haredi. Given an overall retention rate in the ultra-Orthodox community of 88 percent, by 2065 their grandchildren were expected to constitute nearly one-half of all Israeli children.

Yanki Farber, the Haredi digital journalist, dismissed such projections as unfounded scaremongering. In his own family, he said, maybe five of the fifteen siblings had brought ten children into the world. "That's fifty," he said. "The rest have two or three." Haredi journalism, both traditional and digital, including Farber's place of employment, offered a rare and intriguing window into modern-day ultra-Orthodoxy and its internal contradictions. On *Behadrei*'s white Formica conference table, even the used paper cups were declared kosher, stamped with a *Shomrei Shabbat* logo indicating that the disposable tableware company strictly observed the rules of the Sabbath. But nothing here was black and white. Just as the politicians straddled and mediated between the two worlds, so did Haredi journalists, particularly those working in the less rigid digital media or radio as opposed to the traditional party newspapers. A female Haredi journalist edited *Behadrei*'s women's section, though she worked from a separate cubicle. Virulent anti-Zionism had been replaced by a grayer ambivalence. Some reporters and commentators from the ultra-Orthodox media regularly appeared on the main Israeli television panels to analyze and translate Haredi politics and trends for the wider Israeli public, and would bring back news from the outside, suitably repackaged for a Haredi audience. Some Haredi journalists became social media personalities on Twitter, Instagram, and other platforms.

The Haredi printed press was still alive and well, catering to the more conservative mainstream. Given the lack of other entertainment and the almost total absence of television sets in Haredi homes, the party newspapers were pored over like sacred texts, with all that wasn't written almost as important as what appeared in print. The newspapers, each affiliated with a particular political party and patron, remained deferential, shied away from controversy, and refrained from publishing anything that could be deemed offensive to Haredi sensibilities. That included allegations against rabbis or ultra-Orthodox politicians, words like "rape," and photographs of women. Avraham Dov Greenbaum, the editor of the Shas-affiliated newspaper *HaDerech* (The Way), said Haredi journalists did not aspire to be guardians of democracy, like in the secular world; they had different agendas and goals. Featured in a documentary series called *Neias,* Yiddish for "news," aired on Kan, Israel's public broadcast channel, Greenbaum said that the guiding principle of the Haredi press was not the public's right to know, but rather the Haredi public's right not to know.

But undoubtedly one of the biggest revolutions taking place in the Haredi world was the increasing connectivity and access to the Internet, in defiance of the edicts of the rabbis, and the advent of digital media. Since the rabbis who backed the political parties did not endorse broad Internet usage, they could not endorse the news sites; this resulted in the sites' relative independence, and they thrived irreverently on inside scoops and gossip. *Behadrei Haredim* had a main competitor, *Kikar HaShabbat,* Sabbath Square. They and several other sites covered the national news with a Haredi slant. In addition, they recorded the daily comings and goings of the *Admor*s, or rabbinical heads of Hasidic courts, and produced lifestyle, family, and food sections featuring *haimisch* (homely) recipes and more modern ones, like a non-dairy, vegan-friendly version of tiramisu. Haredi "paparazzi" would compete to capture prominent rabbis and ultra-Orthodox politicians in more intimate moments, for example holding meetings in kosher delis or restaurants over a steaming bowl of *cholent*. Enterprising reporters would upload snatched interviews with such august celebrities as Instagram stories.

They knew their audience, however, and had their limits, avoiding overtly offensive items or language. Though some Haredi digital journalists were almost hyperactive on the more news-driven, text-heavy Twitter, other platforms like Facebook were considered out of bounds and were referred to obliquely in news reports as "social networks," in only a semi-acknowledgment of their existence. The Haredi media mostly avoided publishing photographs of women so as to "guard the eyes" of male readers from immodesty and temptation. When unavoidable, in group photographs, for example, some Haredi media resorted to blacking out female images, turning them into silhouettes. One paper, *Hamevaser,* was ridiculed after it clumsily Photoshopped a photograph of world leaders rallying against antisemitism in Paris, cropping out Angela Merkel from the middle of the front row. Even in *Behadrei*'s women's section, images of women were absent. A story about how to choose the right wedding gown was illustrated with a photograph of flowing ivory taffeta; an item about skin hyperpigmentation and overexposure was accompanied by an image of a sunset; an article about childbirth featured a photo of a hospital monitor; and a video demonstrating how to style a wig for special occasions showed only the hands of the stylist at work and an unavoidable part of her torso. And *Behadrei* blurred out the faces—and at least in one case the bare legs, from the knee down—of Israel's female ministers.

More than anything else, though, the shunning of military service alienated the ultra-Orthodox community from the national Jewish consensus. The *Haredim* argued that prayer and Torah study were just as essential for the protection of Israel's citizens, but secular Israelis generally did not buy that argument and the fanaticism of the radical anti-drafters deepened the wedge. On the wall of *Behadrei*'s conference room, opposite Farber, hung a framed photograph of a group of ultra-Orthodox protesters, mock nooses around their necks, wield-

ing banners bearing the legend, in Hebrew and flawed English, "WE
WOULD RATHER DIE AND NOT DRAFT TO THE DEFILED IDF."
Another one read: "If you don't allow us to live as Jews WE WILL DIE
AS JEWS! But we will never surrender to the dictates of the religion-
hating government."

Whether any irony was intended in the office décor or not, for the
reactionaries the army "melting pot" was nothing less than a modern-
day Sodom. Those few who did enlist were generally either on the
fringes of Haredi society to begin with or were looking for a way out
of their stifling ultra-Orthodox environment. Yanki Farber was a little
different. Inspired by a visit to the Western Wall, known in Hebrew
as the *Kotel,* in Jerusalem's Old City during his early years, he said,
his childhood dream was to become a *Kotel* guard and a soldier. He
eventually did both, serving in a specially designated Haredi battalion,
Netzah Yehuda, which catered to ultra-Orthodox needs. Initiated in
1999, the fighting battalion served as part of the Kfir Brigade in the
Ramallah and Jenin sectors of the occupied West Bank. In Farber's case,
there was some family background, which eased his path: His father
had volunteered for the IDF's home front command in 1991, distributing gas masks to civilians during the first Gulf War, when Israel was
hit by Scud rockets from Iraq. A younger brother followed Yanki into
the Haredi battalion and completed the officers' course. More often,
though, mainstreamers who went against the grain and enlisted in the
military risked being cut off by their mortified families. Military service was viewed as a stain on the family, potentially cursing a soldier's
siblings by endangering their acceptance in elite Haredi educational
institutions and harming their marriage prospects.

Early attempts by the army to increase Haredi enlistment had
prompted a vicious backlash by the radicals. A billboard campaign in
the scruffy back alleys of Mea Shearim in Jerusalem depicted ultra-
Orthodox recruiters as grotesque, gun-toting child snatchers. They
were labeled *hardakim,* a combination of *Haredim* and the Hebrew
words for insects and germs. Haredi soldiers who dared to return
home in uniform were verbally abused, spit on, and occasionally
beaten. Notices pasted on the walls, known in Yiddish as *pashkevillim,*
warned of permissiveness in the IDF. Effigies of Haredi soldiers hung
from balconies.

This was despite all the efforts the army made to come toward the community. As well as the Haredi combat battalion, the army had set up the Shahar program in 2007 to train young, married ultra-Orthodox men as technical staff for the air force, navy, intelligence, and other branches of the military. Since Haredi conscripts had often married young and were already parents, Shahar allowed them to go home every night during their two-year army stint and provided them with a family stipend or government salary. Some rabbis even gave their quiet blessing to recruits deemed unsuitable for full-time Torah study. But the public pressure, the Supreme Court's insistence on adhering to the principle of equality, which was anathema in ultra-Orthodoxy, and the past demands of secular politicians like Yair Lapid to criminalize Haredi draft dodging only hardened the mainstream rabbis' positions. One young Haredi lawyer from Jerusalem who served in the army's legal department under the Shahar program told me that he had kept his in-laws in the dark about his day job, unsure of how they would react. Deserters, by contrast, were hailed in some quarters as heroes. When one Haredi man was declared a deserter for refusing to show up at the draft office even to arrange his exemption and was sent for a month-long stint in military prison, he was let out for a Passover furlough. He was picked up in a stretch limo and, surrounded by a black sea of supporters, was brought to receive a special blessing from the leader of the extremist Jerusalem Faction in Jerusalem, carrying a toddler on his lap and wearing a gold silk coat and fur *shtreimel*.

Farber, a nonconformist, said he still performed annual reserve duty, but he did not shy away from the deeper problem. Most mainstream *Haredim*, he said, were simply not cut out to serve, if only for technical reasons like maintaining the most stringently kosher standards for food and Sabbath observance. He asserted a truth that many commanders would only whisper or hint at: that the IDF did not really want nor would it be able to cope with an ultra-Orthodox influx. "What would happen if they came in their thousands?" Farber said. "Girls would be out. They would turn the IDF into a giant yeshiva." But even as he spoke, the very foundations of Haredi life in Israel were already being put to the test.

Store-lined Rabbi Akiva Street, named for the ancient scholar and sage, was Bnei Brak's bustling Champs-Élysées. Its boutiques displayed glittering, if modest and long-sleeved, evening gowns designed to brighten any *simcha,* or celebration. The window displays in menswear shops often featured headless male mannequins modeling stylish suits for adult men, and shirts and waistcoats for boys. The headlessness made sure there was no violation of the Jewish prohibition against idols and graven images of the human form. Charity boxes lined the sidewalks. Phone accessory stores sold cellphone covers with pictures of prominent rabbis. Billboards were plastered with death notices and advertisements for everything from takeout *cholent* to *oybed chochem* air conditioners, *oybed chochem* being Yiddish for "smart." Men scurried by, heads down, with purpose. The women moved more slowly, pushing baby strollers with bunches of young children hanging on to the sides like feeder fish.

Secular Israelis would come here on group tours to sample the Jewish food, buy challahs from the city's famed bakeries, and soak up the atmosphere, like tourists in a foreign capital. Then COVID-19 hit Bnei Brak with the force of a biblical plague just ahead of Passover 2020. The infection had started spreading invisibly and surreptitiously during Purim, a festival of parties, carnivals, and the traditional *mishloah manot,* the swapping of edible gifts between friends and neighbors, with no hand sanitizer in sight. Covering less than three square miles, Bnei Brak, first mentioned in Joshua 19 as one of the towns allotted to the tribe of Dan, was now the most densely populated city in Israel and fertile ground for the virus. An innate suspicion of state authorities, the communal lifestyle of group study and prayer, and social calendars chockablock with circumcision ceremonies, bar mitzvahs, engagements, and weddings—all these added up to a superspreader dream and a social-distancing nightmare. Soon coronavirus was on the rampage.

The Haredi rabbis, whether they were just poorly informed or preferred to put their faith in God, were slow to respond. Yaakov Litzman, the leader of United Torah Judaism and the health minister at the time, was busy with other things—he was under investigation on suspicion of pressuring district psychiatrists to prevent the extradition of Malka Leifer, a member of his Hasidic Gur sect who had been charged in Australia with multiple counts of child rape and molestation. Litzman was also accused of having intervened on behalf of Goldy's, his favorite Jerusalem deli, after it was found in breach of health regulations, and he was said to have applied political pressure on Prime Minister Netanyahu to keep synagogues and ritual baths open amid the pandemic, against the advice of the health professionals. After Litzman and his wife contracted the virus, there were allegations that he himself had broken government lockdown regulations.

The conduct of the rabbis came under unprecedented scrutiny both from within and outside the ultra-Orthodox community, training an unwelcome spotlight on the *Haredim* and, for some, leading to a crisis of faith in the rabbis' judgment when it clashed with that of the state medical professionals. The virus did not recognize boundaries or invisible walls around ghettoes like Bnei Brak, and things turned ugly. Secular Israelis accused the *Haredim* of spreading disease; the *Haredim* accused secular Israel of incitement. At one critical moment in the battle against the virus, the evening after the government had ordered the entire Israeli school system to close down, Rabbi Chaim Kanievsky of Bnei Brak, the revered nonagenarian authority of the Lithuanian branch, was consulted by his grandson, Yaakov, regarding what to do about the schools and yeshivas. In a widely circulated video of the conversation, the grandson could be heard shouting into the ear of the dozy-looking rabbi that "the state" wanted to close down the elementary schools, or *cheders*, and yeshivas until they knew more about "the plague," amid fears that it could easily spread in crowded classrooms. With no reference to science or epidemiology, or rapidly rising infection rates or the fact that thousands of Jews, many of them *Haredim,* were already dying in the United States and Europe, Rabbi Kanievsky issued his ruling: The classrooms should stay open, to avoid the greater danger posed by a cancellation of Torah study. The classrooms remained open for two weeks more. But then the ultra-Orthodox press began printing the names and photographs of scores of Haredi victims who had died of the virus in the United States. A hundred had died over a single weekend. "Everyone was in shock," Farber said of the cloistered population of Bnei Brak. "They began to take precautions."

Once he understood the risk, Kanievsky snapped into action, calling for a half-day fast to halt the spread of the pandemic and ordering all the yeshivas, *cheders*, and synagogues closed. It was too late for many. Bnei Brak's infection rate spiraled to the highest in Israel. Litzman, the health minister, issued a controversial call for the entire city of Bnei Brak to be quarantined, with passage in and out restricted to essential workers and medical cases. The move earned Litzman comparisons to Stalin on the *pashkevillim,* the broadsides posted on billboards in Haredi neighborhoods. The city's ultra-Orthodox mayor, Avraham Rubinstein, denounced the blockade but was desperate for help with extracting the sick. He took an even more drastic step, calling in help from a team of prominent army veterans with logistical expertise. But more assistance was needed to deliver pre-Passover food supplies to keep residents at home and out of crowded stores. Soon the IDF itself would move in. No Israeli city had seen anything like it before. Two brigades took over the streets that were more accustomed to scenes of undulating black rivers of mourners attending a venerated rabbi's funeral or of stormy protests against the military draft. Instead, soldiers in khaki ran from door to door delivering ready-to-eat meals, toys, and groceries and armed with a Hebrew-to-Yiddish dictionary of common words and phrases on their phones. The close encounter between the IDF and the besieged residents was surprisingly congenial and the first wave of the contagion was quickly contained.

With subsequent waves, however, the lessons were unlearned as the fear of spiritual deterioration overtook the needs of public health. The rabbis of some sects openly flouted lockdown rules, keeping schools open and flooding the hospitals. Political pressure by Haredi coalition partners prevented the government from implementing a "traffic light" system to apply tougher restrictions to the worst-hit cities, protesting that Haredi hot spots would be "singled out" and agreeing only to a blanket lockdown of the whole country, regardless of the economic damage, and feeding into the general loathing and resentment of the ultra-Orthodox.

Some Haredi journalists, activists, and politicians called for soul-searching. Aryeh Deri, the Shas interior minister, told a Haredi radio station that *Haredim* had made up some 70 percent of those sickened in the initial wave of the virus in Israel. But the more common ultra-Orthodox response was to blame the health ministry officials and government bureaucrats for failing to address the Haredi sector in its own codes and language. Kanievsky's grandson, Yaakov, and the other "operators" who had the ear of the rabbi also came in for criticism.

Insiders said they had been too scared to take responsibility for shutting down the *cheders* and yeshivas in case the Israeli strain of the virus turned out to be less virulent and deadly than the epidemic abroad.

COVID created a commonality of fear and fate that had rarely existed before. Both within and outside the Haredi community, there were those who saw it as a catalyst for change. The cooperation with the IDF, for one thing, was unprecedented. "Imagine," Farber said, "for thirty years Haredi youths were told that the army will desecrate you, it will turn you secular, it wants to take you to die on the borders, it needs you for cannon fodder, soldiers are bad people, they are not human. Maybe not in those exact words but they tell you the army is no good. Then suddenly along comes corona. The whole city is closed, there's not a dog in the streets—well, there are no dogs anyway, but not a cat in the street. Not a living soul. And what do the children see from the windows? Soldiers. Hundreds of them walked around the city for a month! All through Pesach! And what were they doing? Bringing food. What's a twelve-year-old or fifteen-year-old boy to think?" Even residents who did not appear on the lists drawn up by the municipality for food deliveries would ask the soldiers in the stairwell for help, he said. The soldiers would take their names and addresses and go to their commanders, who would go to the municipal authorities. The next day they would return with supplies, like manna from heaven.

In Jerusalem's hardcore Haredi quarter of Mea Shearim, meanwhile, fear of COVID hardly seemed to have permeated. When the streets of downtown Jerusalem were all but deserted one weekday at noon during a lockdown, the narrow main artery running through Mea Shearim was bustling with people, many unmasked as they scurried in and out of the small, dark stores. Large banners in English declared the opposition of "authentic Jewry" to Zionism and the existence of the state of Israel and exhorted strangers not to pass through the neighborhood in immodest clothing. The *pashkevillim* posters were like anti-public-service announcements. One reminded the girls of Israel that the minimum skirt length required for modesty was no higher than halfway between the knee and the ankle. A new one that cropped up every few meters was titled in bold, black letters: "Yom Kippur War." It warned that "the eternal battle between the sacred and the profane, faith and heresy, and Judaism and Zionism was coming to a decisive point," and it denounced the faint-hearted, compromising Haredi politicians for collaborating with the Zionist government in limiting prayer gatherings on the approaching Day of Atonement, the holiest day of the Jewish calendar.

On the few occasions when police officers did show up on raids to try to enforce lockdown regulations here, extremists, including children, came out to fight them in the streets, throwing stones, spitting and coughing in their faces, and calling them Nazis. And here, the hatred of the army and the state remained undiluted. On Independence Day in 2021, anti-Zionist fanatics stole Memorial Day wreaths from the graves of fallen soldiers and burned them. Later they turned a pile of Israeli flags into a bonfire.

In one of the more symbolic shows of autonomy, one small Haredi charity operating out of a basement in Mea Shearim pioneered a home-care system for elderly ultra-Orthodox COVID-19 patients who dreaded ending up in a hospital ward and wanted to opt out of the national health system. The charity, Hasdei Amram, run by Yitzhak Markovitz, a member of a small anti-Zionist Hasidic sect, organized home visits by private doctors for a fee and follow-up care by volunteer assistants who delivered devices for measuring blood oxygen levels and oxygen generators. The operation was largely off the books: The patients generally avoided taking government COVID tests to evade attention and pressure to go to the hospital. For the same reasons, Markovitz did not report the charity's cases to the authorities.

It would take longer to gauge the broader impact of the pandemic on relations between the *Haredim* and the state. But if the pandemic had any immediate effect that posed a momentous challenge for the rabbis, it was the Haredi public's realization of the need for fast and reliable information, upending years of pious resistance to free access to the Internet. By the time the epidemic arrived, about half the Haredi public in Israel was estimated to already have some kind of Internet access, at least in the workplace. Companies offered kosher Internet services, meaning that they had the stamp of religious councils and were fitted with filters to block access to anything deemed unsuitable, obviously including porn and dating sites. Now, with schools closed and online shopping becoming the safer option, the virus justified and legitimized what had still been a taboo for many: an Internet connection at home.

The Haredi communications revolution had really begun two

decades earlier, under similar circumstances, when the 1991 Gulf War forced the rabbis to sanction bringing radios into the home. The step was considered *pikuach nefesh,* a lifesaving measure that trumped all other religious commandments, as Scud missiles flew in from Iraq and slammed into the Tel Aviv suburbs. The Israeli authorities set up a "quiet channel" for the Sabbath, so that radios could be left on and would remain silent until an incoming missile siren went off. The war ended but the radios stayed put and enterprising *Haredim* soon set up a plethora of pirate radio stations to serve their local audiences.

Mobile phone technology made things more complicated. As smartphones penetrated the Israeli market at the speed of sound, many mainstream *Haredim* had stuck with basic, kosher mobile phones that could only make or receive phone calls, not send text messages, take photos, or connect to the Internet. The strictest *Haredim* had their own ways of remaining updated. For instant news, there were multiple, dial-up Haredi news services known as *Kavei Neias,* Yiddish for "news lines." At least one number marketed itself as a direct line to Kanievsky's court and, during the pandemic, instructed customers to dial 4 for coronavirus reports. Nevertheless, some *Haredim* openly carried smartphones. Some used them only for work purposes, others more generally and surreptitiously. Some Haredi smartphone owners had two separate SIM cards, one with a recognizably kosher number and censored Internet access that could be given to the staff at the children's *cheder* and another that allowed unfettered access to the outside world.

Adding to the confusion, despite the rabbis' exhortations for, and pretense of, abstention, even they and their worldly representatives, the Haredi politicians, were harnessing technology in an effort to ensure the loyalty of the younger generations of voters. For the April 2019 election campaign United Torah Judaism had created a Facebook page and Shas was using a Telegram account. Rabbi Kanievsky, whose followers jostled and fought for a glimpse of him in his rare public appearances, starred in a brief but persuasive United Torah Judaism campaign video. It showed a disciple asking him, in Yiddish, what to tell voters who were considering voting for Zionist parties that "disregarded the laws of the Torah." After a dramatic pause the rabbi growled, "They will have children like that." The clip went viral. In the end, fears that creeping modernization would lead the Haredi masses to defy the rabbis and vote for Zionist parties such as Likud proved largely unfounded. In Modiin Illit, the mostly Lithuanian, urban West Bank settlement of 70,000 souls where a business center employed scores of Haredi women in tech firms and financial services and as paralegals, voter turnout was nearly 84.5 percent that year, more than 16 percentage points above the national average. And a full 97 percent of the votes cast in the settlement went to United Torah Judaism or to Shas. Aided by cyber, the Haredi parties only came out stronger.

The walls of ideology, isolation, and puritanism could not block out the virtual world. During the first wave of the virus, Bezeq, Israel's telecommunications giant, reported a 40 percent increase in Internet traffic from Haredi population centers, with web surfers studying, shopping online, and accessing news. Bezeq said that 8 percent of its new customers were ultra-Orthodox, triple the figure in ordinary times. When Rabbi Gershon Edelstein, the aged head of the prestigious Lithuanian Ponevezh Yeshiva, wanted to address students on the eve of the Shavuot holiday in June 2020, he asked *Kikar HaShabbat,* the other leading Haredi news site, to livestream his remarks. *Kupat Ha'ir,* a charity associated with Rabbi Kanievsky, solicited funds online. A donation of at least 3,000 shekels, or nearly $1,000, in up to thirty installments, to help a family hit by the virus, would be reciprocated with an amulet to guard the benefactors from sickness. Payment could be made with a kosher click of the mouse, via credit card or PayPal. And by the end of the year, Rabbi Kanievsky and his grandson starred again in another video that was circulated on WhatsApp in which the rabbi, after holding consultations with medical experts, urges the faithful to get vaccinated against the virus and assures them there is nothing to be afraid of. When Rabbi Kanievsky died, in the spring of 2022, at the age of ninety-four, he was extolled in eulogies from across Israel's political spectrum. Respected for his extraordinary knowledge of Torah, his extensive writings, and his ultimate leadership in helping the ultra-Orthodox community combat the worst effects of the pandemic, his funeral was one of the biggest mass events in Israel, reflecting his unifying effect within the Haredi world.

Yet the yin and yang of Haredi enthusiasm for the Internet led to an inevitable backlash. The day after Edelstein's livestream, *Yated Nee-*

*man,* the main Lithuanian newspaper published in Bnei Brak, ran a huge advertisement warning against the increased use of the Internet, declaring that the coronavirus was no excuse. When the main rabbinical bodies called for a mass global prayer to stop the spread of the virus, they urged the faithful, among other things, to avoid the "soul corrupting" tools of technology, in a typical case of one click forward and two clicks back.

The question for the country was whether the common threat and experience of the pandemic would ultimately bring the *Haredim* and the rest of Israel any closer together, or if the Haredi displays of autonomy and defiance would end up driving them farther apart. In one harmonious moment of brotherhood, Aviv Geffen, a former bad boy of Israeli rock and once an icon of the secular Israeli left, dedicated a song to the people of Bnei Brak during a televised coronavirus concert, saying that they were not to blame for the spread of the virus and "they are not on Google, they are not always online and updated." As he left the stage, Geffen found his phone flooded with 420 messages of thanks from residents of the city. "Somebody passed my number around Bnei Brak," he later recounted in a Channel 12 interview, recalling the kumbaya moment. "I started reading and simply sat down and cried. For years, they taught us to hate the 'other.' . . . Suddenly I saw them—the *Haredim.*" In response, Bnei Brak City Hall sent a letter to Geffen praising him for displaying the humane, unifying, respectful values that are "the basis for our existence as a people," adding, "Your conduct and words were like cool water for a tired soul."

But as it grew in numbers Haredi society was mutating, and quietly fraying around the edges. There was a small but steady stream of those who had grown up in the Haredi world seeking a new life outside the community. It took courage to step into the unknown without the relevant knowledge or education to live and work in a modern society. One former Haredi compared the experience of leaving the community to being a new immigrant in Israel. Nonprofit groups provided an emergency shelter and halfway accommodation since those who broke away often had nowhere to go. In extreme cases, ultra-Orthodox parents sat *shiva* for their "lost" children, observing the traditional seven-day mourning period as if they were dead.

One leaver, Rachel Ohayon, a young, single woman, had been work-ing at a phone center in Bnei Brak and living with her parents and seven siblings in nearby Petah Tikva. She had drowned out questions about her faith in the past with even stricter observance. But they bub-bled up during lockdown and set her on a journey of self-discovery, to explore her own, long-suppressed individuality. With time on her hands, she joined a local library, a trove of secular knowledge that had been off-limits. After reading the Hebrew translation of one forbidden novel, *The Sweetness of Forgetting* by Kristin Harmel, a story of a Cape Cod woman's secret family history that crosses cultures and religions, she had an epiphany. "I grew up with a sense of the *Haredim* being special and different," Ohayon told me. "I discovered I'm not so special or different, that there are millions like me. That's what suddenly made me say, That's it, I'm leaving." She bought a smartphone and through Google and YouTube discovered oceans of music and history. At her ultra-Orthodox girls' school, she recalled only ever being taught Jew-ish history, and about the evils of the kibbutz as the embodiment of secular Zionism. She had never owned a pair of jeans or seen a movie. Soon an acquaintance who had made a similar journey invited her to Eilat, where she worked for a while as a waitress. After returning to Petah Tikva, she was living with her grandmother. Her parents had not disowned her but preferred her out of the house so she would not be a bad influence on her younger siblings.

As Yanki Farber put it, the broader the highway, the wider the mar-gins. Only a small minority of *Haredim* remained truly cut off from the outside world. Even in Mea Shearim, he said, everyone seemed to know everything, though just how remained "an enigma." Frugality was still an ideal and a norm, but the *Haredim* were not impervious to Israeli materialism. More Haredi men were working. In households where the wives were supporting their husbands' life of study, some aspired to more than a life of abject poverty. "When the children see what their cousins have, they want the same," Farber said. "It never used to be like that. In the past, nobody had."

In another meeting of hearts and minds, the ultra-Orthodox increasingly became an object of curiosity in popular culture. Israeli movies, documentaries, and television drama series delved into their world as an endless source of human interest and even global enter-tainment. One satirical series, *Shababnikim,* followed the antics of

a group of jaunty yeshiva dropouts in Jerusalem; *Kippat Barzel* fic-
tionalized the goings-on in a Haredi army unit, its name a play on
the Hebrew for "Iron Dome," *kippa* being the Hebrew term for both
"dome" and "skullcap." *Shtisel,* the saga of a Haredi family in Jerusalem, found an international following as a Netflix hit. Designer *Haredim* began to emerge in the Israeli media and public sphere. One of
them, Melech Zilbershlag, a sharp-witted millennial Haredi journalist
and son of a rabbi, became a social-media sensation with his humorous
video clips and posts. With dreamy eyes and long ringleted sidelocks,
he took part in a United Colors of Benetton–inspired campaign for
Hoodies, an Israeli basic clothing chain, along with Israeli supermodel
Bar Rafaeli. He then enlisted in the army's new media department,
becoming a pinup boy for *Haredim* in uniform and describing himself in his Twitter bio at the time as "the least decorated soldier in the
IDF." After his release, he changed it to a less reverent status: "Everything would have looked different if I'd had a smartphone during
the Holocaust."

The duality of the Haredi-Israeli interrelationship that drifted
between growing mutual acquaintance and estrangement, national
responsibility and insularity, blind trust in God and autonomy, came
to the fore when disaster struck the community again in the spring of
2021. During the festival of Lag ba'Omer on Mount Meron, a mountain
near the spiritual Galilean city of Safed in the north, some 100,000
mostly ultra-Orthodox pilgrims had crowded the mountain to mark
the *hilulah,* or anniversary of the death, of a revered second-century
rabbi, the mystical Shimon Bar Yochai, known by the Hebrew acronym of Rashbi. His domed stone tomb was the centerpiece of what
had become a shabby, improvised religious and tourist site. Nominally
under the control of the National Center for the Development of Holy
Sites, a division of the Ministry for Religious Services, the site's true
landlords were a handful of associations and charities including the
radically anti-state Toldot Aharon Hasidic sect and some Sephardic
religious trusts. Profiting from selling candles and whatever came into
the charity boxes, they had divided the mountain between them into a
patched-together series of fiefdoms.

Though the Mount Meron *hilulah* was generally the largest single
annual gathering anywhere in Israel, the site's infrastructure was woe-

fully inadequate to safely contain such numbers of people. There was no proper sewage system. The narrow alleys and passageways, including a sloping one with a slippery metal floor, were not built to cope with large crowds. For years police officials, government ombudsmen, and Haredi journalists had sounded alarms of an impending disaster. *Haaretz* revealed that Toldot Aharon had constructed one passageway as a pirate initiative some twenty years earlier, with no planning permission, in order to create a separate male-only entrance and exit path in and out of its compound. Each year, it was declared a miracle that the *hilulah* had passed without major incident. If religious stampedes were usually a problem of third-world nations, this was where the start-up nation met Chelm, the legendary town of fools in Yiddish folklore.

The Lag ba'Omer festival had become an esoteric highlight of the Haredi calendar. Each year, phalanxes of organized buses would bring the faithful to the mountain where ritual bonfires were lit. The festival also traditionally marked the end of a plague that had ravaged the students of Rabbi Akiva, the Rashbi's teacher. In 2020, national coronavirus restrictions had allowed only a very limited, symbolic ceremony on Mount Meron. The next year, amid impassioned petitions from ultra-Orthodox politicians, and with most of the adult population vaccinated, no limits were imposed on entry to the site and safety recommendations were ignored. Though women and families were present in some parts of the site, others were gender segregated. Some 20,000 men and boys crammed into the Toldot Aharon compound for the main bonfire-lighting ceremony at midnight. Singing traditional Hasidic *nigunim,* or tunes, they bobbed and swayed in unison on the bleachers, in a state of spiritual ecstasy. But at around one a.m., as they began funneling out of the compound into the narrow, sloping passageway with the slippery metal floor, the miracles ran out. A few people stumbled and tripped on the stairs at the end of the passage, causing a bottleneck. Pushed from behind, and with nowhere to escape to, people began to fall forward and pile up on top of one another in what some described as a human avalanche. By dawn, forty-five bodies were laid out in rows, loosely wrapped in crinkled, foil-like body bags.

The identification process took place as swiftly as possible so that many of the victims could be buried before the approaching Sabbath. The succession of funerals was so intense that some mourners may have ended up following the wrong body. Through the weekend, while the Haredi public was mostly cut off from the outside world and immersed in observing the Sabbath, the Hebrew news media moved into high gear, feverishly investigating and postulating which government departments or individuals might bear responsibility for the disaster. The Haredi community itself, deep in mourning, responded differently.

On Sunday morning I headed out to Beitar Illit, the large Haredi settlement in the hills south of Jerusalem in the West Bank. There the atmosphere was hushed, somber, and introspective. Four of the victims were from the settlement: Rabbi Shlomo Matlon, thirty-seven, a father of eleven; Elazar Goldberg, thirty-seven; Shmuel Zvi Klagsbald, forty-three; and a teenager, Shmuel Eliyahu Cohen, sixteen. Their names flashed up on an electronic advertising board at the entrance to the sprawling concrete suburb, along with a flickering virtual memorial candle. On a retaining wall by the entrance, a large billboard advertisement announced in the name of the Committee for the Purity of Communications that life was better without movies or the Internet. Prime Minister Netanyahu had declared a day of national mourning, and the Israeli and municipal flags outside the small city hall were flying at half-mast. The city authorities had invested in the settlement, planting colorful flower beds along some of the main roads. A fountain and fruit-themed sculptures, including a bunch of grapes and a pomegranate, adorned the traffic circles. Haredi men and women rushed about, shopping and speaking into cellphones, their eyes mostly downcast. One woman said she was hurrying to a circumcision ceremony. Another, pushing an infant in a stroller and accompanied by a young niece, was on her way to pick up a daughter from kindergarten. Deeper inside the settlement, old posters advertised kabbalistic studies and promised would-be students the miracles and protection of the Rashbi, directing them to a particular rabbi's stall at the *hilulah* at Mount Meron.

Here, there was no blaming or finger-pointing going on. The disaster at Mount Meron, the passersby explained to me, was an act of God. "We are believing Jews," said Aharon Zilberman, a volunteer medic and a member of the Hasidic Sanz sect, who had been at the scene of the tragedy and was visiting his parents in Beitar Illit. "Even when things are difficult to understand, we accept that they are all the doings of the Holy One. We don't ask questions." He agreed that there was also a duty to investigate what happened, to ensure it would not be repeated. "But we are not looking for who to blame," he said. "It was decreed." And even those who acknowledged a need to investigate said the *shiva* was not the time. Yehuda Leib Schreiber, thirty-three, a Hasid from the small Boyen dynasty, whose rabbi traditionally had had the honor of lighting the first bonfire on Mount Meron before the Toldot Aharon muscled in, said the issue of who might be to blame was of no interest to him. Schreiber, who studied in the same Jerusalem *kollel* as one victim of the crush, demonstratively averted his eyes as he spoke, as was customary when dealing with a woman. But his message was stern and clear. "Everything is decreed from above," he said, hurriedly. "The only thing that concerns me is the need to repent." Chavi Zaltsman, twenty-five, the young mother on her way to the kindergarten, took a different approach, reflecting the character of her Karlin Hasidic sect, known for its hospitality. The forty-five victims had been "chosen by God to atone for this whole generation," she said. Her husband and brother had been on the mountain at the time of the disaster. Zaltsman, who was at her parents' home in Haifa that night, spent the hours waiting to hear from them in prayer and reciting psalms, since the cellphone network had crashed in the area of Mount Meron. Eventually, her husband arrived back safely, and her brother phoned.

The tragedy, which counted as Israel's deadliest single event involving civilians, reverberated across the country. The barriers were broken down by a national outpouring of empathy and emotion. Israelis united in shock and grief at the loss of innocent lives, including two sets of young brothers, the youngest of them a round-faced, angelic-looking nine-year-old. Arab residents of the Galilee had set up food and drink stations to aid the survivors, even though the disaster had occurred during the Muslim fasting month of Ramadan. Non-Orthodox Israelis lined up in Tel Aviv's Rabin Square to donate blood. Secular Israelis canceled cultural events that had been planned over the Sabbath. Once Sabbath was over on Saturday night, Haredi commentators joined all the prime-time television panels filling the airwaves. By Sunday, the national day of mourning, the national radio stations played the same melancholy music as after a terrorist attack. Photographs of the victims filled the front page of *Yedioth Ahronoth*. A few secular people even took the bus to Bnei Brak to pay a *shiva* call and were warmly received by the families, despite being total strangers. At least for a moment in time, it felt as if Israel's Haredi and non-Haredi populations were getting better acquainted. There were calls from across the political spectrum, including among the Haredi politicians, for the state to assert its sovereignty and take control over the mountain, though Haredi politicians opposed the establishment of an official commission of inquiry to investigate the event, whether out of fear for themselves or of the wrath of their constituents.

The Haredi parties had sat in most, though not all, Israeli governments since 1977. Over the years, however, the loyalties of the Haredi political factions had shifted from being swing parties willing to enter into any government coalition based on sectoral interest to becoming dependable and crucial partners in Netanyahu's right-wing-religious bloc. There was a certain logic to it, given their social and religious conservatism. After the Oslo peace process dissolved into violence and hopelessness, the Israeli left and center-left had increasingly moved their focus from the quest for a land-for-peace settlement of the Israeli-Palestinian conflict to a more social, civic agenda, promoting issues such as gender equality, civil marriage, LGBTQ rights, public transport on the Sabbath, and accommodation toward the more liberal, progressive streams of Judaism with which the vast majority of affiliated Jews in North America were identified, and which were repudiated by Israel's Orthodox religious authorities. All these liberal causes were anathema to mainstream Haredi voters. The Haredi parties had also pressured Prime Minister Netanyahu into reversing himself on a highly symbolic plan to upgrade a pluralistic, egalitarian prayer area at the Western Wall in Jerusalem, further rupturing the relationship between the Israeli government and the liberal Jewish Diaspora.

Israel Cohen, a political analyst for Hakol Barama, a Haredi radio station in Bnei Brak, explained the Haredi attraction to the Israeli right in terms of its being closer to religious values and to tradition—despite the fact that Netanyahu, as an individual, was unquestionably secular and nonobservant. Cohen, who was close to the Lithuanian leadership in Bnei Brak, had long shared his insights with me, but only over the phone or by voice mail. He was less eager to meet in person. Cohen was not a "blue shirt" like his colleague Yanki Farber; he still wore the white-shirt-black-pants uniform of his more mainstream and conservative Haredi counterparts and gave the impression that he was not eager to be seen around Bnei Brak in the company of a strange, secular woman. Netanyahu's right-wing-religious bloc, he explained, in one of our many telephone talks over the years, was also viewed as representing the "Second Israel" where many *Haredim* felt they belonged. While secular Israelis were fretting about the potential socioeconomic and security impact of the Haredi demographic growth on the future of the country, the *Haredim* themselves were less bothered with national concerns like the economic well-being of the Zionist state and concentrated their efforts on their own interests and dilemmas. "They do not presume to be leaders of the economy or security or anything like that," Cohen said of the Haredi politicians. They had been sent by their rabbis purely to protect the religious aspects of the state and some more material, sectoral matters such as yeshiva budgets and housing.

In return for their support, successive Netanyahu governments had come up with the goods while doing little to pressure the *Haredim* into altering their lifestyle. Despite huge government investment in programs to integrate Haredi men into the workforce, the numbers of formally employed men had come to something of a standstill. Haredi women, on the other hand, were becoming more significant providers, training in accountancy, high-tech skills, and even architecture in tailor-made courses for professions that could earn them three or four times the salary of a preschool teacher. Even among the *Haredim*, there was a realization that dependence on welfare and charity was not sustainable. Haredi families needed money to marry off their children, Cohen said, and a million people could not live on handouts. Understanding that not every Haredi male was cut out for full-time Torah study, some rabbis and yeshiva heads authorized their disciples to seek outside employment.

At the same time, it was every Haredi parent's responsibility to pass on the torch of Haredi culture and education to the next generation and, as Cohen put it, "to preserve the ghetto." The dilemma for the Haredi religious and political leadership was how to find the balance and how much to loosen the reins. One of the more accessible Haredi pols, Yitzhak Pindrus, was a politician from Degel HaTorah, the Lithuanian wing of United Torah Judaism, and the son of immigrants from the United States. He claimed that more Haredi men would join the workforce if more vocational training was offered and if the lack of a college degree was not such an obstacle. Before entering national politics, Pindrus had worked for many years in local government as the former mayor of Beitar Illit and then as a deputy mayor of Jerusalem, responsible for the ultra-Orthodox education and sanitation portfolios. "Take a person like me, with thirty years' experience managing and working for cities," he said. "Because I didn't get a college degree, I couldn't be the head of the parking department in any local government." Many Haredi men were deterred from going to college, he said, because they saw it as a path to integration or assimilation, much like the army, and because the authorities were not willing to enforce gender segregation in public areas on campus. He blamed the policy-makers, saying that, in Haredi eyes, their real goal was not to solve an economic problem but to try to turn *Haredim* into "regular Israelis." The Zionists had failed in that mission for seventy years, he said, adding, "I believe they will fail again."

The Haredi parties stuck by Netanyahu unwaveringly through four successive election campaigns, signing loyalty pledges on demand to the leader and the right-wing bloc. When the Bennett-Lapid government of change was finally sworn in, without the Haredi parties, and promised to usher in a more liberal civil agenda, the Haredi parties cried "*Gevalt*," declaring that the Torah Judaism and the Jewish character of the state were in danger. Pindrus revealed on public radio that in the final hours of Netanyahu's long tenure some of his closest Haredi allies had begged him to stand down and let another Likud leader try to form a right-wing coalition but that Netanyahu had ignored the requests. The Haredi pols had no leverage over him at that point, Pindrus said, because Netanyahu knew they "could not go with the other side." The alternative Bennett-Lapid coalition was to appoint Avigdor Liberman, a nemesis of the *Haredim*, as finance minister. Once in power, it quickly approved the establishment of a state committee of inquiry into the Mount Meron disaster. It also began to crack open the market for the licensing of kosher foods, in which the *Haredim* had lucrative vested interests. When it came to social issues, such as gay rights, the *Haredim* in the opposition were probably closest to the Islamic party, Raam, which sat in the coalition. Pindrus told me that the Haredi parties would try to exploit the differences within the coalition, and that the Haredi parties had survived before in the opposition and would survive again. The Haredi parties had become a resilient, permanent feature of the Israeli political landscape, and the members of the new coalition were wary of taking drastic action, well aware that they might also need the Haredi parties' support for the formation of future governments.

The idea of the classic Haredi was, nevertheless, becoming more flexible. By now, few mainstream families met all the criteria of strict ultra-Orthodoxy and lived entirely off the grid. In the Lithuanian branch, in particular, full-time Torah study was still considered the most prestigious career path, one that brought status, good marriage prospects, and guaranteed entry to educational institutions of choice for the children. Employment within the community came in second. Working outside the community, in secular Israel, lowered one's ranking in the Haredi hierarchy. Yet even in the most stringent circles, the dynamic forces of modernity were challenging the old ways and creating different shades of ultra-Orthodoxy, even within families, and the working Haredi women played a lead role, both as protectors of the faith and as agents of change.

Haredi Israel and secular, democratic Israel had long clashed over Haredi muscle-flexing aimed at excluding women from the public sphere. The Supreme Court was called on to weigh in on whether women could be made to sit at the back of the bus on "kosher" bus lines running along ultra-Orthodox routes or through Haredi neighborhoods and ruled that such segregation was illegal unless it happened voluntarily. Many Haredi women said they preferred sitting at the back in their own zone. Colleges of higher education catering to Haredi students also had to grapple with their demands for gender segregation. In mainstream Haredi society, though women were often the main, or sole, breadwinners, they were still expected to remain in the background. Women were supposed to aspire to ever stricter codes of modesty, including covering one's natural head of hair and wearing clothes that concealed elbows, knees, and throats. Extremists often defaced advertisements on buses or billboards that included images of women, blacking out or tearing out their faces.

In the old part of Beit Shemesh, a mixed town in central Israel with a large ultra-Orthodox constituency, and where religious tensions had sometimes flared, agitators who had migrated from Mea Shearim tyrannized other Haredi or modern Orthodox residents who did not meet their standards. At one point, a female Haredi resident told me, extremist thugs had removed public benches from the sidewalks so that mothers could no longer sit outside with their children, deeming that an immodest activity. The ultra-Orthodox parties refused to run female candidates, despite pushback from some Haredi feminist activists. Other Haredi women blazed their own political trail in secular Zionist parties.

The most prominent one was Omer Yankelevitch, a lawyer and social activist from the rapidly expanding and more modern ultra-Orthodox enclave of Ramat Beit Shemesh, or Beit Shemesh Heights, who ran for the Knesset on the centrist Blue and White slate and became the first Haredi woman to be appointed a government minister, entrusted with Diaspora affairs. Modestly turned out but fashionable and more glamorous than frumpy, her long, chestnut *sheitel*, or wig, looked more Duchess of Cambridge than Vilna. Her politics were a strange hybrid that straddled the secular and religious worlds, and she found herself at odds with the more liberal streams within her own party and out of step with many Israeli feminists. Yankelevitch argued that gender segregation was necessary if Haredi women were to advance and acquire higher education, to provide them with a conducive environment. True liberalism and pluralism, Yankelevitch argued, meant accepting other people's choices and lifestyles, encapsulating the conundrum over religion and state in Israel. The Haredi mainstream did not pay much attention to Yankelevitch or her ilk, saying the women activists were not there to represent them. Some described her disparagingly as a "decoration" or a "token" Haredi to satisfy Blue and White's aspirations of inclusiveness and diversity, as if it were casting for a TV reality show, and dismissed Yankelevitch as Haredi-lite, or not authentic. Others said they had never heard of her.

The diversity of the modern *Haredim,* men and women, could be found within the same family. Sisters-in-law Rachel and Avigayil Heilbronn, for example, had ended up at almost opposite ends of the Haredi spectrum. The Heilbronns, a twelfth-generation Jerusalem family, were proud descendants of the disciples of *HaGra,* a Hebrew acronym for the Vilna Gaon, or Rabbi Eliyahu of Vilna, and anti-Hasidic adherents of the "Polish" school of *misnagdim,* or opponents. The disciples were among the first Jewish migrants from eastern Europe to come and settle in the Holy Land at the beginning of the nineteenth century, reviving a Jewish Ashkenazi presence in Jerusalem. They were hoping to accelerate the Messianic Redemption, and, ironically, along the way they laid the foundations for the future secular Zionist movement.

Rachel grew up in a Haredi neighborhood of Jerusalem, was schooled in the ultra-Orthodox Bais Yaakov school system, then attended a women's seminary. She had married Avigayil's brother Hananel when they were both about twenty-one. The couple had been introduced by a cousin of Rachel's mother, who was a neighbor of Hananel. "We thank him very much to this day," Rachel said of the matchmaker. Thirteen years later, in their mid-thirties, they were living in Neve Yaakov, a settlement on the northern edge of Jerusalem, over the Green Line, where housing was cheaper than elsewhere in the capital, making it popular with ultra-Orthodox and new immigrant families. They were awaiting the birth of their seventh child. Hananel studied Torah in a *kollel* from nine a.m. until one p.m., then from four p.m. until seven p.m., fitting in an additional hour or ninety minutes of study at night. Rachel worked as the bookkeeper at a security firm in Jerusalem. One salary sufficed. "Our standard of living and needs are different from those of the rest of the population," she explained, adding that common Israeli extravagances such as shopping for the latest fashions, vacations, and eating out in restaurants "hardly exist in our circles."

Their neighborhood was largely Haredi; their synagogue mostly Lithuanian, though it embraced its own kind of diversity, with Ashkenazi and Mizrahi members, and some working Haredi males as well as perennial *kollel* students. My conversations with Rachel took place via email, on the account she used for work. She was reluctant to meet. There was the impending birth, she said, and this way she could include what she called the "smarter words" of her husband. I had been introduced to Rachel through Avigayil. Our email correspondence provided a precise, if idealistic-sounding, portrait of the Heilbronn couple and their stringently Orthodox worldview and lifestyle. I had the feeling that the written form of conversation may also have given the couple a chance to vet their responses with their rabbi.

At home, they read only Haredi newspapers and listened to Haredi radio stations. They did what they could to screen out the secular world. They had a computer with Internet access and filters that prevented surfing the net. Neither Rachel nor Hananel had smartphones, just simple "kosher" mobile devices good for making basic calls. One of the things she loved about her community, Rachel wrote, was the sense of mutual responsibility and the neighborhood charitable network. Haredi families customarily donated a tenth of their income to help others in need. The Haredi state-within-a-state had an economic system of its own. Poorer families got by with the help of the *gemach*s, neighborhood free-loan funds. Some would pay back a *gemach* with a loan from another *gemach* in what one Jerusalem resident described as a kind of *gemach* pyramid scheme. Divine intervention had apparently warded off any Madoff-like collapse so far. "We thank G-d that He chose us," Rachel wrote, expressing her gratitude for being part of the Jewish people and Haredi society.

Preserving the values and essence of Haredi life in an ever-changing world meant living even more strictly by the Torah. Rachel saw it as a duty to keep up the old traditions. Practical adaptations to modern life—including women going out to work—were taking hold slowly and only when initiated, or at least approved, by the rabbis. Yet in some respects, Rachel said, Israel's *Haredim* had become more closeted rather than less. Thirty years ago, Haredi children played outside with their secular neighbors in mixed neighborhoods; that was less likely to occur nowadays. *Haredim* tended to cluster together in their own towns, neighborhoods, or settlements. Secular society had strayed too far for many of them. Rachel said there was de facto recognition of Israel in her community, but that identification with the state was "a different story." The problem was that Zionism had come to redefine the Jewish people in a way that no longer required allegiance to God and the Torah. Even the opening words of the Declaration of Independence, "The Land of Israel was the birthplace of the Jewish people," posed problems, she said, noting that the Jewish people came into being when they received the Torah from God at Mount Sinai, in the desert peninsula that was now part of Egypt, and that "a Jew is a person who goes in the path of the Torah and its commandments." Most crucially, she added, "We cannot possibly identify with a Jewish state whose laws are contrary to the Torah of Israel."

Avigayil, Hananel's younger sister, was equally proud of her heritage but life had taken her on a different route. A former high-tech worker and a divorced mother of two, she had become a prominent activist for social change within the ultra-Orthodox community and was working as a public relations consultant. At thirty-one, she was also close to completing an Open University degree in sociology and anthropology. She had not abandoned ultra-Orthodoxy and wanted to be counted as part of the community, embracing its goodness while also calling out its retrograde aspects, representing an alternative voice from within.

Avigayil's activism began almost inadvertently when, in her twenties, she shook up the Haredi world with a Facebook post about sexual abuse and harassment within the ultra-Orthodox community, blowing open a long taboo subject. She explained how that had come about as we sat late one night, after her children had gone to bed, in her spacious apartment in Ramot, another district of north Jerusalem with a large ultra-Orthodox population. She embodied a less austere Orthodoxy: her waist-length hair was loose and uncovered, and her fingernails and toenails were painted a fashionable blue. We settled in for the evening with mugs of green tea.

Avigayil had grown up in Ramot as part of the mainstream Haredi Lithuanian community. High school was geared mainly toward meeting a husband—ideally one who would spend his days in the *kollel*, as her brother Hananel had always aspired to. Her higher education studies in seminary focused on Torah and computing. At twenty, she went to work in Tel Aviv for Realcommerce, a web and application development company, along with another young Haredi woman, Rivki. She would often sleep over at her grandmother's home in Bnei Brak to cut down commuting time to and from Jerusalem. Rivki, after she got married, began coming to work in a wig. The secular bosses went overboard in accommodating the two Haredi women, Avigayil recalled, going beyond what was necessary, even allocating them an office on a separate floor with their own kitchen.

After going on fourteen different blind dates arranged by her parents—or "meetings," as *Haredim* called that stage of the matchmaking process—Avigayil met Yehuda, her husband-to-be. He was considered a *shpitz,* she recounted, Hebrew for a "peak," or "sharp point." That was Haredi slang for a brilliant, top-notch yeshiva student. It was a big romance, she said, complete with butterflies in the stomach. She was twenty-one and he twenty-four. Adhering to the rules, they did not touch each other until they were married. Avigayil quit work in Tel Aviv, the couple settled in Jerusalem, and soon a child was on the way. But something else began happening. Growing up, Avigayil said, she always had questions—about the nature of God and where it was written in the Torah that girls always had to wear tights, even in hot climates. She had never gotten adequate answers. But her new life with Yehuda came with a home computer and access to the Internet. "I get married and I get Google," she said. And the surprise was that as well as a connection with the outside world, she suddenly had virtual access to a part of her own society and religion that had previously been off-limits: the male Haredi universe. Suddenly she was able to study Talmud online, though the texts had always been denied her as a female in the Haredi education system.

Increasingly, after her son, Yishai, was born, she began tapping into her feminist inner self. While nursing, she found she could not go to the synagogue on Rosh Hashana, the Jewish new year and one of the highlights of the religious calendar. "I had a natural instinct for equality," she said, "which is not a good thing in my society." Weepy, and in personal crisis, she began penning questions for her husband to take to the head of his *kollel.* They went back and forth three times. The rabbi answered patiently, with sensitivity, she said, telling her the problem was that she was thinking in male terms, using male structures. That did nothing to solve her problems. At the same time, Yehuda was embarking on a new phase in his own education, studying math and computers online to avoid a coed college environment. He excelled in his exams and went to work in high-tech, joining the ranks of the modern, working *Haredim.* He had to contend with the disappointment of his close community, whose reaction, Avigayil said, was "*Oy,* you left the *kollel!*"

Avigayil, meanwhile, met a whole community of *Haredim* on Face-

book that did not have a name yet: groups of women who studied Talmudic commentaries with a rabbi; *Haredim* who had stopped voting
for Haredi parties and who debated the morality of refusing to serve
in the army. She realized she was not alone, and for once she felt normal. Her personal drama really began during the "knife intifada," the
spate of lone-wolf Palestinian stabbing attacks against Jews that began
in the fall of 2015. Israelis were stripping the store shelves of pepper
spray for self-protection and the streets of Jerusalem were eerily empty.
Avigayil wrote a Facebook post noting that the fear that the men out
at night suddenly felt was already familiar to women, and that sexual
predators were terrorists no less than the knife-wielding Palestinians.
Two years before the #MeToo movement would go viral and become
a global phenomenon, the post burst open a dam within Haredi discourse. Avigayil was instantly inundated by people wanting to share
their stories—Haredi women who had been victims of sexual abuse,
but also men who had been assaulted in *cheder* as children. Rabbis
whom she knew were suddenly accused of being rapists. "I discovered
an underworld," she said, describing the intensity of the outpouring as
traumatizing in itself. She opened a new Facebook page where victims
could share their experiences anonymously. Joined by other activists,
she helped build a small team of therapists and professionals to advise
victims of sexual abuse regarding their rights under the law and she
would even accompany them to the police station to file complaints.
The campaign culminated with the establishment of a dedicated center in Jerusalem to aid and heal Orthodox victims of sexual abuse. A
movement had been founded. It was called Lo Tishtok, Hebrew for
"You Shall Not Be Silent," like an eleventh commandment. The online
campaign joined forces with Magen, a nonprofit organization offering
therapeutic and legal support to victims of sexual abuse in Orthodox
Jewish communities in Israel and around the world. Slowly, the outing
of abuse was embraced by the wider community. "I think my parents
were a bit embarrassed at first," Avigayil said, "but then it became holy
work, within the consensus."

Years later, one of the most recognizable faces of the *Haredim* in
Israel, Yehuda Meshi-Zahav, would also be accused of heinous sexual abuse. A former "operations officer" who organized the protests
of extremist groups from Mea Shearim and then went on to found

ZAKA, the Haredi volunteer emergency response service, Meshi-Zahav had become the Haredi darling of secular Israel. He was disowned by the most radical sects of ultra-Orthodoxy for being a Zionist after he accepted the honor of lighting a torch at Israel's fifty-fifth Independence Day ceremony and after his son joined an IDF combat unit. Generally disliked by many *Haredim*, he was not welcome in the neighborhoods where he had grown up, but he garnered the sympathy of many ordinary Israelis in January 2021 after he lost both his parents to COVID-19 within days of each other. He publicly accused the rabbis who had enabled the flouting of lockdown regulations of having blood on their hands. The allegations of sexual depravity stretching back years were only made public with the subsequent announcement that he was to be awarded the Israel Prize for lifetime achievement, the most prestigious honor the country could offer. Haredi anti-abuse activists and *Haaretz* collaborated to publish testimonies they had gathered from several victims who portrayed Meshi-Zahav as a cruel and obsessed sexual predator who had assaulted men, women, and children for decades. His lawyer denied the allegations, saying Meshi-Zahav had no idea who the mostly anonymous victims were. But hours before *Uvda,* the television documentary program that is Israel's equivalent of CBS's *60 Minutes,* was scheduled to air another investigation into his past conduct, including suggestions that he might also have been a police informer, he tried to hang himself on the balcony of his family apartment, according to media reports. The suicide attempt left him in a coma and he died a year later.

Toward the end of 2021, another prominent Haredi figure, Chaim Walder, of Bnei Brak, was accused of years of sexual abuse and exploitation of Haredi women and children. This time, the allegations rocked the Haredi world to its core. Unlike Meshi-Zahav, Walder was a celebrity in the Haredi world, a charismatic soul healer and prolific children's author whose bestselling "Kids Speak" series came with endorsements from Bnei Brak's leading rabbis. Volumes could be found in almost every Haredi home, both in Israel and, translated into multiple languages, abroad. Walder founded and ran the city's Center for the Child and Family, which offered counseling, and was awarded the Israeli government's Protector of the Child prize in 2003.

After a rabbinic court convened by the chief rabbi of Safed heard testimonies involving twenty-two women and girls and pronounced Walder guilty, he fatally shot himself on the grave of his son, who had died of an illness. Some rabbis initially blamed the complainants for Walder's death, focusing on the sin of gossip and public shaming, further fueling the public outrage. The Haredi media referred only obliquely, if at all, to the Walder episode, sticking to euphemisms such as "the upheaval," since any explicit mention of pedophilia or sexual contact was off-limits. Farber, the *Behadrei Haredim* correspondent, said parents relied on the site to filter the news, and it was not possible to change the world in a day. But like other Haredi commentators he took to the Internet, writing an impassioned Facebook post condemning the code of silence that was intended to shield the Haredi public from sexual matters but had, in effect, protected rapists.

Both Meshi-Zahav and Walder escaped full police investigations—Haredi victims of sexual crimes were in any case reluctant to go to the police, suspicious of the state authorities and fearing exposure—but the Walder case promised to have lasting impact. Avigayil Heilbronn was among a group of activists who raised money in an online crowd-funding campaign to print about a million leaflets raising awareness of sexual abuse and supporting the abused; these were distributed in Haredi communities across the country. In Bnei Brak, there was scant evidence of a revolution underway. Walder's children's books were still prominently displayed in bookstores there, despite calls by two respected rabbis to have them taken off the shelves. But Israel Cohen, the Haredi radio commentator, said that Meshi-Zahav and Walder were high-profile enough to be compared, in Haredi terms, with Harvey Weinstein or Jeffrey Epstein. Fundamental change may come slowly, he said, but he believed that eventually it would come.

The veil had been lifted on sexual abuse in the Haredi sector, so Avigayil focused on new campaigns, including expanding the provision of state Haredi education by the government, alongside the secular and national-religious state school systems. While the traditional Haredi education system was all about being autonomous and independent of the state authorities, a new, if still small, stream of state Haredi education had been established to give forward-looking Haredi families an option to have their children study core curriculum subjects in a state school with a Haredi environment. The few dozen state Haredi schools that existed under a pilot project taught Torah but also chess, English, music, and sports and existed mainly in areas where there were high concentrations of Haredi immigrants from Western countries. Haredi politicians opposed the pilot project, saying they objected on purely ideological grounds. Critics hinted at financial interests at stake, as well as the fear of a loss of control.

In yet another unorthodox departure, Avigayil had established a new tradition of remembering fallen Haredi soldiers on *Yom HaZikaron,* Israel's national Memorial Day, at first online and then in a physical ceremony. In the first year, she said, there were no fallen Haredi soldiers to remember. But that was beginning to change. And while the mainstream Haredi newspapers had always simply ignored Memorial Day, as well as Independence Day, the ultra-Orthodox digital news sites had started displaying black banners and memorial candles on their homepages out of respect for the soldiers.

Sitting on her gray suede L-shaped sofa and reflecting on her own awakening, she said that the only role models when she was growing up were rabbis, but that her daughter, Emuna, then six, would grow up with new ones like Omer Yankelevitch. She avoided elaborating on why she and Yehuda had parted ways. But she expounded eloquently on the realities that put Haredi women like herself in an impossible bind. Yeshiva study for men was all about asking questions, playing devil's advocate, and arguing the point. The girls were educated to do as they were told. Even women who went to work in the high-tech industry, she said, usually remained within the accepted confines of the Haredi mind.

The alternative community she was giving voice to now had a name: the New *Haredim.* They were only a tiny minority of Israel's rapidly expanding ultra-Orthodox society, and some mainstream *Haredim* dismissed them as marginal or no longer counted them as *Haredim.* Yet Avigayil counted herself as still within the fold. She had no television in the house because that would be "too secular." She did not consider herself a Zionist since that would mean putting the state first, above Torah. Avigayil felt that her work on sexual abuse within the community had earned her a special status. She said that a prominent figure from within the Haredi mainstream, whom she did not identify, had recently turned to her for help with a case in his family. "Suddenly

I'm a center of power," she said, "a new elite. Every rebellion starts in the margins."

When asked how she felt about Avigayil's choices, Rachel reacted diplomatically, with a mixture of tolerance and concern. The stricter Haredi mainstream related to the New *Haredim* and the working blue shirts "with understanding," Rachel said, so long as they did not abandon their observance of the commandments of the Torah. Growing in numbers, they could no longer be ignored, and there was a case for embracing them, she said, because "it's important to us that they do not drift too far."

The chinks in the wall were constantly being prized open. But as Rachel saw it, the world was always changing; the challenge was to maintain the values and essence of being a Haredi. The ranks of Torah scholarship had been replenished in a victory over the Nazis. What remained were the questions over the future of Israel and the Haredi contract with the state and society. "We do not deny the need for an army," Rachel allowed, but the *Haredim,* she said, believed that the existence of the world of Torah, the yeshivas and the *kollels,* was even more critical. "We really do not feel like draft dodgers," she said. "We believe that we are contributing to the people of Israel no less." Men who are not studying Torah should not be exempted from military service, she said, noting that a brother of Hananel and Avigayil who was not in a yeshiva served in the IDF's Haredi battalion. For so long as the Messiah tarried, prayers and a life of Torah study would not be enough to fight Israel's wars.

# EIGHT

# HALF THE PEOPLE'S ARMY

STANDING ATOP a flat roof high above the empty parade ground, Colonel Gur Schreibman surveyed his realm. At forty-three, a tall and strapping figure with kind eyes in a starched khaki uniform, he was the commander of Bahad 1, or Base 1, the Israel Defense Forces officers' training academy about half an hour's drive south of Sde Boker, and just north of Mitzpe Rimon, the town overlooking the stunning Ramon crater in the Negev desert. Many of Israel's political leaders had passed through the academy, among them Ehud Barak, Benjamin Netanyahu, and Naftali Bennett. Schreibman extolled it as a hothouse for the country's next generation of military and civil leadership and defined his own role as "like being the principal of the most important school in the country."

The gray concrete buildings and barracks, constructed more than half a century ago in the modernist, minimalist brutalist style, had weathered time and the beating desert sun. The roof offered a panoramic view of the beige wilderness spread out beyond the perimeter of the base, dotted with deep green patches of cultivation. Here, far from the rough and ready bustle of Israeli society, where drivers honked their horns in rude anticipation of a red light turning green and people routinely jumped queue, rules applied, decorum prevailed, and a hushed order reigned. Cadets were forbidden to take shortcuts across the sunbaked parade ground below. It was reserved for ceremonies as if it were a sacred space. Officers in training had to don their berets, color-coded according to unit, whenever they stepped outdoors. Colonel Schreibman wore the purple beret of the Givati infantry brigade.

This hallowed ground was broadly viewed as the heart and soul of the Jewish state, or at least as the state most liked to see itself, the bedrock of mainstream Israeli identity and consensus. As a conscription army made up of the country's sons and daughters, the soldiers were adored, and most Israeli families were, for some time in their lives, intimately, emotionally vested in, and connected to, the military, to the point of corresponding with their children's commanders and one another via WhatsApp groups. A mighty, cutting-edge military force based on the principles of universal draft and equal service, it had long been the glue of a fragmented nation. The most prestigious and trusted institution, it proudly and zealously guarded its brand as a "People's Army," a status that had long guaranteed its success and the country's very survival. But the stately tranquility of Bahad 1 belied the tectonic shifts beneath the surface; the Hebrew version of Sparta was eroding.

Universal conscription had allowed a small, young Israel surrounded by enemies to build a formidable fighting force at relatively low cost, by giving it the pick of the country's best and brightest human capital. The principle of equal service had allowed the IDF to foster an ethos of social solidarity and cohesion—David Ben-Gurion's military melting pot for an immigrant nation—and later, to remain a last bastion of national consensus for a largely native but fractious population. This status afforded the army popular legitimacy, allowing it a wide degree of freedom of action. One of Colonel Schreibman's predecessors at Bahad 1, Elazar Stern, a religious paratrooper who rose through the ranks to become a major general and served as the military's chief education officer and head of its human resources directorate, coined a phrase to describe the symbiotic relationship: "A nation builds an army that builds a nation." It resonated so profoundly with Israelis that it was often mistakenly attributed to Ben-Gurion.

Increasingly, though, the cherished, sacrosanct ideal of the People's Army was becoming a fiction. Conscription rates were dropping, a function of both the shifting demography and societal changes. Israel's Arab citizens, making up 21 percent of the population, were auto-matically exempted from army service by mutual agreement, though members of the tiny Arabic-speaking Druze and Circassian minori-ties, which were fiercely loyal to the state, were drafted. Some Bedouin volunteered, often serving in specialist desert tracking units. A smat-tering of Muslim and Christian citizens volunteered. Orthodox Jewish women were exempted from military service though many from the Zionist national religious camp signed up for a year or more of alter-native civilian national service, volunteering in schools and hospitals.

But one of the most significant disruptors was the exponential growth of the Haredi population, which now included 16 percent of draft-age Israelis. Ben-Gurion's four hundred exemptions for Torah scholars had morphed into tens of thousands of yeshiva students. By the early 2020s, only about 50 percent of Israelis were being drafted, making the IDF an army of half the people. Yet in a demographic para-dox, rather than being short-staffed, the country's growing population meant that there were more people serving than ever before. As the army became more technologically advanced and specialized, and with the mission changing, differential service tracks were becoming the norm amid simmering public resentment over the unequal sharing of the national burden. The army's old model was becoming unsustain-able. Maintaining its consensual role had become as critical as facing the military challenges for the army in the new Israel.

Colonel Schreibman had enlisted at eighteen, as most Israelis of his age did, first into the navy before joining Givati, where he rose to the rank of battalion commander. The army command was based on the concept of *Aharai!,* Hebrew for "Follow me," with commanders set-ting a personal example by leading their troops in the vanguard. Even the chiefs of staff started out as rookies. There was no real aristocracy here. The source of an Israeli commander's authority was born of the ability to inspire others. Schreibman was no exception to this rule. He had risen through the ranks, serving as commander of the Shayetet-13 naval commando unit, Israel's version of the SEALs, one of its elite forces that worked silently behind enemy lines, often in covert opera-tions as part of Israel's unofficial "war between the wars." Israel was one of the only Western countries with a comprehensive draft, officially obligating all Jewish eighteen-year-olds, both male and female, to per-form two to three years of mandatory service. As such, the military was deeply entwined with society and most Israeli Jewish families were personal stakeholders in the civil-military contract. Colonel Schreibman was also an embodiment of that fusion, his life events wrapped into Israel's war calendar. During a tour of the school, he told me that he and his wife, Ya'ara, a high-tech engineer, had gotten engaged during Operation Defensive Shield, Israel's 2002 reinvasion of the cities of the West Bank that took place in the wake of the Palestinian suicide bombing campaign of the Second Intifada. His first child, Or, was born during the 2006 Second Lebanon War. Number two, Dan, arrived soon after Cast Lead, the IDF air war against Gaza's militant groups in the winter of 2008 and 2009. A daughter, Tamar, arrived toward the end of Operation Protective Edge, the fifty-day Gaza war that blighted the summer of 2014.

Born in Neot HaKikar, a small, verdant *moshav* that sat like an oasis in the arid land south of the Dead Sea, he had moved with his family to Kfar Saba, in the bourgeois suburbia of central Israel's coastal plain, and had remained there ever since. Chosen from the ranks to become an officer, and now a career soldier, he exuded a calm, quiet charisma and an innate sense of duty, shouldering responsibility for preparing the next generation to defend the country. He spoke of the ideal of the Israeli officer formed back in the pre-state days by the Haganah and its elite strike force, Palmach: a model of leadership that began, he said, "with the platoon commander who goes forth in the dark with his fifteen soldiers following behind him." The compact size of the country and the relative proximity of its enemies made that responsibility all the more immediate and poignant. The front line was rarely more than a bus ride away. Israelis living in the far north could see the yellow flags of Hezbollah, the Iranian-backed Lebanese paramilitary group, just across the border fence. In the south, Hamas militants manned positions along the Gaza border just a short sprint across the fields from the Israeli forces and border communities. Bahad 1, where we were standing, was probably less than twenty-five miles as the crow flies from both the Jordanian and Egyptian borders. For Schreibman, a stint of study in the United States, with its huge expanses and distant battlefields, brought into sharp relief the immediacy of the threat in Israel, where the lack of strategic depth left few margins for error and added to the responsibility of being an Israeli commander. "When a Canadian is deployed for a tour he flies to Germany, then Afghanistan,"

Schreibman said. "I can be taking part in a military action at night and get home in time to take my kid to kindergarten." Once he was taking part in a raid of a Palestinian explosives laboratory set up in an apartment in the West Bank city of Qalqilya. The city was separated from Israel by a vast concrete wall, a section of the West Bank security barrier running along Route 6, just a few miles east of Kfar Saba. He could literally see his parents' home from the laboratory window. "When we say we are fighting to defend our homes, it is not a cliché," he said, imparting the moral of the story. "Here, it takes on different proportions." And given the high intensity of warfare, this was not something you would do for a salary, he said. Instead, it was a "mission." He said his cadets came with the same motivation to serve.

Like the offices of many senior commanders, Colonel Schreibman's office wall featured an almost de rigueur, framed photograph of the Israeli Air Force's iconic "victory flyby" over Auschwitz-Birkenau. For the first time, in 2003, in coordination with the Polish government, a formation of Israeli fighter jets cut through the skies above the extermination camp in a salute to remembrance and a proud display of triumph over evil. The lead pilot, Amir Eshel, was himself the son of a Holocaust survivor and he went on to become the commander in chief of the Air Force. Delegations of army officers and groups of high school students were taken on visits to the Nazi concentration camps to hone motivation for service and sharpen Israel's survival instinct.

As divisiveness and strident rhetoric ran rampant in the rest of society, the military still retained popular respect as one of the country's last redoubts of its professed values of decency, unity, and camaraderie and as an island of constraint and dependability. The walls of Bahad 1 were inscribed with the inspirational wisdom of the biblical prophets, Ben-Gurion, and the country's war poets. The school's motto, etched in stone, was drawn from Judges 7:17, when Gideon, preparing to take on the Midianites, told his men: "Watch me and follow my lead." On the walls of the education wing an iconic Ben-Gurion quote loomed large: "Every Hebrew mother should know that she has entrusted the lives of her sons in the hands of commanders worthy of the task." When Haim Gouri, that beloved poet of 1948, died, the school held a commemorative ceremony on the parade ground.

Ben-Gurion had envisaged the army as the ultimate "melting pot of the diasporas, a school of civil education and a cradle of a renewed nation" with a single mission and purpose. More recently, though, with most of its recruits now native Israelis, it had become the first, and often only, meeting point where young Israelis from one religious or geographic or ideological sector would encounter their counterparts from other segments of society. So after being educated in separate secular or religious school systems within the same city or having been brought up in almost homogeneous West Bank settlements or the periphery, their military service pulled down at least some of the social barriers. Other than the few Haredi soldiers serving in designated Haredi units, soldiers of many different backgrounds ate and slept together, learned to rely on one another, and were prepared to die for one another.

The messages of the past were patently clear, but the present was getting more complicated. The ultra-Orthodox were not the only ones escaping the draft. In recent years, the army had also seen a rise in males applying for, and obtaining, exemptions on mental health grounds, at times amounting to about 12 percent of eligible conscripts. A mental health exemption would once have been a source of shame and hobbled career prospects, but not serving had become less of a taboo. In all, only about two-thirds of eligible Jewish men were being drafted and only half the country's Jewish women were performing military service. Some 13 percent of the conscripted men did not complete their military service.

The dropping percentages and challenges to the IDF's claim to embody the consensus were not only a function of demographics, but also of the changing nature of the people and the mission. Life in Israel had grown more comfortable and less austere, while its wars were becoming less decisive and conclusive and more asymmetric, and the threats from most enemies beyond the borders were non-existential. The glory and rush of the victory of 1967 was not to be repeated. The army had not been immune to criticism in the past. The surprise Egyptian and Syrian opening attacks of the 1973 war, when sirens split the quiet of Yom Kippur, resulted from failed intelligence assessments and left Israelis fearing annihilation. The trauma, relived in a gripping Israeli television drama series, *Valley of Tears,* in late 2020, complete with blockbuster re-creations of harrowing battle scenes, pried open a collective national wound and exposed it for the first time to the younger generation. But since then the army's missions had become more amorphous and controversial. The First Lebanon War, launched in 1982, was defined by Prime Minister Menachem Begin at the time as a "war of choice" against the PLO militias in Lebanon, largely to halt non-existential attacks on Israel's northern communities. The campaign did not achieve all its goals, it spawned the creation of Hezbollah, and, as casualties mounted, it generated unprecedented domestic opposition. In some ways it became Israel's Afghanistan, bogging down its soldiers in a southern Lebanese "security zone" until 2000. Thrust into the Second Lebanon War, in 2006, the army was revealed to be woefully unprepared as the newspapers filled with reports of soldiers fighting in southern Lebanon while short of food and water. Though the army had prepared multibillion-dollar plans to attack Iran's nuclear facilities, the struggle against Iran and its proxies largely took the form of a distant shadow war. At the same time, and most contentiously, the military was caught in the middle of the country's political and diplomatic stalemate, charged with policing the territories conquered in the 1967 war and maintaining the occupation.

The First Intifada, which broke out in 1987, more often than not pitted heavily armed Israeli soldiers and snipers against stone-throwing Palestinian youths and children. The Second Intifada's bombings of Israeli cafés and markets prompted Operation Defensive Shield in 2002, the military's reinvasion of the Palestinian cities of the West Bank, its largest campaign in that territory since 1967. And after Israel's 2005 unilateral withdrawal from Gaza and the Hamas takeover there two years later the military was repeatedly called upon to carry out military operations and fight air and ground wars as successive Israeli governments failed to achieve any more solid truce or comprehensive policy to dismantle or disarm the militant groups in the blockaded Palestinian coastal enclave. Hamas's MOs included embedding its fighters and rocket launchers among the densely packed Palestinian civilian population in the enclave, or underneath them in an extensive tunnel network. These tactics came together with a growing lack of tolerance in Israel for casualties among its soldiers and a dread of ground invasions. Many Israelis, particularly in the *kibbutzim* along the Gaza border, expressed regret for the loss of innocent Palestinian lives, but also largely viewed the toll on the other side as an inevitable result of Hamas's warmongering and its tactics. The IDF, aware of the harm caused by collateral damage from its air strikes, both in terms of its international image and the ability to keep fighting in the face of international pressure to stop, armed its frontline units with legal advisers who had to approve targets. Nevertheless, the self-declared "most moral army in the world" repeatedly found itself exposed to international allegations of possible war crimes.

The more sophisticated the military's hardware and cyber-aided "jointness," or connectivity, among the intelligence, aerial, naval, and ground forces, the more it was confounded by the Gaza militants' low-tech solutions. Israel's innovative Iron Dome system was developed in partnership with the United States, which provided Israel with more than $3 billion in annual military assistance, mostly to be spent in the United States. Iron Dome had about a 90 percent success rate in identifying and intercepting short-to-medium-range rockets and even mortars headed for populated areas. The next generation of air defense, a laser interception system called Iron Beam, had shot down drones, rockets, and mortars in live tests and was moving into production, to be deployed along the Gaza border within a few years. But advanced weapons were of little help when masses of Gazans protested and rioted along the border fence or when Hamas reverted to medieval-style warfare using underground tunnels or sending flaming kites and booby-trapped balloons over the border, setting ablaze swaths of kibbutz farmland. This was an arms race with a twist. Israel, a regional nuclear superpower, developed solutions to intercept Iranian ballistic missiles in the stratosphere but was periodically paralyzed by guerrilla fighters armed with crude rockets who did not adhere to any laws of war.

The "temporary" occupation of the West Bank, meanwhile, had dragged on for more than half a century, long after the triumphal euphoria of 1967 had worn off, forcing the IDF to walk a tightrope across the historical chasm dividing Israeli society. Over the years, hundreds of retired generals and commanders had campaigned for a political solution to the territorial conflict with the Palestinians based on partition. Others argued for retaining as much of the strategic West

Bank territory as possible. By the second decade of the 2000s, the army intake consisted of a generation of recruits who had grown up scarred, their childhoods overshadowed by the bloody suicide bombings of the Second Intifada. Many of those who enlisted were highly motivated to serve and protect their homes and cities from terrorism. But some also harbored misgivings about other parts of the mission, such as defending the Israeli settlements and unauthorized outposts, particularly when unruly hilltop youths and radical settlers attacked them or tried to co-opt them. In the summer of 2021, a hundred former conscripts signed an open letter to the defense minister protesting settler violence against both Palestinians and the soldiers in the West Bank and the lack of means to contend with it, since the army command shied away from authorizing soldiers to arrest Israeli civilians. The signatories were denounced by other former soldiers, who dismissed them on social networks as Ashkenazi liberal lefties. The army worked hard to keep politics out of its ranks, but Israel's fighters quickly reverted to the business of identity politics and culture wars once out of uniform.

The willingness to sacrifice in combat—the essence of the vow taken by recruits at their swearing-in ceremony—also appeared to be declining in certain quarters, at least on paper, as Israeli society evolved and the sense of immediate, existential threats receded. A 2015 study by Yagil Levy, a respected Israeli professor specializing in military-civil relations, found that the affluent, secular, upper-middle classes and the old kibbutz social-military elite were making up less of the casualty list, and were increasingly being replaced by religious soldiers, new immigrants, and those from the poorer margins of Israeli society. The rate of recruits volunteering for frontline combat units had decreased from 79 percent in 2011 to 67 percent in 2018, after which the IDF appeared to have stopped issuing such data. The privileged, better-educated elites from the center of the country were increasingly opting for cyber and other technological intelligence units, where prestigious, yet safe, desk jobs came with the added allure of lucrative job opportunities after the army in the private high-tech sector. They came better prepared for the army's entry tests, often after paying for specialized pre-enlistment courses. One recruitment officer described the new intakes to me as the "MILI" generation, a Hebrew acronym for the phrase *Mah yitzeh li mi'zeh?* or "What's in it for me?"

I met Professor Levy in the noisy cafeteria on the central campus of the Open University in the central city of Ra'anana. What he had to convey was dramatic, but delivered in clipped, matter-of-fact tones over a cappuccino. The army was in a "twilight zone," he said, with its cherished model of universal conscription undergoing an inevitable process of erosion. Israel was, in fact, no different from other Western countries, nor impervious to the trends of the broader modern world. Military sacrifice was "contrary to the social DNA," he said, noting that the more a society became competitive, individualistic, and controlled by market forces, the more anomalous the demand for obligatory mandatory service.

The problem was not so much with the numbers of those enlisting; rather it was the impact of those who were not enlisting on the ethos of universal and equal service in the people's army. With Israel's population having grown to more than nine million, there were enough conscripts to fill the ranks with a reported annual intake in 2020 of roughly 50,000. In fact, given the rapid population growth, the army was on course for a likely surplus of recruits by 2030, when there would be 17,000 more eighteen-year-olds in the enlistment pool than a decade earlier.

For the longer term, however, the projections were more worrying. With almost half the country's first-graders now registered in the Arabic or ultra-Orthodox school systems, and with the Haredi sector multiplying faster than any other, the ratio of the population constituting the future recruitment pool was liable to shrink. The commanders believed that at least some measure of Haredi draft would become imperative, regardless of the difficulties raised by Haredi demands for specially supervised kosher food and a female-free environment. An increasing number of Israelis, ultra-Orthodox politicians among them, believed the only proper solution was to cancel the universal draft and turn the army into a professional volunteer force where recruits would choose to sign up and receive a proper salary. A survey carried out by the Israel Democracy Institute in late 2021 found that 47 percent of the Jewish public favored shifting to a professional army model and 42 percent disagreed. The army command had long opposed the idea.

Colonel Schreibman told me there was "too much fighting" for a professional army working on salary. Experts assessed that there would never be enough volunteers, and canceling conscription meant that Israel would lose its crucial advantage of being able to recruit and take its pick of the country's highest-quality human assets. Even the most sophisticated of technologies had to be developed and operated by humans. Robots were no replacement for commanders making the decisions. The army was not ready to give up on the people.

That position was firmly reinforced by Major General Moti Almoz, who served as the commander of the IDF's human resources directorate from 2017 until early 2021. We met in 2018 in his office on an upper floor of the general command headquarters in Tel Aviv, during a period when the army was grappling with particular tensions regarding the radical Haredi public, as well as frictions within the army concerning Orthodox soldiers and the issue of equal service for women. That summer he wrote a letter to commanders warning them to stick to the army's policy and orders preventing discrimination against women soldiers after the Israel Women's Network published a report exposing numerous cases of commanders freelancing and imposing "modesty" strictures to take religious male sensibilities into account, such as confining the women to separate smoking areas or, on some bases, banning them from wearing white T-shirts for fear they could be seen through.

Major General Almoz was trying to hold it all together and was clear that he considered universal, equal service essential for national security. "We are defending our lives," he said. "Only the people who live here can do that. All of them." The policy of not being ready to give up on anyone, in the interests of upholding at least a vestige of equal service, and despite the grim reality, sometimes led to absurd situations, mass demonstrations, and even riots. In one case, military police arrested a young woman who had obtained an exemption on religious grounds, claiming to be part of an ultra-Orthodox community, but who had also posted scantily clad selfies on Facebook. The arrest sparked ultra-Orthodox riots in Jerusalem. The protesters, who insisted the pictures were old and that the woman had since returned to religion, tried to set fire to the local draft office. The military police would also chase down Haredi "deserters" who belonged to extreme anti-Zionist rabbinical sects and refused even to show up at the recruitment offices to obtain their exemptions. Pointing to the female soldiers taking notes at the table, he said it would be unfair to them if others of their age were simply let off without any accountability.

Facing the conflicting scenarios of both a glut of recruits in the next few years and, at the same time, a future where only a fraction of the population would be liable for service, Major General Almoz headed up a committee looking forward to 2030, which he pointedly named the People's Army Committee. The idea, he said, was to find a balance between the looming demographic realities and the IDF's ethos and spirit. "If we aren't the people's army, we don't exist here," he declared passionately. "We need all the soldiers. This is not some social program. The tech doesn't work without the spirit. You need the right people."

So the People's Army model was not up for debate. It was only a question of how to manage it. Already changes were underway. The army had once relied on a vast bank of reservists in wartime, with demobilized citizens often performing annual reserve duty well into middle age. Long a means of preserving the citizen's sense of camaraderie over decades, *miluim,* or reserve duty, was part of the fabric of Israeli life and culture. *Givat Halfon Eina Ona,* or Halfon Hill Doesn't Answer, a cult comedy movie made in 1976, three years after the surprise crossing of the Suez Canal by Egyptian forces, immortalized and satirized the experience, lampooning the IDF through the antics of a reserve company left much to their own devices in the Sinai desert. Now, though, the reliance on reserve forces and reserve training had been scaled back significantly, and mostly involved specialized forces. Mandatory service had been shortened for the male rank and file from three years to thirty-two months. The idea was to continue drafting all eligible Israelis in principle, but the definition of universal and equal service was being stretched thin. The army was already introducing incentives, differential salaries, and service tracks to contend with the requirements of a more technologically advanced and specialized fighting force, with soldiers serving in elite fighting units now required to sign up for eight years of service.

In its quest for inclusiveness and a vestige of equality, the army offered fast-track conversion courses and circumcisions for Russian-speaking immigrant soldiers who had qualified for citizenship and the draft, but who were not technically Jewish according to Jewish law. The army also catered to vegans, providing appropriate food and alternatives to the standard leather boots; introduced outreach programs for gay and transgender recruits; and ran special programs to integrate youths with autism or with criminal records.

Weeks after my meeting with Major General Almoz, in the fall of 2018, the IDF launched a massive public relations effort to preserve the sense of consensus and the popular brand. Marking the seventieth anniversary of its establishment, the army went all out with an innovative exhibit highlighting both its technological prowess and its trademark of being of, and for, the people. Titled "Our IDF," it opened in a vast sports arena in Holon, a Tel Aviv suburb, then toured the country over the next year. When online registration first opened, the initial 100,000 tickets were snapped up within hours. I attended the festive opening in Holon and made my way through the exhibit. A slick, twenty-first-century digital version of a traditional military parade, it was set up as a kind of military theme park. Instead of rides, there were different stations offering virtual reality challenges for the whole family. Visitors could test their joystick skills on a massive screen that covered a whole wall by shooting down incoming rockets as they headed for buildings, like a giant computer game; they could simulate maneuvering themselves in a parachute; and they could try their luck at identifying sonar signals in a mock submarine. At the end of the course, each player could receive a computer-generated certificate with their scores. The Home Front command distributed educational card games, 3-D stickers, and comic books with X-ray specs to prepare children for rocket attacks or earthquakes. The arena in Holon was filled with patriotic, emotional parents and grandparents and children who scrambled over the armored vehicles on display.

Outside there were warplanes and, in a long pool of water, patrol boats. Hannah Dekel, sixty-seven, a retired teacher, had come from northern Israel to see the exhibit with her daughter, a former officer in the education corps, and her grandson, Lior, six, who she said was interested in tanks and technology. "We are a small country with lots of enemies," she said, adding of the IDF, "It's what binds us together." She was expressing a broad sentiment among the visitors to the exhibition but also one with a narrow interpretation of "us" and with limited validity. The hall was filled with secular and religious families from the Zionist, modern Orthodox sector on the day I visited. I did not encounter any Arab families there. The only *Haredim* in sight, a father-and-son duo from Holon, were Hasidic Chabad adherents who appeared to be there to proselytize.

The army's efforts at public relations and populism reached new peaks two years later, during the winter intake of 2020. The IDF invited television cameras into an induction base to document the enlistment of Noa Kirel, a teen model and pop star with a million followers on Instagram, prompting one Israeli columnist to describe the photo op as "another symptom of a confused army that is experiencing a serious identity crisis." Like her teen pop star boyfriend Jonathan Mergui, Kirel had enlisted in the IDF's new VIP "talent" track. In order to attract and cater to the YouTube and TikTok generation of young celebrities, it offered a select number of perks like the ability to shower in private and ninety days' special annual leave to pursue their civilian careers, double the number of furlough days granted to other gifted artists. In its early days, the IDF had helped shape modern Israeli culture with its entertainment troupes whose members went on to become popular stars. The army troupes produced meaningful, patriotic numbers and some of the country's most iconic peace songs. Now, though, the IDF was importing teen pop. To the astonishment of many Israelis, two days after the spectacle of Kirel being photographed at her induction in a seemingly bespoke, starched army uniform, supposedly headed off to basic training and then service in an entertainment troupe attached to the Education Corps, she flew off, instead, to Thailand for a holiday. Responding to the outpouring of criticism, Kirel's publicity machine responded that the trip had been planned in advance and that she was "proud to serve her country and to serve as a personal example to thousands of other draft-age Israelis." That wasn't the end of the bizarre concept of celebrity army service. The IDF's seventy-second Independence Day celebrations included a concert by Kirel at the Tzrifin military base accompanied by two male khaki-clad backup dancers. After a video of the gyrating soldiers rehearsing in their fatigues surfaced on social media and went viral, and was greeted with mirth and ridicule, Major General Almoz decided the sight was unbecoming and retired the dancers, reassigning them to a more traditional service track for artists. During her service, Kirel went on to sign a mega-contract with the American label Atlantic Records, but not before she caused another kerfuffle. That's when she appeared, with the army's permission, in a TV advertisement for a cable company singing a commercial parody of "Let the Sun Shine In," from *Hair*, the classic anti–Vietnam War musical, and playing the part of an American rookie, dressed in a foreign military's uniform, to the embarrassment of the Israeli high command.

Despite the shifting ground, the rituals around the army were still a rare unifier, at least for the mainstream Jews of Israel. Memorial Day had an air of sanctity, with all cafés and places of entertainment closed. The collective mourning abruptly transitioned into Independence Day celebrations, which also had a military hue. One highlight of the changeover ceremony at nightfall was a beloved flag parade representing all the military units, followed by intricately choreographed conformations onstage. The next day featured a televised ceremony at President's House honoring that year's outstanding soldiers, a cross-country flyover and acrobatic display by the air force, and family visits to tank museums and army bases that were opened up for the day, as well as the traditional barbecues and picnics in the park. On these national days, as during wartime, the intense sense of solidarity reminded many Israelis of who they really were and what the country was all about.

When soldiers fell in wars and one televised military funeral followed another on the evening news, raw emotion swept through suburban living rooms. Analysts questioned whether the practice of broadcasting so many burials was harmful for the morale of the people and the soldiers, much like the dilemma in 1948 of the Palmach's gravediggers along the road to Jerusalem. Some of the dead became household names, and many were revered as national heroes. The most gravely injured who prevailed against the odds became storied role models. So did some of the bereaved parents. Miriam Peretz, a warm, earthy, Moroccan-born educator who lost two sons, Eliraz and Uriel, twelve years apart, in combat in Lebanon and in Gaza, respectively, and whose partner, Eliezer, died "of heartache," became an Israeli everywoman, a heroic symbol of national resilience and social cohesion. She was awarded the country's top honors, including the prestigious

Israel Prize in 2018, in the categories of lifetime achievement and special contribution to society. Speaking on behalf of all that year's laureates, including the celebrated writer David Grossman, another publicly aching bereaved parent who lost his son Uri in Lebanon, her rousing speech pleading for unity, faith, hope, and kindness earned a standing ovation from the august audience that packed the hall of Jerusalem's International Congress Center. Having come to Israel with her family in the mid-1960s, she said, "As a girl, I felt I did nothing for my country. I came to a ready-made country and didn't know that there would come a day when I would give my dearest to the country—my sons Uriel and Eliraz. But a homeland is not only built with pain and tears. It is also built with labor and continued generosity," she said.

Most Israeli parents could identify with Peretz. Service in the IDF was part of the Israeli experience not only for the soldiers but also for their parents who were enlisted vicariously. As the mother of two sons who performed their military service, I, too, had attended ritualistic swearing-in ceremonies, driven across the country on parental missions to far-flung army bases in the rain and snow, and spent weekends laundering muddy khaki uniforms and socks stiff with sweat and threaded with thorns. When the authorities issued a controversial directive to close the gates of the military cemeteries to bereaved families on Memorial Day in 2020 at the height of the coronavirus pandemic, Peretz was recruited to become the face of a public campaign defending the decision, which prompted outrage as street-front stores, hair and nail salons, and Ikea furniture emporiums were being allowed to open up. "I have chosen life," Peretz said on television, urging people to stay away from the cemeteries. "The graves can wait." Many Israelis had wanted to see her as the country's next president, though she lost the vote in the Knesset to the former Labor leader Isaac Herzog, who succeeded President Rivlin.

Part of the army's ethos was to convince the soldiers and the proverbial Hebrew mother that their lives were sacrosanct, ingrained in the principle of never abandoning a soldier in the field. That was put to the test when Gilad Shalit, a soldier serving along the Gaza border, was abducted by Hamas militants in a cross-border raid in 2006 and was held captive in Gaza for the next five years. Much of Israel rallied to the cause. Popular musicians composed songs about the staff sergeant.

Thousands of dedicated activists filled protest tents and held demonstrations and marches across the country. Public relations professionals
volunteered their services. The Hebrew news media adopted the cause,
portraying Shalit as "everybody's child" and printing cute photos of
him as a boy. "We had to keep Gilad in the public consciousness," one
PR professional who was helping the family told me, "and to build him
into a national icon." When in the fall of 2011 he was finally redeemed
by the Netanyahu government in exchange for more than a thousand
Palestinian prisoners, some of them convicted of heinous murders,
millions of Israelis supported the deal, despite its brazen lopsidedness.

That sense of public cohesiveness frayed, however, with each additional month of the politicized violence bred of the corrosive occupation. One shameful act of a single, low-ranking Israeli soldier in the
dour West Bank city of Hebron showed just how divisive it had become
and rocked the pedestal on which the IDF usually stood. In March
2016, at the height of the deadly Palestinian stabbing campaign known
as the "knives intifada," Sergeant Elor Azaria, a nineteen-year-old
Israeli conscript and medic, fatally shot a wounded Palestinian assail-
ant in the head as he lay incapacitated on the ground. The Palestinian
had, a short while earlier, stabbed and wounded one of Azaria's comrades, had already been shot and wounded, and was barely moving.
Azaria told others at the scene that he thought the Palestinian, Abdel
al-Fatah al-Sharif, deserved to die. After Azaria shot him in the head,
Sharif's blood ran out in a rivulet on the asphalt. Another Palestinian
resident of the neighborhood caught the act on a video camera that
had been provided by B'Tselem, the Israeli human rights organization,
and the footage quickly went viral. In damage control mode, the military swiftly condemned Azaria's actions and arrested the soldier. He
was tried in a military court and convicted of manslaughter. He served
about two-thirds of a fourteen-month prison sentence.

But the episode stirred a public backlash that put the IDF, its military ethics, and its core values in the dock, and polarized Israelis over
their most trusted institution. The high command had denounced
Azaria's cold-blooded act as a direct violation of the "purity of arms,"
a central doctrine of the "Spirit of the IDF," the military's ethical code.
The code, which General Elazar Stern also had a hand in drafting,
stated that soldiers must exercise restraint in the use of armed force,

using their weapons "only for the purpose of subduing the enemy to the necessary extent," without inflicting unnecessary harm to human life or limb, dignity, or property. At the time, though, there was little public sympathy for the Palestinians wielding knives, nor for the idea of restraint. Politicians were questioning the army's open-fire regulations, frequently citing the Talmudic injunction for self-defense: "If someone comes to kill you, rise up and kill him first."

The soldier's supporters accused the generals of prejudging him. He tried to mount a defense based on claims that he feared that Sharif, who had stirred, was concealing an explosive belt under his jacket and posed a danger to other troops casually standing around in the street. The public storm also took on ethnic overtones, pitting the overtly Mizrahi Azaria family against the "elitist" establishment—despite the fact that the chief of staff at the time, Lieutenant General Gadi Eisenkot, a down-to-earth military man, was of Moroccan descent, notwithstanding his Germanic-sounding surname. Eisenkot had already been pilloried for what his critics perceived as being soft on knife terrorism. After a police officer was filmed by security cameras in Jerusalem chasing a Palestinian schoolgirl who had tried to stab passersby with scissors and shooting her as she lay on the ground, Eisenkot said he would not want a soldier of his "to empty a magazine at a thirteen-year-old girl with scissors." A poll conducted by the Israel Democracy Institute at the time found that 50 percent of the Jewish public disagreed with General Eisenkot's position while 48 percent supported it. In the supercharged emotion of the cycle of stabbings and shootings, the raging Azaria affair cast the IDF as being against the "ordinary people" who hailed Azaria as a hero. Tens of thousands signed an online petition calling for him to be given a medal. Some young soldiers said the only thing he had done wrong was to have been caught in the act on camera. And Azaria's case was in many ways an exception. Yesh Din, the Israeli human rights organization, found that in recent years 80 percent of the complaints of violence filed by Palestinians against the army were closed without a criminal investigation. Criminal investigations were generally not launched when a Palestinian was hurt or killed in what the military categorized broadly as a combat situation. Even when a veteran Palestinian-American journalist, Shireen Abu Akleh, of Al Jazeera, was fatally shot in May 2022 while covering an

Israeli army counter-terrorism raid in the West Bank city of Jenin, prompting an international uproar, the military did not rush to open a criminal investigation. Numerous probes, including one conducted by the Americans, concluded that she had most likely been killed accidentally by an Israeli sniper while the Palestinian Authority and eyewitnesses insisted that she had been targeted intentionally.

More egregious in the Azaria case was the intervention of the politicians. As one would have expected, Netanyahu, the prime minister at the time, initially backed up the army. But typically feeling the heat from politicians to his right and appealing to a base that already felt the army was too soft on the Palestinians, he soon phoned Azaria's parents to offer his sympathy and later even called for the convicted soldier to be pardoned. The hardline defense minister, Avigdor Liberman, showed up at the military court to support Azaria. The IDF clarified its open-fire regulations at all levels of service in case there was any confusion. Soon after the incident, I visited a cramped "pillbox," one of the army's cylindrical concrete guard posts, in a tiny, barricaded position by a checkpoint on the outskirts of Ramallah in the West Bank. I clambered up the narrow, spiral staircase inside the squat tower where conscripts took turns sleeping in nooks and crannies. At the top, in the guard's 360-degree lookout, the arrest procedure and open-fire regulations were taped to a grubby window stipulating that warning shots must first be fired into the air and only after that at a suspect's lower limbs.

If the army came under fire from the right during the Azaria affair, the occupation had certainly put it in the sights of the left. It was the military's silent war that it could not win, eroding its morality and the morale of many soldiers by turning them into an oppressive policing force. Two generations of Israeli soldiers had enforced government policy in the occupied West Bank, raiding towns and villages to arrest militants, entering houses late at night to "map" out their layout and show a presence, searching for weapons, dragging Palestinian minors suspected of throwing stones at troops from their beds, protecting the settlements and outposts, policing checkpoints, and securing the roads.

Buffeted by years of criticism from Israeli and international human rights organizations who charged it with brutality in suppressing Palestinian resistance and using excessive force, the IDF that convicted

Azaria was more frequently accused of whitewashing alleged war crimes. After Israel's unilateral withdrawal from the Gaza Strip in 2005, and the evacuation and demolition of all its settlements there, the IDF had fought four asymmetrical wars against the militant warlords of the impoverished territory, as well as been engulfed in repeated bursts of cross-border fighting that could last two or three days. However precisely the Israeli air force tried to work, its arguments were soon buried in the rubble along with the hundreds of civilians inevitably killed as collateral damage as the militants operated from densely packed residential areas. There was more carnage when Israeli snipers shot dead more than sixty mostly unarmed Palestinians during protests along the Gaza border fence in May 2018 after Palestinian activists threatened a mass "march of the return" to break the siege of Gaza and reclaim— or at least draw attention to—the refugees' lost ancestral lands. The protests and riots continued for months on consecutive Fridays, with dozens more killed. One protester was filmed being shot in the back; another protester was shot in a wheelchair. The few investigations opened by the army were painfully slow.

There was a time when military officials dared to say they were glad for B'Tselem, feeling they had nothing to hide and that such watchdogs kept Israel democratic and moral. But in more recent years, left-wing Israelis who decried what they viewed as the army's brutality, impunity, and lack of accountability were branded by other Israelis as disloyal and unpatriotic. Those who worked for groups like B'Tselem or Breaking the Silence, an organization made up of disillusioned army veterans opposed to the occupation, were demonized as traitors, particularly for their fundraising activities abroad and presentations to United Nations fact-finding commissions, which were viewed as "firing inside the APC"—APC stands for armored personnel carrier—or airing the dirty linen in public and defaming the military and Israel. Ex-soldiers who spoke out against the occupation faced off against nationalist grassroots groups like Im Tirzu, which presented its goals as true Zionism, and another group of former soldiers, Reservists at the Front, whose mission was to defend the military and Israel against the so-called defamation.

Despite the deep and cardinal fault line that the occupation carved through Israeli society, the army worked hard to keep the dispute out of its ranks. Genuine pacifists could apply to a special committee that granted a small number of exemptions each year on the grounds of conscientious objection, but those slots were reserved for people who objected to joining any army and to any use of force. Recruits who were prepared to serve in general, just not in the occupied territories, in what the army called selective objection or selective conscience, were given no alternatives. Some objectors found themselves serving months-long terms in military prison until they were eventually discharged, on the grounds that they'd been judged incompatible and unfit for army service. In the delicate balance among individual rights, duty, and equality, the military was wary of making public concessions to one ideological viewpoint over another. If it made concessions to those who opposed the occupation, the argument went, it would also have to show tolerance toward soldiers who supported the settlement enterprise and allow them to sit out any actions to curb settlement activity or, theoretically, to allow them to refuse orders to evacuate settlements.

Still, it was impossible to keep the culture wars being waged outside from seeping into the ranks of the military, especially as the old kibbutz elite was being overtaken by religious officers for whom defending the settlements meant defending their homes. If religious Jews had once shunned Ben-Gurion's "melting pot" army for fear of coming out of it secularized, the modern Orthodox national religious camp had come to embrace military service as a means of influence, replacing the secular crème de la crème of the fighting forces and making a concerted effort to penetrate its top ranks. The change came when the army allowed a system combining service in the military with years of Torah study in approved modern Orthodox seminaries, often entailing a deferral of army service and in turn allowing the seminary rabbis a mediating role between the religious conscripts and the military. But the mix brought new tensions. One religiously observant brigade commander, Ofer Winter, a graduate of one such prestigious pre-army religious academy in the West Bank settlement of Eli, gained notoriety during the 2014 Gaza war when he sent a letter to his troops to rally them in what he called a battle against "a blasphemous enemy that defiles the God of Israel."

When we spoke, Colonel Schreibman had refused to break down the identity or religious affiliation of the cadets at officers' school, saying he could see the skullcaps but did not count them. But at least a third of the officers' corps was now reported to be made up of "knitted *kippot*," meaning those who were identified as belonging to the national religious camp by means of their trademark crocheted skullcaps. And the more strictly observant some Orthodox officers became, even outside the specially designated ultra-Orthodox units, the louder the demands for gender-segregated service, since religious male soldiers sometimes heeded the instructions and guidance offered by their rabbis above that of their commanders, at least in spiritual matters.

The religious vector collided head-on with another distinctly Israeli phenomenon: Despite the more typical antipathy toward militarism of feminists internationally, the IDF had become a prime vehicle for Israeli feminism. Israeli women's activists pushed for gender equality, and for all combat roles to be opened up to women. Though women had fought in Israel's War of Independence, and a few had served as pilots in the earliest years, by the early 1950s women had been barred from combat positions for fear of what would happen if they were captured behind enemy lines. Instead they were assigned to clerical and educational roles, providing training and combat support and freeing up the men for the fighting. It took until the mid-1990s for change to come after Alice Miller, a South African–born student of aerospace engineering who held a civilian pilot license and had a passion for flying, successfully petitioned the Supreme Court to be allowed to try out for the air force's then male-only flight academy. In a landmark verdict that changed the face of the IDF, and impacted Israeli society as a whole, the court ruled that preventing her would be discriminatory and unconstitutional. Miller was ultimately rejected from the course on medical grounds but paved the way for others. By 1998, Sheri Rahat, an F-16 combat navigator, became the first female graduate of the army's flight school in decades. Three years later Roni Zuckerman, the granddaughter of Yitzhak "Antek" Zuckerman and Zivia Lubetkin, leaders of the Warsaw Ghetto uprising and founders of Kibbutz Lohamei HaGetaot, became a combat pilot, in the kind of historic justice the IDF excelled at, and in 2019 the air force appointed its first female commander of a surveillance flight squadron.

Still, the traditional frontline infantry units that operated across enemy lines in wartime remained closed to females. Military officials argued that because of the physiological limitations, it was not worth the expense of opening up the intake process to women for the sake of a few who would be physically capable of keeping up with the men. No doubt there was an element of ingrained chauvinism involved. Though Israel was one of the few countries left that drafted women, several other Western countries, including the United States, France, and Germany, had opened up all units to women. In Israel's case, however, the policy also had the added value for commanders of avoiding all-out confrontation with religious male soldiers who increasingly shunned serving in close quarters with women. In the end, it was a case of either/ or, Yagil Levy, the civil-military affairs expert, told me. Total integration of women would mean the traditional frontline units like the Paratroopers, Givati, and Golani could not include religious men, he said, "and women aren't really a replacement for them." Female recruits continued to press for more challenging roles, however, and several petitioned the Supreme Court again in the process. In 2000, the army established the first of four coed combat battalions, usually composed of about one-third men and two-thirds women, to patrol the Egyptian and Jordanian borders and carry out routine security.

But the issue of women's roles continued to roil the military and society. In late 2020, at a meeting of the Knesset's Foreign Affairs and Defense Committee devoted to the subject, Orna Barbivai, the first woman to attain the rank of major general, the second-highest rank in the IDF, who then became a lawmaker from the centrist Yesh Atid party, argued that the social legitimacy of the IDF would suffer if it continued "to sanctify male service and fight for the enlistment of every last Haredi, and at the same time, does not see the value of women in realizing the goal of victory."

Barbivai was a prime beneficiary of the upward mobility offered by the military. She had grown up as the oldest of seven siblings from a broken home in the hardscrabble northern town of Afula. Her mother, Tzila, was born in Iraq; her father, Eli Shochetman, was an immigrant from Romania. After her parents divorced, Barbivai cleaned floors and babysat for doctors at a local hospital to help her mother make ends meet. As she rose through the ranks, one Israeli television interviewer described her as "a Cinderella in army boots."

We met in her party's 2020 election campaign headquarters in a business district in the Tel Aviv suburbs, when she was running as part of the alliance led by Benny Gantz in a bid to unseat Netanyahu, and in a period when the generals had made a comeback in Israeli politics. Her first break had come in her youth, she said, when an inspirational teacher took her under her wing and encouraged her to take advantage of a scholarship for poor, gifted teens at a boarding school. After two years she missed home too much, with all its rowdiness. She went back to Afula and fell in love with Moshe, a neighbor in her apartment building and one of the few officers in their northern town. She married at nineteen and decided she, too, wanted to become an officer. Drafted in 1981, she began to climb the ranks of the human resources director- ate. After it became clear to the couple that she had the better chance of a significant promotion, Moshe began to take primary responsibil- ity for the care of their three children. A BA and MBA later, she was appointed to head the directorate, in the position that Major General Almoz would hold years later. She was instrumental in drafting the Joint Service ordinance regulating coed service, working closely with commanders in the field, and was sometimes criticized for not doing enough to promote other women in the military. But she advocated opening up all army combat roles to women. She rebuffed the argu- ment that full women's service in the traditional frontline infantry bri- gades would cause too much friction with religious soldiers since, she said, only a few women would likely qualify. "Just as there are men who are not physiologically able," she said, "there are women who are able."

Armed with a Micro-Tavor assault rifle, her long blond mane gathered up in a ponytail, Lieutenant Ya'ar Perlow, twenty-one, a platoon com- mander in the mixed Caracal Battalion, named for a desert cat, was on a five-month deployment with her thirty troops—male and female—at the Anatot base just north of Jerusalem, in the West Bank. The mission was keeping the peace in the area for both the Palestinian residents and the Jewish settlers. A handwritten banner on the wall of her office in the barracks read "Sweat saves blood." Sweating did not preclude wearing pale nail varnish—one of the shades permitted by the high command. Outside, on a patch of grass under the shade of two trees, her soldiers sat cleaning their weapons. A couple more were on duty in a small control room, monitoring the surrounding area on screens. Beyond the base, female soldiers were patrolling the sector on foot and guarding a small position on a rocky incline above the main road.

The unit was ordinarily stationed along the Egyptian border, patrolling and lying in ambush for drug and weapons smugglers. "There, it's just us, the desert and the bad guys," Perlow said. Caracal's beret, with its dappled shades of yellow and brown camouflage, was designed for the sandy terrain. Here, in the West Bank, the contact between the soldiers and the local population, both the settler occupiers and the occupied Palestinians, was deeply intertwined. During a recent search of a house in a nearby Palestinian town, Hizmeh, Perlow and a comrade found a toddler sleeping in his parents' bed as they searched the bedroom. "We're in vests, helmets. He woke up," she said. "We said hi and smiled and waved a lot. With all the abnormality of the situation, he seemed happy. We were just doing the job the best way we could. We don't scream and yell."

Lieutenant Perlow grew up in the Misgav region of the upper Galilee, in a home where love of the IDF was ingrained, she said. She was the only female out of her grade of 250 students to opt for a combat unit. It was hard getting under a stretcher toward the end of a six-hour march during training, she acknowledged, but teammates helped push her up the mountain from behind. During her eight-month-long officers' course at Bahad 1, she said, male soldiers who were not used to seeing female combat soldiers sweat, jump, and run "were in shock. Really in shock."

Over the years, the mix of religion and gender conflicts in the military had at times become potent and explosive. In one case that gained national attention, dozens of religiously observant male paratroopers turned their backs on a parachuting instructor—the daughter of a senior general, no less—as she attempted to give them a demonstration. They had turned away with the permission of their commanding officer. Female soldiers reported stringently modest dress codes including having to wear tights or leggings beneath their shorts for fitness training and the ban on white T-shirts mentioned earlier. A pilot program to train all-female tank crews for routine security roles within Israel's frontiers drew ire from some vociferous, ultraconservative rabbis of pre-military seminaries who were against the principle of gender-equal service in the first place. They were enraged by the rising number of modern Orthodox women from the religious Zionist camp who were opting to serve. "They are Jewish when they go in, but they aren't Jews by the end—not in the genetic sense, but all of their values and priorities have been upset," railed one prominent critic, Rabbi Yigal Levinstein, from the academy in the settlement of Eli, adding, "I don't know who will marry them." Some rabbis called on religious male soldiers to refuse to serve in units alongside women. And a small pressure group of Orthodox male reservists launched a public campaign called "Brothers in Arms," claiming that women combat soldiers dragged army standards down, endangering the security of Israel. By the summer of 2021, the first all-women company of tank operators was stationed along the Egyptian border, under the command of the Caracal Battalion.

Three years earlier, the IDF had issued a final version of its Joint Service ordinance after amendments resulting from pressure from rabbis. Israeli women's organizations also took part in its formulation. It stipulated that male soldiers were required to serve in mixed combat units if that's where they were assigned. But before being posted, religious officers were allowed to submit a request for a transfer. Lieutenant Perlow took a matter-of-fact approach to the gender wars and said there was usually a way to work things out. At one base, near the Egyptian border, she recalled, her platoon had to wait for an Orthodox male unit to finish eating before they could enter the mess tent. "Some of them had a problem with us eating together," she said. "We solved the problem by eating at different times."

The high command downplayed the tensions on a day-to-day basis, refusing to be drawn into religious and gender wars. Colonel Schreibman tried to evade the subject, though he said he had kicked one religious cadet out of officers' school when he refused to work together with a female cadet, on the grounds that he had not found a way to complete his mission. "We are not here to serve as a youth movement or to educate Israeli society and solve its problems," he said. "My mission is to get ready for the next war." In June 2022 the chief of the general staff announced that some additional combat positions had opened up for women, including the elite 669 search-and-rescue unit, subject to them meeting certain physiological criteria for screening. Gur Schreibman, by then a brigadier general in the reserves, told a parliamentary meeting convened by a caucus for the advancement of women that he supported the idea of women being allowed to compete to serve in all capacities in the military, but that uniform criteria needed to be established for both men and women seeking admittance to special units, derived from operational scenarios.

Despite the difficulties of military inclusiveness, few Israeli leaders seemed willing to take a bet on a professional army based on voluntary enlistment. Elazar Stern, the retired general who had helped author the "Spirit of the IDF," the army's ethical code, and saw the army as building the nation, and vice versa, told me one day in his office in the Knesset that he believed that in the absence of mandatory conscription even his own sons would not have chosen to serve. But even for those who were passionate about maintaining the People's Army brand, it was clear that the current conscription model, which ended up enlisting fewer than half the Israelis of draft age, was no longer workable and it was, ultimately, up to the politicians to set policy, legislate amendments to the draft law, and tackle one of the most delicate issues facing Israeli society. The buzzword was "selective conscription."

In late January 2021, after yet another Supreme Court deadline for regulating the ultra-Orthodox draft had expired, Benny Gantz, as an "alternative" prime-minister-in-waiting in Netanyahu's discordant "unity" government, laid out his party's proposal to resolve the conscription conundrum. The plan called for all Israelis to perform some manner of national service, whether military or civilian. Every Israeli eighteen-year-old, Jewish and Arab, would be reviewed by a new joint military-civilian administration. The military would get first pick of whom it wanted to draft for military service. All the others could perform civilian national service in the police or in the community. As well as solving the military's human resources problems, this model was meant to create some common ground among the warring sectors of Israeli society and help those on the margins, including the *Haredim,* have access to training and education and become productive members of the workforce.

"The face of society is in a process of change," Gantz said, "and the IDF long ago stopped being the people's army to become half the people's army." He added a stark warning: "The people who serve and the combat fighters have come to feel like suckers. Israel's resilience is at risk. Israel's future—economic, civil, and social—hangs in the balance."

Months later, Gantz was defense minister in the government that included left-wingers, centrists, and right-wingers as well as Raam, the Islamic party. It did not include the Haredi parties, though Prime Minister Bennett and some of his allies were hoping to keep the door open for future cooperation in the post-Netanyahu era. The Blue and White former generals of the so-called cockpit that had steered the anti-Netanyahu political camp in earlier elections had failed in their mission. Netanyahu had managed to splinter the opposition and left the generals fighting one another. Among the new Bennett-Lapid government's main goals was domestic peace and national healing. Within its first hundred days, the cabinet approved the plan to lower the age of exemption from military service for yeshiva students to twenty-one from twenty-four. Prime Minister Bennett said the idea was to free up thousands of ultra-Orthodox young men "without coercion and without tanks in Bnei Brak." Avigdor Liberman, then the finance minister, said the decision was meant to balance the ideal of the melting pot with economic needs. At the same time, a government committee was to build an outline for a comprehensive new law regulating national and civilian service and present its conclusions in about a year. The new consensus was unlikely to involve forcing the issue of universal and equal service out of a recognition that coercing Haredi men into fatigues would only exacerbate Israel's internal conflicts and that the army was in any case unable and unwilling to cater to the dietary and gender-related demands of tens of thousands of *Haredim*.

But even in the relative calm of the early months of the Bennett era, it became clear that the army would continue to have to fight for its legitimacy and status in a still-polarized Israel. An illustration of that came in the late summer of 2021 when Barel Hadaria Shmueli, an Israeli sniper from a special Border Police unit, was shot and critically injured at point-blank range by a Palestinian militant who fired his pistol through a hole in a concrete security wall during a riot along the Gaza border. The incident was amplified by the fact that it was captured on video from the Palestinian side and the images made their way to Israeli TV screens. Netanyahu and his supporters immediately seized upon the incident and tried to make political capital out of it. Hours after Shmueli arrived at the hospital, the former prime minister, whose social media machine was still whirring nonstop, made sure to phone the family from his vacation spot at a friend's exclusive Hawaiian island resort. Bennett had already called, but the conversation was a disaster. The soldier's father, beside himself with worry and rage, launched a verbal assault on the stunned prime minister, calling Bennett and his government cowards and accusing his son's commanders of staying back and holding back instead of using all their firepower to distance the rioters, turning his son into a sitting duck. On Bennett's end of the line there were excruciating, awkward silences that made him sound unprepared or distracted, and when the prime minister did speak he got the soldier's name wrong and asked which hospital he was in, though that information had been widely reported. Shmueli's mother went on the radio the next morning to describe the family's disgust over the prime minister's botched phone call. But that was not the end of it. Shortly after noon, an audio recording of the embarrassing call was posted on social media by The Shadow, a rap singer and far-right political activist. As the audio went viral, the *New York Times* bureau chief in Jerusalem, Patrick Kingsley, and I were sitting in the prime minister's office opposite Bennett, mid-interview on the eve of his first visit to Washington as Israeli premier. An aide burst in declaring a crisis that needed immediate attention. Bennett broke off to draft a humble apology to the soldier's family.

Days later, Shmueli succumbed to his injuries. His funeral was disrupted by a small but vocal group of hardcore pro-Netanyahu supporters who cursed Bennett and blamed him for having "killed the soldier," purportedly by reining in the army and having them curb their fire to keep things quiet during his visit to the White House— even though Shmueli had fired at several Palestinian rioters before being shot. The refrain about too much restraint was frequently aired on the right, along with allegations that the Azaria affair had made soldiers scared to use their weapons for fear of legal repercussions. Bennett himself, before becoming prime minister, had once claimed that the soldiers were more afraid of the military prosecutor than they were of the leader of Hamas in Gaza. As prime minister, he changed his tune and backed up the commanders. He publicly apologized to the Shmueli family again for making a mistake and adding to their pain, in interviews he gave to the Israeli media on the eve of Yom Kippur. But he hinted at the waning Israeli tolerance for losses among its troops, emphasizing that Shmueli had not been "murdered" but had fallen in battle, and he denounced the politicians and activists who'd been dancing on Shmueli's fresh grave, warning them to keep the IDF out of the political game. The military, for its part, insisted there had been no change in the open-fire regulations and, while the deployment of forces may have been faulty, there was no evidence of commanders pulling back. One minister told me that Shmueli's division commander was standing right next to him on the front line and could easily have been the one killed.

Days after Shmueli's death, and clearly concerned over the cynical, politicized assault on the military and the legitimacy of an army meant to be of and for the people, Lieutenant General Aviv Kochavi, the military chief of staff, issued an unusual statement backing up his troops. It was rich in profoundly resonant messages that were reminiscent of Moshe Dayan's eulogy delivered at Nahal Oz, by the Gaza border, in the 1950s. "The state of Israel is flourishing and growing in a region wracked with violence, social crises and multiple security threats," Kochavi's statement began. "This is testimony to the great success of the IDF over seventy-three years." It was the army's job, he continued, to deploy along the borders and serve as protection for Israeli civilians even at the cost of the lives of soldiers—soldiers who are equipped with the means to fight and the permission to use those means in any situation deemed life-threatening. The commanders continued to command from the front, and the army would continue to be a moral army. But the statement also came with an ominous and existential warning: "A society that does not back up its soldiers and commanders, even if they have erred, will find that there is nobody left to fight for it. The willingness to bear losses is a condition for national resilience, and that resilience is a condition for our continued existence." At the end of the day, just as the people needed the army, the People's Army needed the people.

# NINE

# THE RUSSIANS

THE FACEBOOK posts kept pouring in. They spoke of trauma—not from Israel's wars, but from the reception their authors got as children arriving in the country from the former Soviet Union. Thirty years had passed since the beginning of the great wave of Russian *aliyah,* or immigration, of the 1990s, an influx that transformed Israel. Perhaps it was the thirty-year anniversary in the winter of 2019 that sparked the explosion of memories, good and bad, that flooded a Facebook group wryly called "Humorless Russian Women and Their Friends."

Now adults, those immigrants called themselves the 1.5 generation, a sociological term for those who arrive in a new country as children or adolescents, growing up in two cultures. These Russian-speaking Israelis had been brought to the country by their parents as young children or teens, by no choice of their own. Some rejected being described as *olim,* or *olot,* the Israeli masculine and feminine terms for immigrants with connotations of ascending to a better life and location, preferring to call themselves simply "migrants." Nevertheless, they shared their *aliyah* stories, laced with wit and pain, in posts written in flawless Hebrew.

These were recollections of culture shock and embarrassment. Recurring themes included being dropped off at preschool or elementary school dressed as if for a formal family portrait, with hair neatly combed or plaited and topped with an outsize bow or festive pompom. Many of their parents committed the cardinal sin of dressing them in open sandals with socks. The Israeli schools were most un-Soviet, adding to their feeling of being outsiders. The classrooms were noisy and chaotic, filled with unruly native Israeli children who showed little respect for their teachers and routinely addressed them by their first names. Russian-sounding names like Irena, Dmitri, and Yulia were dead giveaways, and, like previous waves of immigrants from other parts of the world, the newcomers came with little or no Hebrew. They recounted how they were immediately and sometimes cruelly teased by their casual, suntanned Sabra classmates who basked in their Israeliness. There was also a built-in sense of insult and shame. Many immigrant parents who came with qualifications ended up cleaning houses, and money was usually tight. Known simply as "the Russians," the generic term was applied to the roughly one million immigrants who flowed into the country from 1989 to 1999, no matter which corner of the former Soviet republics they came from.

"I remember that we received many things from good people around us—kitchenware, clothes," wrote one member of the Facebook group, Ira Lapardin, who came from Moldova with her family at the age of nine, at the height of the influx in 1991. "Afterwards," she continued, "they laughed at me in school because I came dressed in an old sweater that had belonged to a girl in my class who lived in my apartment building." Others remembered being called a "Russian whore" or a "smelly Russian," accused of stinking of sausage, pickled cabbage, and herring.

As if a dam had broken, the monologues kept flowing. By 2021, the Facebook group had swelled to more than 40,000 members. Ola Belensky, a student of psychology who had also emigrated at age nine from Lugansk, Ukraine, wrote of how the Israeli teacher had found her name and that of her twin sister too complicated and, to the amusement of the other pupils, simply referred to them as "the Russians," as in, "Yes, Russian, did you want to say something?" She also posted an old black-and-white photograph of herself and her twin sister when they were young, posing with bunches of flowers, bows in their hair, dressed in traditional lacy aprons. Besides the recollections of hurtful classmates and fights with bullies, however, many of the stories had happy endings. For Ola, salvation came with her enlistment in the military. For the first time, she wrote, the army made her feel that she belonged to the country she lived in—even if the country was still not sure she belonged to it.

The digital stocktaking was just one reflection of how "the Russians," the largest wave of immigrants to have arrived in Israel since the 1950s, were still challenging the system as much as they were still challenged by the realities of life in Israel. All immigrants to Israel have undergone some degree of culture shock in their absorption process. But the great Russian *aliyah*, an overwhelmingly secular one, was exceptional in that many of the immigrants were not Jewish. Many of them qualified for automatic citizenship through descent or family ties under the Law of Return but did not qualify as Jews in accordance with Jewish law, nor were they recognized as such by the state. This placed them in the crosshairs of the religious authorities and at the crux of the country's secular-religious divide. The non-Jews among them could not officially marry in Israel, since there was no provision for civil marriage. They could not be buried next to a Jew in a consecrated graveyard; their difference lasted after death, even when they died in the service of the state. Yet the impact of the Russian *aliyah* was profound. Well-educated and often with a sense of cultural superiority, the Russians disrupted the political, religious, cultural, economic, and demographic trajectory of Israel.

Unlike the hardy Russian pioneers who had come out to settle the land a century earlier and who often came from a religious background, even if they rejected it for secular socialism, these newcomers were mostly not motivated by any idealistic, Zionist longing to return to the ancestral homeland. Instead, fleeing a crumbling Soviet empire and seeking a better life, many came to Israel by default, and not as their first choice. For years, as Jews trickled out, more and more opted to go to the United States rather than Israel, dealing a blow to Israel's ideological claim to be a safe haven for Jews and leading to feverish policy debates within the American Jewish organizations, which had originally lobbied for the right of Soviet Jewish emigration to Israel, and within the U.S. administration, over the émigrés' refugee status. By the time the floodgates opened in the late 1980s, in the wake of perestroika, glasnost, and the collapse of the Iron Curtain, more than 80 percent of Soviet Jewish émigrés had been opting for the United States rather than Israel. In 1987, Prime Minister Yitzhak Shamir, determined not to pass up the boon of such valuable human capital, had urged the American administration not to grant refugee status to Soviet Jews coming out on Israeli visas and to further limit resettlement funding. Once the Jews began leaving en masse, those policies, together with the mechanisms of direct flights and other benefits, funneled the majority of the émigrés to Israel.

The Israeli population jumped from about 4.5 million in 1989 to just over six million a decade later. The injection of mostly secular, often highly skilled immigrants boosted the economy and its nascent high-tech enterprises. In that first decade, according to the Ministry of Immigration and Absorption, the Soviet immigration brought in 100,000 engineers, 20,000 doctors and dentists, and 20,000 musicians, artists, and athletes, even if many did not find employment in their professions. The impact was particularly felt in many of the development towns on the country's periphery, where the immigrants found cheaper housing.

Those who did come out of Zionism lacked the ideological fervor that had underpinned the early Zionist *olim* from Russia and other parts of eastern Europe to Ottoman Palestine in the late nineteenth and early twentieth centuries. They had come to help build the state and quickly shed their Russian and Yiddish, reinventing themselves as new Hebrews. By the time the ex-Soviets arrived in the 1990s, modern Israel had basically been built. But its character, its identity, and even its permanent borders were still in the making, giving the new arrivals a stake in shaping its future. Demographically, the injection of a million mostly secular "Russians" allowed Israel to maintain the balance over the years between its Jewish and Arab populations and temporarily diluted, or slowed, the rising power of the ultra-Orthodox, while triggering a seismic shift in the delicate domestic construct of religion and state and in national and regional politics.

The complications were built into the crevices of the so-called status quo agreement, the uneasy secular-religious arrangement on which the state was founded, and which gave the Orthodox rabbinical establishment a monopoly over life-cycle events including legally recognized

Jewish marriage, divorce, and burial. Jews, Muslims, and Christians were to be married by their own religious authorities. Decades later, however, the population increasingly failed to fit into this rubric. Israel's Law of Return, the legislation governing Jewish immigration and a fundamental pillar of the Jewish state, had been amended in 1970 to grant automatic citizenship not only to Jews born of a Jewish mother, in accordance with the matrilineal descent stipulated in Jewish law, or to converts to Judaism, but also to the children and grandchildren of mixed marriages, and the non-Jewish spouses of the children and grandchildren. The idea was to prevent split families and was based on the criteria laid down by the Nazi-era Nuremberg laws, whereby having one Jewish grandparent and being a "quarter Jewish," or being married to a Jew, was enough to warrant persecution—and therefore, by the state's logic, enough to warrant a place of refuge in Israel. The prevalence of mixed families in the former Soviet Union meant that about a quarter of the immigrants who came in the 1990s were considered Jewish enough for citizenship by the secular state authorities but were not considered Jewish by the rabbis according to the *Halacha*, or Orthodox Jewish law. A generation on, nearly half a million Israelis of eastern European descent were not recognized as Jewish by the Orthodox state rabbinical authorities who still maintained their grip on official marriage and burial in Israel.

The Orthodox rabbis insisted on sticking rigidly to the rules, they said, to preserve Jewish unity and maintain one halachic standard, protecting future generations from canonical chaos and the complications that could arise from unclear genealogy and lineage. Many immigrants who had always considered themselves Jewish and who wanted a state-approved wedding were subjected to special background checks and often had to go to great lengths to prove their Jewish credentials, or did not qualify at all.

For the more than 400,000 immigrants and their offspring from the former Soviet Union who were not considered halachically Jewish and could not marry through the Chief Rabbinate without undergoing conversion, there were various ways around the state-sanctioned chuppah, or marriage canopy. Many traveled to nearby Cyprus for a quick wedding package that combined a civil ceremony and a brief honeymoon. On their return, the marriage would be registered with the

Israeli Interior Ministry. Weddings performed legally abroad were recognized by the government. Other couples held alternative weddings
in Israel, sometimes with the help of nonprofit organizations fighting
religious coercion. An increasing number of non-Russian couples were
also opting for non-state-sanctioned weddings in a tuxedo-and-lace
rebellion against the monopoly of the rabbinate and the disproportionate power wielded by ultra-Orthodox politicians.

If the immigrant parents were too busy trying to learn Hebrew and
make ends meet, their children, the so-called 1.5 generation who were
brought on *aliyah* without having had much say in it, would be the
ones to grapple with the consequences. Having spent their formative
years split between Russia and Israel and, once in Israel, navigating
between heavily Russian home lives and the Hebrew-speaking society
outside, the age-old questions of "Who is a Jew?" and what is an Israeli
took on a new relevance and urgency as they entered adulthood. On
the whole the integration of the Russian *aliyah* was considered a great
success. But many found they had been leading a kind of double life:
They had tried their best to fit in, but also, as staunchly secular Jews or
even as non-Jews, they had ended up on the front lines of the country's
religious culture wars.

Pola (Polina) Barkan, one of the 1.5 generation, had turned her
mixed identity into a career move. She had come to Israel in 1992,
at the age of two, from Kyiv, Ukraine, with her father, Alex, a military man; her mother, Faina, a literature teacher; and an older sister.
A Yiddish-speaking great-grandmother, two grandmothers, and an
aunt came too. Her parents were still in their twenties and a younger
brother was born in Israel. The family spent the first two years on a
religious *moshav* before moving to Kiryat Malachi, the southern town
that had grown out of a Mizrahi immigrant transit camp in the 1950s.
"Most of us came to the periphery, where it was not cool to be a Russian," said Barkan over coffee and juice in a Jerusalem café. Her soft,
Semitic-looking features, her long brown hair, and her faintly freck-
led face reminded me of the Ashkenazi friends of eastern European
descent whom I had grown up with in Manchester, England. My own
grandfather on my father's side had come to Manchester from Russia.
What Barkan remembered of her childhood was trying to be "more
Israeli than the Israelis." Life at home, with four generations of the fam-

ily squeezed in, remained Russian. The grandmothers never acquired much Hebrew. "My whole childhood was accompanied by a kind of embarrassment," Barkan recalled, voicing the cultural dissonance felt by many a child of immigrants.

The family had arrived with little more than pots, sheets, some wardrobes, and a forty-year-old table, the closest they had to an heirloom. Faina first found work in a factory producing wet wipes, then trained as a bookkeeper. Alex took a course in supermarket management. There wasn't much money to spare but realizing that Pola was unlikely to get a high-quality education in Kiryat Malachi, and driven by a Soviet zeal for excellence, her parents agreed to send her to a school in an agricultural youth village a ninety-minute commute away that catered mainly to Russian-speakers. By the time Barkan was in twelfth grade her parents had divorced and Alex had returned to Russia, where he felt he'd have more opportunities.

Barkan served in the army as an instructor of a course offering fast-track conversions for non-Jewish soldiers, most of them immigrants from the former Soviet Union. The course included seminars on Zionist history and prayer and the Jewish holidays. Circumcisions were also available for those who wanted them. Next came university in Beersheba and a student trip to Belarus, where Barkan visited the childhood home of Shimon Peres. There, she said, at the home of the Russian-speaking Israeli statesman who hailed from Vishniev, it dawned on her that instead of having to choose between her two identities she could be both.

After a stint working for the Hillel student organization as a "professional Jew" who spoke Russian with a Hebrew accent, she was tapped to direct a new initiative launched by Russian-Israeli activists of the 1.5 generation called the *Brigada Tarbutit,* or Cultural Brigade. The mission was to bring their Russian cultural heritage and traditions to a wider Israeli public in the hope of making them a legitimate part of Israeli culture. If Ben-Gurion's melting pot had required new immigrants to abandon their native language and their roots from the old country in the quest to build the new Hebrew culture, this was a reversal or a revision reminiscent of the Ars Poetica movement, which sought to honor and revive Mizrahi heritage and create a more tolerant, culturally diverse Israeli society.

One of the Brigada's first campaigns was to educate mainstream Israelis about *Novy God*, a joyous New Year's Eve celebration when Russian families traditionally gathered before midnight on December 31 to feast on nostalgia along with delicacies like herring, caviar, and jellied calf's foot, and to ring in the Gregorian New Year with champagne and vodka. A purely secular holiday, it was particularly relished in the Soviet Union, where religious celebrations were frowned upon. In an added bonus for many, it also had nothing to do with the Communist Party. The émigrés brought their Novy God traditions with them to Israel, decorating their homes with evergreen *yulka* trees adorned with tinsel and baubles and *Ded Moroz* (Grandfather Frost) dolls looking like a blue-coated Santa Claus. But they were dismayed to find themselves celebrating in shame, behind drawn curtains, as disapproving neighbors thought they were observing Christmas.

The Novy God conundrum tapped into deep prejudices and suspicions among many veteran, traditional Israelis that the Russians were not really Jewish. In an unfortunate twist, the country's Orthodox Jews, who lived by the Hebrew calendar, had long repudiated civil New Year celebrations, referring to the night of December 31 as "Sylvester," because it coincided with a traditional European feast day for an eponymous fourth-century pope who was considered an anti-Semite. The date was carved in Jewish memory as a time when gentiles would get drunk and carry out pogroms. At best, Israelis at first viewed Novy God as a time when the Russian immigrants got drunk. At worst, they imagined them performing clandestine, pagan rituals almost on a par with devil worship. The Chief Rabbinate, the Orthodox-run state religious authority, had threatened in years past to revoke the kosher food licenses of hotels or restaurants celebrating the secular New Year.

In an effort to demystify the holiday, the Brigada launched its "Israeli Novy God" campaign, producing humorous videos familiarizing Israelis with the customs and offering to host them at Russian family gatherings. Within a couple of years, the Brigada succeeded in turning Novy God into a widely recognized and legitimate fete. Many non-Russian Israelis adopted it as an excuse for a party, Prime Minister Netanyahu began broadcasting Novy God greetings in Russian, the IDF granted furloughs to Russian-speaking recruits for the holiday, and the mainstream Hebrew press began printing recipes for mayonnaise-soaked

Russian salads. Vodka was on special offer at the supermarkets. Novy God had come out of hiding.

Still, there were pockets of resistance. One recent year, a spat broke out in the southern port city of Ashdod over a glittery Novy God tree placed along a central avenue of the city's BIG open-air shopping mall. Though almost a quarter of the city's residents were Russian-speakers, the city's ultra-Orthodox deputy mayor, Avi Amsalem, railed against the modest spruce tree in a Facebook post, calling it an affront to "whoever defines themselves as Jewish." When I visited one sunny December afternoon, a bare-bones, outsize menorah had been placed alongside the bush by the BIG management to try to ameliorate the situation, but Amsalem complained that the lamp had only gone up a day after Hanukkah ended. Similar tensions over trees played out in other cities, including the Tel Aviv seaside suburb of Bat Yam. Nevertheless, the BIG tree stayed put, adorned with gold and red baubles. Israelis of all stripes posed in front of it for selfies, and probably in greater numbers because of the ruckus. An adjacent stall run by two non-Russian saleswomen was doing a brisk trade in Santa dolls, trinkets, and piggy banks, since it was also the Chinese year of the pig. Most people seemed unfazed by the fuss. "We're a free country," said Daniel Atias, sixty, a maintenance manager at the mall. "You can never please 100 percent of the people," he added, eagerly telling me that he was of Moroccan descent. "As long as the world exists, there'll be a New Year," he said.

Unsurprisingly, there was no real snow to be seen in Ashdod, slightly ruining the Yuletide atmosphere. Nevertheless, holiday preparations were in full swing. Families were ordering Rent-a-Santa visits by local entrepreneurs in costume who would drop in with gifts for the children. A nighttime visit cost more than $100. At the Ashdod branch of Tiv Taam, a famously non-kosher supermarket chain where the deli sections sold smoked fish and all manner of sausage glistening with fat, there had been a rush on tinned caviar. I met Sofia Roisin, a well-groomed sixty-two-year-old, at the freezer section buying veal trotters for her Novy God jellied calf's foot, a once-a-year special. The Israeli attitude toward Novy God had softened, she said, compared with when she first arrived from Moldova in 1989. "They see it does no harm," she said. Her aunt had always told her Israel was Asia, and full of sand.

"Today it's different," she said confidently. "We brought European culture here."

After the Novy God success, the Brigada went on to launch a project to honor Israel's Red Army veterans and to organize festivals of contemporary Russian-Israeli culture inspired by the legacies of St. Petersburg and Odessa, the birthplace of some giants of early Zionism and the cradle of modern Hebrew. Barkan had invited me to the St. Petersburg festival, which was held at the old Diaspora Museum in Tel Aviv as it was undergoing renovations. A showcase of 1.5 Gen creativity, it provided a window into a largely in-house, buzzing cultural hub and included art installations, lectures, and a concert by young Russian-Israeli rock musicians as well as a dramatic reenactment of transcripts from the 1964 trial in St. Petersburg of the poet Joseph Brodsky, who was charged with "parasitism" and was known for his courtroom repartee. Young Russian-speaking Israelis and Israeli veterans milled around among the exhibits. One of the highlights of the evening came as Alex Rif, a new Russian-Israeli poet and a co-founder of the Brigada, recounted her own *aliyah*—or *hagirah,* migration—story to a rapt crowd in a packed auditorium. Delivering a lecture in accentless Hebrew and reciting from her upcoming book of poetry, Rif encapsulated the experience of many of her generation. Immigrating with her family at age five, she described arriving for her first day at an Israeli kindergarten, hand in hand with her mother. She was wearing a pure white dress, thick tights and sandals, and an enormous red bow in her blond hair. "Suddenly," she recalled, "there was silence. From that day I decided I didn't want to be Russian anymore, only Israeli." But twenty years later, after the army, she said she realized something was missing: "Me."

The cultural awakening of the 1.5 generation brought with it a growing self-confidence and lack of tolerance for the dictates of the country's religious czars. Among the many affronts, there were few more emotionally charged than one that became apparent early on in the absorption process: that some Russian-speaking army conscripts were Israeli enough to die for their country but not Jewish enough to be buried inside the military cemeteries. In the Jewish tradition, non-Jews were not supposed to be buried alongside Jews in sanctified ground but had to be laid to rest outside the cemetery gates or fence. The practice became a flashpoint in Israel after one notorious case in 1993, when Sergeant Lev Pesachov, an IDF soldier who was shot and killed at a West Bank checkpoint, was interred at the edge of a military cemetery in the city of Beit Shean in northern Israel. An uproar ensued, leading to calls for less hurtful compromise solutions. Some lenient rabbis ruled that gentiles who fought together with Jews should not be shunned in death. In some cemeteries pleasantly land-scaped areas were set aside for non-Jewish immigrants. In others, the graves of soldiers whose Jewishness was in question were dug a bit farther away from their Jewish counterparts and separated by a bench or shrubbery. Finally, after nearly three decades, the military rabbis approved a less obvious way of differentiating between the Jewish and less Jewish corpses. Those who did not qualify as fully Jewish would be buried about a foot deeper and a discreet divider would be placed underground between the graves.

Aboveground, meanwhile, in the land of the living, matrimony had become the new battlefront. One summer Friday afternoon Adam Mendelsohn-Lessel, thirty-six, and Julia Eizenman, twenty-nine, wed under a chuppah among fig and pomegranate trees in the presence of family and friends at a venue on Kibbutz Hulda in central Israel. They replaced the traditional seven blessings with their own vows. Mendelsohn-Lessel broke a glass to a hearty *Mazel tov* from the crowd. Instead of a rabbi, the officiator was a stage and television actor best known as the face of a popular travel app commercial. The couple had hired him with the help of a nonprofit called Be Free Israel. Eizen-man, a graphic designer born in Moldova to a Jewish father and a non-Jewish mother, did not qualify to marry through the official channels without undergoing a conversion. Mendelsohn-Lessel, a native Israeli who worked in a factory producing coffee roasters, was happy to avoid the rabbinate because in general, like a growing number of secular and even some modern Orthodox Israelis, he did not like "the establish-ment and institutions."

Some secular couples didn't bother getting married at all, setting up housekeeping and becoming common-law spouses, with or without a civil union agreement witnessed by a lawyer. That also worked for same-sex couples, under the noses of the religious authorities. And yet others who qualified as Jews insisted on being recognized by the religious establishment even when the establishment made it difficult. Pola Barkan of the Brigada married Mark, an environmental engineer who'd arrived from Volgograd in 1996, aged six, and who still spoke Hebrew with a Russian accent. Her Jewishness was not in doubt. He was set on having an Orthodox marriage, but he had to somehow prove his Jewishness to the chief rabbinate. He eventually managed to do so with the help of an old family photograph from the Soviet Union showing him wearing a skullcap. After his family had fought to remain Jewish in the USSR, Barkan explained, he was not about to give up on a Jewish wedding in Israel. As they stood under the canopy in the spring of 2017, Barkan added an eighth blessing: She said she wished to be able to dance at the weddings of all her friends in Israel. She lamented the fate of those taxpaying citizens who did not have the chance and who had to run off to Cyprus to "marry like mice."

Between 1989 and the end of 1991, some 346,000 immigrants from the former Soviet Union had settled in Israel. The hectic logistics of housing the newcomers led to a battle of wills between the government of Yitzhak Shamir and the George H. W. Bush administration. Shamir was seeking $10 billion in U.S. loan guarantees to finance housing construction for the tide of new arrivals. Seeking to promote peace negotiations among Israel, the Palestinians, and the Arab states in the aftermath of the first Gulf War, the U.S. administration was conditioning the loan guarantees on an Israeli freeze on settlement expansion in the occupied territories, an anathema to the right-wing Israeli government and still a point of contention three decades later. So great was the influx that Israel's housing minister at the time, Ariel Sharon, scrambled to find trailers and mobile homes to provide shelter for the newcomers, setting them up in huge trailer parks. He also devised an ambitious "Seven Stars" plan of construction zigzagging along the pre-1967 Green Line with the intention of blurring and emptying it of any meaning in the Israeli consciousness. Sharon scoffed at any notion of preventing new immigrants from moving to the West Bank settlements to satisfy the Americans, saying that in any case after a year they would no longer be new immigrants and were free to live wherever they liked. Shamir posited that the Arab states opposed any Jewish immigration to Israel, regardless of where the immigrants ended up. Ultimately only a fraction of the Soviet *olim* ended up in the West Bank, but many moved into the new—and cheaper—Jewish neighborhoods across the Green Line in expanded East Jerusalem, helping Israel consolidate its claim and control over the whole city.

Given the sheer numbers, the Russian-speaking immigrants were bound to have an impact on Israeli geopolitics, identity, and society. The first effects were felt in the 1992 election. Frustrated over the handling of their absorption and housing needs by the Shamir-led Likud government, they came to the ballot box determined to take "electoral revenge" on the system, in the words of Lily Galili, a *Haaretz* journalist who covered the wave of immigration intensively, and Roman Bronfman, a Ukrainian-born former politician, co-authors of a book about the Soviet immigration, *The Million That Changed the Middle East*.

About half the votes of the new immigrants in that election went to Labor, enough for about 4 additional seats in the 120-seat Knesset. That, the authors argued, provided Labor leader Yitzhak Rabin with the margin he needed to overthrow the Likud and come to power. The Russian love affair with Labor did not last long. The *olim* fleeing the former Soviet Union were inclined against anything that smacked of socialism. But wittingly or not, that fleeting injection of support may have been instrumental in changing Middle East history by enabling Rabin to embark on the historic Oslo peace process with the Palestinians. But if the "white" Ashkenazi liberal elite had initially assumed, or hoped, that their Israel would be saved by the secular, educated wave of Russian immigrants, they would be disappointed. Equally dismayed with the Labor Party, the immigrants largely voted against Rabin's successor, Shimon Peres, four years later.

Over time, the immigrants appeared to tilt the system firmly to the right. It was hardly surprising, having fled the collapsing Soviet Union. They brought with them a strong nationalist sentiment, coming from the vast tracts of the USSR to a seemingly tiny and vulnerable strip of land surrounded by hostile neighbors. Rather than supporting the idea of territorial concessions to the Palestinians, some of them went to live in the settlements. It was the time of the First Intifada, and the demand for settlement homes had dropped among veteran Israelis for fear of their cars being stoned or firebombed on the roads. Immigrants came to fill the vacuum. One particular magnet was Ariel, the urban, largely secular settlement in the central West Bank, established by a group of security hawks intent on blocking the prospect of any future contiguous Palestinian state. Immigrants I met there spoke less of ideology than quality of life, saying they had come in search of clean air and affordable housing. Seeing an opportunity, Ron Nachman, the mayor of Ariel and one of its founders, had sent representatives to the airport to recruit new—and probably somewhat disoriented—settlers fresh off the flights. He also sent emissaries to Moscow and the former Soviet republics to entice would-be immigrants even before their departure. Russian-speakers came to make up about half the population of Ariel, a city of some 20,000 that also went on to house the first Israeli university in the occupied West Bank. On one of my visits to the settlement, I asked a young woman at a bus stop who had arrived not long before from a former Soviet republic how she felt about living over the Green Line. An unwitting settler who spoke in halting Hebrew, she seemed to have not thought much about it and appeared to have little clue that she was living in contested territory.

In a political arena where the tribes of Israel increasingly sought representation by their own niche parties, the Russians were no exception. Their first immigrant party, the right-of-center Yisrael B'Aliyah, was founded in 1996 by Natan Sharansky, one of the most famous Soviet "refuseniks," those who were refused permission to emigrate to Israel by Soviet authorities; he had been denied an exit visa to Israel in the 1970s, was charged and convicted of treason, and spent nine years in prison, partly in the Siberian gulag, for his Zionist and human rights activities. Released in an East–West prisoner exchange in 1986, he came to live in Israel, joining his wife, Avital, who had campaigned intensively on his behalf. The party, which grew out of an advocacy group, the Zionist Forum, won seven seats in the 1996 election and joined Netanyahu's first government. A few years later, after its popularity waned, it merged with Likud. But that was not the end of "Russian" politics in Israel. The Russian-speaking politician most identified with his roots was Avigdor "Yvet" Liberman, a burly, blunt-talking immigrant who had come from Moldova in the late 1970s. As a student he had famously worked as a bouncer in a bar. He launched his political career as Netanyahu's operator. An odd couple, they paired up in the 1980s when the suave Netanyahu returned from his post as Israel's ambassador to the United Nations. Netanyahu had ambitions of taking over Likud and Liberman became his political henchman, connecting him with the party's grassroots, schlepping him to weddings, bar mitzvahs, and salon gatherings, and taking on all the backroom dealing and dirty work. Working from the ground up, Liberman rehabilitated the Likud's local branch offices, overhauled the party's finances, and proved instrumental in propelling Netanyahu into office. In return, when Netanyahu came to power in 1996, he promoted Liberman to the prestigious role of director-general of the prime minister's bureau, a pinnacle of power for a once-penniless immigrant from Kishinev.

But Netanyahu was notorious for using loyalists and then casting them aside, and Liberman was no exception. He and his patron had a dramatic falling out. Feeling slighted by Netanyahu after doing the heavy lifting in the ranks of the Likud, Liberman formed his own ultra-nationalist immigrant party, Yisrael Beiteinu, which means "Israel, our home." At first it competed with Yisrael B'Aliyah for the votes of the Russian-speaking constituency, but it outlived Sharansky's party. One of its early campaign slogans, "*Da* Liberman!"—Russian for "Yes to Liberman!"—catapulted him into the spotlight. At its peak, in the 2009 election, Yisrael Beiteinu won fifteen seats, making Liberman a kingmaker.

With his straight talk, thickly accented Hebrew, and sardonic wit, Liberman quickly became one of Israel's most intriguing and unpredictable politicians and arguably its most powerful Russian-speaking immigrant, serving as foreign minister, defense minister, and deputy prime minister in consecutive Netanyahu governments. However bad his prospects seemed at any given time, he would answer queries about them with the assurance "*Hakol dvash,*" meaning "Everything is honey," or would simply reply "*Gan Eden,*" meaning "Paradise."

Unabashedly hardline, he had taken his young family to live in a trailer on a hillside in a remote settlement in the Judean hills in the occupied West Bank. He either quit or was fired from half a dozen governments from 2001 on, in most cases ostensibly because of disputes over policy toward the Palestinians. The trailer was swapped for a villa, and a new road was built linking his Judean desert settlement, Nokdim, with southern Jerusalem, popularly known as Liberman Highway. He initially took a tough nationalist line against Israel's Arab minority, at one time campaigning for citizenship to be conditional on a loyalty oath, a pledge of allegiance to Israel as a Jewish state. One of his more contentious campaign slogans was "Only Liberman understands Arabic."

The Israeli establishment initially received him with suspicion and stereotyped him as a kind of mafioso figure. A popular satirical television show, *Eretz Nehederet* (A Wonderful Country), depicted him as a bloodthirsty, leather-clad thug called Vladimir. Critics depicted him as a KGB agent or Rasputin. His image was not helped by the corruption allegations and police investigations that dogged him for more than a decade, mainly stemming from a period in the late 1990s when he went into business with international tycoons during a brief hiatus from politics. There were colorful rumors about witnesses who disappeared, suddenly lost their memory, or conveniently died, including one said to have committed suicide with two shots to the head. Liberman complained that he was being persecuted by the authorities because he was Russian. The years of investigations eventually yielded one relatively minor indictment related to the appointment of an ambassador to Belarus. Liberman was acquitted in court. His legal tribulations played well with his Russian base, however, with many empathizing with his claims of victimization.

His loyal base of Russian-speaking immigrants began to age, however, and to die off. Of the original million who came in the 1990s, Roman Bronfman told me, an estimated 200,000 had left Israel, some having gone back to Russia after collecting their immigration benefits, others to third countries. Over the next three decades another 200,000 died. Liberman changed tack and refashioned himself as a self-declared liberal and champion of the struggle against religious coercion in an effort to appeal to mainstream, secular Israelis. The resentment in middle-class circles of the ultra-Orthodox politicians and public, who were widely seen as exploiting the system, helped Liberman remain relevant even as the electoral power of his Russian constituency waned.

The 1.5 generation of Russian-speakers were by now consuming Hebrew news media and had spread across the Israeli political map. Pola Barkan said she had been approached by the whole gamut of political parties to run as their token representative of the Russian voice. "Me? Russian voice?" she told them. "I'm Israeli." And Liberman finally got his revenge against Netanyahu, served on ice: In a final break with his former patron, Liberman defected from the Netanyahu-led right-wing and religious bloc in 2019 and subsequently refused to join a Netanyahu-led coalition, ultimately denying Netanyahu a majority and helping drive him out of office in 2021. Having transformed himself from the bogeyman of the Israeli liberal elite to an unlikely savior, Liberman pledged to sit only in a broad government without the ultra-Orthodox, extremists, and "messianists," as he referred to the far right. After the 2021 ballot he joined the alternative Bennett-Lapid government as finance minister and sat in the coalition with Raam, the Arab Islamic party.

Two decades before the influx of the 1990s, a smaller but more Zionist and ideological group had arrived from the Soviet Union and would come to serve as a bridge between the newcomers and the right-wing establishment in Israel. Russian Zionism, largely dormant since the early pioneer movement in Ottoman times, had reemerged in the wake of Israel's victory in the 1967 war. Growing numbers of Soviet Jews applied for exit visas, and some 160,000 made their way to Israel. Those who were prohibited from leaving, often on the spurious grounds of posing a threat to Soviet national security, became known as the "refuseniks," symbols of the struggle for freedom, and many of them became household names in Israel and the Diaspora. Those who spent time in prison, like Sharansky, were celebrated as "Prisoners of Zion." A dozen dissidents had plotted to hijack a small commercial plane from Leningrad to Sweden to highlight their cause, inspiring others. After years in the gulag, they, too, eventually landed in Israel as heroes.

Itzak Ben Dov was one of those fired up by the failed hijacking plot. He had lived well in St. Petersburg, growing up there in the 1950s and 1960s and graduating from university in economics and mathematics. His father, an army officer and lecturer at the military university, and his mother, a dentist, earned decent enough salaries. "It was a good life," he said, filled with student friends, beauty and culture, and a vibrant underground of unpublished poets and artists. His father, whose Hebrew name was Dov, was a religious man and would pray quietly in the mornings, without phylacteries or the need for a tell-tale prayer book—he knew the blessings by heart. The hijacking plot created a buzz, and one of Ben Dov's relatives and a friend were both arrested for involvement in it. Jewish life was vitalized, as was the Zionist movement. People started agitating to be allowed to emigrate.

Ben Dov, a libertarian, recalled chafing at being part of a minority and said he came to view the Soviet regime as "criminal." He wanted to taste the freedom of being the majority. He obtained an exit visa at the age of twenty-four and landed in Vienna. He could have gone anywhere at that point, but there was no question in his mind. Motivated by Zionism, he was headed for Israel, a place about which he knew little. He arrived in the middle of the 1973 war, describing himself to me as a "male, right-wing, chauvinist pig" and an avowed anti-socialist. But extra hands were needed on the *kibbutzim* so he ended up at one for three months, working in its rubber factory.

I came across Ben Dov by chance, after wandering into a Russian café, Vatrushka, that he owned on Tel Aviv's Ben Yehuda Street. By then he was in his late sixties, balding, with a groomed white beard, living in the Opera Tower, a landmark apartment building along the Tel Aviv seafront. He also ran a medical tourism business, with most of his clients coming from the former Soviet Union for private treatment in Israel. I was a curious stranger and he was happy to reminisce about his own *aliyah* and the differences between his generation and the immigrant wave of the 1990s. We arranged to have coffee.

His emigration, followed by his brother's, had cost their father his job. With nothing left to lose, the rest of the family arrived in Israel two years later. Ben Dov soon relocated to Jerusalem, performed army service, found a job in the Ministry of Transportation, and began to ascend the ranks of the Israeli civil service and social ladder. As an economist he went on to posts in the Finance Ministry, the prime minister's office, and the airport authority and as director of the public housing association. Having retired from public service, he and his partner of the past few years, Yelena, were running Vatrushka as a small Russian eatery and cultural hub, serving up fine Russian cuisine in an intellectual atmosphere. Popular with artists, actors, and journalists, the café was decorated like a cozy living room, with vintage cushions and old china. Its salon-style cultural evenings hosted jazz students and Russian-speaking writers. Ben Dov was unsentimental about the enterprise. "It's a business," he said. "You make money out of what you know and love." Soon after we met, Vatrushka closed down. Ben Dov said he was seeking larger premises and was thinking of opening a members' club—but nothing like the popular Russian bars and water-ing holes frequented by immigrants in some of the more working-class areas of Haifa or Bat Yam, which he said catered to the "proletariat."

Ben Dov had been a Likudnik since the 1977 political revolution. Long before his days in Tel Aviv's Opera Tower, in the early 1980s, he had helped found a settlement in the central West Bank called Barkan, not far from Ariel. The settlement was secular; its acceptance com-mittee kept religiously observant applicants out, he recalled, by tell-ing them they were welcome to join but would have to participate in group-building activities on Saturday mornings that would not be tak-ing place in a synagogue. It was not worth mixing things up in such a tight community, Ben Dov said, fearing the tyranny of finding him-self back in the minority. When he felt the settlement had become too small a world for his growing children, he left.

In general, he said, he believed the impact of the 1970s wave of Soviet immigrants on the country was relatively minor, because of their limited numbers and their more individualistic approach, each aspiring to burrow into Israeli society within their own field. There was no desire to organize in groups, like the 1.5 generation would do, he said. In fact, Ben Dov appeared to find them somewhat wallowing and self-indulgent. "Maybe they suffered as kids and maybe not," he said. "They are very Israeli, but they are searching for some form of distinction."

The masses of immigrants who came in the 1990s were altogether of a different cloth, he said. Some harbored resentment at not having been allowed into the United States and blamed Israel for the closing of the gates. The vote for Yitzhak Rabin in 1992, and the vote against his Labor Party successor, Shimon Peres, four years later were functions of an anti-establishment mentality. Yet the staunch Zionist Soviet *olim* of the 1970s had provided a backbone for the immigrants of the 1990s. The veterans helped create a vibrant, if often blatantly right-wing, Russian-language news media and paved the way for the newcomers to enter the political arena. And in the end, Ben Dov argued, the 1990s wave had integrated even better than his did, both economically and politically. Other than Liberman and Yuli Edelstein, a former refuse-nik who rose to the top echelons of the Likud party, all the "Russian" representatives in the Knesset had arrived in the 1990s.

Without compromising on their sense of cultural superiority, the immigrants also became an integral part of the Israeli cultural scene. The Gesher Theater, established in 1991 by Yevgeny Arye, a director from Moscow, and a group of newly arrived Russian actors, started out staging Russian-language productions. "It all started like a scene from the theatre of the absurd," the theater's website recounted. "A group of actors crowded in a small cellar in Tel-Aviv, rehearsing Hebrew texts transcribed into Cyrillic alphabet, running in their costumes and gas-masks to the nearest shelter each time the sirens started wailing to warn of an Iraqi missile attack." Growing into a venerable Tel Aviv institution, its repertoire had since changed over to mostly Hebrew productions, and it had lived up to its name, Gesher, Hebrew for "a bridge," spanning across Russian and Israeli culture. One hit that premiered in 2017, a sharp political satire called *In the Tunnel,* could not have been more Israeli: The plot centered on two Israeli soldiers who found themselves trapped in a tunnel across the Gaza border along with two Hamas militants, while aboveground, a feckless bunch of Israeli and Palestinian politicians continued their antics. A performance I attended one weeknight was sold out; a large portion of the audience was made up of Russian-speaking theatergoers. Russian classics were now staged in Hebrew, with Russian subtitles.

Still, the Russian *aliyah* of the 1990s remained one of contradictions. Immigrant musicians filled classical orchestras and audiences in the newly built concert halls. They also staffed the supermarket checkout counters. One of *Eretz Nehederet*'s all-time favorite characters was Luba, the stereotypically brusque, blond, and stout babushka who berated the customers. The newcomers were variously viewed as academic assets, vodka-swilling mobsters, cultural snobs, and prostitutes. Some oligarchs hosted flashy Novy God parties and invited the television cameras in. Others preferred to remain in the shadows.

A watershed moment for the immigrants and their shared fate with their adopted country came abruptly and tragically one Friday night in June 2001, at the height of the Second Intifada, when a Palestinian suicide bomber detonated a bomb filled with ball bearings outside the Dolphinarium discotheque on the Tel Aviv beachfront. A majority of the twenty-one victims who had been queuing to enter the club were teenage Russian-speaking girls, like Yevgenia Dorfman, fifteen, from

Bat Yam, and Maria Tagiltseva, fourteen, from Netanya. Scores were wounded. It was a baptism of blood into the harshest of Israeli realities.

In time, the negative stereotypes faded. At a cabinet meeting in 2009 marking twenty years since the fall of the Iron Curtain, Prime Minister Netanyahu described the immigration from the former Soviet Union as "one of the greatest miracles to happen in the State of Israel." The four Russian-speaking ministers in his cabinet and Natan Sharansky, then the chairman of the Jewish Agency, who was present at the meeting, were, Netanyahu said, "the best testimony" to the immigrants' integration into the leadership of the country.

The solo exhibition by immigrant artist Zoya Cherkassky-Nnadi at the venerable Israel Museum radiated with cynicism, eschewing any Zionist sentimentalism that Israelis may still have harbored about the *aliyah* experience of the 1990s. Grimly provocative, even as it celebrated Cherkassky's own great accomplishment, the jarring contrast was perhaps emblematic of the new, less idealistic, more skeptical Israel. Cherkassky, born in Kyiv, Ukraine, in 1976, had come to Israel in 1991, as a teenager. The first painting that hit you in the face as you entered the exhibit was autobiographical, depicting Cherkassky and her family disembarking an El Al plane, incongruously wrapped in layers of winter clothing against a background of palm trees and balmy blue skies as an Israeli official waited on the tarmac to hand them miniature Israeli flags. It was sardonically titled *New Victims*. Cherkassky explained that the immigrant families were only allowed to bring forty kilograms of luggage each, so they wore as much as they could, regardless of the season. The title came from her grandmother, who had apparently never been keen on emigrating to Israel. For months, Cherkassky related, her grandmother would sit by the window of the family apartment in Israel and every time she saw a plane coming in, "she would sigh and say new victims are arriving."

Like others, Cherkassky referred to her own journey to Israel as *hagirah,* migration, rather than *aliyah,* with its connotations of elevation, while addressing another packed auditorium at an event marking the closing of the exhibit. When I asked her about her choice of the term *hagirah* at the end of the evening, she replied crisply, "*Aliyah* is an ideological term. *Hagirah* is a fact." The exhibit, titled *Pravda,* had run for ten months in 2018 and was a dizzying success, establishing Cherkassky as a leading Israeli contemporary artist. At auction, her paintings could fetch tens of thousands of dollars. Cherkassky's direct, figurative style portrayed the Russian immigrant experience in an often humorous if sarcastic, shocking, and defiant light. The curator, Amitai Mendelsohn, said it had raised difficult questions, annoyed a lot of people, and made others laugh. "It was time to have that conversation and not hide from it," he said, adding that one member of the 1.5 generation had told him the exhibit saved her hours of psychological treatment. "Me too," Cherkassky chimed in.

Cherkassky was unconventional by any Israeli standard. She wore Dr. Martens and had married Sunny Nnadi, a migrant from Nigeria. She said she had picked him out of a group of migrants on a street in Tel Aviv when she was looking for a model to sit for a portrait, Nnadi being the most handsome one. One legend etched onto her heavily tattooed arm said it all: "Attitude." With her art, she underlined and satirized many of the absurdities and hypocrisies of the immigration story, particularly those involving identity, religion, and the state religious authorities. One work portrayed a visit by a black-hatted kosher food inspector to the apartment of a young immigrant family apparently undergoing conversion. They had dressed the part, modestly and with Orthodox-style head coverings. But the giveaway was on the stove, where a pig's snout was sticking out of a soup pot. *The Circumcision of Uncle Yasha* depicted a bloody horror scene of an adult on a gurney surrounded by surgeons with beards and sidelocks. And the painting *Itzik* had stirred a mini uproar when Cherkassky first posted an image of it on Facebook. Depicting a dark-skinned, thick-lipped, Mizrahi falafel-store owner groping his defenseless, blond-haired, Russian waitress, it provided a crudely grotesque commentary on contemporary Israeli racism, Orientalism, and prejudice. The layers of paint also probed the paradox of the development towns on the Israeli periphery, where the mismatched veterans and newer waves of immigrants, in many ways opposites in the Israeli social kaleidoscope, competed for resources but also found common cause.

Perhaps the most controversial work of all was a side-by-side diptych, *Friday in the Projects; Ukraine 1991*, offering an equally grim, split-screen vision of there and here. On one side was a stark, snowy scene of a drab Ukrainian housing project, gang violence, and a woman falling into a pothole; on the other, a dusty, dismal housing project somewhere in southern Israel with thugs in the street and, up above, a rocket heading in from Gaza. The message was subversive, undermining the entire premise of classical Zionism and the dream of a Jewish homeland: It was bad there; it's just as bad here. The exhibition riled some Israeli veterans—"those who came and built the country," as the curator put it, who bridled at the cheek of it. One of the docents told me that many Russian-speaking immigrants had also left the exhibit, upset by some of its caricaturish stereotypes and insisting that there was much to be thankful for in Israel.

Indeed, rather than dwelling on hardships, an outstanding feature of the Russian-speaking community was its quest for excellence, at least when it came to the children. Parents sacrificed to pay for extra tuition and chess, music, and ballroom dancing lessons. Alex Rif, the Brigada Tarbutit co-founder and poet, related how her parents had spent money for every after-school activity going, though it had taken them twenty-five years to be able to afford air conditioning.

For the family of Dima Bogoslaviz, who had immigrated as a baby in 1994 with his parents, one set of grandparents, and an uncle from Odessa, the first stop was an immigrant absorption center in Beit Shemesh, the mixed town between Tel Aviv and Jerusalem of traditional Moroccan veterans, a fast-growing ultra-Orthodox population, and the secular new arrivals from the former Soviet Union. The town made headlines when the "pork wars" broke out there in the late 1990s. By then, about a fifth of its inhabitants were Russian-speaking recent arrivals. They opened local stores and began catering to their taste for pork, sparking resistance from the Orthodox Jews. A large demonstration against the pork-sellers in 1999 led to a broader offensive against the immigrants. After an emotional parliamentary debate about "looking into other people's plates," a compromise was reached: The sale of pork would be restricted to industrial zones on the city's outskirts under municipal bylaws.

I had known Bogoslaviz for years as my son's fair, blue-eyed, gentle school friend. Now a young adult, he had become an inseparable part of the "gang" of former classmates. Curious to hear about his childhood, I met him in a hip café near the old Bezalel Art Academy in downtown Jerusalem. As a child, Bogoslaviz said, his parents worked all hours, so he spent his early years living with his grandparents in their rented Beit Shemesh apartment. His grandfather found work as a crane operator, his grandmother in a bakery producing Russian rye bread. His class at school was about half Russian and half Mizrahi. The Russians mainly kept to themselves, he recalled. He took tennis lessons, frequented the chess club, and joined the Scouts. His grandparents' attitude, he said, was "This is the Land of Israel. We'll make the best of it. It's better here than there." There they went to the theater and here they rarely left Beit Shemesh. They kept to a strict routine. And though they had difficulty integrating, they invested all their efforts in the children, Bogoslaviz said. "It was all about me and my cousins succeeding."

Bogoslaviz's grandfather was an old-school, by-the-book Soviet who loved order and strength and admired Vladimir Putin and Benjamin Netanyahu. He disapproved of tattoos, which reminded him of Russian criminal gangs and the Holocaust. Dima had to explain that it was fashionable to buy ripped jeans. By high school, he had moved to Jerusalem to live with his mother, who had divorced and remarried a native Israeli. For the grandparents, integration only came with Dima's induction into the army, where he served in an elite reconnaissance unit of the Paratroopers Brigade. "What pride it brought them," he said. They finally felt a sense of belonging. They had become Israeli. Marking his enlistment, his grandfather hung an Israeli flag from his balcony in Beit Shemesh. It remained there for years, well after Bogoslaviz completed his army service. "Till now he cries with emotion at being here," said Dima, who went on to study industrial design in Jerusalem. "The kids succeeded. He feels he has dividends."

But for Bogoslaviz himself, like for many young Israelis, the future came "with a question mark." There was always the Palestinian conflict in the background. But as troubling for him were the internal inequalities and discord. His personal status as a Jew in Israel was not in question. Though his father was not Jewish, his mother was, so he was. Still, he said, Israel was unfair to those who did not qualify. "I'm not saying let everyone in," he said, "but if you are already here . . ." Being an Israeli but not being allowed to officially marry was "like going into a café but not being allowed to order a coffee," he said, staring into his own cappuccino. Success did not solve all the problems of the immigrants, nor all of Israel's problems.

In the fall of 2021, Brigada activists led by Alex Rif launched their next phase of activity to promote the country's Russian-speakers, called the Million Lobby. "After thirty years now is the time to put the heritage and identity of the Soviet Jews at the center of discourse in school programs, academia, and culture," they wrote, ahead of a conference on the subject. Thirty years on, many Russians still felt they were being stereotyped. In late 2021 the "Humorless Russian Women and Their Friends" Facebook group was again flooded with emotional and indignant posts after a popular Mizrahi singer, Omer Adam, released a new single called *Kak dela,* a colloquial Russian term for "How's it going?," with lyrics that appeared to depict Russian-speaking women as promiscuous heavy drinkers.

The Million Lobby argued that Israelis learned little in school about the history of Soviet Jewry and its heroes in a country that some claimed cared more about immigration than its immigrants. Ida Nudel, one of the symbols of the refusenik movement, who waged a personal struggle to emigrate to Israel that led to her being banished to Siberia in the late 1970s for her activities, had died in Israel at the age of ninety in September 2021. She was eulogized by Israel's leaders as a lioness among the Prisoners of Zion, but as if to prove the Million Lobby's point, the Israeli news media reported that only about forty people attended her funeral.

The Lobby's political demands included equalizing conditions for elderly Holocaust survivors, many from behind the Iron Curtain, who had immigrated after 1953 and, by law, did not receive the same benefits as those who had come before; establishing a heritage center telling the story of Soviet Jewry; and finding civil solutions for people who could not officially get married in Israel. That problem had been highlighted when Artem Dolgopyat, a gymnast who immigrated to Israel at the age of twelve from Ukraine, won Israel's second-ever Olympic gold medal at that summer's Tokyo games. The national anthem, "Hatikvah," played as he stood proudly on the podium. He was welcomed back home like a national hero. But his mother, who is not Jewish, lamented on the radio that the champion was unable to marry his girlfriend of three years in Israel.

The next episode of the Russian *aliyah* saga began when the Russian army invaded Ukraine in early 2022. The conflict further galvanized the 1.5 generation and highlighted its growing prominence in the public arena. About a third of the Russian-speaking immigrants of the previous decades had come from Ukraine and a third from Russia, with the last third hailing from a variety of the former Soviet republics. There was little nationalist division among them. Most had grown up in the Soviet Union, where Russian culture was dominant, and many families had relatives split between Russia and Ukraine. In Jerusalem, the Russian-born owners of the popular Putin Pub removed the gilded P-U-T-I-N letters from the façade and announced that they were seeking a new name for their bar. It became the Generation Pub. And the now-grown immigrant children of the 1990s came out on the streets of Israel to protest against a strict government quota that was initially placed on the entry of non-Jewish refugees fleeing the horror in Ukraine, though most of them had relatives or friends in Israel. The policy ignited an emotional debate in Israel over what it meant to be a Jewish state. On the religious right, some placed the need to maintain Israel's Jewish character above welcoming those in need. More liberal Israelis like Nachman Shai, then the Labor minister for Diaspora affairs, said there was no point in a Jewish state that did not adhere to basic Jewish values of charity and kindness to others, particularly given the Jews' long history of being refugees themselves.

By contrast, as the Israeli government maneuvered awkwardly between its support for Ukraine and its national security need to maintain relations with President Putin, government ministers enthusiastically anticipated the prospect of tens of thousands of potential new immigrants from both Ukraine and Russia who would qualify under the Law of Return, describing the new pool of well-educated human capital as a strategic asset for Israel. The immigration authorities moved into high gear, extricating families from the battle zone and reserving thousands of hotel rooms for the new arrivals. Alex Rif and Pola Barkan were among a small group of leaders of the 1.5 generation who met with Prime Minister Bennett and urged him not to repeat the mistakes of the 1990s. Chief among them, Rif told me, was failing to integrate the newcomers into the economy and ensuring they could work in their professions, forcing doctors and engineers to clean houses to make a living.

# TEN

# HIGH-TECH IN THE SAND

THE GROUP gathering at Ben-Gurion Airport was as excited as schoolchildren about to embark on their first class trip abroad. However, the passengers were very much grown-ups, well-traveled and sophisticated members of Israel's upper percentile. All members of the smart and well-heeled high-tech set, they were about to leave their usual stomping ground of Tel Aviv as the first delegation of Israeli tech entrepreneurs to be openly visiting the dazzling Arab emirate of Dubai.

It was the fall of 2020, just weeks after the festive ceremony on the White House South Lawn where Prime Minister Netanyahu and the foreign ministers of the United Arab Emirates and Bahrain had signed their surprise agreement, brokered by the Trump administration, to formalize diplomatic relations. The first tech delegation was the brain-child of Erel Margalit, a leading Israeli venture capitalist considered one of the architects of the start-up nation and the founder and chair-man of JVP, a major Jerusalem-based venture capital fund. There were no direct flights yet, and the coronavirus had curtailed international travel, so Margalit had chartered a private plane with about fifty seats and was bringing along the top executives of more than a dozen of the most promising Israeli companies in JVP's portfolio.

Some journalists had been invited along to get an immersive, up-close, and behind-the-scenes glimpse into this historic and very public foray into the Arabian Gulf, which was once enemy territory and off-limits to Israelis. The sense of thrill and anticipation only increased as the jet took off, as if it were the first time the passengers were taking to the skies on some intrepid expedition. A few of the passengers had, in fact, visited the Emirates before, covertly. Others had never set foot in an Arab country. Executives took selfies in the cockpit or against the oval windows of the jet as it glided over the Saudi Arabian sands—another novelty, since Saudi airspace had long been closed to Israeli planes—and swooped over Dubai's artificial Palm Island before landing in the afternoon heat of the emirate of glittering towers.

For more than two decades Israel and the Emiratis had conducted unofficial, under-the-table intelligence, diplomatic, and business dealings, usually carried out by Israeli spies, discreet diplomats, and businesspeople with a second, foreign passport or via third parties. But Margalit and his entourage were making a decidedly conspicuous entrance. After landing, and before checking in at a luxury hotel in the financial district, the local guide took the busful of Israelis to the beach for selfies at sunset against the backdrop of the iconic Burj Al Arab hotel.

During the flight Margalit, fifty-nine, sat in an empty row up front and held a series of audiences with those on board who sought his ear or were invited to join him. When my turn came and I asked about the goals of the trip, he began to expound on his worldview and plans in visionary terms. It might all have sounded somewhat delusional, only Margalit was a social as well as business entrepreneur and he had some credibility. He had already established innovative economic and social hubs, or colonies, known as Margalit Startup Cities, in Jerusalem and Manhattan, combining accelerator space for promising tech companies together with cultural and leisure facilities. One of his typically grandiose mottos was "If innovation can change a city, it can change a country, it can change a region, and can serve as a bridge to the world." He was looking to expand in Europe. But for the new Israelis like Margalit, the Middle East, long stymied by conflict, was the latest frontier.

The Emiratis had been traders since ancient times, Margalit noted, and now had a reach that stretched from North Africa and the Middle East to Pakistan. Israel's new relations with the Emirates could serve as a bridge to potential markets of three billion people within a two-hour flight of Dubai. The marriage of Israeli technology and Emirati entrepreneurship would be a boon for Israeli start-ups looking to scale up. Even more ambitiously, he argued, by maximizing the potential of Israeli ag-tech, food-tech, and water solutions, a combined force of Israeli ingenuity and Emirati initiative could help feed the world. "We bring our expertise, they bring theirs, plus their market knowledge, and it's a much bigger story," said Margalit. He envisaged being able to provide food security for the poorer countries of the region, including Lebanon, Israel's economically collapsing enemy to the north. After all, Israel had proven itself in arid agriculture. "If you can do it in the desert," Margalit said, "you can probably do it on Mars." The portfolio companies on the plane were, he said, the "next generation of unicorns," tech-speak for those rare start-up companies valued at more than a billion dollars.

Israeli innovation had come a long way since David Ben-Gurion's dreams of a blooming desert. Driven to invention by a paucity of natural resources and the hostile geopolitical environment, the Israelis turned the challenge of their precarious existence into a calling card. Many also credited the nation's healthy disregard for formalities or hierarchy, and even the Jewish tradition of Talmudic debate and free-thinking inquiry, with helping turn it into a regional, even global, cyber power. The national security imperative of maintaining Israel's qualitative military edge and the serendipity of the influx of Russian engineers in the 1990s combined to take the economy to the next level as the state founded by socialist idealists embraced capitalism. By the early 2020s Israel was becoming a top producer of unicorns and, despite the pandemic, foreign investment was pouring in, keeping the economy afloat and filling the national tax coffers. In the first nine months of 2021, Israeli high-tech firms raised a historic peak of nearly $18 billion in capital from funding rounds and made nearly $19 billion in merger and acquisition deals or initial public offerings of shares, both popularly known as exits in Israel, and up by 92 percent from the annual 2020 figure.

Iran deserved some credit. The existential threat posed by its nuclear ambitions had focused Israeli minds and fueled the military's technological units. Now, as this next phase beckoned, Israel and the Sunni

Muslim Gulf states, also in Iran's sights, had bonded over their joint interest in curbing Iranian influence in the region and cooperating in counterintelligence. The lure of these new frontiers would not compensate for all the ills in the troubled country, just as the People's Army did not encompass all the people. After a quarter century of growth, Israel's high-tech boom had barely trickled down or spread much beyond the privileged enclaves of First Israel. Instead, the digital renaissance had underscored—even exacerbated—the socioeconomic gaps in Israeli society, further distinguishing the more educated, affluent, liberal, and secular population of the notional "state of Tel Aviv" from the periphery.

Still, it was all a far cry from the country that, in the late 1950s, had manufactured the ill-fated Susita, a fiberglass-shelled car with a British-made engine that was decried as a plastic death trap and derided as a snack for camels. The new Israel was a world leader in driverless car technology. It appeared that the kind of optical, radar, sonar, and sensor systems used to detect incoming missiles and to guide tanks proved useful for scanning roads for dangerous obstacles. In 2017, Intel spent $15.3 billion on Mobileye, a Jerusalem-based autonomous vehicle tech company led by Amnon Shashua, a Hebrew University professor, in what then constituted the biggest acquisition in Israel's high-tech industry.

The bonanza had begun nearly two decades earlier. In 1998, America Online bought Mirabilis, an Israeli pioneer in instant Internet messaging. The people who spoke the revived tongue of the Bible had invented ICQ, the first online chat program, then sold it for more than $400 million. It was an almost inconceivable fortune at the time for an invisible product with no business plan to drive it; as Israel's first big exit, it was hailed as a high-tech milestone. By 2021, cyber-security start-ups had raised a record-breaking $1.5 billion in the first quarter.

Israelis were often asked what the secret ingredient was. One of the founding fathers of the Israeli high-tech enterprise, Yossi Vardi, a Tel Aviv–born early-stage angel investor who liked to play the industry comedian, had a simple answer: "Israel's most important natural resource is the 12,000 tons of gray material that exist in the heads of the people," he told me. He got to the figure by multiplying the average weight of a brain (some 1.3 kilograms) by 9 million. He also credited the culture of Jewish parents and their investment in their children. "After all we've done for you, to bring one Nobel Prize is too much?" he quipped, imitating a stock Jewish mother. He himself had invested in Mirabilis, founded in 1996 by his eldest son, Arik, and three Israeli friends from military intelligence, all in their twenties. One of them left Mirabilis early on to go to university. The remaining three launched ICQ after working out of an apartment in San Jose, California, where Internet access was then much cheaper than in Israel. Another ingredient was undoubtedly Israel's ability to locate and nurture young tech talent and genius, first through programs for gifted pupils at school, then through the IDF's annual intake system of screening and testing of so many of the country's seventeen- and eighteen-year-olds. And all this was built on the trauma of the Holocaust and the national security doctrine of self-reliance.

The role of the army and its top-tier tech units became instrumental in developing the industry. Like the tales of *One Thousand and One Nights,* a seemingly endless fount of new ideas for high-tech companies sprang from the minds of the graduates of the IDF's once-shadowy, now-famed technological intelligence unit known as 8200, as well as from lesser-known army frameworks such as the Talpiot program, which turned out an elite squad of technological problem solvers for the fighting units, or Unit 81, the technological arm of military intelligence, or Mamram, an acronym for the army's center for data and computer systems. All had become established breeding grounds, or boot camps, for the country's start-up ecosystem. Joining these units often required signing up for more years of service, but they provided invaluable experience and the basis for a professional network in civilian life. Retired commanders and officers set up companies, then would recruit their former soldiers. Creative and close-knit teams of people who were already accustomed to working together and aware of one another's particular talents gave many an Israeli start-up a clear advantage. The secrecy of the work they had done in the army only enhanced the aura of invincibility, exclusivity, and mystique for outsiders.

In some ways the beginnings of Israeli high-tech could be traced to one particular failure. In the 1980s, as young people around the world were logging on to their first desktop computers, Israel brought together some of its best engineers to work on an ambitious project:

the Lavi fighter jet, a made-in-Israel aircraft and part of the doctrine of self-reliance. A catalyst for groundbreaking technology in avionics and electronics, it proved to be a spectacularly expensive escapade and was shut down in 1987 under intense pressure from the Americans, who preferred Israel to spend their military aid on American aircraft. Hundreds of highly specialized scientists and engineers were released into the Israeli civilian market. The injection of the aforementioned Soviet immigrant engineers in the 1990s boosted the genesis of the start-up phenomenon, encouraged by prescient government support and incentives. The country's new moniker and brand was minted with the publication in 2009 of a proud, blue-and-white-covered volume titled *Start-Up Nation* that chronicled what its authors, Dan Senor and Saul Singer, called the story of Israel's economic miracle. It fast became a bestseller.

The start-up scene was split between "good guys" and "bad guys." Israel was a global leader in cyber weapons and spyware. While many of the companies were producing innovations for the good of humankind and the planet, a few, like NSO, gained notoriety after a number of foreign clients were found to be exploiting spyware programs meant to thwart terrorism and serious crime for more nefarious purposes, such as monitoring journalists, human rights activists, and political opponents. Either way, much of the know-how was gained in the army. Computer geeks and freelance hackers were often spotted during high school and plucked from the annual intake of conscripts for the army's cyber units. Speaking at a cyber-security conference at Tel Aviv University in 2022, the deputy commander of Unit 8200 said that nearly three-quarters of the current personnel were under the age of twenty-three, which he described as a magic ingredient that set the unit apart from other agencies abroad.

These hothouses of innovation had invented ways of nurturing talent. There was seemingly a contradiction between an army's ingrained military structure and rigid chains of command and the looser kind of environment that generally encouraged creativity and out-of-the-box thinking. But the army proved adaptable—and Israeli—enough to embrace the start-up culture and encourage a freewheeling, trial-and-error approach. The youthful savvy of the recruits, the typically Israeli *yihye be'seder* (it'll be okay) attitude toward calculated risk, the knack for improvisation, and the lack of fear of failure all helped turn the IDF into a national high-tech incubator with premier offensive and defensive cyber capabilities and digital connectivity among its fighting forces, a powerful force multiplier in a world where war was increasingly fought on screens.

Like much of the world, small Israel could not compete with China or India when it came to the sheer quantity of engineering graduates. It could compete in quality, though, and what the technological commanders called the "start-up spirit" of entrepreneurship. Many of those selected for the technological units would earn degrees along the way, weaving a seamless thread among the military, academia, and the private IT sector. The conscription model gave the army the advantage of youth. Recruits to the military's C4i corps, dealing with command and control, communications, information technology, and electronic warfare, had been born into the digital age. The army's system for incoming rocket alerts, honed to target increasingly specific locations under threat, was created by nineteen-year-olds. Every cockpit had become a data center. Big data made intelligence accumulated over many years easily accessible.

Lieutenant Colonel Rami Shaked presided for several years over the IDF's IT and cyber defense academy. Bearing little resemblance to any Google-type workspace, it was housed in an outwardly drab, walled-in concrete army compound in a residential area of Ramat Gan, in the Tel Aviv suburbs. Shaked's office did not feature any brightly colored pipes or a Ping-Pong table and there were no bean bags in sight—just the usual framed photograph of the Auschwitz flyover and, in a glass cabinet, a vintage Gameboy and Atari console. It was 2016, and Shaked spoke animatedly about needing to "develop the people to develop the technology to win the next war." The Gaza war of 2014 had been the most technological war that Israel had fought, he said, with air, land, and naval units all able to see the same picture of the battlefield. Generation Z, he said, was often viewed as having a low attention span and suffering from information overload. For the lieutenant colonel, this was pure gold. He saw his recruits as multi-taskers and curious self-learners who could create connections around the globe. Adapting the learning environment and tapping into their emotional, creative side was much more effective than Ritalin in focusing their abilities. Lieutenant Colonel Shaked aimed to teach in a way that had relevancy for real life. He wanted to turn out *"start-upistim"* and "revolutionaries" from what he called his "school of enterprise."

The academy's intensive six-month courses included twenty-four- or thirty-six-hour hackathons and online learning. The recruits could engage from anywhere, anytime, including on their smartphones. To give me a taste of the training tools, I was shown a miniature mock-up of a city, like an elaborate train set, that was used to figure out the knock-on effects of a cyber attack on the local train system. Another exercise involved calculating the blast effect and collateral damage that would be caused by blowing up a tunnel in Gaza. Working with simulations of incoming rocket fire heading for built-up neighborhoods, students worked out algorithms for intercepting the rockets. Lieutenant Colonel Shaked said the school accommodated some ultra-Orthodox male recruits, who learned in rooms cloistered from any females, as well as some Druze and Arab recruits. And in 2016, for the first time, females outnumbered males in the academy.

But the statistics showed that the most prestigious technological units of the army, the surest entry ticket into the start-up world, were still largely the domain of the more privileged recruits from the prosperous strongholds of the coastal plain. Their parents were able to fund private lessons and invest in specialized extracurricular courses designed to prepare them for the entry tests. Such courses, run by graduates of the coveted units, were available mostly to those in the know.

Despite Israel's prowess, some worried about an industry bubble. By 2019, a decade after the publication of *Start-Up Nation*, there were signs of a slowdown. Israeli high-tech export had reached an all-time annual record of $45.8 billion, representing about 46 percent of the country's exports, consisting mainly of R&D and software, according to the annual report of the governmental Israel Innovation Authority. But the high-tech "engine," it said, had become a "railcar," growing with the economy rather than pushing it forward; the number of newly launched start-ups was the lowest in a decade. Then there were the two Israels: one Israel still basking in its successful brand as one of the world's leading go-to places for venture capitalists, an outlier in the Middle East with the third most companies listed on the NASDAQ after the United States and China, and another Israel whose school-children scored toward the bottom of a long list of developed countries in math, science, and reading. Pupils in the Arabic education system did worse than those in many predominantly Muslim and developing countries. The ultra-Orthodox schools, where boys barely studied such core subjects, were not even included in the testing process. The overwhelmingly secular, Jewish, ex-military delegation that landed in Dubai represented both the vanguard of Israeli high-tech and its problem.

Experts such as Dan Ben-David, an energetic, mustached economics professor, had been warning for years of an eventual implosion of the Israeli economy if Israel's demographic and pedagogical trajectory continued, as well as its brain drain given the tempting opportunities and superior infrastructure available abroad. Domestically, given Israel's high fertility rate, low mortality rates, and continuing commitment to Jewish immigration, projections showed that it would become one of the most crowded countries on earth. The population was expected to reach more than 12 million by 2040 and some 20 million by 2065. According to one forecast calculated by the Central Bureau of Statistics, by 2065 Haredi Jews and Arab citizens and residents, including the Palestinians of East Jerusalem, will constitute more than half of the population of Israel, with all the implications that will have for the future labor force, army enlistment, and social cohesiveness. And that is without counting the Palestinians of the West Bank and the Gaza Strip. The majority of the population of Israel proper was bound to remain Jewish, but the future character and security of the country were in question, along with the nature of its economy and democracy, given the varying degrees of affiliation with, or outright opposition to, the state.

As noted earlier, ultra-Orthodox and Arab children already accounted for almost half the pupils in Israeli schools, and many of those from the fastest-growing population sectors were receiving an inferior education. When the coronavirus epidemic shuttered the classrooms and mandated remote learning, the gaps became even more apparent. It transpired that 23 percent of the country's Arab pupils had no access to a computer or Internet at home and, compared with 2 percent of non-Haredi Jews, 41 percent of ultra-Orthodox Jews had no way of learning online.

The seeds of the high-tech boom were laid under the Rabin government of the early 1990s, when government bureaucrats set up the Yozma (Initiative) Group to partner with the private sector and offer matching funds, kick-starting an Israeli venture capital industry. Netanyahu first came to power the year that Mirabilis was born. He was credited with saving the Israeli economy from collapse when he served as finance minister from 2003 to 2005, in the grim aftermath of the Second Intifada. Fond of repeating the analogy of a fat man, meaning the public sector, riding on the back of a thin man, the private sector, Netanyahu privatized key state assets such as El Al, the national airline; boosted Israel's free-market economy with tax reductions and budget cuts that ate away at the welfare state; and essentially laid the groundwork for an Israeli financial sector.

It was in the early 1990s that Erel Margalit took the leap out of public service and founded JVP. Barely a decade later, in 2004, he became the first Israeli to make the prestigious Forbes Midas List, ranking 59th out of the world's top 100 venture capitalists. A year later he came in 48th. Born in 1961 in Kibbutz Naan in central Israel, Margalit did not grow up with the typical profile of a tech entrepreneur. As a young child he spent a few years with his family in the United States. When they returned to Israel they lived in Karmiel in the Galilee and then moved to Jerusalem, where Margalit attended high school. After serving as a combat soldier in a special unit of the Golani infantry brigade, he studied for his degree in philosophy and English literature at Hebrew University of Jerusalem and went on to study for a PhD in philosophy at Columbia University in New York. "These studies had to be paid for," he wrote in a short memoir for *Yedioth Ahronoth*'s 2021 Rosh Hashana edition. "Mother was a teacher, father the manager of a community center. . . . It was on my back. Literally." Margalit paid his way with muscle and sweat, schlepping for Moishe's Moving company, the decades-old Manhattan house-mover empire founded by another Israeli entrepreneur.

After his father died unexpectedly, Margalit, by now married to Debbie and a father of young children, moved back to Israel, landing with nothing. "I wanted to work in high-tech, which was then in diapers," he wrote, "but I was not an engineer, had no background in business management and nobody seemed to rate philosophy as a pre-requisite." After six months of fruitless job-hunting he met Teddy

Kollek, the legendary mayor of Jerusalem, and by the age of twenty-nine he had been put in charge of business development and a campaign to lure tech companies to the city and transform its image from that of a dour redoubt of rabbis and imams, scholars and civil servants. When Kollek lost the 1993 election, Margalit struck out on his own and established JVP, with seed money from the Yozma program. The fund has since created and supported more than 150 companies, and facilitated a dozen public offerings on NASDAQ, including those of CyberArk, QLIK Technologies, and Chromatis, each at a market value of more than $4 billion. In 2019 Margalit was back in Manhattan to inaugurate a cyber-security center. His social activism included an educational program to close gaps among Jewish and Arab disadvantaged communities in Jerusalem and elsewhere in Israel.

Not everything worked out. A vision of turning Jerusalem into a global animation and media hub fell flat. Margalit successfully ran for Knesset as a Labor Party candidate and served as a lawmaker from 2013 to 2017, but he quit after an unsuccessful bid for the party leadership. I once went to see Margalit in his small office in the Knesset after he had come back from a trip to Germany. Ever resourceful, and with his eye on the leadership, he had gone off to investigate for himself the murky questions surrounding the Netanyahu government's purchase of additional submarines and missile boats for the Israeli fleet from ThyssenKrupp, the German shipbuilder, a deal that was being dubbed by critics as possibly the worst corruption scandal in Israeli history. A member of the parliamentary committee that approved budgets for military acquisitions, Margalit recalled an unusually rushed vote to approve a purchase on the eve of Yom Kippur. He also led an ultimately unsuccessful petition against what he called the "very fishy" deal in the Supreme Court.

Once he got out of politics it was back into business. Margalit had more grand plans, besides those in the Persian Gulf, for expanding the economic and secular entertainment hub of Margalit Startup City in central Jerusalem, where he already owned a space including an innovation center, a trendy restaurant, and a music club. And in 2021 he opened a food-tech center in the northern town of Kiryat Shemona, near the Lebanese border, declaring the global meat industry to be unsustainable and food-tech innovation to be the next big thing in Israeli high-tech.

More broadly, though, instead of the "thin man," Israeli socio-economic experts were worrying about the "thin layer"—the elite minority of highly accomplished and productive Israelis. In all, about 300,000 Israelis were employed in high-tech, representing about 9 percent of the workforce. But the working immigrants of the 1990s were reaching retirement age, the education system had not kept up, and the shortage of qualified engineers drove up salaries. In order to fill the gap and increase profits, Israeli companies were outsourcing, hiring engineers in places like India, Ukraine, and Romania. The Central Bureau of Statistics estimated that the local high-tech industry was short about 12,500 skilled professionals. A survey conducted by Start-Up Nation Central, a Tel Aviv–based nonprofit promoting the industry and its image, put the missing number even higher, at about 18,500. Much of the recruitment was by word of mouth. Some companies paid employees large bonuses for bringing in new talent. The wealth could be felt in every corner of Israel, with nary a room to be found in the ever more luxurious and expensive boutique hotels going up, from the Galilee in the north to the sandy expanses of the southern desert. New events companies sprung up overnight with multimillion-dollar turnovers to cater to the high-tech companies as they competed with one another in throwing ever more lavish and creative staff parties to keep their teams on board and attract new brainpower.

There was a slight sense of it all being a bit like a ball aboard the *Titanic*. As with everything else in Israel, the makeup of the high-tech force had social implications. The Innovation Authority listed the population sectors that were underrepresented in the high-tech industry as the ultra-Orthodox, the Arab minority, Israelis of Ethiopian descent, and residents of the country's periphery—including those with college degrees—as well as people with disabilities and women in general.

By early 2021, despite the investment of tens of millions of shekels by the government and philanthropic organizations, *Haredim* made up only about 3 percent of the country's high-tech workforce, and of that number some 71 percent were ultra-Orthodox women working mostly in lower-level, lower-salaried jobs such as quality assurance, checking for possible faults in software programs, according to research conducted by Israel Advanced Technology Industries, an umbrella group, and KamaTech, an accelerator for ultra-Orthodox-run start-ups. There was no shortage of organizations trying to promote social change, but change was slow to come. Tsofen, a nonprofit of Jewish and Arab high-tech professionals and economists dedicated to promoting the industry among the Arab population, found that Arab employees represented about 3.5 percent of Israel's high-tech workforce, despite constituting about 21 percent of the population. Though the number of Arab employees in high-tech had tripled from 2,200 in 2012 to 6,100 in 2019, a Bank of Israel report found that Jewish high-tech workers earned on average 31 percent more than their Arab counterparts, in part because more Arab employees worked in branches servicing the industry rather than in actual programming or engineering. The start-up nation was more of a split-up nation and the other Israel was also struggling to live up to the image of a futuristic, high-tech powerhouse.

With the highest fertility rate among the long list of developed nations, and the center of the country already packed with people and cars, the government could hardly build new roads, overpasses, and tunnels fast enough. High-rise neighborhoods and new towns sprang up without enough ways in and out, leading to chronic traffic congestion and productivity losses. Despite the highly digitized and advanced health system that had made Israel a global model for its COVID vaccination rollout, hospital wards, emergency rooms, and even corridors often groaned with patients. Nor was the country prepared for freak weather or the serious earthquake that experts said was bound to come. A couple of hours of heavy rainfall could sometimes be disastrous and even deadly. In the southern Negev desert, several fighter jets were damaged when a hangar in an air force base flooded.

Critics dismissed the doomsday scenarios as alarmist. Professionals said the human shortage was a worldwide problem, and Israel's Ministry of Immigration and Absorption had located thousands of engineers, many of them in the former Soviet Union, who had expressed an interest in immigrating to Israel. The slowdown in the number of new start-ups was hardly felt amid the excitement of the massive funding rounds and public offerings, which local entrepreneurs saw as a sign of maturity as Israel moved from being a start-up nation of quick exits to a scale-up nation.

If Tel Aviv was the thrumming heart of Israeli high-tech, and one of the most concentrated start-up ecosystems in the world with more than 2,000 start-ups—roughly one for every 215 residents—Rabaa Al-Hawashleh lived on the flip side, having grown up in the economic underbelly of Israel. Her story is a redeeming one of Israeli meritocracy and untapped potential.

She was born in Abu Krinat, a ramshackle Bedouin village, or encampment, in the Negev desert. From there, the glass façades of the high-tech giants in metropolitan Tel Aviv and beyond were like a distant planet. A collection of tin-roofed dwellings, shacks, and animal pens, Abu Krinat was tucked into folds of beige-brown scrubland down a long unpaved path off a main highway about forty-five minutes' drive southeast of Beersheba. The village predated the state of Israel and had been officially recognized by the government in 2003, unlike many others that still lacked any official status and were under constant threat of demolition, but Abu Krinat was still not connected to the electricity grid. Hawashleh's home got electricity by day from a couple of solar panels in the yard but there was no way of storing it after dark. When we met, Hawashleh was working in quality assurance at an all-Bedouin technology firm, Sadel Tech, which offered Internet and mobile solutions and occupied modest quarters in a clean industrial park about five miles outside Beersheba. If she brought work home from the office, she could only work on her laptop at night for as long as the battery held out. A sunny personality, she took such obstacles in her stride as she navigated the challenges of family, clan, and the societal norms of the conservative tribe she lived among. Hawashleh, then twenty-four, took two buses each way to work and back, a journey of ninety minutes. She did not have a driver's license because her relatives did not approve of single women driving. One afternoon I gave her a ride back from the office to her small hamlet, where I was welcomed into her humble home by her kindly mother. It grew gloomier inside as the sun went down. We sat on thin, embroidered mattresses along the rough walls, which were decorated with framed needlepoint tapestries of Quranic verses—Hawashleh's handiwork. A delicate, willowy woman, she was dressed in a long robe and a lapeled business jacket, her face framed by a plain hijab. Her mother, Hasen, fifty and illiterate, was dressed more traditionally in a long black gown with cross-stitch ornament and a large floral headscarf. Hawashleh's father was a truck driver. His second wife and family lived in a separate abode in the compound. Hawashleh was one of eleven siblings from her mother's side, and there were another five half siblings from her father's second marriage.

Bedouins who volunteered for service in the IDF were more likely to serve as trackers in a desert unit than in 8200. Hawashleh, who did not serve, was navigating between her conservative society and her personal ambitions and freedoms. In some ways she was like a one-woman start-up, a startling example of Israeli meritocracy. In other ways, she was fighting against odds that were something of an indictment of modern Israel. Even though the village had been officially recognized for more than fifteen years, most families still lacked the required legal permits to build permanent houses. She had attended her local school, probably the only two-story permanent building in the village of some five thousand residents. A star pupil, she said she had only had herself to compete with in class. She went on to study a year of math and computer science at Ben-Gurion University in Beersheba but dropped out because she needed to help support the family. She taught in the village school, fulfilling her parents' ideal of her becoming a teacher and then, they hoped, getting married, until a friend who worked at Sadel brought her into the company. Though the job was outside the usual comfort zone for women in her community, her parents were proud of her.

Sadel was established in 2013 by Ibrahim Sana, a Bedouin from the Negev who was sent by his father, who owned an animal feed store in Beersheba, to be educated in a private Arabic school in the north. He then graduated from the Technion in Haifa and received a master's degree at Ben-Gurion University. Something of a trailblazer, Sana worked at Cisco, the American network equipment company, in central Israel and at various start-ups before founding Sadel. He now employed a dozen young people, mostly software graduates who otherwise could have ended up pumping gas, he said. Aside from overcoming the usual prejudices, getting into high-tech was all the more difficult for Arabic-speakers with no post-army network and for whom English was usually a third language after Hebrew. Bedouin, in particular, often lived in remote villages without much infrastructure. Sana found one of his employees, who had graduated with distinction, stocking supermarket shelves. Another had been working as an apprentice locksmith. "Israel is a leader in high-tech, and we want a piece of that," Sana said. In 2015, the Ministry of Economy introduced a program that helped train and place hundreds of Arab tech graduates in the workforce at companies like Amdocs, Check Point, and the Israeli branch of Intel.

Hawashleh left Sadel and went on to work in digital marketing to promote a grassroots organization, *Marcaz Tamar,* the Tamar Center Negev, and coordinate its projects in the eastern Negev. She was also studying information systems engineering at a southern college and teaching after-school math at local high schools. The Tamar Center, headquartered in Beersheba, described its mission as bridging the socioeconomic gaps between the Bedouin and the rest of Israeli society through education and increasing the number of Bedouin studying science and engineering in college. It offered courses to promote excellence in science for high school pupils and to strengthen their Hebrew and English skills and created its own alumni network. It was funded in part by the government and partly by donations. Its chairman, Ibrahim Nsasra, a business and social entrepreneur from the Bedouin town of Lakia, was the son of a Bedouin judge. In his late thirties, he described listening to traditional trials as a child, feeding the family's sheep before school, and shepherding them on weekends. His own children, he said, were attached to screens, a measure of the rapid modernization of Bedouin society.

I reconnected with Hawashleh on Zoom at the height of the coronavirus epidemic. She was back at work after being temporarily laid off during the lockdown. Working remotely, in her case, was not really an option. The government had poured millions of shekels into programs in the Negev, she said, "but we don't see or feel the effects of those millions. If we are talking specifically about education, a lot of those programs don't work. If a program is built in Tel Aviv," she said, "it does not necessarily work for the Bedouin community. We understand our society best."

The first forty-seven alumni of the Tamar program, from the class of 2018, all graduated high school with high marks in English, math, and physics. Almost 60 percent of them went on to higher education. Some didn't get accepted to college because of poor grades in Hebrew. Within another two years, the center was providing extracurricular enrichment and empowerment training for hundreds of Bedouin high school students. The initiative was a glimmer of light in the small and neglected backwaters of the Bedouin communities spread throughout the Negev. Numbering about a quarter of a million people, more than two-thirds of them were under the age of twenty-one. Still, the school dropout rate was almost 25 percent and the ratio of students graduating high school with a certificate or completing academic degrees was way below that of the rest of Arab society, let alone Jewish Israeli society.

As a woman, Hawashleh, who had beaten the educational odds, was treading a careful path between family expectations and experimenting with life as a modern Israeli. Bedouin society was in flux, yet she remained something of a local oddity. Now twenty-nine, she still lived at her parental home. A more open-minded uncle had allowed one of her female cousins to obtain a driver's license, paving the way for her to learn to drive. Her relatives kept proposing potential husbands, not pushing too hard, and so far she had refused them all. "I don't want to just marry," she said. "I am looking for a partner. I haven't yet found the man. But on the other hand, I don't want to stay in my father's house with no way out. I am beginning to think about options for leaving without marrying." Such a proposition would be shocking to many Bedouin, but Hawashleh felt she now had a special status and worried less about what people thought. "It is accepted that Rabaa does such and such," she said, "though that is not necessarily the right thing for others."

The enterprising spirit that sprang from Abu Krinat may have been something of an exception, but the army, as well as social entrepreneurs like Yossi Vardi and a plethora of non-governmental organizations, were also engaged in enrichment programs to raise standards and encourage excellence in the periphery. Large companies were venturing out of the Tel Aviv area. Intel Israel had established one of the company's most advanced electronics manufacturing facilities in Kiryat Gat, a development town of 60,000 about halfway between Tel Aviv and Beersheba, saying it was committed to contributing to local economic development. A small high-tech hub was thriving in the Galilean city of Nazareth, the "capital" of Israel's Arab population. In 2019 a group of venture investors including Our Crowd, an equity crowdfunding platform for people looking to invest in Israel, and two major food and beverage manufacturers had established another billion-shekel food-tech incubator in Kiryat Shemona, on the Lebanese border.

For government and industry chiefs, the ultra-Orthodox yeshiva world was another, largely latent, source of human capital despite the more conservative rabbis' fiery denunciations of digital temptations. In 2020, nearly 5,000 *Haredim* were receiving technological training, about a third of them men. A couple of Haredi entrepreneurs had established ultra-Orthodox, single-sex shared office spaces for those who did not want to work from home. But success appeared to be relative. That same year, nearly 150,000 ultra-Orthodox adult males were studying in yeshivas and *kollel*s.

Once on the ground in Dubai, the Israelis were immediately impressed by the vision of the Emiratis. We rode through a futuristic metropolis that before the oil wells were discovered was little more than a Bedouin fishing village with an economy based on pearl diving. The skyline was breathtaking, the city spotless. A refined, most un-Israeli hush prevailed on the streets. Luxury cars glided by but there was almost nobody out walking. Along the way, the local guide, a Polish resident, pointed out the metallic metro stops that were air-conditioned. The wonders of Dubai flashed by and were mostly artificial—the world's tallest twisted residential building, the longest indoor ski slope, a vivid green golf course in the desert. It was as if the Israelis had met their match in entrepreneurship, audacity, and ambition—a novel experience for those whose idea of the Arab world was shaped by the West Bank and Gaza, the dysfunctional state Lebanon had become, Jordan, or Egypt. The emirate's veneer oozed opulence, sophistication, and decorum, though beneath the surface it depended on the foreign workforce that made up some 85 to 90 percent of its largely unseen population.

A quarter century of covert relations between Israel and the Gulf states had yielded some solid relationships in the intelligence and business worlds, with one often leading seamlessly into the other. Accompanying Margalit's JVP delegation was David Meidan, a large-framed, retired senior Mossad official who had turned to business after leaving the spy agency and had become an expert in international technology

marketing and a partner in several successful start-ups. Having slipped
in and out of the Emirates for years on the quiet, in both his official
and his business capacity, he had come this time to help open doors
and smooth the way for the newcomers. Meidan had just brokered a
deal of his own between an Israeli cyber intelligence company, Celle-
brite, and an Emirati government agency in the capital, Abu Dhabi; it
was estimated to be worth $3 million. Cellebrite's customers reportedly
included the security agencies of foreign regimes, which used its systems to gather and analyze data from mobile phones, personal computers, cloud computing, and even civilian drones captured by security
forces.

Margalit had orchestrated some of the country's largest, multibillion-
dollar exits and had a reputation at home for aggressive business tactics. He believed in holding out against premature exits that provided
quick but relatively small profits. He was the alpha male of the group;
his delegation was largely made up of trim executives who looked like
marathon runners and included veterans of the army's most prestigious intelligence, technological, and fighting units.

The technology-hungry, transactional Emiratis clearly had no
problem with that. It seemed that all had been forgiven since 2010,
when Mossad agents assassinated a Hamas arms smuggler, Mahmoud
al-Mabhouh, in a Dubai hotel room and then were embarrassingly
exposed by the Emirati authorities. To the Israelis' surprise, the Dubai
police had published comical images culled from ubiquitous closed-
circuit TV cameras showing bumbling agents following the target
disguised in bad wigs and tennis gear and one spy who entered a bathroom clean shaven and emerged wearing a false beard. It was even
possible that the Emiratis had cracked the plot thanks to technology
they had bought from Israeli companies.

Now it was all about peace and progress. For the Arab monarchies
and sheikhdoms there was also an element of self-preservation following the turbulence of the Arab Spring, a shared interest with Israel in
thwarting the threats from Iran, and a hankering for regional prestige
and influence. Plummeting oil prices and the coronavirus pandemic
had underscored the Gulf states' need to diversify and become more
self-sufficient, while Israeli technology was looking for new partners
and markets. The stars were aligned to take relations to new heights.

At a more fundamental level, Israel and Dubai did not have so much in common. In fact, beneath the veneer of shared interests and entrepreneurship, they were in many respects the antithesis of each other. Oil-rich Dubai relied heavily on foreign workers while resource-poor Israel was more xenophobic about foreign nationals staying in the country, zealously guarding its Jewish majority. The Israeli disregard for hierarchy and inherent unruliness contrasted with Emirati formality and intolerance of any criticism of or display of opposition to the country's rulers. The minister of state for food security, Mariam bint Mohammed Saeed Hareb Almheiri, who met with the Israeli delegation, was an example of Emirati Western-educated sophistication with her master's degree in mechanical engineering from Germany. But a handout for members of the delegation about the ruling family of Dubai noted prominently that His Highness Sheikh Mohammed bin Rashid Al Maktoum "has been married six times and has a total of 30 children."

The Emiratis made gracious hosts and the Israelis were on their best behavior. They tried to conform to the formality and hushed atmosphere. When some became too animated and loud while waiting for an elevator in the hotel, a porter gestured for them to keep their voices down. On sightseeing forays, they marched across the marbled expanses of the Dubai Mall, rode the silent elevators to the viewing lounges of the soaring Burj Khalifa tower, took a boat ride across the Creek, a natural waterway coursing through Dubai, and shopped in the squeaky-clean alleys of the gold and spice markets that were emptied of tourists because of the pandemic. They told inside army jokes in Hebrew, assuming they could not be understood by the local plain-clothes security detail that was discreetly tailing us.

Though urbane and seasoned travelers, some of the first-timers were still pinching themselves, hardly believing they were actually in the United Arab Emirates, with Iran just across the narrow waters of the Persian Gulf. They marveled at how safe they felt souvenir shopping in the market. Dror Liwer, a mild-mannered and modest senior executive and a retired officer of the IDF's Mamram unit, said he found it all "mind-boggling." Liwer's company, Coronet, provided an end-to-end cyber-security envelope to small and medium-sized businesses that normally fell below what he called the "cyber poverty line." He had moved to the United States on a two-year contract that turned into twenty years, had returned to Israel a decade ago, and now had a daughter in the army. He spoke with emotion soon after landing. "I'm standing in front of the Burj Al Arab hotel on the beach at sunset," he said, "and I'm thinking, Really? We flew over Saudi Arabia today and through Bahraini airspace! The significance of the moment is not lost on me." Liwer said his father had traded in arms with Iran in the days of the shah, before the 1979 Islamic revolution. Now, he said, he was in Dubai because "my enemy's enemy has turned out to be a friend." He said he had some butterflies about being in an Arab country for the first time but was more excited than afraid, proclaiming it "a new era" and "stepping into the unknown. Our history, unfortunately, is one in which we always viewed the other as the enemy," he continued, sitting next to me on the bus as the skyscrapers of Dubai whizzed by and began to light up at dusk. "To come with a hand extended, as a friend, is quite amazing to me." He felt more comfortable walking around alone in the Dubai gold market than he did in the Muslim Quarter *souk* of Jerusalem's fraught Old City.

The Israeli innovators were welcomed graciously, with the kind of embrace the Jewish state had long yearned for in the Arab world. A few executives already had some local contacts and were treated to private desert jeep tours and sumptuous dinners in the homes of sheikhs. For others, this was virgin territory. Liwer said his company, Coronet, had held conversations about doing business with potential partners in the Gulf in the past, but they had remained theoretical because the lack of diplomatic relations made it too complicated. Now, he said, the playing field had completely changed. He and his partner were meeting with local distributors who could market Coronet products throughout the Middle East, viewing the Emirates as a gateway. "Look at what they've built here in fifty years," he enthused. "Seriously, look at this." There was a lot to be learned here, he said, for Israel, too.

It was so rare, and refreshing, to hear worldly Israelis concede that their country could learn something from Arabs, and it felt as if at least some of the perceptions underpinning the Israel-Arab conflict had been upended. This new partnership was unlike any other Israel had known in the Arab world. Decades after peace treaties had been signed with Egypt and Jordan, a "cold peace" still reigned. Those countries maintained strong security ties with Israel but at the popular level there was hostility against any "normalization" of relations, few business ties, and little interaction, all stymied by Israeli policies toward the Palestinians. Any tourism was largely one-way, with Israelis keen to visit the archaeological wonders of Egypt and Jordan but avoiding speaking Hebrew in public when they were there.

It obviously helped that there was no bloody history between Israel and the Emirates. Unlike the Egyptians and Jordanians, the Emiratis had never faced Israelis on the battlefield. In addition, the Emirates, a conservative, authoritarian country with only one million nationals, was cosmopolitan, with its imported labor force hailing from some two hundred countries, the majority of workers Muslims from South Asia. Indians made up much of the white-collar management, and there was a contingent of resident Americans and Europeans. Despite the occasional culture clash incident that could still land a foreigner in jail, Emiratis prided themselves on their tolerance and multicultural business environment. It was verboten to mix politics with commerce. The Palestinian issue was barely mentioned. The Emiratis had moved on.

A welcome letter from the hotel's local ownership, slipped under the door of each of the Israeli guests, began with a Hebrew greeting, *Shalom Aleichem,* "Peace be upon you"—and a pitch to be in touch if there was any interest in exploring joint business opportunities. A Dubai-based rabbi was running around granting kosher food licenses to local establishments ahead of an onslaught of tens of thousands of Israeli tourists with the introduction of direct flights over the Hanukkah holidays. More broadly, the Emirates, with their strategic outlook, formidable infrastructure, and strong trade and logistics connections in the Middle East and beyond, saw opportunity.

With oil reserves dwindling and other sources of revenue, such as tourism and trade, shown to be vulnerable by the pandemic, the pampered sheikhdoms were eager to become more self-reliant. They were importing up to 90 percent of their food supply and had seen prices of basics rise sharply as airports closed down during the initial coronavirus panic. Forward thinking, the Emirati government included ministers for artificial intelligence and food-tech. So perhaps it was not surprising that the morning after the JVP group's arrival, when the company executives gathered in the hotel ballroom to present their

wares to some prominent Emirati investors, the companies that created the most immediate buzz were those dealing with edibles, food
security, and desert agriculture.

The Emirati men were all dressed in gleaming white, starched robes,
or *kanduras,* and flowing headdresses. The Israelis were in Western business attire. Among them was Taly Nechushtan, the CEO of
InnovoPro, an Israeli company that had developed a technology to
extract concentrated protein out of chickpeas, conveniently known as
*hummus* in both Arabic and Hebrew. We had talked chickpeas on the
plane over. With more than ten billion mouths to feed by 2050, and
the rise of vegetarianism, veganism, and environmental awareness, the
global demand for plant-based alternatives to meat and animal products was growing. The humble chickpea had proven to be an adaptable,
gluten-free, allergen-free, nutritionally rich, and neutral-tasting source
of protein. A Swiss company was already using InnovoPro's extract to
produce dairy-free yogurt and ice cream. Nechushtan could not bring
samples of those in her suitcase, but she did bring dozens of bite-sized,
chickpea-based sweet and savory snacks, which she distributed like
party favors to the Emirati investors seated at round tables, like at a
bar mitzvah.

On the flight over, Nechushtan, petite and to the point, had told me it
felt almost funny to be bringing a basic staple like *hummus* to the Arab
world, like bringing ice to the North Pole. She said a large Japanese
food distributor based in Dubai had contacted her six months earlier
and invited her to visit but she had turned down the offer because she
had only an Israeli passport. (Before the normalization deal, Israelis
could usually enter the Emirates on a non-Israeli passport. The JVP
delegation arrived before new entry protocols were in place, so special
arrangements were made for handling their entry on landing.) Now
Nechushtan was confidently presenting her PowerPoint pitch in the
ballroom. Her presentation followed a long line of cyber companies',
and investors instantly perked up and asked pertinent questions about
logistics and whether the chickpea protein set off an allergy that was
common in the region to certain legumes. She seemed taken aback by
the interest, remarking, as we crossed paths, "Who'd have thought?"
The next task, she said, was "to build trust, which is like building peace."

The investors' interest was similarly piqued by Yehonatan Ben-

Hamozeg, a gray-haired, retired veteran of Unit 8200 and now the CEO of an agricultural intelligence company, Agrint. Dubbed the "tree listener," he had developed a sensor for the early detection of red weevils, a pest that ate away at date palms from the inside, ultimately destroying them. Of the four billion palm trees in the world, some forty-three million were said to be in the United Arab Emirates, where a third of the world's dates were grown. Ben-Hamozeg's $12 sensors could be attached to each tree and the monitoring system linked to the cloud, allowing farmers to pinpoint infested trees via an app on their phones.

There was much talk between the Israeli visitors and the Emiratis about the Bedouin culture of hospitality and about being long-lost cousins. One investor, originally from Bahrain, said he had once done a DNA test and found matches in Tel Aviv. Margalit became the first Israeli to be invited to the swish studios of the government-owned Dubai TV, where he was interviewed for a program called *Message for Peace* by the popular host Youssef Abdulbari, an imposing Emirati anchor with a rich baritone. Off-camera, the charming Abdulbari practiced how to pronounce "Erel," Margalit's first name. Waxing lyrical about his first time interviewing an Israeli, he told me, "It is something new and intriguing. You can say it's like falling in love."

The interview took place against a panoramic backdrop of the skylines of Dubai and Tel Aviv. Margalit, who had asked Abdulbari to write down the similar-sounding names of the Emirati rulers for him to avoid any mistakes, spoke emotionally about the Israelis wanting to be part of the region, "the place we wanted to reach for such a long time." He spoke of the need for food security, healthcare IT, water, and jobs. "The content of peace can be provided by the entrepreneurs," he added, "after the politicians have signed." He suggested helping Egypt with water technology and, in the region where wheat was first domesticated, helping Lebanon with food. He spoke of *tikkun olam,* the Jewish concept of repairing the world, adding, "We can mend our region by working together." Abdulbari replied on camera, "You do strike me as a visionary man." On the plane back Margalit was exuberant. "You did it!" he told the entrepreneurs in a speech summing up the trip. This was, he said, the "true story of the next phase for Israel."

A broader peace did not immediately break out in the Middle East but the Abraham Accords expanded to include Morocco and had weathered a deadly war between Israel and the Islamic militants in Gaza. In the fall of 2021 Israel opened its pavilion at the Dubai Expo with a display inspired by desert dunes signifying the shared features of the region and the vast space for future cooperation. Marking the first anniversary of the accords, two hundred senior Israeli business-men joined dozens of their Emirati counterparts for a business confer-ence in Abu Dhabi and were serenaded on the opening night by an Arab-Jewish Israeli duo with an ethereal rendition of Leonard Cohen's "Hallelujah." Over the past year trade between Israel and the UAE had amounted to $1 billion and the next year the two countries would ini-tial an extensive free trade agreement.

I checked back in with some of the JVP portfolio executives, curious to hear what had transpired with their dreams of high-tech castles in the sand. Nechushtan of InnovoPro had emerged a year earlier from a meeting with the Emirates' food security minister declaring that the Emirates had the three pillars needed to create a chickpea growing and manufacturing empire: land, sea, and sun. Now, though, she sounded more sober. She said her company had done a comprehensive mar-ket analysis and was focusing on the European and American market, which it had identified as the most developed and relevant for its prod-uct. InnovoPro had just launched what it claimed to be the first ever texturized vegetable protein made from chickpeas, to be used as a base for meat alternatives such as burgers and nuggets. The company would approach the Emirates once the market there was set with the same sustainability and nutritional goals, Nechushtan said, "hopefully soon."

Two other companies in that first JVP delegation to Dubai had since opened offices in the emirate. And Dror Liwer, of Coronet, said the cyber company's dealings in Dubai had far exceeded expectations. Speaking by Zoom from Tel Aviv against a real backdrop of rows of employees at computer screens, Liwer described with excitement how the company now had two distributors based in Dubai, one run by an Emirati, and had made deals spanning much of the Middle East and extending into Southeast Asia. "It is definitely not a mirage," he said of the partnership with Dubai. "It is very much real."

Things had moved more slowly than the company was used to in dealings in the United States. "There is not the same level of a sense of urgency," Liwer said. But due diligence had been thorough, and business was now being done. The company found everyone was comfortable working in English, and in similar time zones. Some deals had been done with Egypt and many others in African countries, with the new facilitators able to leverage their familiarity with local languages, customs, bureaucracy, and market behavior in order to make sales.

With most people still working remotely because of the pandemic, the collaboration had taken place largely via Zoom. Liwer had not yet been back to Dubai. Still, he said, "What blew me away was how natural and easy and comfortable everybody was with everybody. There was almost an instant sense of camaraderie. I thought it would take longer to build mutual trust, but it all happened so quickly. Everybody is so happy that these artificial barriers and walls were torn apart. Everybody wanted to make it work."

In one of the more surprising and positive legacies left by the Trump and Netanyahu administrations, new horizons had opened up, which nobody would have thought feasible just a couple of years earlier. "We are seeing in front of us a redefinition of what the Middle East could be, both economically and politically," Liwer said. The language was technology; the currency—business and opportunity. The Abraham Accords had proven that even in this turbulent and historically burdened region, partnership, however transactional, was possible.

# ELEVEN

# A MODERN EXODUS

I T WAS A DAZZLING SPECTACLE of the ingathering of exiles. Each November, multitudes of Ethiopian Israelis would gather at the Hass Promenade, an elevated point in southeast Jerusalem, to celebrate the ancient holiday of Sigd, a spiritual and social ritual they had brought with them from the highlands of Ethiopia. Sigd bound them to their ancient traditions, and to one another. Many were dressed in white robes with decorative trim. The *kessim,* or priests, were regal and resplendent in their turbans. Adding to the visual festivity, they held up glittering multicolored umbrellas for shade in one hand and horsehair fly swatters, a symbol of the sanctity of life, in the other. The promenade, with its majestic views across the holy city, was transformed into a vivid, living human tapestry. The monotonous, haunting chorus of communal prayer carried in the fall breeze far across the biblical Hinnon and Kidron Valleys, in the direction of the Old City.

On the fiftieth day after Yom Kippur, the Jews in Ethiopia would climb a high mountain, reminiscent of Mount Sinai. They would fast and pray to renew their covenant with God and their wish to return to the Land of Israel, to Jerusalem, to Zion. And here it was, spread out like a vast carpet before them. The top of the promenade in the Armon Hanatziv neighborhood of Jerusalem, a favorite spot for tourists and lovers, offered a spectacular view of the city's landmarks, old and new. Straight ahead was Mount Zion, the traditional site of King David's tomb; the walled Old City, with its iconic golden cupola of the Dome of the Rock marking out the Temple Mount; and the Palestinian neighborhoods, their gray houses and apartment blocks seemingly piled on top of one another and threatening to tumble down the hillsides. To the east rose the ridges of Mount Scopus and the Mount of Olives, with their three hallmark towers and ancient Jewish graveyard, the gilded onion-domed Church of Mary Magdalene, and the Garden of Gethsemane; and to the north and west the urban sprawl of the new city.

The grassy slopes below the promenade took on the atmosphere of a fete. Stalls were set up, selling ethnic arts and crafts. In a tent, youth counselors conducted discussion circles. Menberu Shimon, an Ethiopian Israeli resident of Jerusalem, was selling copies of his illustrated children's book explaining the meaning of Sigd, a name taken from the Hebrew word for prostration. He wrote it in Hebrew, he said, to educate about and ensure the future of the Sigd, because among the young, Sabra generation of Israelis of Ethiopian descent the tradition was already fading. Friends and relatives who had come from across the country squealed with delight at meeting up with one another. Families broke their fasts and picnicked on the lawn.

Of all the great waves of *aliyah* to Israel—from the massive influx from North Africa and the Middle East that doubled Israel's population in the 1950s through to the transformative effects of the exodus from the former Soviet Union—none appeared as miraculous or as symbolic of the Zionist ethos as the rescue of the Beta Israel, the long-lost Jews of Ethiopia, nor, in many ways, as testing. For while the determination and perilous journeys and daring operations that brought them to Israel were inspiring and uplifting, the excitement turned over time to a more mixed, and at times anguished, reality.

It was not just the absorption difficulties experienced by all immigrants, and all the more so for families, many of them illiterate, airlifted from a rural life in the mountains of northern Ethiopia to a fast-paced modern society. It was not just their small numbers. The roughly 150,000 Jews of Ethiopian descent in Israel made up less than 2 percent of Israel's population, which denied them the political clout of the ultra-Orthodox, the Arab minority, or even the settlers. Nor was it about the struggle for resources or attention after years of dedicated committees and programs led by Jewish organizations and the Israeli government. Rather, for the Ethiopian Jews, more than any other of the tribes of Israel, it was the otherness they had to bear as a Black community that had long been cut off from world Jewry, its difference as obvious and impossible to erase as skin color.

The community first had to contend with questions about its Jewishness—not, like the Russian immigrants, on an individual basis, but as a whole. And decades after the rescue was initially declared over, subsequent Israeli governments faced an ongoing dilemma as relatives of relatives of those already in Israel—including many converts to Christianity who did not qualify for immigration under the Law of Return—waited in camps in Ethiopia to be reunited with their families. A newer, more multicultural Israel grappled with some of the Jewish state's most perennial and vexing questions, such as "Who is a Jew?," pitting humanity against *halacha*. And once in Israel, could Jews, who had suffered so much from antisemitism, be racist and discriminate against one another? The Ethiopian *aliyah* held the ultimate mirror up to Israeli society as an ancient community's centuries of dreams and yearning for Zion encountered the realities of Zionism.

The Beta Israel, meaning "the house of Israel," was the stuff of exotic legends, its origins a mystery wrapped up in biblical traditions about King Solomon's encounter with the Queen of Sheba and an ancient story of being the lost Israelite tribe of Dan. Known as *Falashas* in Ethiopia, a pejorative term denoting wandering peasants or strangers, they had lived across the ages believing they were the last surviving Jews while Jews around the world were largely oblivious to their existence. "Discovered" by Europeans in the late eighteenth century, they became targets of missions bent on converting them to Christianity.

Only a trickle of Ethiopian Jews made their way to Israel in the early decades of the state. The first few dozen came to study Hebrew and Judaism with the intention of going back to teach in Ethiopia. There, the Beta Israel practiced a pre-rabbinic form of Judaism from the First Temple period, based only on the Torah. They had been cut off from the later oral rabbinic law and rituals of the Talmud and their holy tongue was Geez, not Hebrew, facts that had fueled suspicions about their Jewishness in the halls of Israel's Orthodox Chief Rabbinate.

The community had also been diluted over the centuries by conversion, made easier by the Ethiopian Church's adoption of some Jewish symbols and traditions. The royal dynasty ending with Emperor Haile Selassie, who was deposed in 1974, claimed lineage from King Solomon and the Queen of Sheba and adopted the symbol of the Lion of Judah. Some of the converts had continued to practice their Judaism in stealth, high in the mountains, like the Spanish and Portuguese Marranos who converted on pain of death during the Middle Ages. They carried with them a history of antisemitism and persecution, having mostly been banned from owning land for centuries, and being associated with the evil eye and sorcery because of their traditional ironsmith skills.

In the 1970s, while Jews around the world were lobbying and marching to get the Soviets to open the gates for Jewish emigration, the fate of endangered Ethiopian Jewry whipped up much less fervor. The Labor governments had shown interest in the Yemenite Jews of the ancient Sheba, or South Arabia, who looked Middle Eastern, knew the Talmud, and prayed in Hebrew. Not so the Ethiopian Jews, despite reports of arrests, executions, and persecution at the hands of local militias. Only in 1973 did the Sephardic chief rabbi of Israel, Ovadia Yosef, issue a halachic ruling that the Ethiopian Jews were Jewish, descendants of the lost tribe of Dan, a decision he based on the opinions of some great sages and rabbis before him. Government recognition came three years later, making Ethiopia's Jews eligible for *aliyah*.

Israel, at the same time, was trying to buttress relations in Africa, sending out medical, technical, and agricultural experts and helping Haile Selassie, for one, with his army and secret police. The emperor, like a modern-day pharaoh, had vowed not to let the Jews go, apparently viewing it as his mission to convert them to Christianity, or holding them hostage in return for weapons. Israel continued to cooperate with the Marxist regime that followed.

It was an Ethiopian Jew, Ferede Aklum, a largely unsung hero who had escaped to Sudan, who initially raised the alarm. He sent letters begging for the rescue of the community, caught up in the country's civil wars, drought, and famine. Menachem Begin determined to bring the Ethiopian Jews to Israel and the drama of the exodus began. The Mossad and other Israeli, American, and international bodies sprang into action and, over more than two decades, undertook a string of clandestine operations to complete the mission. Activists and agents from the Mossad urged Ethiopia's Jews to trek across the border to refugee camps in Sudan, from which they would be transported via Europe to Israel. Whole villages would empty, silently, overnight. Many thousands made the grueling journey to the camps and an estimated four thousand died there, or along the way. In 1984 and early 1985, about eight thousand Ethiopian Jews were flown to Israel in a secretive airlift code-named Operation Moses. Another plan to smuggle them out involved a Hollywood-like fake diving resort on the Red Sea coast run by a team of Mossad agents.

But after a long, American-arbitrated negotiation with the Ethiopian regime and a reported payment of $35 million in return for their freedom, the years-old effort to bring out the Ethiopian Jews culminated in a massive emergency airlift that was engineered in secrecy by the government of Yitzhak Shamir in May 1991. The 1,500-mile, five-and-a-half-hour transfer from Addis Ababa to Tel Aviv involved some forty flights on unmarked planes crammed with passengers and was named Operation Solomon. The Ethiopians brought no luggage and wore stickers with numbers on their foreheads to aid the process, which had mostly taken place during the Sabbath. Once the strict media blackout in Israel was lifted at the end of the Sabbath, it transpired that some 14,500 Ethiopian Jews had been spirited in over a period of less than thirty-four hours. There were no religious protests about the violation of the sanctity of the Sabbath: This was a case of saving lives, which always took precedence in Jewish law.

Once the military censorship was lifted, wondrous footage emerged of the new arrivals, many of them in traditional robes and barefoot, carrying little or nothing beyond their infants or their elderly. One baby had been born on a plane, and several others soon before boarding or after landing. The country rejoiced in an explosion of pride and goodwill. People rushed to deliver bags of clothing and toys to the hotels and absorption centers where the newcomers were being accommodated.

The culture shock was intense. Farming families and shepherds from remote mountain villages with no running water were suddenly transported to sixth-floor apartments in a far more earthly Jerusalem than they had imagined—or to the run-down development town of Kiryat

Malachi to the south, or even more incongruously to the Red Sea holiday resort of Eilat. One young woman I met, Tamar Lilay, recalled her mother crying bitterly as they were being driven from the airport to a hotel in Eilat, where they were "surrounded by women in bikinis."

"We came from a village, a modest life," Lilay told me. "All our stories were about holy Jerusalem, not Eilat. We were not prepared for that." Lilay said she did not know how to hold a pencil when she first landed as a girl of eleven. She had since gone on to obtain a degree in special education at Haifa University and by the time we met was working in a program for the empowerment of Ethiopian women.

Lilay's mother was not alone in her rude awakening. Israel was not exactly the paradise the Ethiopian Jews had dreamed of. "It was not what we expected," Devre Warko, a hospital nurse and mother of four from Mazkeret Batya, a small village near Rehovot, in central Israel, told me during one of the Sigd gatherings on the Jerusalem promenade, as she sat on a rock along a manicured pathway.

Most of Ethiopian Jewry was by now in Israel and a new generation had already grown up in the land: Of the 150,000-strong community, about 65,000 were born in Israel. Yet many of them still felt marginalized and faced prejudice and suspicion. While there had been no soft landings for the Russians or the *Mizrahim* before them, nor for the Holocaust survivors or the early pioneers who cleared the malarial swamps and laid the ground for the state, the Ethiopian Jews may well have traveled the farthest distance between expectations and actuality.

Warko had come at the age of eight from the mountainous Simien region on the secret airlift of 1991. "It was a shock for my parents, and also for us, as children," she said of their arrival in Israel. "Parents told their children that everyone was good there, that there were no bad people, as if the Messiah had come," Warko said, adding that some even described a Jerusalem of gold. "We came here and it wasn't like that," she said. As she spoke, the Sigd crowds milled around. Along with the matriarchs and patriarchs of the community were young people in fashionably ripped jeans and some soldiers in uniform, assault rifles casually slung over their shoulders. Warko recalled how she, her parents, and five siblings had been whisked from the airport to a trailer home in Nehora, a small *moshav* near Kiryat Gat, in southern Israel. Their home was cold in the winter and sweltering in the summer. The family stayed in Nehora for three years until they could buy an apartment nearby, in Mazkeret Batya, with a special government mortgage. Like many Ethiopian immigrant children, Warko was sent to a boarding school in a youth village in the north, far from her parents, "because they told us that was best," she said, hinting at a paternalistic approach from the authorities. She said that some of her Ethiopian neighbors had been so disappointed with their new life in Zion that they wished they could go back to where they came from. None of them did. The talk of disillusionment struck a sad and discordant note on this clear Jerusalem day years after the Israeli Knesset, in a gesture to the community and its rich heritage, declared the annual Sigd a national holiday.

Once in Israel, the ancestral homeland, the old family structures came under tremendous strain. A proud community that had struggled for centuries to maintain its Judaism in isolation felt patronized, expected to keep quiet and be grateful for having been rescued. The *kessim* felt humiliated by the rabbinical authorities, who did not recognize their right to officiate as religious leaders in matters such as marriage and divorce, as they did in Ethiopia, because of their lack of a background in rabbinic Judaism and oral law. It took until 2018 for a government committee to recognize the status of the *kessim* as spiritual shepherds of the community and announce a plan to integrate fully fledged rabbis of Ethiopian descent who had qualified in Israel into the official religious council system. Most gallingly, though, despite millions of dollars spent by the government and charities largely financed by American Jews to try to ease the transition and help Ethiopian Jews settle, decades later even those born in Israel felt the sting of mostly unofficial, but semi-institutional, social discrimination and racism.

The brief history of the Ethiopians in Israel could be measured in bursts of protest. They punctuated the years preceding the great *aliyah* of Operation Solomon and the three decades that followed it. The earliest to arrive demonstrated periodically to persuade Israel to make more of an effort to save the rest of the community. Buttressed by the thousands who arrived in the airlifts, the Ethiopian Israelis exploded in rage when it emerged in 1996 that Israel's medical services were secretly dumping their blood donations for fear they were contaminated with HIV. Then, in 2012, after a number of ugly racist episodes made national headlines, second-generation activists who had grown up in Israel, professionals among them, spent months protesting on the sidewalk outside the prime minister's residence in Jerusalem. There was the story of four buildings in Kiryat Malachi whose residents had signed an agreement not to rent or sell apartments to Ethiopians, telling television crews that the Ethiopians smelled bad and ate strange food. Three years after that, soon after riots erupted in Baltimore and Ferguson, Missouri, triggered by the killing of unarmed Black men by police, Ethiopian Israelis blocked main junctions and routes in Tel Aviv after two police officers were caught on a street-side security camera beating up Demas Fikadey, a young soldier of Ethiopian descent in uniform, for no apparent reason. He had been on his way home from the army one afternoon when he was set upon by the officers. The security camera video of the assault went viral and made its way to national television and the Ethiopian community took to the streets.

The demonstration began peacefully enough. The protesters started gathering one weekday afternoon in the spring of 2015 outside the Azrieli Center, a Tel Aviv landmark strategically situated at one of the city's busiest junctions. Almost everyone I spoke to there had a story of humiliation and insult. Eli Malassa, from the Negev town of Netivot, said he had been beaten by police while he was a soldier, and that they had asked him where he had stolen his uniform from. Uri Muallem, a slight man no more than five feet tall, told me he had been drinking at a family event a few years before and had gone outside to relieve himself when three police officers set upon him with pepper spray and handcuffed him. Accused of assaulting a policeman, he spent three nights in detention. Now wearing a baseball cap, a T-shirt with a New York slogan, and a thick, rapper-style chain around his neck, he said, "We came to our homeland to be with our brothers. There, they called us dirty Jews and told us to go to our people," he said of Ethiopia. "Here, in my own country, I hide from the police so they won't arrest me. It's humiliating." A truck driver, he worried how he would provide for his four-year-old daughter since the police took away his driver's license for speeding.

Bracha Tamano, a medical secretary, introduced herself as the sister of Pnina Tamano-Shata, an Ethiopian-born lawyer and journalist who had been elected to the Knesset in 2013. Tamano said she had been born in Sudan as the family made its way to Israel and had also experienced racism. There were kiosks that refused to sell her cigarettes, she said, adding that some people looked at her suspiciously. Some white Israeli sympathizers and activists had also shown up in solidarity, though in Israel "white" came in many shades of brown. Nir Malach, who said he had volunteered in the past with the Ethiopian community in the coastal city of Netanya, was there with his two young children and a placard that read "Don't discriminate against brothers."

The sense of hurt swelled with the crowd as the protest turned into a vibrant display of Black anger and solidarity. The theme of police brutality channeled the anger of Black Americans and the young protesters adopted aspects of that culture, though the two had little in common. The Ethiopian Israelis had been brought home by virtue of their ancestry, far removed from the legacy of slavery. But they flooded onto the road with their fists raised above their heads, arms crossed in an X, in a symbol of defiance reminiscent of the anti-regime protests in Ethiopia. Central Tel Aviv came to a standstill. It also became clear that the Ethiopian Israeli community had its own internal signals and grievances that many other Israelis were not even aware of, and that the beating of Fikadey was not the only cause of the protest. The protesters began chanting "Salamse! Salamse!," demanding justice for someone that few outside the community had ever heard of. Yosef Salamse, it turned out, was an Ethiopian Israeli from the small northern town of Binyamina, who had been found dead in a quarry in the summer of 2014, months after being the victim of police harassment and brutality. The police determined he had died by suicide, but his family did not believe that. The ignorance about the case beyond the tiny Ethiopian community only attested to the sense of marginalization fueling the protest.

Then there was the enigmatic T-shirt worn by some of the protesters. Printed with the silhouette of a man's head and a question mark, it hinted at another episode roiling the Ethiopian Israeli community that was being kept under wraps by the security services and would be made public only a couple of months later. The silhouette, it would later become clear, symbolized Avera Mengistu, an anguished and mentally disturbed Ethiopian Israeli from Ashkelon, on the southern Mediterranean coast, who was being held captive by Hamas in Gaza. The case had been classified for months but eventually it was made public. There was even video of Mengistu striding down the beach one day in 2014 in a clearly agitated state. At the border with Gaza he waded into the sea and crossed a flimsy fence. Soldiers had seen him heading for the enemy territory but had not stopped him. Once on the other side, he headed for a tent on the dunes, then disappeared.

The demonstrators marched off from the Azrieli Center toward Rabin Square. There, and in the side streets around the square, they were confronted by the police and the protest devolved into violence and chaos. Demonstrators hurled stones, overturned a patrol car, and clashed with officers who fired stun grenades and water cannons and charged the crowds on horseback. The TV images were shocking; the area looked like a battleground. The rest of Israel was finding out that the young generation of Ethiopian Israelis was not as meek and grateful as that of their parents.

The accidental hero whose encounter with police brutality had triggered this outburst, Demas Fikadey, was unable to be present. As a conscript in active service, he was prohibited by army rules from demonstrating. Fikadey, twenty-one at the time, was a slender, bashful soldier. An outstanding high school student, he was serving as a computer technician in the military's computing and communications corps. He had come to Israel seven years earlier from the Gojam region in Ethiopia. Both his parents had died, and he lived with his siblings in an apartment in Holon, a Tel Aviv suburb.

I met Fikadey the day after the stormy protest in Tel Aviv. The country had woken up shaken. Prime Minister Netanyahu, eager to defuse the Ethiopian community's rage, had invited Fikadey to his office for a well-publicized meeting and a commitment to address the community's problems. Jews protesting against racism in their own homeland was a deep mark of shame. Fikadey's lawyer had arranged for Fikadey to give a few media interviews after the meeting in the Rose Garden, a park opposite the prime minister's office. Wearing a skullcap and an army shirt with sleeves that were too long, Fikadey, a soft-spoken and somewhat reluctant symbol of the rage, said he had told the prime minister he must work to end racism and discrimination. "We dreamed for so many years to come to Israel," Fikadey said. "He must work to solve the problem."

Fikadey did not see himself as a hero and was against all violence, though he said his heart was with the protesters. He went on to describe the incident that had sparked the protest. It was about 6:30 in the evening, he said, and he was on his way home from duty. The road ahead was closed, and he had gotten off his bicycle when a police officer stopped him and told him to turn around and leave, without offering any explanation. Fikadey did not know that the road had been closed because of a suspicious object. He said he waited for the police officer to get off his cellphone and then tried to get past him to reach home. The officer threw Fikadey's bicycle down and started to shove him. "When I asked him why he was pushing me, he began hitting me in the face," Fikadey recounted. A volunteer policeman joined in and Fikadey ended up on the ground. Fikadey's lawyer said the officer later told his superiors that Fikadey had hit him and thrown a stone at him.

"If it hadn't all been caught on camera from beginning to end, I would be in some prison now," Fikadey said. As he spoke, a group of schoolgirls, including several of Ethiopian descent, spotted him and ran up to him screeching, as if he were a rock star. He spoke to them with quiet words, encouraging them to serve their country. Ultimately, after an internal police investigation, the Justice Ministry closed the case, saying that tempers had flared on both sides and that both Fikadey and the police officers were to blame for the melee.

In the wake of the 2015 protest, the government formed a commission to stamp out racism; it was led by Emi Palmor, the director general of the Justice Ministry. Its conclusions, submitted in the summer of 2016, were quite damning, finding discriminatory policies and practices that distinguished Ethiopian Israelis from other citizens in fields including education, medical treatment, employment, and army enlistment, as well as policing. In 2015, it said, the percentage of indictments against Ethiopian Israelis was twice as high as that for the general population and four times as high among minors, while the percentage of Ethiopian Israeli minors in detention was almost ten times that of the rest of the population. One of the commission's recommendations was to equip police patrols with body cameras. The police committed to reduce overpolicing based on racial profiling and introduced anti-racism training workshops.

The report did not provide an instant fix. The rate of Israelis of Ethiopian descent in the criminal justice system remained disproportionately high. In the eyes of the community, the police continued to stoke tensions with a quick finger on the trigger. And Ethiopian Israelis were still struggling in other areas of life. About 87 percent of their marriages were within the community, but the divorce rate was nearly twice as high as that of the general population, as was the number of single-parent families. Net income was about 20 percent lower in households of Ethiopian descent compared to the rest of the population.

So once again, in 2019, more stormy protests broke out around the country, sparked this time by the fatal police shooting of an unarmed Ethiopian Israeli teenager near Haifa. Drawing energy from the Black Lives Matter movement in the United States, angry young Ethiopian Israelis took to the streets again, joined by community professionals and political activists, crying out against overpolicing, racial profiling, and being treated as "automatic suspects." Ethiopian parents spoke of the fear they harbored for their children at the hands of the police, a sentiment not generally felt by other Israelis.

That year had begun with the January killing of Yehuda Biadga, a twenty-four-year-old from Bat Yam, just south of Tel Aviv, who suffered from a mental disorder. His family had called the police for help as he ran amok wielding a knife. An officer who responded to the call ended up shooting Biadga dead in the street after the disturbed youth lunged at him. Six months later, Solomon Tekah, eighteen, was fatally shot by an off-duty policeman in a suburb of Haifa. Tekah was a round-faced youth who had come as a child from the Gondar region of Ethiopia. He was hanging out with his friends one evening in a park near a youth center they attended. The police officer was in the same park with his wife and three young children. An altercation ensued. The officer said he had tried to break up a fight involving the Ethiopian youths, and that they had thrown stones that struck him, putting himself and his family in danger. He drew his gun, aimed at the youths, then fired toward the sidewalk, according to the charge sheet. The bullet apparently ricocheted and struck Tekah in the upper torso. The police officer was indicted on suspicion of negligent homicide. Tekah's friends had a different version of that evening's events. They said they were just trying to get away after the officer began harassing them.

Whatever the exact circumstances, Tekah's supporters noted, an armed Israeli police officer would have been far less likely to feel "threatened" enough to open fire in a residential area had the youths in question not been dark-skinned. The killing occurred just weeks after George Floyd took his last breaths in Minneapolis, setting off a wave of protests that convulsed America. In Israel, the community's resentment had only grown and erupted with a new level of pent-up fury. Tekah's death sparked days of rioting by Israelis of Ethiopian descent across Israel. Rush-hour traffic was paralyzed for hours; police vehicles were overturned and set alight. Police fired stun grenades, tear gas, and hard sponge bullets and sent in officers on horseback.

Initially, there was widespread sympathy for the Ethiopian community, but with the violence much of that dissipated and turned to denunciation. The most vitriolic critics took to social media, telling their Ethiopian fellow Jews to "go back to Africa." Some of the Ethiopians remarked that their detractors seemed more bothered about being stuck in traffic than by the death of an innocent teenager. Grief-stricken, the Tekah family called for calm, at least until after the *shiva*. In an emotional and noble piece written for *Ynet*, the popular Hebrew news site, just after the *shiva*, Solomon's father, Worka Tekah, said the family fully supported the legitimate right to protest but condemned the violence. "We didn't want anyone else to be hurt—not a protestor nor a policeman," he wrote. "Perhaps my most important message is this: Let this be the end of racism. I hope that my son Solomon is the last victim."

Ethiopian Israelis acknowledged that things had been tough for the waves of immigrants who came before them. Some compared their protest to that of the Mizrahi awakening and the Black Panthers resistance in the 1970s. But they also noted that the *Mizrahim* and the Yemenites and others who had traumatic immigration stories had come to Israel when it was a young state in its first decade, struggling to establish itself through years of austerity and rationing. By the time the Ethiopians and Russians arrived in the 1980s and 1990s, the state was relatively powerful and prosperous.

Yet their *aliyah* had come with its own set of complexities, indignities, and denigrations.

Many of the Ethiopians had to go through some kind of conversion back to Judaism after arriving in Israel, particularly if they were from families who had returned to the faith after having converted to Christianity. They were required to dip in a ritual bath, undergo symbolic circumcision, or even remarry because their marriage customs did not conform to those prescribed in religious Jewish law, raising doubts about the halachic status of offspring of possibly adulterous unions. Improbably, it took until late 2019 for the Chief Rabbinate in Jerusalem to officially adopt Ovadia Yosef's ruling on the Beta Israel's Jewish status, a decision that only came to light after Israel's public broadcast network, Kan, requested it be made public. The decision came after another series of ugly incidents that caused a public uproar, including a kosher winery that forbade Ethiopian Israeli workers to touch the wine since a gentile's touch would render it unkosher.

The transition to modern Israeli society had been a long and difficult one. The traditional hierarchy had been turned upside down. Children in Ethiopia were expected to keep quiet and obey their parents. Here, the parents who did not speak Hebrew relied on their children to help them navigate the system. With almost half the community born in Israel by the 2020s, many of the children did not speak their parents' native tongue, hampering any nuanced verbal communication and emotional support. Roles were reversed as women went out to work and got ahead, often proving more adaptable than their husbands. Many marriages broke down, while others were prone to domestic violence. The concentration of Ethiopian immigrants in areas with cheap housing created foci of poverty that some in the community referred to as ghettoes and made integration more challenging. The Israeli-born children became more outspoken and assertive and, even as they grappled with identity issues, demanded acceptance as full-fledged Jewish Israelis. The rioting was a cry for help and a heartbreaking indictment of the conduct of the police and of broader swaths of Israeli society.

In the Rehovot neighborhood of Kiryat Moshe, Ethiopian Israelis made up more than half the residents of the squat, cement-gray projects built in the 1950s, originally to house Holocaust survivors and immigrants from North Africa. Days after the 2019 riots, Laoul Tashala, twenty-four, was leaning against a motorbike, hanging around with a few friends on the sidewalk outside an apartment building where an Ethiopian family was sitting *shiva* for a deceased relative. Groups of mourners, the women dressed in traditional white robes, filed off buses and into the courtyard to pay their respects. Tashala wore long dread-locks tied up in a thick bunch. He was working for the national railway and now lived in Tel Aviv, but had grown up in one of the apartment blocks across the street. He had arrived in Israel with his family in 1996, when he was four, though he said the immigration authorities regis-tered him as being two years old because he was so small. His father was a *kess*, a spiritual leader, he said, and he was one of nine siblings.

His first encounter with the police came when he was about eleven, he recalled. He said he was sitting with friends in a *sukkah*, a temporary hut set up for the holiday of the Feast of Tabernacles near his house, when the police came in and searched them, seized his cellphone, which he had purchased with money he had made from gardening and other odd jobs, and detained them. It was a Nokia or something, a good one for then, he said. The phone was finally returned to him two months later, looking worse for wear.

After a stint at boarding school, he enlisted at eighteen in the IDF's elite Duvdevan unit, which was known for its undercover operations in Palestinian areas. "It was crazy, a very good experience," he said. "The army really is a melting pot. But when you get out of the army and you take off your uniform, you go back to being an Ethiopian to them—to the whites." He went on to illustrate the point with a story of humilia-tion I would hear again and again from young Ethiopian Israelis, one so shameful it was hard to believe. The realization would come, he said, when he went to a club with his army friends and the bouncers—or "selectors," as they were known in Hebrew—"give all sorts of reasons why you can't go in. Excuses, like there's no room." It happened to Tashala while he was a soldier out on a short furlough after fighting in the Gaza war of 2014. He went with his friends to a club in the Tel Aviv port. When it was his turn to enter, he was told it was a private party for invitees only. "That's the humiliation, right there in your face," he said. The only saving grace was that his "white" army buddies left with him.

While the Arab community suffered from police neglect, the Ethio-pian youths consistently complained of overpolicing and harassment. The black neighborhoods were hardly no-go fiefdoms or the domain of violent gangs. Yes, fights between drunken youths had ended in the occasional deadly stabbing in Kiryat Moshe, and some Ethiopian Israelis had been recruited as foot soldiers in the service of some of the organized crime families and their turf wars. But the local youths complained of the police focusing on smaller matters, such as breaking up groups of teens innocently hanging out in the parks, automatically suspecting bored kids of being up to no good or of having stolen their cellphones. One police chief, Roni Alsheich, who had expressed a commitment to integrate more minorities into the police force, stirred condemnation in 2016 when he answered a question about police brutality and racism toward Ethiopian Israelis with a rambling explanation of how studies abroad showed there was a "natural" inclination to be more suspicious of young people from immigrant backgrounds. Even model citizens, such as one of Tashala's friends, a youth counselor at the community center in Kiryat Moshe, complained of being repeatedly arrested, searched, and released.

It was not only the police, Tashala went on, becoming more animated and impassioned. It was the entire establishment. "Take the *kessim*," he said. "They have no authority." In Ethiopia, they performed circumcisions, weddings, funerals, but here they were only authorized to give a blessing. "My father is eighty-two. He blesses everyone and that's it," Tashala said. "Then a rabbi conducts the wedding. Still, he's out all day visiting people on the verge of divorce, holding *shiva*s or circumcisions."

Another childhood friend from the neighborhood, Uri Sarche, chimed in, calling the police "criminals in uniform, with guns." Also sporting long dreadlocks, his body laced with tattoos about money and freedom and some Bob Marley lyrics, Sarche had skipped army service, for which he spent some time in a military prison. "I'm not a *freier*," he said, using the Hebrew slang for sucker. "The moment I was out of uniform, would I have security?" He did do a stint of national service in the end, volunteering in a school. Two younger brothers had served in combat units. One of them, he said, had been fingerprinted by the police at the age of fifteen and was made to give a saliva sample "in case he does something in the future." Sarche's parents had arrived in 1991. He was born in Israel, had attended school on a kibbutz in the area, and had sleepovers with his "white" friends. His parents had since divorced. He lived with his mother, who worked as a cleaner and caregiver, along with her partner and several young siblings in a walk-up with a crumbling façade surrounded by a garbage-strewn yard. The building's residents were all Ethiopian, he said, apart from one Arab family who lived on the ground floor.

It was school holidays. Upstairs in the apartment, two young siblings were alone, playing on phones in a cramped lounge dominated by a TV, a sofa, and a bed along one wall. The old, narrow kitchen contained a special grill for making *injera,* the spongy sourdough flatbread that was an Ethiopian staple. Sarche took me to the tiny bathroom to show me the view from the shower cubicle of the community police station just across the road. "They know me by name, but they still stop me and ask to see my identity card," Sarche said. He, too, had stories of being handcuffed and punched in the back of a patrol car by a police officer—in this case an Ethiopian one with rank who was apparently trying to prove himself to his comrades. Sarche avoided going to nightclubs "to avoid the shame," he said. "You know what's the funniest thing?" he asked. "Moses wandered for forty years in the desert. Do you think he had blond hair and blue eyes?"

The face and name of Avera Mengistu, the captive in Gaza, were stenciled like a motif on walls in Ethiopian neighborhoods in a haunting reminder of his continued absence. He, too, had come from a fractured family and grew up in a dilapidated quarter of the seaside city of Ashkelon, about ten miles north of the Gaza Strip, in a public housing block with a grimy stairwell and broken mailboxes. A neighbor complained that the building was not fit to stable horses in. Mengistu had been adrift long before he approached the Gaza border after the summer war of 2014. Born in the Gondar region, he was airlifted to Israel with his family in 1991, at the age of five, the fourth of eight siblings. In Israel he had proven to be a clever student, his oldest brother, Yallo, told me. But the family broke down. His parents divorced and his father became largely absent. Then, in 2011, another brother, Michael, whom Avera adored, died of some form of anorexia, sending Avera into a depression. He had spent short spells in psychiatric wards. A medical committee found him unfit to serve and he was exempted from military duty. He had gone missing on occasion before. The day he disappeared into Gaza, he had been agitated, pacing, and wrapped up in his thoughts, another brother, Ilan, told me about a year later. Mengistu did not return. Security agents who visited the family the next day told them he had left behind a bag on the beach containing his identity card, a Hebrew Bible, a towel, slippers, and a math book.

Mengistu's relatives had been torn between launching a public campaign to pressure Hamas to free Avera and keeping quiet, as the Israeli authorities preferred, for fear of driving up Mengistu's price in the eyes of Hamas. After the heavily weighted prisoner deals of the past, including the 2011 exchange of 1,000 Palestinian prisoners, many convicted of deadly terrorist attacks, for Gilad Shalit, the Israeli public had turned against giving in to such extortion. Hamas had set the bar high, demanding the release of dozens of hardcore prisoners just for information about Mengistu and another Israeli captive, Hisham Al Said, a Bedouin from the Negev, as well as the remains of two Israeli soldiers, Hadar Goldin and Oron Shaul, who the authorities had determined were both killed in action in the summer of 2014. Years on, in 2022, in an apparent pressure tactic aimed at the Israeli government, Hamas released a brief video of Hisham Al Said lying in bed and breathing through an oxygen mask.

Mengistu was still believed to be alive, in the absence of evidence to the contrary, but his plight had commanded less public sympathy from the outset than the MIAs since he was not a soldier and had walked into Gaza of his own volition. Being from an Ethiopian family of paltry means on the very margins of Israeli society did not help his cause. The robust public campaign for the release of Shalit had centered around the slogan that he was "Everybody's Child." Beyond the Ethiopian community, Mengistu was largely out of sight and out of mind. Ethiopian Israeli activists had long asserted that things would have looked different if Mengistu's name was Rubinstein.

Unlike the prejudice felt by Palestinian citizens of Israel, the smarting discrimination and disillusionment felt by many in the Ethiopian community could not be mitigated or explained away in terms of security or national conflict. There was simply no excuse for it. Thinking that perhaps an older representative of the community might have a longer, more positive perspective, I went to see Zion Getahun, a wise community leader and educator in Jerusalem. Getahun, fifty, ran a community center attached to a small Ethiopian synagogue on the poorer side of the Talpiot neighborhood and was employed by City Hall. He was working on a project to introduce nearby synagogues to Ethiopian Jewry, to showcase Ethiopian art, and, he said, to help highlight "the beautiful mosaic that exists only in Israel." Sitting in a small office in the community center, Getahun first spoke of the treacherous journey he had undertaken to get here. The family had never felt deprived in Ethiopia, he said, but he had grown up with his grandmother's stories of their "home" in Jerusalem, the center of the world.

In 1984, at fourteen, he set out on foot with a group from his village toward the Sudanese border. They didn't know if it would take them two days or two months to get to Israel. Friends died along the way or lost most of their families. "When we went without food and water or encountered robbers," he recalled, "in the darkness we saw the light of Jerusalem." He told of rapes, killing, and trauma in the camps in Sudan, likening it to a holocaust. Once, he recounted, he and the other Jews in the camp were forced into a pit with a bulldozer standing by, but he said they were saved by someone from the Red Cross who stopped the horror in time. Getahun got on the last rescue flight out of Sudan. Israel had made that possible. But he felt the heroism of the Ethiopian Jews had been lost on most Israelis. "To make that journey at twelve or fourteen, is that not a sign of strength and power?" he asked. "Nobody tells that story of the strength of the community."

One of the lucky ones, Getahun somehow got to Jerusalem. But his memories of the welcome he received were tinged with sadness. As he landed, immigration clerks discarded his Ethiopian name, Aychgar, which his parents back in Ethiopia had chosen for him, and told him that from then on, his name was Zion. He was sent to boarding school in the far north. He then found his Judaism was in doubt and that the community's *kessim* were "worth nothing."

Decades later, Getahun sat on the Palmor committee to examine racism after the 2015 protests. He said the Ethiopians had even surpassed the country's Arab citizens as victims of discrimination. The fact that the beating of Demas Fikadey had been caught on camera was, he said, a sign "that God had apparently wanted it all to come out." Then came the killing of Solomon Tekah. "Should things be this way in the Israel we dreamed of? It's a question I ask," Getahun said, not really needing an answer.

The Ethiopian Israeli community certainly had its success stories. Belaynesh Zevadia, the first Israeli ambassador of Ethiopian origin, was appointed to head the mission in Addis Ababa in 2012. Pnina Tamano-Shata, the politician, went on to become Israel's first government minister of Ethiopian origin, charged with immigration and absorption, and Ethiopian artists, doctors, army officers, and reality TV stars served as role models. A popular, bittersweet Israeli sitcom, *Nevsu,* won an International Emmy Award in 2018 for comedy. Co-created by Ethiopian Israeli writer and actor Yossi Vasa, the first episode opened with the police detaining the main, eponymous character, an Ethiopian Israeli, married to a blonde Ashkenazi woman and living in an upscale neighborhood, for trying to get into his own car. The very act of laughing at the prejudices and travails Israelis of Ethiopian descent faced seemed to indicate that the worst was behind them.

Ethiopian musicians who broke through to the mainstream, such as Esther Rada and the fun-loving rap duo Strong Black Coffee, ushered in a new level of the multiculturalism that was redefining Israeli society, moving away from the early Zionist ideal of a uniform Hebrew culture to one that celebrated the assorted tribes of Israel as a creative antidote to its political, ethnic, and religious polarization. When Eden Alene, a young pop singer of Ethiopian descent, was chosen to represent Israel in the 2020 Eurovision Song Contest, she was supposed to perform a catchy love song written especially for her with lyrics in Hebrew, English, Arabic, and Amharic and titled "Feker Libi," Amharic for "love of my heart," in the spirit of Israeli diversity. That year's contest was canceled because of the coronavirus pandemic. The next year she competed with a more generic dance-pop number, "Set Me Free," her hair spectacularly braided, projecting a breezy, modern face of Israel.

Encouraging *aliyah* was still at the very core of Israel's being. More than 3,340,000 immigrants had come since 1948. In 2016, the Knesset declared an annual Aliyah Day, to be marked in schools during the week of the Hebrew calendar coinciding with the Torah portion of *Lech Lecha,* in which God commands Abraham to go to the Land of Israel. In the first nine months of 2021, according to government data, more than 20,360 immigrants had arrived, even as Israel had closed its borders to tourists because of the pandemic. The largest number came from Russia, followed by the United States, France, and Ukraine. The aim of the holiday, according to the government and the quasi-governmental Jewish Agency, was "to celebrate the development of Israel as a multicultural society and emphasize the importance of *aliyah* to Israel."

One community that had struggled to be included were those still waiting in limbo in the camps in Ethiopia. They included thousands of descendants of Ethiopian Jews who had converted to Christianity and, as willing converts, did not qualify for immigration and automatic citizenship under the Law of Return. Many said they regretted their conversions and practiced Judaism. Many had first-degree relatives already in Israel. In Jewish religious law, the blood descendants of Jews who no longer qualified halachically as Jews were known as *Zera Israel,* the Seed of Israel.

The Jewish Agency, which oversaw many aspects of the immigration process, had announced in 2013 that it had completed its mission of bringing Ethiopian Jewry to Israel. Yet the camps in Addis Ababa and Gondar kept filling up with thousands of people who had sold their property in the expectation of leaving. Some had been waiting to get on a plane for almost twenty years. Families were split in what became an open and festering collective wound. In 2018, after years of campaigning by community activists and their supporters, and broken promises and foot-dragging by the government, the immigration authorities declared that nearly eight thousand individuals would be allowed to immigrate, not under the Law of Return but under the rubric of family reunification. In the fall of 2020, the Netanyahu government announced that it had allocated a budget of $100 million to airlift the first two thousand to Israel in the coming months. This operation was to be called *Zur Israel,* Rock of Israel.

It would not pass entirely without controversy. In the summer of 2021, in the weekend magazine of *Yedioth Ahronoth,* Ben-Dror Yemini, an iconoclastic Israeli columnist, wrote a piece attacking the operation titled "The Never-Ending Migrants." "Are those 8,000 waiting in Ethiopia to come to Israel the end of the story? Not a chance," he wrote. "Like previous times, the camps will empty out, relatives of the migrants will fill them up again, the demands will be renewed, as will the protests."

He said that veterans of Beta Israel had tried to expose the scheme, but that critics were cowed into silence for fear of being branded as racists.

Tamano-Shata, the minister of immigration and absorption, argued back in a Facebook post that as the granddaughter of a *kess* and the scion of a long line of *kessim* who had dedicated their lives to preserving Ethiopian Jewry, even at risk of death, there was nobody who viewed the Jewish character of the state of Israel as more important than she did. Thousands of those waiting were the sons and daughters of Israeli citizens, she wrote, Ethiopians who had made *aliyah* as the grandchildren of Jews under the Law of Return but had had to make the agonizing choice of leaving their own children behind.

Tamano-Shata, who had pushed hard for the plan, traveled to Ethiopia to accompany the first five hundred of the expected two thousand on their journey to Israel. Fighting in the Tigray province and the threat of a coronavirus outbreak in the camps had only added to the urgency. The final flight landed one gray and blustery morning in March 2021 with about three hundred on board. There had been a last-minute political flap. Prime Minister Netanyahu and his transportation minister, Miri Regev, had planned to come to the airport to greet the newcomers in a transparent effort to score a few more political points in yet another election campaign. Tamano-Shata, a Blue and White centrist running against the Likud, had threatened to call off the welcoming ceremony and make do with a modest reception committee. In the end, Netanyahu and Regev found other things to do.

The Ethiopian Airlines jumbo landed and taxied toward the marked spot behind a small podium in a far corner of the nearly deserted airport. A phalanx of Israeli press photographers stood at the ready. The sound system blasted out rousing and patriotic songs such as "Hallelujah," Israel's winning number in the 1979 Eurovision Song Contest performed by Milk and Honey. The welcoming lineup included Tamano-Shata, the Jewish Agency head Isaac Herzog, and other *aliyah* officials as well as two *kessim* wearing white turbans and prayer shawls and holding horsehair fly swatters, one of whom was Tamano-Shata's uncle from Ashdod. They waved Israeli flags. Eventually the plane door opened and the tired and dazed new immigrants began to disembark. For many it had been their first flight. Unlike the bundled-up Russian immigrants in Zoya Cherkassky's *New Victims,* many were flimsily dressed in traditional robes. An elderly couple descended the steps slowly, clutching the hands of a small boy. As they reached the bottom, the couple bowed down and kissed the tarmac. The photographers also lunged down to the ground to capture what felt like a choreographed moment.

But as the arrival scene unfolded, even the most cynical Israeli would likely have been moved and uplifted. As Tamano-Shata gave a brief welcoming speech in Amharic, the immigrants kept disembarking: stunningly beautiful women in brightly trimmed robes, some with infants swaddled in shawls and strapped to their backs; young men with sharp haircuts in denim jackets and jeans; whole families with children in tow. As they filed toward the buses waiting to take them to Haifa, out of view of the cameras, one after another dropped to their knees, bowed down, and kissed the ground. Some paused to kneel, covered their eyes with one hand, and uttered a prayer. For these new Israelis, this was still a blessed land.

# EPILOGUE

### THE EIGHTH DECADE

O N ISRAEL'S SEVENTY-THIRD Independence Day, in the spring of 2021, Lieutenant General Aviv Kochavi delivered the traditional IDF chief of staff's speech at the festive annual ceremony in the gardens of the president's official residence in Jerusalem. He began with an unexpected message, stating that this was only the third time in all of Jewish history that a unified nation of Israel was sovereign in its country and the previous two times had ended disastrously.

The ominous theme was picked up by Naftali Bennett, who repeated it in his inauguration speech weeks later as he was installed as prime minister, and again at the graveside of Yitzhak Rabin. The biblical United Monarchy of David and Solomon had lasted just eighty years, he reminded the Israelis, while a second attempt at full sovereignty under the Hasmonean dynasty had lasted for about seventy-five years before it disintegrated in a frenzy of civil war and fanaticism.

The modern state of Israel was likely the final chance the Jews had to be masters of their fate, on their land, with their own laws and preserving their faith, Bennett told the nation that fall, during the twenty-sixth annual memorial ceremony for Rabin at Mount Herzl, the resting place of many of the great leaders of Israel and its fallen soldiers. "We have never succeeded in getting beyond the eighth decade, united and sovereign in our land," he declared. In the spring of 2022, on the eve of Memorial Day, he would reiterate the message yet again, as his governing coalition, having lost its parliamentary majority, teetered on the verge of collapse. Days earlier, Bennett's wife and teenage son had received letters containing death threats and two live bullets. Incitement against the government was rampant, with Benjamin Netanyahu demonizing it from the opposition as weak, fraudulent, and dependent on "supporters of terrorism," referring to the small Islamic party in the coalition, and bent on a political comeback.

Even in the age of the prophets, the stiff-necked Jews barely heeded their leaders. In any case, Israel's modern leaders offered few answers to some of the most pressing problems, the political divisions engendering a kind of paralysis, and the lessons of the past could not chart a course ahead. Netanyahu's army-of-bots propaganda machine had never let up. In June 2022, after serving just one year in office, Prime Minister Bennett resigned as his coalition imploded around him and he moved to dissolve the Parliament. The Israelis were heading back to the ballot box for a fifth time in under four years. Yair Lapid, the centrist leader, took over as prime minister of the caretaker government. In a televised address dubbed the "We Believe" speech, he spoke of a common goal of a "Jewish, democratic, liberal, strong, advanced, and prosperous Israel." So why, he asked, were the levels of hate and anxiety so high, and the polarization of Israeli society more threatening than ever? In Israel, he said, extremism was "flowing like lava" from the top down, "from politics to the streets." The looming challenges instilled fear in those who dared look over the precipice: a demographic trajectory pointing to a population more ambivalent and conflicted about Zionism and less equipped to contribute to a robust and modern economy; a potential nuclear arms race in the region, and a people's army fighting to preserve its popular legitimacy; the rise of the far-right political fringes and the threats to liberal democracy. Perhaps most daunting of all was the fading prospect of a comprehensive peace with the Palestinians as the likelihood of partition gives way to creeping annexation and a binational reality, with resolution deferred at least until the Palestinians, and the Israelis, can make some peace among themselves. Some Israelis and Palestinians appeared intent on turning the national and territorial conflict into a religious war.

When Netanyahu emerged victorious from the November 2022 election, Israel's fifth in less than four years, he pledged to be the prime minister of all Israel's citizens and to seek to broaden the circle of peace in the Middle East. That message was fiercely at odds with the fervently right-wing and religious wave that had propelled him back to power: His ultra-Orthodox allies immediately demanded doubling government stipends for yeshiva students and legislation to formalize their exemption from military service. The historic Labor Party scraped through with just four parliamentary seats, the minimum required to enter the Knesset, while a far-right, religious Zionist alliance including Itamar Ben-Gvir's Jewish Power became the third largest political force in the country, promising to authorize all settlement outposts, curb the independence of the judiciary, and bolster the rule of the Jewish majority.

But still, there is the hope, built on the unlikely birth of the state of Israel, with all its imperfections, and its proven knack for improvisation, innovation, resilience, and survival. The growing acceptance of the Jewish state in the Arabian Peninsula offers new horizons. The multifaceted and multicultural Israeli society that is emerging is vibrant and engaged, the constituents fiercely protective of their rights and freedoms.

As the drama plays out, the actors are staying put. The air is thick with memory and premonition. This land, thrumming with obstinate, exuberant life, is their home. The Israelis—Jews and Arabs, religious and secular, Eastern and Western, immigrants and veterans, liberals and zealots—are all by now intrinsic elements of the landscape. The Sabra nation, their roots reach into the soil. They bear the fruits of those who came before them and for the generations to come, adapting, enduring, still ripening in the sun.

# ACKNOWLEDGMENTS

Who are the people living in Israel now? And what do they want? These questions were intriguing Jonathan Segal, my editor at Alfred A. Knopf. I had the good fortune to become the author who would try to answer them; this book is the result. I am eternally grateful to Jonathan for conceiving this project in the first place, then for his endless patience as he waited for me to produce the manuscript. I am indebted to Martin Indyk, who recommended me to Jonathan and made the match.

As well as his calm forbearance in the face of missed and long-gone deadlines, Jonathan provided brilliant guidance and wisdom at critical junctures as the project came along. The manuscript has benefited from his fine editing and sharp eye for detail. I am also extremely grateful to Sarah Perrin, Jonathan's editorial assistant who so expertly helmed the editing and production process, to Nicole Pedersen, the production editor, and to Susanna Sturgis, who skillfully copyedited the manuscript. Any shortcomings are mine alone.

I thank my agent, David R. Patterson, of the Stuart Krichevsky Literary Agency in New York, as well as Chandler Wickers, for their invaluable help and care. And for my author photo, a special thank-you to Rina Castelnuovo, photographer, artist, longtime colleague, and valued friend.

I am also indebted to my wonderful editors at *The New York Times* for nurturing me and allowing me the time I needed to write the book.

Successive bureau chiefs and my colleagues at the *Times*'s Jerusalem Bureau have buttressed me over the years with their individual excellence, friendship, and support. It's a village, its members too numerous to name, but you know who you are.

The main reading room of the National Library of Israel provided me with an inspiring and tranquil sanctuary where I could go to write.

I thank from the bottom of my heart every one of the people who appear in this book and who let me into their lives and their homes.

My family, across continents, has always been there for me. My beloved parents, Harold *z'l* and Doreen, to whom this book is dedicated, and my fabulous siblings, Helena, Maxine, and Mark, have all helped shape who I am. My Israeli uncles, aunts, and tribe of cousins who, like all good Israeli families, span the political and religious spectrum, have endowed me with insights that I will treasure, always. Shai, Maya, Moti, and Daria have enriched my life here in so many ways.

This book would never have been written without the constant devotion, encouragement, spurring on, and precious advice of my husband, Hirsh Goodman, my partner in creativity, love, and life. Gavriel and Lev, our beautiful Sabra sons, and their friends on all sides of the divides, hold the future of the country in their hands. May they use their many talents wisely and help bring peace to the land.

# NOTES

CHAPTER 2  CIVIL WARS

34  Rabin later said: Shlomo Nakdimon, "The Myth and the Lie: What Rabin's Real Role Was in the Sinking of the *Altalena*," *Haaretz*, June 15, 2016.

38  Arens chronicled the rivalry: Moshe Arens, *Flags over the Warsaw Ghetto: The Untold Story of the Warsaw Ghetto Uprising* (Jerusalem: Gefen Publishing House and Menachem Begin Heritage Center, 2011).

41  Arens wrote a searing commentary: Moshe Arens, "The Jewish Nation-State Bill Alienates Israel's Arab Citizens for Nothing," *Haaretz*, July 15, 2018.

48  *I'm a civil war:* Translated by Stanley F. Chyet in *Words in My Lovesick Blood: Poems by Haim Gouri* (Detroit: Wayne State University, 1996).

51  documentary aired in 2016: *Uvda*, Channel 2 Television, broadcast on April 14, 2016.

57  letter he received from Ben-Gurion: Tom Segev, "The Love-Hate Relationship Between Ben-Gurion and Menachem Begin," *Haaretz*, July 3, 2009.


CHAPTER 3  RIVER OF DISCONTENT

67  in the genteel Rehavia neighborhood: "If I Forget Thee, Oh Musrara," *Yedioth Ahronoth*, Special Independence Day supplement, April 14, 2021.

75  revealed in a television documentary: Amnon Levy, *True Face: The Ethnic Demon*, Channel 10, 2013.


CHAPTER 4  A TALE OF TWO *KIBBUTZIM*

107  "The volunteers bring in": Ruth Sinai, "Kibbutz Closes Gates to Volunteers from Abroad," Associated Press, March 23, 1986.

108 "like millionaires lolling": "Begin Assailed for Disparaging Kibbutz Members," Jewish Telegraphic Agency report, October 2, 1981.

## CHAPTER 5 OUTPOST MILLENNIALS

149 "joined the thieves": Michael Sfard, *The Wall and the Gate: Israel, Palestine and the Legal Battle for Human Rights* (New York: Metropolitan Books, Henry Holt, 2018).

## CHAPTER 6 SABRAS AND OLIVE TREES

160 The first to arrive: Gershom Gorenberg, *The Unmaking of Israel* (New York: HarperCollins, 2011).
166 Even the quality of the Arabic language: Interview with Nasreen Hadad Haj-Yahya, an education expert at the Israel Democracy Institute in Jerusalem, spring 2020.
184 "Is it really so hard": Muhammad Zoabi, "As Usual, Ayman Odeh Stammers When It Comes to LGBT," *Ynet*, July 11, 2020.
193 "I screamed that I was choking": Itamar Eichner, "The First Bedouin Diplomat Complained That He Was Attacked by Security Guards," *Ynet,* June 15, 2020.
196 "diagnosed with the cancer that killed him": Yigal Zalmona, "100 Years of Israeli Art," The Israel Museum, Jerusalem, 2010.

## CHAPTER 7 HAREDI AND ISRAELI: HAVING IT ALL

206 the ultra-Orthodox gained political leverage: Dr. Asaf Malchi, "The 'People's Army'?," Israel Democracy Institute, October 16, 2018.
208 Less than 10 percent: Israel Democracy Institute Statistical Report on Ultra-Orthodox Society in Israel, 2019.
208 nearly one-half of all Israeli children: Shoresh Institution for Socioeconomic Research, Policy Brief, November 2019.
215 The move earned Litzman: Sarit Rosenblum, "Litzman: 'Impose a Closure on Bnei Brak, the Situation There is Awful,' " *Yedioth Ahronoth*, March 31, 2020.
219 Bezeq said that 8 percent: Gad Perez, "Covid-19 Crisis Draws Haredi Community to Internet," *Globes*, April 6, 2020.
230 True liberalism and pluralism: Etty Suissa Ben Ami, "On Art, Faith and Politics," interview with Omer Yankelevitch, *Etika*, February 15, 2019.

## CHAPTER 8 HALF THE PEOPLE'S ARMY

241 "A nation builds an army that builds a nation": Elazar Stern, *Struggling over Israel's Soul: An IDF General Speaks of His Controversial Moral Decisions* (Jerusalem: Gefen Publishing House, 2012).
248 A 2015 study by Yagil Levy: Yagil Levy, "Has the 'Spider Web' Theory Really Collapsed?" *Military and Strategic Affairs* 7, no. 3 (December 2015).

253 "another symptom of a confused army": Chen Artzi Sror, "Noa Kirel as a Symbol of an Army in an Identity Crisis," *Yedioth Ahronoth*, February 4, 2020.

## CHAPTER 9 THE RUSSIANS

282 "electoral revenge": Lily Galili and Roman Bronfman, *The Million That Changed the Middle East: The Soviet Immigration to Israel* (Tel Aviv: Matar Publishing House, 2013).

292 a compromise was reached: Daphne Barak-Erez, *Outlawed Pigs: Law, Religion and Culture in Israel* (Madison: University of Wisconsin Press, 2007).

## CHAPTER 10 HIGH-TECH IN THE SAND

298 Israeli high-tech firms raised a historic peak: Report by Meitar Law Offices and IVC Research Center, October 2021.

301 Israel's economic miracle: Dan Senor and Saul Singer, *Start-Up Nation: The Story of Israel's Economic Miracle,* a Council on Foreign Relations Book (New York: Twelve, 2009).

304 23 percent of the country's Arab pupils: Taub Center for Social Policy Studies in Israel, State of the Nation Report 2020.

305 Netanyahu privatized key state assets: Analysis in Meirav Arlosoroff, "From Oranges to High Tech?," *Haaretz*, November 11, 2019.

313 In 2020, nearly 5,000 *Haredim:* Israel Democracy Institute, Statistical Report on Ultra-Orthodox Society in Israel, December 2021.

314 estimated to be worth $3 million: Uri Berkovitz, "Israeli Cyber Intelligence Co Cellebrite Signs Deal in UAE," *Globes,* October 22, 2020.

## CHAPTER 11 A MODERN EXODUS

324 "Discovered" by Europeans: Louis Rapaport, *The Lost Jews: Last of the Ethiopian Falashas* (New York: Stein and Day, 1980).

333 About 87 percent of their marriages: Israeli government Central Bureau of Statistics report on the occasion of the Sigd, November 2019.

334 In an emotional and noble piece: Worka Tekah, "May My Son Solomon Tekah Be the Last Victim of Racism," *Ynet,* September 7, 2019.

# INDEX

Isabel Kershner was born and raised in Manchester, England, and graduated from Oxford University with a degree in Arabic from the faculty of Asian and Middle Eastern studies. After working for a political risk consultancy in London, she migrated to Israel. In 2007 she became a correspondent for *The New York Times* in Jerusalem, covering both Israeli and Palestinian politics and society. Previously, she was a senior editor for Middle East and Palestinian affairs at *The Jerusalem Report*. She is the author of *Barrier: The Seam of the Israeli-Palestinian Conflict*. She has been living with her family in Jerusalem since 1990.

A NOTE ON THE TYPE

This book was set in Minion, a typeface produced by the Adobe Corporation specifically for the Macintosh personal computer, and released in 1990. Designed by Robert Slimbach, Minion combines the classic characteristics of old-style faces with the full complement of weights required for modern typesetting.

*Composed by North Market Street Graphics, Lancaster, Pennsylvania*

*Printed and bound by Berryville Graphics, Berryville, Virginia*

*Designed by Maggie Hinders*

*Map by Joe LeMonnier*